Uncertainty and Insecurity in the New Age

EDITED BY
Vincent N. Parrillo

JOHN D. CALANDRA ITALIAN AMERICAN INSTITUTE, QUEENS COLLEGE, CUNY
NEW YORK, NEW YORK

This book is dedicated to the memory of our wonderful friend and colleague Rocco Caporale, who was an important part of the conference from which these papers emanate as well as of the four conferences that preceded this one.

CONTENTS

ix   Foreword
       VINCENT N. PARRILLO

PART ONE: SOCIETY AND SOCIAL RELATIONS

3   The National Basis of a Sociology Without Borders
       ANDREA BORGHINI

11   The Marketing of Global Control
       VALENTINA CREMONESINI

29   The Social Dramaturgy of Risk Communication: The Case of the LNG Tanker Galleon off the Coast of Livorno, Italy
       GABRIELE DE ANGELIS

43   Social Resources in the Global Age: The Concept of Social Capital
       STEFANIA MILELLA

53   'And Yet It Moves': Civil Society in Southern Italy
       FERDINANDO SPINA

PART TWO: COMMUNITY AND ISOLATION

69   Social Networks and Insecurity
       SIMONE GABBRIELLINI

75   Why Does the Glass Ceiling Still Exist?
       RITA BIANCHERI

83   Communities and Social Change: Pasolini's Works as Sociological Resources
       LUCA CARBONE

97   Acceptance or Rejection: The Uncertainty and Insecurity of Homosexual Italian Americans
       MICHAEL CAROSONE

107 Some Aspects of Social and Spatial Inequalities in Megacities
SONIA PAONE

115 The Adaptation of Old vs. New Immigrants: Italians and Mexicans in Perspective
SUSANNA TARDI

PART THREE: IDENTITY AND CULTURE

131 Flexibility and Memory: Individuals and Society in the Age of Risk
MARIA GRAZIA RICCI

143 Preserving Italian American History and Culture: Great Resources in Search of an Audience
DOMINIC CANDELORO

159 Local Development, Cultural Identity, and Popular Culture in Peripheral Areas
ANGELO SALENTO

169 The Use of Cultural Heritage in Italy and in the United States
SARAH SICILIANO

185 Globalization and Negotiated Global Awareness: Whither Individualization?
INO ROSSI

199 The Maintenance of a Commons
CHRISTINE ZINNI

PART FOUR: PERCEPTION AND POLITICS

219 The Disappearing Italian Expatriate Voter and the Census of Italians Abroad
ROCCO CAPORALE

231 *Contadini, Sovversivi,* and Electors: Italian-American Radicalism and Municipal Elections in 1940s New York City
MICHELE ROSA-CLOT

245 White Ethnics and White Privilege
KARYN LOSCOCCO

257 The More Things Change: Comparing Italians in World War II
and Arabs in the War on Terror
PAUL MAGRO

271 Thirty Years of Italian-American Public Employment in
New York City and New York State
VINCENZO MILIONE, CARMINE PIZZIRUSSO, AND ITALA PELIZZOLI

PART FIVE: THE WORLD OF WORK

291 The Idea of Work in the Postmodern Age
MARIO ALDO TOSCANO

295 Employment and Social Inclusion: A European Perspective
RACHELE BENEDETTI

309 The Industrial Districts: The Case Study of Santa Croce
sull'Arno (Tuscany)
SOFIA CAPUANO

317 Life Histories at Risk: Work and Identity in Flexible Capitalism
VINCENZO MELE

331 Work Harassment as Health Risk Regime
NOELLE MOLÉ

341 Possibility and Insecurity in the European Learning Society:
Considerations on the Italian Situation
GERARDO PASTORE

349 Contributors

359 Index

Foreword

The Industrial Revolution—beginning in England in the eighteenth century and spreading throughout Europe and North America in the nineteenth—caused major social changes in every society it touched. The twin processes of industrialization and urbanization generated a fundamental alteration of the social structure as rural, agricultural economies were transformed into urban, capitalist economies, and household, family-based economies were replaced by industry-based economies. Technological innovations prompted a profound cultural shift with the emergence of new occupations, changed living conditions, exploitation of the working class (including child labor abuses), labor strife, the rise of a middle class, and general access to mass-produced consumer goods. Out of this profound societal metamorphosis, the discipline of sociology was born, as social analysts—August Comte (1798-1857), Émile Durkheim (1858-1917), Karl Marx (1818-1883), and Ferdinand Tönnies (1855-1936) among them—attempted to theorize about and explain what was happening. Here is where we find the origins of structural-functionalism and conflict theory.

In our lifetime we are experiencing another significant shift in our way of life. The Electronic Revolution, as some call it, has given us the world of telecommunications and the Internet, which break down cultural and political borders, while providing instantaneous contact and information even more quickly than the spread of gossip in a gemeinschaft small village. The still-continuing expansion of a global economy—with numerous multi-national or transnational corporations generating revenues greater than the Gross Domestic Product (GDP) of many countries—is having an increasing impact on local economies and cultures. As with the Industrial Revolution, social observers—Noam Chomsky, Thomas L. Friedman, and Amartya Sen, to name just a few—seek to inform us about these social forces. Emerging also from these changing times is a new theoretical school of thought to explain this process: postmodernism. Among its leading figures are Jean Baudrillard (1929-2007), Ulrich Beck, Judith Butler, Jacques Derrida (1930-2004), Michel Foucault (1926-1984), and Jean-Francis Lyotard (1924-1998).

In a small way, this volume offers commentaries and analyses about different aspects of life affected by the events and unfolding socio-economic processes of the current epoch. Although change is an ongoing part of life, we don't always welcome it, particularly if its impact alters our existence in any significant way. Even the possibility of any dramatic change, not just its realization, can breed feelings of anxiety and uncertainty about one's future, hence the title of this book.

LA STORIA DIETRO QUESTO LIBRO

In May 2007, the Fifth Italo-American Conference held at William Paterson University and the John D. Calandra Italian American Institute at Queens College, CUNY, brought together both veteran and young scholars from Italy and the United States to share an intellectual exchange on issues facing us in the twenty-first century. This volume, like its predecessors from the previous four conferences, contains the full papers from the conference participants who had to shorten their presentations, given the time constraints from the seven sessions during the three-day conference. Thus the intent of this book is twofold: to enable a wider audience to benefit from the thoughtful discussion of important issues facing us all, and to provide the conference participants themselves with the opportunity to offer more detailed observations while simultaneously gaining further insights from their colleagues.

Such exchanges are important, for as our world shrinks more and more into a global village, we need to maintain not only an intercontinental dialogue but also that sense of cultural identity in terms of who we are and how we are interconnected. That Italian and Italian-American academics united as a community, discussing mutually important concerns, was a valuable experience. That they constituted an interdisciplinary array from the fields of anthropology, communications, demography, economics, history, law, marketing, philosophy, political science, and sociology, was particularly helpful in all gaining a more complete understanding. That the presenter/authors were a combination of both older and newer scholars, resulted in experienced viewpoints as well as fresh insights, and provide for continuity for further intellectual exchanges as the years pass.

This community of scholars, stronger than ever before, evolved out of a series of past conference experiences—the first three held in Pisa and the last two in the United States. Begun in 1993 with the theme of origins and emigration, the Italo-American Conference next occurred in 1995, examining the interplay of local and global dynamics, followed in 1997 with a focus on the relationship between public and private entities and processes. The 1999 conference took up the comprehensive theme of society, identity, and communication technology as they affected Italy and the United States in the twenty-first century. After an interval of eight years, caused by economic and other unforeseen issues, the 2007 conference theme was that of the title of this book.

The origin and development of these intellectual exchanges, cultural experiences, and published papers are due to the vision of one man, Professor Mario A. Toscano at the University of Pisa. His idea occurred, interestingly, in Kobe, Japan, while attending the biennial congress of the International Institute of Sociology that brought together scholars from the eastern and western hemispheres. "Why not experiment with a conference for Italian and Italian-American social scientists?" he wondered. It would be a venue to talk, analyze, and confront the issues; recollect vanishing individual and collective memories; and explore the possibility of a community without frontiers. Further, he wanted the program to have a special pedagogy, one that constructed both a transnational community founded on old experiences and cultural roots, and also socialized young scholars into it in the name of intellectual interchange and democracy. In naming this program, Professor Toscano gave the Latin-sounding acronym IPSEIDEM, drawing from Italy's glorious past with a touch of humor, to call it the International Pedagogy for Socializing Experiences and Intellectual Democracy. And so, he set about planning the event with colleagues in Italy and the United States, raising the necessary funding, and holding a most successful conference that became the foundation for all that has since occurred. Professor Toscano is the one who established the three-day structure for the conference—its paper sessions, cultural events, and the amenities provided for conference participants. It was that standard that, as U.S. coordinator for the 1999 and 2007 conferences, I sought to emulate. Happily, these conferences have now been formalized within the framework of a signed international agreement (*convenzione*) between William Paterson University and the University of Pisa, which will serve as the basis for the continuity of this significant initiative.

Professor Toscano was the Italian coordinator for this latest conference, as he had been in 1999. The importance of his successful efforts to secure funding to enable so many young Italian scholars to come to the United States to present their research, learn from their American counterparts, and establish a transatlantic network of academics, cannot be overstated. Moreover, not content with simply remembering past successes, Professor Toscano hopes to host the next conference in Pisa in 2009 to advance further his dream of a transnational community of scholars who maintain an active network of collaboration, cooperation, and mutual understanding.

IL PROGRAMMA DI QUESTO LIBRO

To sharpen the focus in discussing the theme of uncertainty and insecurity in the new age, this book is divided into five parts. In "Part One: Society and Social Relations," the authors examine the impact of globalization on local cultures and ways in which they respond to these social forces. "Part Two: Community and Isolation" contains varying discussions on how individuals fare when confronted with conflicting values and social change. Coping strategies to preserve one's sense of self and one's heritage are also an important consideration to the authors contributing to "Part Three: Identity and Culture." How we view ourselves and others, as well as the actions we take to improve or maintain our societal position, is the emphasis in "Part Four: Perception and Politics." Finally, but by no means less important, is how the changing times affect employment stability and the workplace environment, as the authors discuss in "Part Five: The World of Work."

In *The Sociological Imagination* (1959; 2000), C. Wright Mills explained that ordinary people often see their personal troubles as private matters, not realizing that what we experience in diverse and distinct social settings is often traceable to structural changes and institutional contradictions. In other words, the public issues of the social structure transcend the local environments. With all the talk today about globalization and the reality of the worldwide pervasiveness of telecommunications and the Internet, many people are at least vaguely aware of the occurring global and technological changes that may be affecting them. In particular, economic changes—such as megamergers, downsizing, outsourcing, and competing foreign markets—may directly and negatively impact individuals and local industries, and so they are keenly aware. Even so, personal experience and/or observation alone cannot enable us to comprehend the social forces permeating our daily lives. Through theoretical application and real-life examples, the authors in this book provide us with insights to enhance our understanding of what we are experiencing.

IL SUPPORTO DI MOLTI

Conferences such as these are expensive and impossible to hold without the support of many people and organizations. William Paterson University provided extensive logistical support, including site facilities, housing and linen, shuttle bus transportation, and administrative assistance. The John D. Calandra Italian American Institute hosted the Saturday sessions, a luncheon, and published this book. Two individuals who worked tirelessly—Sam Fumosa and Rosemary Feterick Vasta—were responsible for securing funding from numerous Italian-American organizations. Indeed, without their help, the conference could not have reached the level of success that it did.

We gratefully acknowledge the financial support from the National Italian American Foundation; National Association of Italian American Women; National Order Sons of Italy in America; New Jersey Italian and Italian American Heritage Commission; Vice Consulate of Italy in Newark; American Italian Historical Association; Grand Lodge of New Jersey, Order Sons of Italy in America; Padre Pio Lodge #2350, OSIA; Cavaliere Dottore Angelo Bianchi Lodge #2654, OSIA; Department of Sociology, William Paterson University; Garibaldi Meucci Museum; Marlton Lodge #2315, OSIA; Mercer County Italian American Festival Association; Morris County Lodge #2561, OSIA; and Sylvia Sammartino Lodge #2671, OSIA.

Giving generously of their time and efforts to help make this conference a success were: Center for Italian and Italian-American Culture, Cedar Grove, NJ; Sydney Barksdale-Howe, Joseph Caffarelli, Nicholas DiMinni, Diana Krohnert, Cathy Marston, Meredith McCarthy, Clyde Roberts, Anthony Scally, Marc Schaeffer, Barbara Stomper, Gradie Stone, Anthony Julian Tamburri, Susanna Tardi, and Allen Williams.

We also express our appreciation that the Italo-American Conference 2007 enjoyed well-wishing messages from Italian President Giorgio Napolitano, Italian Minister of Foreign Affairs Massimo D'Alema, Tuscany Regional President Claudio Martini, and U.S. Congressman William Pascrell. We are also most appreciative of the presence and words spoken at the conference from Paolo Toschi, Vice Consul of Italy in Newark; Agostino Fragai, Councilman for Institutional Policies, Regional Council of Tuscany; and Mary Ann Re, Executive Director of the NJ Italian and Italian American Heritage Commission.

On a personal note, I would like to thank Anthony Julian Tamburri, Dean of the John D. Calandra Italian American Institute of Queens College, CUNY, and Professor of Italian and Italian American Studies, for making the publication of this book possible. My deep appreciation goes to Lisa Cicchetti, who has been the consummate professional in preparing the book for production and guiding it through that process. Finally, I want to acknowledge my gratitude to my wife, Beth, for her ongoing understanding and support for the time and effort needed to bring this project to completion.

VINCENT N. PARRILLO
William Paterson University

PART ONE
Society and Social Relations

The National Basis of a Sociology Without Borders

ANDREA BORGHINI
University of Pisa

This paper discusses a recent trend in contemporary sociology based on the idea that new global problems, such as ecological crises and immigration flows, need a global view and global institutions. The need to deal with these new challenges, which have nurtured global uncertainty, has impelled many sociologists from several countries in the world—especially Europe and United States—to broaden their cultural vision and discover new paths for sociology. These efforts have led to use of the phrase *sociology without borders*. Indeed, if we consider globalization as a relatively new phenomenon affecting the world as a whole, we are compelled to find new methodological instruments to tackle our realization of this transitional period.

Sociology without borders advances a cosmopolitan sociology and vision. At its center are human rights and collective goods. Human rights include the right to decent employment; social security; education; housing; food; security; health care; cultural, racial, religious, and ethnic identity; and sexual preference. Human rights also include gender equality and the principle that vulnerable groups need special protection. Enabling these human rights are the advance and protection of collective goods, including a sustainable environment, transparent laws and government, public control of natural resources, community-based information grids, fair trade, food sovereignty, and participatory democracy. Indeed, a just society and human rights are themselves collective goods because they are indivisible and inclusive (Blau and Moncada 2006).

Such considerations suggest the necessity of redefining some values beyond the territorial scale and national belonging. Sociologists without borders claim that we are witnessing growing interdependencies and solidarities around the world and that these do not emanate from nation–states, but from the enormous capabilities and resourcefulness of ordinary people.

EPISTEMOLOGICAL PREMISES

It is important to underline the epistemological premises of this cultural stance, which is the focus of this paper. Sociology without borders implies leaving out the epistemology of state centrism or, as European sociologist Ulrich Beck said, moving away from *methodological nationalism* to methodological cosmopolitanism.

By methodological nationalism, Beck means a social vision that studies cultural, social and political dimensions through alternative and opposite categories such as *either . . . or*. In Beck's opinion this tradition comes from sociology's tendency to study society in relation to the nation-state to which it belongs. Nation-states create and contain society and, therefore, they also define the frontiers of sociology.

Beck contrasts this version with methodological cosmopolitanism. Like other authors who espouse this new vision of sociology, Beck shares a similar reading of sociology's history, emphasizing an approach based on the inclusive comparisons of *and . . . and*. In Beck's opinion the same reality is ongoing at a cosmopolitan level. For instance, he refers to public demonstrations around the world against the Iraq war in 2003. We thus need a new cosmopolitan vision, centered on a borderless world. We need to challenge the iron grip of the nation-state on the social imagination (Beck 2003).

> Indeed, as Bryan S. Turner (2006) asserts, classical sociology involved the systematic study of the social, not society and hence this tradition is not negated by the current interest in sociological accounts of globality, network and flows. Sociology has a direct purchase on the contemporary debate on globalization because it was not a science of (national) society but the study of the social. In addition, because the social was always a moral field, sociology can contribute directly to the study and promotion of cosmopolitanism, which must also reflect on the ethical dimension of the social, especially in developing a hermeneutics of Otherness (2006:140-41).

Turner also tells us that Weber's study of the social meanings of action and interaction and his methodology are compatible with a cosmopolitan ethic of care. In addition, Durkheim's idea of true patriotism revealed a cosmopolitan view: "In a global social world the hermeneutics of social action forces us ever to engage with other cultures in a context of growing hybridity and culture interpenetration" (Turner 2006:141).

This epistemological challenge posed by a sociology without borders is the most problematic aspect. To give up an epistemology of state centrism is not straightforward because the state surrounds us, it is inside of us, and it can condition public and private identity significantly. For many centuries, the nation-state has represented the natural framework for society, and individuals have grown and found security and well-being within it. Hobbes eloquently captures this reality:

> Out of it [the State], we are protected by our own forces, in it by the power of all. Out of it no man is sure of the fruit of his labours; in it, all men are. Finally, out of it, there is a Dominion of Passion, war, fear, poverty, solitude, barbarisme, ignorance, cruelty. In it the Dominion of peace, security, riches, decency, society, elegancy, sciences and benevolence (Hobbes, 2000:130).

This paper holds that the persistence of the nation-state is due to its symbolic value, and the strong ties that it keeps with the private and public collective. We are not yet in an era characterized by the end of the state, but in an era in which this political form is undergoing transformation.

GLOCALISM AND GOVERNANCE: SOME CRITICAL ASPECTS

Some examples are useful at this point, beginning with the concept of *glocal*. The term, coined by Roland Robertson (1995), clarifies better than the term globalization the need to group global and local. As George Ritzer says,

> Glocalization can be defined as the interpenetration of the global and the local, resulting in unique outcomes in different geographic areas. This view emphasizes global heterogeneity and tends to reject the idea that forces emanating from the West in general and United States in particular are leading to economic, political, institutional and—most importantly—cultural homogeneity (2003:193-194).

This term contrasts the thesis of the hard version of cosmopolitanism that sees the world as a whole. The cultural, political, and economic glocal interactions, (for instance between cities or regions), intersect the space and the territory of the nation-state. This is not to say that the state is at an end, because it reacts to this new situation. Here it is the *glocal state*, the *network state*:

> . . . still plays a critical role in shaping markets by mediating these connections between the local and the global and by influencing how local specific assets are mobilized within the range of opportunities

> available in the global economy . . . State is increasingly moving toward a position as a network state, embedded in a variety of levels and types of governance institution (Riain 2000:203).

The re-scaling of the state is not only a defensive response to intensified global economic competition, but a concerted strategy to create new scales of state regulation to facilitate and coordinate the globalization process. On one scale, states have promoted economic globalization with the formation of supranational economic blocs: EU, NAFTA, ASEAN; on sub-state scales, meanwhile, states have devolved substantial aspects of their governance capacities to regional and local institutions, which are better positioned to restructure major urban regions (Brenner 1999).

> The organizational structure and strategy of these glocal states are only now beginning to be explored. The state that connects a wide range of local networks to a diverse set of global actors and networks must itself be more decentralised and flexible than states that presided over a centrally negotiated national development coalition (Riain 2000:203).

Italian author Antonio Cassese (2002) also stresses the capacity of the state to penetrate global institutions, becoming market builders in new sectors; or by the strategy of infranationalism, that enables the state to keep the EU under control through middle range officials that establish a meso-level of governance.

The second example concerns the idea of *governance*. The theory of the new institutional perspective of governance addresses the problem of a lack of authority to coordinate decisions among the number of actors participating in this strategy. The problem is similar at local, national, supranational and global levels. In relation to multilevel governance, for instance, Gary Marks and Liesbet Hooghes (2003) remark that the reallocation of authority away from the central state is an ongoing process but it poses a *coordination dilemma*. As the number of actors rises, it becomes more difficult to punish defectors. Free riding is the dominant strategy for large groups in the absence of a leviathan or countervailing norms that can induce actors to monitor and punish defection.

The same problem is evident at a global level. Governance appears to be a useful instrument only if it is applied in a milieu ranging from the local to the international level, where actors involved share the same reference points and communication codes. Since at a global level all the actors do not share the same values, governance naturally lacks that centrality and coherence of action. Conversely, the more that globalization advances, the more that individuals will organize action according to their own particular characteristics.

Problems regarding issues such as order, accountability, legitimacy, democracy, security and transparency of procedure appear even more serious at a global level. The success of global governance must necessarily lie in the sharing of a collective identity or solidarity that is still out of reach. At present, it is extremely difficult to reconcile the hierarchical dimension of power with the cooperative dimension, because of the difficulty of identifying institutions that can assume the important role of coordinating decisions, and especially, the difficulty of identifying apparatuses to control law and order within a complex intertwining of powers and functions generated by such an institutional strategy. It is practically impossible to outline a precise identity, neat boundaries and clearly assigned rights and duties. The powers of non-state actors are therefore endangered by their lack of accountability, sovereignty and democratic structures (Borghini 2004:52).

The examples mentioned above show that the State persists in relation to its symbolic importance and values. This is the starting point of new reflections about the need to investigate some aspects of the State's formation and the reallocation of power in the global era. The State is an actor capable of shaping globalization and conditioning the private and collective identity of citizens. This is possible because the State is a rational-irrational admixture that adapts itself readily to the political-social nature of human beings (Smith 1991).

THE NATION-STATE: SYMBOLIC ASPECTS

What emerges from these examples is therefore an aspect that does not seem to have been thoroughly investigated—and which was hinted at in the introduction to this paper: the mythological-symbolic motivational nucleus, which perhaps sustains the institutional apparatuses that we observe and know. Here, literature and philosophy can come to our aid: Friedrich Nietzsche (*State is the name of the coldest of all cold monsters*), Martin Van Creveld (*the State is an abstract entity that corresponds neither to those who make the rules nor to those who submit to them*) and so on.

These are but a few examples that point us to the idea of the State as a social construction (society, therefore!) deeply rooted within individual consciousness and in governed communities, and which therefore culminates in the State as a socially created image. In this context, the suggestions taken from the works of Pierre Bourdieu on the *Pensée d'Etat* (the State's Thought) seem particularly intriguing.

The *Pensée d'Etat* is a concept elaborated by Pierre Bourdieu (1993), who took his lead from the tradition that predated him (Cassirer and Foucault, specifically). Bourdieu blends within his concept the idea of the State that "thinks for itself" and produces the categories with which anything else can be thought—society, for example: "One of the powers of the State is that of producing (particularly through schools) the categories of thought that we spontaneously apply to everything around us, beginning with the State itself" (Bourdieu 1993:49). What is interesting to underscore in this connection is that, in Bourdieu's analysis, the State proceeds not solely with respect to its legal-normative guise as the origin of externally imposed order, but rather on a more internal, molecular level of institutions positioned to transform, constitute, and condition the mental structures of individuals by means of socialization channels already established to accomplish such tasks: the school and family. Borrowing from Weber, Bourdieu states that the "State is an X that successfully claims the right to a monopoly on the legitimate use of physical and symbolic violence against a particular territory and against the entire population that belongs to it" (1993:51). The examples that Bourdieu adumbrates in support of his thesis are numerous: Spelling reform, for example, a decision originally made centuries before in the form of a state decree and which remains as a decree of the same organism in a different form, provokes

> strident protest by a large percentage of those who are in some way connected to writing, whether those who live by writing or those who use writing ... all of these defenders of spelling orthodoxy are mobilized in the name of the fact that the existing system of spelling is natural, in name of the satisfaction ... that a perfect accord between mental and objective structures provides (Bourdieu 1993:49).

Other examples include those related to changes of any kind proposed in the regulations governing school subject matter, which always encounter intense resistance that is not only tied to corporate interests, but also to something that runs much more deeply, in other words to "cultural phenomena, with their connected hierarchies, [that] are elevated to the rank of the natural by the action of the State which, introducing such hierarchies into cultural objects as well as into our brains, confers upon cultural authority all the illusions of naturalness" (Bourdieu 1993:50).

Endeavoring to explain such a phenomenology, Bourdieu resorts to a distinction among various forms of capital: physical, economic, informational, and symbolic, positing the State as the holder of meta-capital. The State, as it developed across the centuries, is accepted from people as a natural phenomenon without the need for it, in most cases, to resort to force in order to obtain obedience to its norms. In fact, it relies upon the *ritual subjugation to established order* (*soumission doxique à l'ordre établi*). The State provides us with our social identities, modeling them for us, and it becomes difficult, if not impossible, to escape because both formal and cognitive levels refer to one another continuously and adherence seems both immediate and impulsive because subjects consider it to be consonant with the actual structures of daily life.

In conclusion, we must point to the importance of the symbolic nature of the State and the State as a social image. The latter is a dimension to develop not to confute sociology without borders, but rather to highlight an ongoing social, piecemeal engineering in building it. It is important to give centrality to government factors in all their complexity, in order to give some durable foundation to the development of this new sociological perspective, and some new perspectives of certainty in an increasingly uncertain world.

References

Beck, Ulrich. 2003. *La Società Cosmopolita*. Bologna: Il Mulino.

Blau, Judith and Alberto Moncada. 2006. *Societies Without Borders* 1.

Borghini, Andrea. 2004. "Governance and Nation-State." Pp.47-56 in *Globalization, Armed Conflicts and Security* edited by Alessandro Gobbicchi. Soveria Mannelli, CZ: Rubbettino.

Bourdieu, Pierre. 1993. "Le Pensèe d'Etat." *Actes de la Recherche en Science Sociales*. 3:49-62.

Brenner, Neil. 1999. "Beyond State-Centrism? Space, Territoriality and Geographical Scale in Globalization Studies." *Theory and Society* 28(1):39-78.

Cassese, Antonio. 2002. *La crisi dello Stato*. Roma-Bari: Laterza.

Hobbes, Thomas. [1642]. 2000. *De Cive*. Roma: Editori Riuniti.

Marks, Gary and Liesbet Hooghes. 2003. "Unraveling the Central State, but How? Types of Multi-Level Governance." *American Political Science Review* 97(2):233-243.

Riain, Sean.O. 2000. "States and Markets in an Era of Globalization." *Annual Review of Sociology*. 26:187-213.

Ritzer, George. 2003. "Rethinking Globalization: Glocalization/Globalization and Something/Nothing." *Sociological Theory* 21(3):193-209.

Robertson, Roland. 1995. "Glocalization: Time-space and Homogeneity-heterogeneity." Pp. 25-44 in *Global Modernities*, edited by Mike Featherstone et al. London: Sage.

Smith, Gordon. 1991. "A Future for the Nation-state?" Pp. 197-207 in *The Nation-state: The Formation of Modern Politics*, edited by Leonard Tivey. Oxford: Robertson.

Turner, Bryan. S. 2006. "Classical Sociology and Cosmopolitanism: A Critical Defence of the Social." *British Journal of Sociology* 57(1):133-151.

The Marketing of Global Control

VALENTINA CREMONESINI
University of Salento

This essay discusses the impact of multinational companies on local cultures. It focuses on the modalities through which that impact takes place and the possible consequences in the cultural terms of self-perception and social reality. It also focuses on the *modus operandi* of multinationals, in particular, their strategies and tools to interpret, define and project themselves. Finally, this paper also examines the global society in an exchange relationship. Consequently, this text above all centers on marketing.

Globalization is an ongoing process we are all experiencing. The European sociological debate on what this process is or represents is divided between those who believe that globalization is a *social fact*, an *historical process* (Giddens 1990; Bauman 1998; Beck 1999) and those who maintain that the same phenomenon is a *doxa*, an ideology (Bourdieu 1998) and a *field of enunciation*, (Foucault 1982), in which the discourses of neoliberal power are produced and acquire meaning.

This author agrees with the second conceptual trend, affirming that globalization is simultaneously a *descriptive and performative* concept (Bourdieu and Wacquant 1998). Globalization does not conceal the complexity of "real processes." On the contrary, it legitimizes a false interpretation of social phenomena, producing those effects that it should in fact describe. It is this ambiguity that represents the symbolic strength of this concept. Globalization is one of the principal elements of the neoliberal symbolic imperialism, in which *reality* and *truth* of the present materialize.

The function of the term globalization is so *naturalizing*, according to Roland Barthes (1972), that it allows the unifying process of the economic field to be transformed into an ineluctable destiny and a universal liberation project. In this way, the above-mentioned function obscures the phenomenon of globalization as the result of precise political choices made by the boards of directors of the major multinational companies, rather than by institutions. Multinationals are the new political and economic entities, capable of ruling reality (Burham 1941).

Globalization thus constitutes an ideological product, one that allows the discourses of neoliberal power—the discourses of the market—to produce both perceived and real effects that become described as a consequence of a global, unifying natural process. In this sense, we can recognize a sort of imperialism that multinationals impose on reality on a global scale. This is a type of imperialism that does not show its negative form. Rather, it easily shifts into a more desirable metamorphosis through the sale of reality and the truths of power, thanks to an exchange between the subjects involved with reality.

According to this point of view, "the marketing action" taken by the manager becomes the prevailing visible action. Accordingly, we must analyze marketing not only as an operative tool but also, and above all, as a mentality. It means that marketing is knowledge made up of institutionalized attitudes, regulations, and behaviors. Marketing is the typical mentality of the so-called *managerial revolution* (Burham 1941).

The conversion of marketing from a mere economic function connected with the market into a real and concrete mentality is the most visible cultural feature in the global scenario dominated by multinational companies. Thanks to a new leading class—that of managers who present themselves as candidates to manage most of our everyday reality—this mentality has become the protagonist. Unlike what happens in the United States, this conversion is highly visible in Italy. This is due to the fact that it is historically more recent, with more recognizable effects and it places a more significant burden on traditional local culture.

My study therefore analyzes marketing as a mentality, following Sennett (2006), by means of the reconstruction of its knowledge, purposes, strategies, and tools, to understand some the possible outcomes.

MARKETING AS A DEVICE OF KNOWLEDGE

The adoption of a "marketing mentality" is the result of overall transformations that have evolved in both the economic and the production systems. Contemporary capitalist companies more and more tend to disengage from the production of objects. They contract with a third party for the productive process, and concentrate on research to develop new, creative ways to build and strengthen their own image. This is how the run towards the so-called "lightweight companies" starts, with the process of *core business*. This implies light and highly flexible structures that manage the external production of objects, aimed at projecting their own image internally, their own brand and strong identity that enable companies to sell the products.

The same concept of the market, in its relationship with multinationals, has changed radically. This is the *marketing concept*: a global vision of both exterior and interior firms, where the market is part of the same process of projecting and organizing the company. This evolution of the marketing concept, the universality of its principles and methods, and its classification as a social science—as claimed by its theorists, and especially by Philip Kotler (1986)—go beyond the traditional economic field.

Kotler (2003) asserted that marketing concerns every relationship where a value exchange on a product, a service, an idea, an opinion, and information takes place. The cultural impact of multinational companies on local cultures depends on their goals: globalization at the same time of production and consumption, opening and expanding new markets, or seeking to control these same markets. The appropriate analysis and the management strategy of the market represent a vital issue for multinational companies, with analysis as the first and the main marketing tool, most particularly target and need analysis.

My research centered on the deconstruction, as suggested by Jacques Derrida (2001), of the field of analytical interest of marketing. Methodologically, my analysis is based on Michel Foucault's device analysis. This type of analysis examines the discipline of marketing as a *device of knowledge* (Foucault 1981), elaborating on social reality and self-objectification. Thanks to Foucault's theoretical contribution and methodological guidelines, even though never explicitly confirmed by the French philosopher yet contained in his *genealogy of power* (Foucault 1995), I tried to show how the discourses of marketing empirically redefine the geography of thinking that is the framework of values and cognitive schemes of each of us. The marketing device of knowledge produces discourses—objectification of the subjects and their actions—that not only redefine the hierarchical organization of values, accessible to everybody and generating what Foucault named *effects in terms of knowledge*, but also, at the same time, activate a mechanism of selection and exclusion, producing what Foucault defined *effects in terms of power*.

The discourses of marketing are not homogeneous, in the sense that the proposed social significances and the hierarchy of values depend on single productive and communicative decisions made by each company. Rather, the same discourses become homogeneous because they are possible in a wider frame of the production of *truth*. As a matter of fact, marketing as a device of knowledge implies a *will of truth*, as in Foucault's opinion.

In a framework of production of general truths, companies can manufacture the reality of the needs they intend to fulfill in several ways, thanks to different social significances. The marketing effects of power are such that they successfully promulgate these truths to condition all of us, so that the company thrives by meeting those newly created needs.

Even though we are not the consumers of a specific product, we participate in the social process of accepting the same truths by which that product has been produced. Moreover we are part of the more evident dynamics of cultural homogenization that contemporary capitalism imposes on local cultures. I would argue that this process of homogenization is not the result of a homogeneous operation carried out by multinationals, or by the discipline of marketing in a general sense. The marketing strategies used by multinational companies are not aimed at remodelling society, even though they actual do remodel both society and social actors in order to invent and sell their new products, and so increase their sales. Instead, consumption is the heterogeneous purpose that marketing pursues. In any case though, the forms and objects of consumption remodel the frame of those values and cognitive schemes that define our society and ourselves.

I propose that the postmodern form of capitalism begins with the above-mentioned principle. Bernard Stiegler (2004) defined this as cultural and services capitalism, "that entirely generates patterns of life, transforming the ordinary in order to subject it to its direct interests, and standardizing existences by means of marketing concepts." For these reasons, it may be said that consumption has gone beyond the level of just product consumption by becoming a form of knowledge of the world. The postmodern consumer consumes the categories of sense, among which an unlimited variety of products *naturally* becomes important. He consumes the standardization of himself and his way of living, by means of the formatting and artificial manufacture of his desires and needs, and the exposition—pervasive to simulation—of the same desires made by communication marketing strategies. What multinationals want us to consume, even before selling us their lines of products, are the social *significances* and the *truth* that allow their existence to be possible and necessary.

These reasons are why I think that consumption now goes beyond mere product consumption and becomes a discursive strategy, that is, the possibility for multinationals to establish a relationship with us, wherever and whenever. I want to briefly explain those principles by means of an example. A multinational producer of cosmetics, before putting on the market a skin care products line (such as eye contour night cream, eye contour day cream, moisturizing cream, anti-wrinkle cream, lip contour cream, lip moisturizing, ad infinitum) must sell the consumers two things:

First, to the population segment of women (or men) who invest in their physical appearance via the consumption of beauty products, multinationals present images of women's beauty and the social significance of beauty: women must be beautiful. The specific standards of how they must be beautiful may change according to the communication choices of a company, with respect to these significances. The social actor can choose to follow them or not. I can choose to take care of my physical appearance, aspiring to that pattern of women's beauty, that prototype that may correspond to the one proposed by a company. According to the analytical pattern I propose, this constitutes an effect in terms of knowledge. But that company wants to sell something else.

Second, it wants to sell the truth according to which, in order to be good-looking, we must have a perception of our body as if it was a unity divided into a thousand parts. Beauty, regardless of an individual's interpretation, requires the division of the body into an almost unlimited series of parts in order to identify the blemish to cure. The division of body unity is a cultural feature becoming more and more established in almost all societies. This almost universal transformation of the body is producing dramatic effects on self-perception. Apart from this, the cosmetic company wants to sell another truth too, that beauty is something that needs to be cured. The historic (though widely differing) search for beauty found in all societies has acquired significance closer to medical and scientific knowledge in the discourses of marketing. Taking take care of oneself is converted into a cure to treat by means of adequate therapeutic tools, necessary to the recovery. This recovery is from the new social disease of ugliness. Another example, apart from ugliness itself, involves old age, as my study shows that ugliness and old age are two symptoms of the same disease that have to be kept away, cured and prevented. The epistemological importance of these conceptual transformations demands analysis.

Multinational companies, by means of marketing strategies, homogenize local cultures in a frame of global consumption, providing social significances (effects of knowledge) that usually mix and integrate with local cultures. However, these *glo-local* social significances are included on a plane of production of truth and remodeling of the categories of thought—and in effects of power then—that are becoming the same for everybody. From this point of view, what is changing is the same way of experiencing reality, as cited in the above-mentioned example of getting experience in beauty or old age or the various categories of pragmatic thought. In my opinion, this transformation is useful to show the homogenizing practice of multinationals in a more visible perspective. That is how the transformation of marketing in a contemporary tool of social control can be detected, as a global and globalizing cultural control that, pressing the local cultural dimension, makes it converge in forms of social reality and self-objectification, communicatively produced on a global scale.

The discipline of marketing would constitute control devices prevailing in our societies, partially because it persuades us not only to buy, but also to think in a specific way. It offers parts of reality, pieces of categories of possible reality, and truth conjugations that live with us every day and become part of our lives, surrounding and redefining our spaces and times, our relationships and ourselves. Marketing is a deceptively light but nevertheless an effective and pervasive, reticular control that cages contemporary individuals, acting like a global cobweb of categories, concepts, values and typifications. This cobweb has a net with a jolly, colored, and attractive appearance of those objects of contemporary consumption. The discipline of marketing controls a great part of our lives as consumers. Its effect on local culture is heterogeneous but fatal.

MARKETING AS A DISCURSIVE STRATEGY OF GLOBAL CONTROL

Marketing experts analyze individuals and their typical social actions in detail, by means of a segmentation process of consumers, that is, the reconstruction of the cognitive schemes of social actors, distinguished according to the target of reference. By doing so, they objectify both subjective and social features in reproducible forms, creating a taxonomy of individuals and social action. Alfred Schutz examined this aspect, particularly the indicators, in his posthumous work *The Problem of Relevance* (1970).

Nowadays the object of consumption has changed, resulting in the juxtaposition of brand, packaging and advertising. Creating thematic fields, marketers present objects through interpretative references, or what sociologists call membership categorization devices (Sacks 1974). Marketing experts seek ways to make the public perceive their products as more desirable in a competitive market. Thus, they attempt to generate new maps of conceptual categories by remodeling the social subject. They try to control our minds, redefining the categories of thought by investigating and studying who we are. They dissect our dreams, wishes and needs in order to categorize individuals or groups of individuals in targets and market segments. They redefine the local cultural plane into the process of global homogenization. The cognitive processes that enable individuals to recognizably order their existence in the world thus become transformed into a simple economic function—marketing—in which knowledge and power interpenetrate with devastating effectiveness.

This paper examines those marketing techniques and strategies that attempt to "colonize" our cognitive processes every day, for the strategic juxtaposition of brand, packaging and advertising has become an important field of control. I consider them as *finished provinces of meaning* (Schutz, 1962), discursive universes with their own logic. The process of cognitive colonization juxtaposes discursive reality of the objects of consumption on our cognitive reality, activating and transferring interpretative elements to socially construct them in a way to make them appear relevant to each of us.

Such redefinitions and re-formatting do not offer more significance and possibilities, but rather make us more submissive and resigned to the fact that everything works this way. Marketing reconstructs individual and social cognitive panorama, where companies can conceptually position their brands and products to increase the number of consumers.

In my study I conducted an empirical and phenomenological analysis on 10 objects of daily consumption in Italy. I chose useless objects of daily use with an accessible price and available in every supermarket, produced by famous brands or multinationals. I then applied these 10 products to the following modalities: *to sin; to reveal one's personality; to protect oneself; to divide one's body; to obtain self importance; to clean and perfume; to diet quickly; to project the external world as a risk; to produce incessantly; and to raise individuals in a scientific arena.*

In Italy, the redefinition of these *concepts*—elements that allow the transfer of interpretative elements of the objects of consumption in daily life — is happening. Although the effects of this redefining, in terms of the transformation of traditional local culture, are not completely identifiable, we can state such transformation is indeed impacting on at least a part of Italian cultural heritage. A condition of cognitive and valuable uncertainty and insecurity has emerged, and I suggest that the marketing strategies of multinational companies contribute to this situation through their efforts at subjection and control.

As these companies mask their processes of subjection, destruction, separation and differentiation, they seek not to overcome cultural differences, but to convert them into a wider matrix of unique thought. Instead of the global production of symbols and cultural information, social significances and categories of sense leading to a "global culture," however, they move to a common world of goods, a homogenization of needs, and a standardization of products. Everything will be the same, just in different places.

PHENOMENOLOGY OF CONSUMPTION: EMPIRICAL RESEARCH

I began by considering the object of consumption — seen as the communication result of the juxtaposition of brand, packaging and advertising — that entirely reveals its discursive structure in numerous advertisements. Advertising is essentially the simulated reconstruction of an individual and/or social experience, in which the object of consumption inserts its own cognitive reality on daily life, inserting new interpretative elements into its definition and redefinition.

The content analysis came from an initial survey of TV commercials and the resulting selection of the objects of consumption from a sample of 10,571 commercials telecast on the seven main Italian TV channels (Rai 1, Rai 2, Rai 3, Rete 4, Canale 5, Italia 1, and La 7) in five time slots (8-10, 12.30-14.30, 15-17, 19-21, and 21-23), during seven days (from Monday, May 9, to Monday, May 16, 2005). As already stated, the selection of the objects of consumption rested on two criteria: as objects of daily consumption and their availability in supermarkets at relatively low prices. As a result, the criteria dropped this exorbitant number of 10,571 commercials in one week to 70 brands, which nonetheless covered almost 50 percent of all the scheduled advertising of that week.

Next, the methodological criterion for selection of a limited sample of these brands rested on considering marketing as a device of knowledge. In particular, I referred to the pattern of the so-called *creative templates*, elaborated by economists Jacob Goldenberg and David Mazursky (2001). That pattern constitutes a matrix of expectations in which the creative process of producing new products takes place, one that also produces its own advertising focus. Identifying the presence of these templates in the advertisements selected led to the discovery of some specific abstract *patterns* in successful commercials. What was particularly interesting about these patterns was identifying the operators connected with each advertisement and reconstructing relevant *sets* (Goldenberg and Mazursky, 1999).

In reconstructing the thematic fields of the individuals involved, we can specify *finished provinces of meaning*, as represented by the objects of consumption and their meaning in the daily life of social actors. From this point of view, the concept of operator of connection becomes of vital importance to "dismantle" this process by using it to divide the TV commercials of these 70 brands chosen into two relevant sets.

On the one hand, there were the *interpretative attributes* of the experience of the object of consumption, and on the other hand, there were the *interpretive attributes* activated in the advertising to simulate a typical situation of daily life, where the interpretative elements of the objects of consumption could be relevant. In this phase of discerning the social significance that advertising visibly attaches to each product, I interpreted this as an effect in terms of *knowledge*, that is, in the advertising supposedly presenting information as "knowledge."

Next, I sought to verify my intuition through identification of an operator of connection in a specific brand's commercial to understand the structure of the relevant sets and their relative significance. It was also possible to detect the *interpretative data* selected by the operator and produce a cognitive connection between a specific product and a specific experience of daily life. This interpretative data, used to establish a connection, allow the natural introduction of the experience of a product into the individual experience. Moreover, these data enable us to identify the effects in terms of *power* that marketing discursively produces to justify its existence, as significant not in opinion but generally as *truth*. This is the significance that every marketing-oriented company must *instill* in society to legitimize its existence and ensure its survival and expansion.

The 10 brands selected, each comprising a 10-commercial set, were: Bacardi, Campari, Chilly, Clinians, Dixan, Elvive, L'Oréal, Kelloggs, Mellin, Mentadent, and Mulino Bianco. Each advertisement was analyzed structurally in passages corresponding to the two preliminary objectives:

identifying relevant sets and operators of connection. Accordingly, each advertisement was analyzed within three frameworks: 1) definition of the situation/situations, allowing us to identify the relevant sets; 2) identification of the operator of connection, enabling us to divide the commercial into two segments; and 3) redefinition of the situation by means of the operator of connection, allowing us to identify the effects in terms of knowledge and power. Identifying the most frequently employed templates in the commercials as a compass, I used Goldenberg and Mazursky's classification of needs[1] to identify each operator of connection.

THE SYSTEM OF OBJECTS IN DAILY CONSUMPTION

For purposes of this paper, the Bacardi rum case study allowed us to analyze the first modality mentioned earlier: "to sin." This advertisement is a highly sophisticated creation that follows the *Extreme Situation Template* pattern, in particular, the *Absurd Alternative* pattern.

FIGURE 1 FIGURE 2

The advertisement starts with the image of a sunset (Figure 1). An off-screen voice solemnly intones: "I am the light, the heat . . . while . . . you . . . " [dissolve into the second picture showing a city at night] (Figure 2) " . . . live the night." In the first image, the alternative is still proposed thanks to a first operator of connection, represented by the adverb "while." The use of the pronoun "I" allows us to understand that the sun is speaking about itself ("I"), a natural power, simple and essential with two attributes—light and heat. The use of the pronoun "you" refers, on the contrary, to human

---

[1] Goldenberg and Mazursky identified 6 vital Templates with 16 versions, as follows: 1) Pictorial Analogy: a) Replacement; b) Extreme Analogy; 2) Extreme Situation: a) Absurd Alternative; b) Extreme Attribute; c) Extreme Value; 3) Consequences: a) Extreme Consequences; b) Opposite Consequences; 4) Competition: a) Attributes in Competition; b) Value in Competition; c) Unusual Use; 5) Interactive Experiment: a) Activation; b) Imaginary Experiment; and 6) Dimensionality Alteration: a) New Connection Parameter; b) Multiplication; c) Division; d) Temporal Jump. (1999:344)

beings who live the night and, in a way, express its attributes. So the advertisement suggests two alternative lines of meaning: the sun (light and heat) that "sleeps" during the night, and the "typical" night experiences of human beings who dwell in it because they do not go to sleep. But the off-screen voice of the sun, as if it were not sleeping but watching what happens, tells/shows different, sensual ways of living the night. The provocative commercial flows according to the following schematic of dialogue and subsequent images;

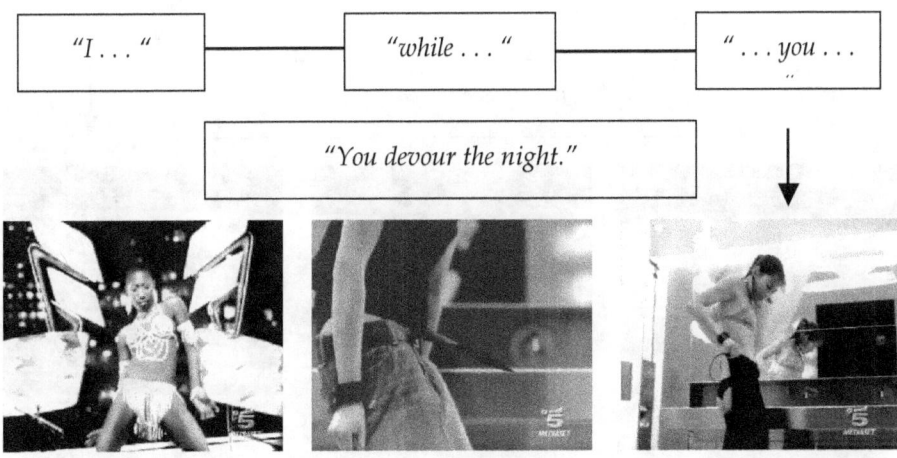

FIGURES 3, 4, 5

FIGURES 6, 7

"You celebrate the ambiguous."

FIGURE 8

"You let passion seduce you."

FIGURES 9, 10, 11

"You hunt by the senses."

FIGURE 12

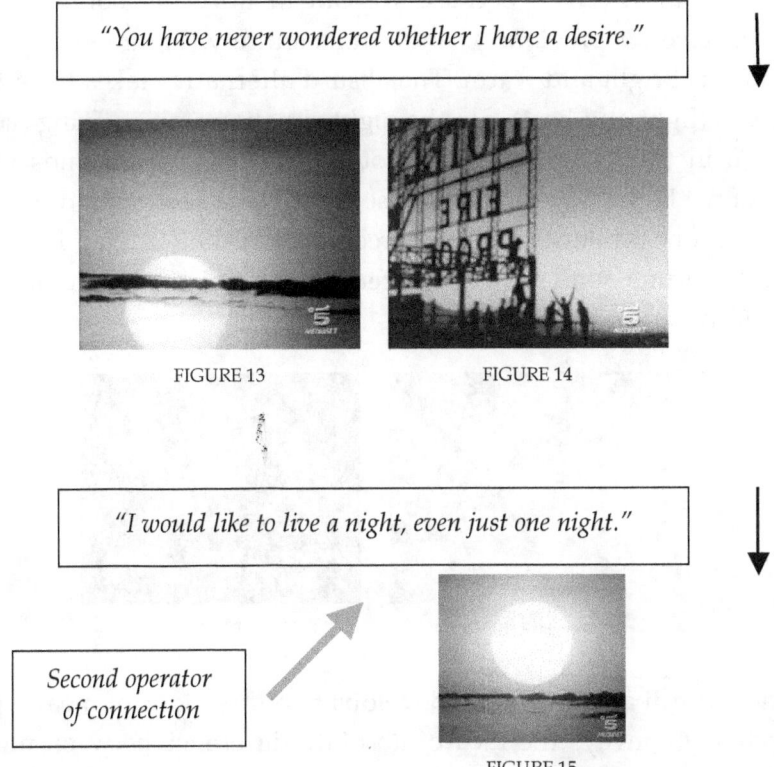

FIGURE 13   FIGURE 14

FIGURE 15

Figure 13 launches an absurd alternative, as night has ended and the sun is rising, its light and heat already beginning to "push back" the night and its inhabitants who are awaiting the sunrise (Figure 14). At this point, the off-screen voice of the sun ("I") asks the inhabitants of the night: "You have never wondered whether I have a desire".

This absurd reification of the sun to have a desire and express it to be, "I would like to live a night, even just a single night," enables marketers to show the sun and the night as naturally antithetical. One can never occur within the context of the place of the other. At night our desires, even sinful ones, can find expression, but things look differently in the light of day.

REDEFINITION OF THE SITUATION

After the sun expresses its wish, it is as if this wish is granted, for images of the night return. This time, however, we see liquor, suggestably rum, pouring from a bottle into a glass (Figure 16). This image is briefly on screen but effective, because we can identify the bottle as Bacardi Reserva, since we previously saw it in its entirety (Figure 9). The color of the liquid is bright and warm. The absurd alternative takes the attributes of the sun (light and heat) into the night situations, objectifying them into that rum in the Bacardi Reserva bottle. The commercial ends with the image of the Bacardi Reserva bottle set on a black background (Figure 17), with only one sentence on the screen: "Bacardi Reserva. The night is ours." The same sentence is repeated by the voice of a woman with a particularly sensual voice.

FIGURE 16   FIGURE 17

The Bacardi advertisement develops two directions of meaning. First, it effectively conveys the idea of absolute difference between night and day that we can symbolically appreciate as incompatible, par excellence. That absolute difference is humanized as the sun speaks (I) and demarcates its own difference—not directly to the night, its opposite, but in relation to those who live the night (You). Moreover, living the night means to have adventurous and/or sensual experiences, suggested as ones of a sinful nature. Note the suggestiveness of the voiceover: "You who devour the night," (who do not sleep then because you live the night); "You who follow the mystery" (who live the mysteries of the night); "You who celebrate the ambiguousness" (who leave normality at night to reveal your ambiguous true nature). And again: "You who let passion seduce you," (who are human, and for capable of passions); "Hunt by the senses"(the obscure and sinful intrinsic nature of human beings, allowing emotions to suppress reason).

Another contrast involves normal behaviors against alternative ones. The first part of the commercial lets us know that there is a transgressive situation: at night people are more likely to take risks or break the rules, unlike a greater reluctance to do so in daylight. With this interpretation, two contrasts are evident: sun/night establishing the absolute difference of worlds, and normality/transgression serving to qualify this difference. By advertising rum as if it were one of the inhabitants of the night, the Bacardi commercial poses the problem of drinking alcoholic drinks. Consuming alcoholic drinks constitutes a transgression for those *alternative* people, who distinguish themselves from normality, as happens with night and day.

The second part of the advertisement redefines the situation. The conversion of the total otherness between the two elements (the sun and people who live the night) into an absurd alternative by means of the operator of connection, that is, the wish expressed by the sun ("I would like to live a night, even just one night"). This radically changes the perspective. This change is even more radical because it is impossible: it is impossible the sun could live a night, but even with this imaginative idea, the sun expresses an envy for those who "let go." With alcoholic drinking redefined as transgressive, people flout normality this way, implying this action allows an escape for those who otherwise may live normal lives and that most normal people wish to transgress and be different at least once. Figure 16 suggests that deviation; pouring rum corresponds to that change of pattern that most people sometimes crave. The message is clear: transgress, drink an alcoholic drink and feel, just once, part of that world of the night, completely different from the normality of daily life. Drinking Bacardi Reserva rum can help you do that, since Bacardi is an element of the night (Figure 9–16). Only in the final part of the advertisement, though, when the bottle appears on a black background (black as the night) is it confirmed that Bacardi belongs to the night world ("The night is ours"). So, become part of the night tribe, drink Bacardi rum, and leave normality behind.

THE CONNECTION TO KNOWLEDGE AND POWER

The knowledge provided by the Bacardi commercial to the viewer is that of the just-stated interpretation. Transgress a little, be different, live the night and its adventures, feel different, and you will be like us. This typification of "like us" means "alternative" actions: diverse, non-conforming people live it up through the night until sunrise, they drink alcoholic drinks, they let passions seduce them, they let senses devour them, and they live ambiguous situations. From this point of view, the social significances that are carried out this way are quite interesting.

The effects of power produced by the commercial are structured — thanks to the operator of connection — in relation to specific situations: 1) alternatives are good in the sense of sin and transgression; 2) a variety of experiences is something to which almost everyone aspires; 3) a break from the routine is also welcome. These three effects seem to be the most visible effects of power, but there is one more, perhaps the most interesting effect concerning the Bacardi company and its use of the oppositions of I and You. Here, "I" is synonymous with normality, by means of the operator of connection, the desire to live even just one night. Because the "I" wishes the experience, the abnormality of the inhabitants of the night, it wishes to be "You." This wish for a new experience is the main theme, but its expression through a generic "You" becomes transformed into "We" in the final sentence, "The night is ours" and "become one of us." The collective grouping implies the marketing strategy of portraying different people as essentially the same: sinners and would-be sinners. So it is true that transgressing and being different is the stimulus, in terms of effects of knowledge that is integrated in order to increase the sale of the rum. However, it is also true that—in terms of effects of power—this differentiation is affected by the significance of transgression as a homogenizing sin: precisely, all sinners the same differently.

CONCLUSION

The phenomenological analyses of ten brand advertisements (but only one in this paper) and the identification of the effects in terms of knowledge and power allowed us to circumscribe the prevailing contents of a limited part of marketing and not its entire system. My research did not aim at defining problem-solving solutions or revealing present-day truths. I tried to display some of marketing and to outline how easily marketing mentality penetrates so many current social situations. In this sense, Jurgen Habermas (1984) was right when he stated that the economic system is colonizing concretely the *world of life*. This colonization is a radical action involving our cognitive processes. Marketing mentality orders our way of knowing and experiencing the world. It orders our store of common sense knowledge and subjects social relationships to the logic of the economic exchange.

My research attempts to show, both from a theoretical viewpoint and empirical examination, that marketing is a tool of social control in our society. Gilles Deleuze (1990) outlined how marketing is indeed a prevalent social control device that could establish a new dictatorship in a progressive and widespread way. Starting from this theoretical suggestion,

I tried to reconstruct some possible strategic procedures in which this device is spreading in our society and to outline some mechanisms that marketing uses to control. Marketing is a tool of power because it is an instrument of knowledge, since, as Foucault would say, it constitutes the body of those on which it exercises its power, and it models the individuality of each body.

References

Barthes, Roland. 1972. *Mythologies*. Translated by Annette Lavers. London: Paladin.

Bauman, Zygmunt. 1998. *Globalization: The Human Consequences*. New York: Columbia University Press.

Beck, Ulrich. 1999. *What Is Globalization?* Cambridge: Polity Press.

Bourdieu, Pierre and Wacquant Loic. 1998. "Les Ruses de la Raison Impérialiste." *Actes de la Recherche en Sciences Sociales* 121-122(03):109-118.

Bourdieu, Pierre. 1998. *Contre-feux*. Paris: Liber.

Deleuze, Gilles. 1990. *Pourparlers* (1972-1990). Paris: Minuit.

Derrida, Jacques. 2001. *Writing and Difference*. London: Routledge Classics.

Foucault, Michel. 1981. *The History of Sexuality: Volume 1: An Introduction*. Harmondsworth: Penguin Books.

—. 1982. *The Archaeology of Knowledge*. New York: Pantheon.

—. 1995. *Discipline and Punish*. New York: Vintage.

Giddens, Anthony. 1990. *The Consequences of Modernity*. Cambridge: Polity Press.

Goldenberg, Jacob and Mazursky, David. 1999. "The Fundamental Templates of Quality Ads." *Marketing Science* 18(3):333-351.

—. 2001. *Creativity Templates in New Products*. New York: Cambridge University Press.

Habermas, Jurgen. 1984. *The Theory of Communicative Action, I: Reason and the Rationalization of Society*. Boston: Beacon Press.

Kotler, Philip. [1967] 2003. *Marketing Management*. N.J.: Prentice Hall.

—. 1986. "Megamarketing." *Harvard Business Review* 64:117-24.

Sacks, Harvey. 1974. "On the Analyzability of Stories by Children." Pp. 216-232 in *Ethnomethodology*, edited by R. Turner. Harmondsworth: Penguin Books.

Schutz, Alfred. 1962. *Collected Papers, I: The Problem of Social Reality*. Edited by Maurice Natanson. The Hague: Martinus Nijhoff Publishers.

—. 1970. *Reflections on the Problem of Relevance*. Edited by Richard Zaner. New Haven, CT: Yale University Press.

Sennett, Richard. 2006. *The Culture of the New Capitalism*. New Haven, CT: Yale University Press.

Stiegler, Bernard. 2004. "Le Désir Asphyxié, ou Comment l'Industrie Culturelle Détruit l'Individu." *Le Monde Diplomatique*, Archives June.

The Social Dramaturgy of Risk Communication: The Case of the LNG Tanker Galleon off the Coast of Livorno, Italy

GABRIELE DE ANGELIS
University of Pisa

Due to the important role that environmental issues play in advanced societies in crystallizing public attention in general, and episodes of social contention in particular, risk communication is attracting increasing interest among social scientists. Accordingly, risk communication emerged as a major social science subject, including the psychology of risk perception, the sociology of social movements, and both fields in the arena of mass communication. Research on risk communication serves different goals. Depending on the interests and specializations of the scholars, it suggests how to design and implement risk communication strategies, or it analyzes media coverage of actual or hypothesized catastrophic events. Risk communication concerns objects as different as the psychological, sociological, and ecological questions linked to, or the various actors dealing with, the different technological branches that can produce environmental risks. Risk communication as a scientific discipline deals further with understanding and assessing risks among different social groups; it analyzes risk-behavior as well as the means of influencing it through public communication (Plough and Krimsky 1987). Risk communication involves, therefore, a considerable number of different tasks and objects.

The analysis of risk communication also offers scholars the opportunity to focus on the complex interplay of interests clashing with one another in all conflicts that develop around environmental issues. In doing so, such analysis can shed light on the dynamics of social action and their sphere of influence within social systems theory, as developed by Niklas Luhmann (1996, 2003).

Social contention is a chief issue of risk communication. Indeed, the great thrust towards tackling environmental questions as questions of public choice has been made by social movements since the 1970s. It has been the increasing resistance against political and private decisions involving environmental or health risk among ever larger social groups that has furthered the attentiveness towards environmental questions that is nowadays obvious to most of us.

I will, therefore, illustrate some key elements of risk communication as they emerge from episodes of contention. To simplify the matter, I will concentrate on the hypothetical, but also quite exemplary case of an environmental issue consisting in making the decision to build or not to build an industrial plant. I will first attempt to outline the key analytical tools necessary to inquire into the relationship between risk and contention. Then, some key questions concerning the dynamics of risk communication will be considered inasmuch as they impact on the dynamics of contention. Further, I will make the case of the debate currently developing with regard to the liquid natural gas (LNG) tanker galleon whose construction is planned off the shores of Livorno, Italy. This will finally lead to some general remarks on risk communication and its political relevance.

RISK AND SOCIAL CONTENTION

During the twentieth century, social conflicts in industrialized countries mostly revolved around issues of redistribution of economic resources. Environmental risks seem now to have replaced the "social question" as the main issue apt to crystallize episodes of contention (Beck 1992). As the social movements against globalization (or promoting an alternative form of globalization) clearly show, environmental risk issues can also be combined with the more classical matters of redistribution, inequality, and imperialism (Della Porta and Mosca 2003).

Nevertheless, it would be hard to find a reasonable classification for the broad range of social movements and the numerous episodes of contention that address environmental issues. Indeed, contrary to the more genuinely politicized movements that crossed the European political scenes of the 1960s and 1970s, the most striking characteristic of the large mobilization around environmental issues is the ability to attract participants with different ideologies who pursue different strategic goals and avail themselves of different forms and repertoires of contention. Just one Italian example is the movement against construction of a high-speed railroad, with its different meanings for different participants. The local people aim at preserving their surrounding environment independently of the usefulness or uselessness of the railroad itself, whereas the participants coming from further afar denounce a form of technological advancement they believe only serves the goals of capitalism in spite of the people's true interests.

If we classify environmental movements by their participants, the range of their goals, or their repertoires of contention, chances are that we would be at a loss as to which classification would suit our purpose. In this respect, the question could be helpful as to what unites all the different participants with their different goals, so as to bring them to participate in the *same* movement. We must look for phenomena that help these different participants share in the same perspective on the issues at stake despite the many differences among them. Niklas Luhmann (2003) suggested concentrating on the so-called "semantics of protest" to find the unifying element of contention on environmental issues.

With this suggestion, Luhmann maintains that social contention unites around a distinction between the potential or current participants and their opponents. Accordingly, the ability to maintain and display this distinction through episodes of contention is a basic requirement for the movement to acquire a definite identity and thus continue its activity. So the quest for the characteristics that can give stability to a social movement comes down to looking for a basic distinction to mark the participants from those they oppose. In case of the environmental movements, Luhmann suggests that the fundamental distinction is the one between those who make decisions and those who are affected by the consequences of those decisions. The fundamental oppositions that emerge from environmental struggles, the ones between decision-makers and affected persons, are omnipresent in all possible specific variations (Luhmann 2003:111-12).

To analyze a movement protesting against a political decision to build an industrial plant, we must first look at the *sources of risk* that the movements identify as the main question at stake. Then, we must identify whom the movement holds accountable for the project, i.e., the *addressee of the protest*. Further, we must take note of the solutions that the movement proposes as an alternative to the project, i.e., the *goals of the protest*. Then, we must identify the *repertoires of contention*, i.e., the means that the movement undertakes to attract public attention on the issue and to put pressure on the decision-makers. The repertoires of protest will channel the *self-representation of the movement*, i.e., the kind of actors and their common interest the movement intends to represent (for instance, workers defending the safety of their workplace or a local community defending the integrity of the environment in which they live).

Asserting the central role that the semantics of protest play in integrating a social movement, I suggest that the whole "discourse of protest" seeks to reinforce the latter aspect of the movement, i.e., its self-representation. By *discourse of protest* I mean all communication acts produced by the movements to shape and organize its own activities according to the aspects highlighted above. Thus, I assume that identifying the sources of risk, vindicating the motives of protest, aggregating supporters and participants around the reasons for protest, and finally expressing protest by means of a repertoire of contention, are all activities that flow into the constant assertion of who the participants are. The bulk of the utterances produced within the movement will be addressed either to the participants themselves or to their audience of bystanders, to the non-participating local population, or to the decision-makers as the addressee of protest. I expect all these utterances to revolve around the constant reassertion of what the movement represents, why it is necessary to gather in protest, and what the goals are. As Luhmann suggests, the unifying aspect of all these different utterances should be some simple juxtapositions, such as the one between decision-makers and those who suffer the consequences of the decision made by others. These fundamental juxtapositions will be the means to ensure that the movement will keep together despite the strategies of communication enacted by the opponents.

THE DYNAMICS OF COMMUNICATION

Scholars analyzing risk communication in contentious situations can help themselves by distinguishing between different analytical aspects of the communication process. They must identify the issue at stake, the actors involved, their explicit requests and goals, how they assess the risk they debate on, and finally which means and strategies of communication they rely upon.

Leading this analysis can be the following questions: 1) What kind of risk is being considered and discussed? 2) What kind of actors is involved? 3) What are the most common, implicit or explicit, understandings of "risk" among them? 4) How far do the actors involved diverge in their views of the risks, their definition, and assessment? 5) What are the (manifest or latent) goals of the actors? 6) What kind of communication strategies do the actors pursue and by which means? 7) Which actors can be defined as the main opponents in the struggle?[1]

Moreover, the strategies of communication can be classified according to the following four *fundamental attitudes*: Communication strategies can 1) aim at providing the audience with *information* among the (potentially or currently) affected population; 2) aim at consolidating or regaining *trustworthiness* (for instance by opening to visitors the doors of the plant, by promoting ethically relevant initiatives, etc.); 3) aim at strengthening *cooperation* between actors, for instance by means of partnerships between ecologists and industries or public authorities; and 4) pursue the goal of *managing* the conflict, i.e., actors can attempt to win the confrontation by splitting the opposition front, managing news, undermining the opponent's trustworthiness, etc. (Wiedemann 1991:375-76).

The study of communication strategies involves the identification of the *actors* involved. They usually belong to one of the following four categories: 1) *politicians* in charge of the decision; 2) more or less organized *citizens* rebelling against or uttering worries about the consequences of the decision in question; 3) *stakeholders* bearing some economic interest in the decision to be made; and 4) *professional communicators*, journalists, etc., reporting over the debate and the forms of contention.

We could add more types of participants: the *justices* possibly called on to block an administrative procedure or a political decision, the *political parties* possibly backing or opposing the decision, and the *editors* or *owners* of newspapers or TV-channels (Rohrmann 1991:355). Indeed, risk communication is a confrontation between many different actors bearing diverging interests and looking at the issue from different points of view. Depending on their specific research interest, scholars can focus on the one actor or the other, and they can reduce or extend the range of actors to which they choose to pay attention.

The first analytical task consists in defining the fundamental interests playing into the dynamic of confrontation. We might assume that they diverge from case to case and must therefore be assessed specifically for every single case. This is, of course, true if what we have in mind are the actors' specific interests in promoting or opposing some decisions. Nevertheless, it is possible to outline some recurring fundamental interests typical of the social roles that the actors fulfill. What I wish to highlight is

---

[1] This is a modified list of fundamental analytical questions as drawn by Wiedemann, Rohrmann and Jungermann 1991:8-9.

that the whole point of Luhmann's system theory consists in offering us the chance to perform such a schematic. Often characterizing the conflicts that arise around environmental issues are actors wielding recurring arguments that mark some constant interests at stake. So we can assume that entrepreneurs will tend to underline the economic efficiency of the project opposed by environmentalists, its positive effects on employment, etc. Protest movements, environmentalists, and their associations will tend to emphasize environmental and health risks, and will also claim to represent the non-vested interests of the people. We can expect politicians to more or less tentatively join one side or the other, but we can assume that their ultimate goal is to gain the voters' support and thus to interpret the struggle as a political chance or as a political danger. Workers and unions will likely join the entrepreneurs in valuing the positive effects on employment, but are also likely to issue concerns about the safety of the workplace. In the end, the actors involved tend to look at the struggle through a specific interpretive frame that enables them to sort the matter ideally according to a simple alternative. Every time an actor faces an option, a decision, a request, or an offer from the opponent, he or she will attempt to judge it according to a specific binary code: this option is economically favorable or unfavorable, safe or unsafe, politically (ultimately electorally) desirable or undesirable, etc.

Analysis of the actors' interpretive frames can, indeed, go much deeper, but the aspects sketched above at least represent the first steps in the definition of interpretive codes that can be generalized among classes of actors. Nevertheless, when analyzing any specific environmental struggle, it is useful to keep in mind how the statements of the actors involved can refer to a deeper layer of fundamental interests that can be either explicit or tacit, especially on the side of political or economic actors.

THE CASE OF THE LNG TANKER GALLEON OFF THE COAST OF LIVORNO

To illustrate how the tools above can be used for empirical analysis, I will focus on a struggle currently taking place around the construction of an LNG tanker galleon off the coast of Livorno (Italy). A LNG tanker galleon is a platform for the storage and treatment of liquid gas. Inside the galleon the liquid is gasified and fed into the continental pipelines that convey the gas to different plants for the production of energy.

The Italian government has given the project high priority, not least because of its geopolitical importance: LNG tanker galleons would eliminate the reliance on the natural gas pipelines running from Russia through Belarus or Ukraine to Italy. These pipelines are objects of continuous tensions between Russia and its neighbors, leading over the past several years to recurrent gas shortages due to a controversy concerning the Russian gas supply to Ukraine and taxes due to Belarus for the gas conveyance. To lessen Italian dependence on the not-too-reliable East European pipelines, an extensive program for an alternative natural gas supply has evolved, of which the Italian government considers the tanker galleons an important part. The government plans two plants for LNG gasification, one of them to be built off the shores of Livorno. The construction was due to begin in January 2006,[2] but it was subsequently delayed. At present, due partly to the need for further risk assessment to meet the requests of citizens and protesters, the construction has not yet begun. All local authorities as well as both the center-left and the center-right coalitions, agree on construction of the tanker galleon. The decision was made when the center-right coalition was in power and is now continued by the current center-left government.

For this analysis, I will consider just the two principal actors: the movement opposing the decision and the political actors (the region government of Tuscany and the federal government) promoting the tanker galleon. This restriction is justified by the fact that the decision to construct the tanker galleon was made and could theoretically be repealed only by the public authorities, although the plant would be administrated by a private corporation. Moreover, media coverage was thus far almost exclusively local and limited to reporting the will of the government and local authorities to build the plant, as well as to reporting the increasing worries about the possible risks by the population. In all probability, the media will play a more important role if and when the episodes of contention go beyond their current scope, as participation has been relatively scarce and the movement has failed to catch sufficient attention from the media.[3]

The movement against the construction of the LNG tanker galleon off the coast of Livorno, Italy, is coordinated by a committee externally supported by several political groupings and organizations ranging from the local Green Party (the party is, however, a member of the now [May

---

[2] Bulletin of the *Ministero delle Attività Produttive* (Ministry for Productive Activities), December 16th, 2005.

[3] The following remarks rely mainly on analysis of the documents and sources that can be found at www.offshorenograzie.it.

2006] serving center-left coalition that supports the construction) to centers of youth aggregation commonly associated with the "extra-parliamentary left." The committee has enacted its own strategy of scientific communication by availing itself of the help of university personnel in the role of experts who are among the founders of the committee itself.

The protesters make use of a large range of means of communication. They have an up-to-date Internet site, issue press statements, and promote demonstrations and sit-ins. Their first communicative strategy was a symbolic action showing the proportions of the project. In these impressive pictures the tanker galleon appears as high as an eight-story building that looms far above the surrounding constructions. As a contrast, on the websites of contractors and administrators of LNG tanker galleons, and on flyers with pictures they provide, are images showing the galleon on the high seas with no comparative objects nearby.

Beyond the use of impressive pictures and computer-reconstructions as eye-catchers, the protesters point to the dangers linked to the construction and the use of the galleon: the pollution of the sea and the possibility of catastrophic events. They avail themselves of pictures showing past incidents as well as of computer-generated images displaying the possible sources of risk: aircraft incidents given the nearness of the airport in Pisa, ship collisions given the commercial traffic that crowds the port of Livorno, and the proximity to oil refineries that would amplify the effects of a possible accident. To catch the attention of the population potentially exposed to the risks of the galleon, the committee organized protest actions in the most significant places they maintain would be affected by a major catastrophe, such as the leaning tower of Pisa, for instance. They attempt to impress their possible allies by displaying on leaflets and posters the scope of the possible consequences of an accident.

A further means to catch public attention consists in the attempt to raise associations with movements most people approve. Protesters, for example, march behind a long peace flag, the symbol of the peace movement highly appreciated in Italy. Further associations concern the widely shared fear in Italy about nuclear energy and weapons. Many local communities of the Pisa and Livorno area were "denuclearized" years ago, meaning that they rejected the building of atomic plants, which is anyhow impossible after the 1987 referendum against nuclear energy and would have been out of the question in those seismic areas. Although the local administrations were perfectly conscious of the practical superfluity of their measure, they so acted in the late 1980s when the danger of a nuclear war was still present. It is commonly acknowledged that their decision gave expression to the will and the moral sentiment of the broad majority of the people, and this sentiment is likely to be still alive in everybody's mind despite the decline of the east-west confrontation.

The third most frequently used symbol belonging to the repertoire of protest is the appeal to "democracy," i.e., direct democracy and the will of the people as opposed to the decisions made by political representatives that, though democratically elected, are depicted as removed from reality and the sentiment of the affected populations. The appeal to direct democracy also relates to the final goal of the protesters, promoting a referendum by which the communities located where the galleon is to be built can decide on the destiny of the project. Needless to say, they expect to win such a referendum.

As to the identity, the "who we are" of the movement, a broad range of symbols depicts the protesters themselves. These images have the double effect of attracting possible co-protesters who identify with these images and reaffirming in fellow protesters the rightfulness of their endeavor. Protesters depict themselves as "parents who want to protect the health and safety of their children" (and also future generations), as dockworkers protecting their working environment, as environmentalists protecting the sea and its inhabitants, and as fishermen worried about their future due to the negative effects of pollution caused by the tanker galleon.

It is indeed difficult to assess whether the protesters actually belong to all of those groups or if those groups recognize themselves in the motives and aims of the protest. As often happens in controversial issues, the debate carries on for a long time, and the number of activists as well as participation in episodes of contention vary over time, depending on whether or not something happens to flare up the protest, such as bad news from the central or local government that makes the possibility of a referendum look more uncertain. Furthermore, uncertainty about the number of participants in the larger demonstrations (the organizers claim a few thousand, the police a few hundred) makes it difficult to assess whether the movement has a constant and effective following among the local population. The self-identifications reported might be reliable self-descriptions, as well as an attempt to interest groups of people whose readiness to join in the protest has been meager thus far, as it is the with regard to the dockworkers and fishermen.

The protest movement is complex and multifaceted and its organizers attempt to involve larger groups of people by differentiating the repertoire of contention, the symbols they use, and their self-identifications. The statements issued during the on-going confrontation with the local authorities show the constant features of the "semantics of protest." The documents produced contrast the "safety" of the environment to the "risk" of constructing the tanker galleon.

Those local authorities and political parties who take a definite position regarding the matter point out that the tanker is "safe." The few who go deeper into the matter or who address the worries concerning the galleon assure the public that further risk assessment will show that the tanker is safe or, alternatively, will make clear how the tanker can be made safer. What characterizes these more articulated statements is the rejection of the dichotomy between risk and safety in favor of a more nuanced insistence on a "reasonable risk."[4] The strategy of the local authorities thus far is to underplay the importance of a protest movement that has found difficulty in getting a footing as they try to deaden the resonance of the protest. For instance, representatives of the regional government do not show up when the protest committee invites them to public debates.

The dichotomy between risk and safety is what the protesters emphasize to highlight the common interest of the diverse figures and social groups they want to get involved in the protest. As the movement continues and the installation of the LNG tanker galleon is not yet accomplished, further analysis is still possible to check the scope of the catalyst function of the "semantics of protest." This is anyway the most suitable candidate to explain the strategy and the style of communication adopted by the protest movement.

THE POLITICS OF RISK COMMUNICATION

Since the 1980s social scientists have paid ever-increasing attention to the issues of risk and risk communication. Characterizing contemporary attitudes towards environmental and health risks are greater sensitivity and worries about risks (Beck 1992), though the lack of comparative empirical data makes it difficult to compare the risk awareness of different epochs. On the other hand, scholars observe an increased

---

[4] See La Margherita - L'Ulivo, Comunicato del 24/05/2006, on the internet site of the Region Tuscany (www.consiglio.regione.toscana.it/).

readiness to transform dangers into risks, i.e., to understand situations implying possible damages to health or environment as the outcome of somebody's will, negligence or sabotage. This is a consequence of the greater capacities for human intervention in nature. For instance, floods have usually been understood as the natural events but the technological ability to reduce their impact on people and infrastructure leads to imputing that possible catastrophes result from someone's negligence because of the expectation that the evil effects of floods can be effectively prevented. If it may be allowed to misuse collective tragedies for making a scientific point, the political consequences of Hurricane Katrina are telling enough.

Thus, higher expectations about risk prevention affect risk perception and communication. Scholars notice an increased willingness in dealing with risks that can be imputed to somebody rather than dealing with risks for which accountability is more difficult (Douglas and Wildawsky 1982). The risk perception of experts and laypeople varies accordingly: the first rely on statistics and quantitative risk calculations, whereas monopolizing the latter's attention is usually some catastrophic event. Influencing public judgment is usually some qualitative factor, such as the magnitude of the catastrophic event independent of its probability, or the mental associations that the source of risks calls to mind (nuclear power as a case in point).

In recent decades scientific risk analysis emerged as the epitome of the rational approach, whereas the risk perception of laypeople was dismissed as irrational and non-scientific. Accordingly, risk communication aimed to re-orient public risk perception through information campaigns. The determination of citizens to be involved in decision-making when environmental and health risks are concerned, as well as the frequent controversies among experts as to methods and results of scientific risk assessment, have led to serious attention to the risk perception of laypeople. Risk communication as a scientific discipline evolved accordingly.

Even so, the fundamental questions that risk communication as a scientific discipline addresses still revolve around the delicate balance that decision-makers must maintain when informing those affected by their decisions. In particular, they must decide how much information to release, which means of communication to choose, how to sharpen awareness about certain risks yet allay unreasonable fears, if and how to involve affected populations in the decision-making, and how to deal with discrepancies among experts in communicating with the public.

Various actors promote public communication on environmental issues: companies, public authorities, multinational and international organizations, and NGOs. The case discussed in this paper concerns public authorities. It illustrates that politicians are often the addressees of a clear-cut expectation: to take full responsibility and to choose between concurring interests. Rarely do protest movements promote a compromise between the interests they advocate and the ones they oppose. Besides, in the language of social and protest movements, interests are usually understood as something barely material and suspicious, and therefore mainly attributed to the opponent. Politicians and authorities are therefore subject to a double request: certainty of choice and certainty of outcome. This is the epitome of "political responsibility" as it often emerges from the language of movements.

Protests concerning environmental issues can be therefore analyzed according to the scheme: "requests to political decision-makers" and "answers of political decision-makers." Schematically, we can distinguish between two fundamental attitudes that political decision-makers can take when facing these requests: we can name them "decisionism" and "quest for trust."

Decisionism is an attitude consisting of a willingness to make political decisions without regard for public involvement. Opposition is seen as a matter to deal with through a strategy of conflict management so as to sidestep public protest or to confront it in such a way as to enact the decision made without compromising with the opponents.

In contrast, *quest for trust* is an attitude consisting of a desire to meet the risk perception of laypeople as well as the worries raised by environmentally risky decisions either by involving the affected population in the process of decision-making or by "staging trustworthiness." We can understand "aimed at staging trustworthiness" as all those communication acts by which decision-makers display their readiness to take seriously the worries raised by risky decisions.

Staging trustworthiness implies attempting to gain trust by showing attentiveness to the worries, requests, and protests of those who oppose a decision. Trust must be gained independently of the results achieved by the decisions made. Indeed, trust as a result of the positive outcomes of decisions would not do in the case of protest movements, for the obvious reason that the whole point in opposing decisions that imply an environmental or health risk is to thwart the attempt to make the decision. In such cases, the goal of the decision-makers is therefore to allay the fears, to reassure the population, to show readiness to narrow the chances that the project in question produces negative outcomes. This can be done by considering, for instance, the possibility of modifying the project itself or by gathering experts for additional risk assessment. The last measure is indeed the most frequent one public authorities adopt to meet the requests of protesters or rather to "stage trustworthiness."

As part of a strategy aimed at "staging trust," committees of experts usually serve the goal of mitigating contention and taking the edge off political confrontation, since experts are supposed to be non-political and therefore ease the pressure on political decision-makers. Consensus can thus be facilitated by referring to their judgment to allay worries and undermine the arguments of opponents. Nevertheless, they also represent a risk in itself, since the gathering of a committee of experts implies a delay in the process of decision-making. Moreover, the results of their consultations can be less certain than the promoters assume, particularly since the composition of the committee is often the object of sharp controversies, as each party tries to bring in experts they trust and who are likely to judge in accordance with the wishes of their clients. Although it cannot be unequivocally said that committees of experts implicitly facilitate the goals of decision-makers at the expense of the protesters, they are nevertheless likely to ease the efforts of decision-makers to delay decisions until the ebbing of the movement, in case the latter is too strong to be simply ignored, or to mask the fact that decisions have already been taken and only wait to be put into practice.

However, both the "quest for trust" and the decisionist attitude epitomize the political difficulties inherent in risk communication, i.e., the discrepancies between the "criteria of relevance" that shape the actions of the actors involved and the way they evaluate the situation according to the specific "institutional" interests of politics and movements. The communication process, far from serving the goal of conciliating diverging interests, is often a means of delaying decisions and staging a search for consensus that is often more illusional than factual.

The case portrayed in this paper shows how diverging semantics mark the differences between the diverging interests at stake. The opposition between risk and safety—understood as the "zero risk-option" — as well as between decision-makers and affected population constitutes a barrier between the actors involved, i.e., in the case illustrated above, between protesters and public authorities.

References

Beck, Ulrich. 1992. *Risk Society: Towards a New Modernity*. New Dehli, India.

Della Porta, Donatella, and L. Mosca, eds. 2003. *Globalizzazione e Movimenti Sociali*. Rome, Italy: Manifestolibri.

Douglas, Mary and Aaron Wildawsky. 1982. *Risk and Culture*. Berkley, CA: University of California Press.

Luhmann, Niklas. 2003. "Soziologie des Risikos." Pp. 201-215 in *Protest. Systemtheorie und Neue Soziale Bewegungen*, edited by Kai-Uwe Hellmann. Frankfurt am Main, Germany: Suhrkamp.

—. 1996. "Alternative ohne Alternative." Pp. 75-78 in *Protest. Systemtheorie und Neue Soziale Bewegungen*. Frankfurt am Main, Germany: Suhrkamp.

Plough A. and S. Krimsky. 1987. "The Emergence of Risk Communication Studies." *Science, Technology, and Human Values* 12:4-10.

Rohrmann, Bernd. 1991. "Akteure der Risiko-Kommunikation," in P.M. Wiedemann, B. Rohrmann, H. Jungermann, eds. *Risikokontroversen. Konzepte, Konflikte, Kommunikation*. Berlin, Germany: Springer Verlag, 355-370.

Wiedemann, Peter M. 1991. "Strategien der Risiko-Kommunikation und ihre Probleme," in P.M. Wiedemann, B. Rohrmann and H. Jungermann (eds.), *Risikokontroversen*, 371-394.

Wiedemann, Peter M., Bernd Rohrmann and Helmut Jungermann 1991. "Das Forschungsgebiet Risiko-Kommunikation," in Eadem, eds., *Risikokontroversen*, 1-10.

Social Resources in the Global Age: The Concept of Social Capital

STEFANIA MILELLA
University of Pisa

In the global age, the topic of social resources that emanate from social relations has become important because they may represent an answer to the phenomena of the social isolation and individualism prompted by globalization.

Usually called *social capital*, these resources are the material and symbolic resources embedded in social networks, e.g., social support, information, and help in the search for a new job. Recent sociological studies in Italy and abroad have underlined the importance of the relational dimension for the individual and show the existence of potential re-sources within social networks accessed and mobilized by network members through their social relationships. The concept of social capital has thus become popular in the social sciences and, in particular, in sociological analysis of social phenomena. In the last decade, in fact, social capital acquired an important position at the center of sociological debate, as illustrated by the publication of numerous theoretical studies.

In this paper we identify some meaningful dimensions of this concept, offering an overview of its most important and theoretical contributions, as well as discussing some theoretical and methodological issues.

Some preliminary considerations are first necessary. Social capital is a complex and multidimensional concept, marked by the interaction between an individual and a collective dimension, but one that has led, not surprisingly, to a multiplicity of definitions and conceptualizations, thereby widening even more the semantic field of the concept (Chiesi 2003). The heuristic complexity and the multidimensional nature of social capital, however, make it difficult to formulate an unambiguous definition. Therefore, it is perhaps best to use the term as an "umbrella," for this metaphor allows us to embrace any aspect of the social structure that produces benefits to the individual (Lin 2003).

Also, an overabundant literature on this subject does not necessarily reflect a rigorous and univocal definition of the term. As a result, social capital is characterized by an insufficient conceptual rigor, making difficult any unambiguous definition, and in turn affecting any methodological approach (Lin 2003).

SOME THEORETICAL APPROACHES

Sociological analysis treats social capital both as an individual resource and as a collective resource. Among the numerous interpretations of social capital are two primary ones: the micro-relational approach and the macro-relational approach. The two levels cannot be analytically separated because they are strongly interlinked and share a common point of view. Lin (2003), one of the leading scholars of social capital, argues that social relations are the nexus of any definition of social capital.

First introduced in the 1970s, the concept of social capital emerged from the inquiries of economic sociology into labor market dynamics and how individual social networks person may affect the job search. Mark S. Granovetter (1974), for example, examined how individuals are more likely to gain useful information about job openings through weak ties, that is, more open but not necessarily strong social networks. Granovetter himself did not use the term *social capital*. James S. Coleman attributes that distinction to economist Glenn C. Loury (1977), who used it to indicate the social network of family and social relations that actors may use to increase their human capital, that is, all knowledge, contacts, and skills that can be used to get a job.

THE MICRO-RELATIONAL APPROACH

The micro-relational approach rises from both rational choice theory and exchange theory, and considers social capital from the individual's point of view, as a set of resources that social actors get from their social networks (Bourdieu 1980; Coleman 1990). This perspective focuses on the resources deriving from the social relations tissue in which a person is inserted. Authors belonging to this perspective include Pierre Bourdieu, James Coleman, and Nan Lin.

PIERRE BOURDIEU

A first attempt to elaborate upon social capital came from French sociologist Pierre Bourdieu (1980), who used the concept to explain social class reproduction processes as a third kind of capital alongside cultural capital and economic capital. Bourdieu suggested that social capital consists of access opportunity to material and symbolic resources derived from belonging to a social group, through the construction of social relations. The first source of social capital is family, within which actors increase and continually modify their endowments of social capital through access to their different relatives. Bourdieu's analysis is important because he underlines the role of social relations to explain the social classes, reproduction processes, but on the other hand, it does not provide any specifics as to what kind of resources constitute social capital. That information would come from others.

JAMES COLEMAN

James Coleman (1990), utilizing the methodological individualism perspective, identified three distinct elements: 1) physical capital (the set of tangible assets); 2) human capital (the person's capabilities and abilities); and 3) social capital (the set of social relations that provide material and immaterial value to help social actors pursue certain aims). In Coleman's vision, social capital constitutes the resources deriving from the social relation tissue in which the social actors are embedded; it is embodied in the relations among persons. While human capital is an individual attribute, social capital is inherent in the social structure since it exists *in* and *among* the social relations. Defined by its function, social capital provides resources that can be used by the social actors to achieve interests and goals that would not be attainable in its absence (Coleman 1990). This, then, is the aspect of productivity of social capital; it appears as a structural phenomenon, since it is based on a social network of relations placed at people's disposal.

It is important to note that Coleman's vision assumes the existence of a rational actor, who intentionally uses the relations net to realize certain goals. In fact, the relations networks represent the outcome of social strategies oriented to build and reproduce durable and useful relations to obtain material and symbolic profits (Piselli 2001). This outcome not only brings benefit to the individual social actor, but also to the entire social tissue. Coleman thus shows how social capital has also the nature of a public good.

However, there are some problematic aspects in Coleman's theorization. First, his analysis combines different elements that should be kept separate: the actor relations dimension and the institutional dimension of social norms and trust. Second, he also does not provide a clear definition of the term *social capital,* since he considers it both as a set of relations and as the resources one can get from the social relations network.

NAN LIN

An important contemporary scholar of social capital, Nan Lin, offers a theory about the social structure and the goal of social capital actions, that is, a mobilization and investment of resources that are embedded in the social networks in pursuit of a profit (Lin 2001). Lin emphasizes the individual dimension, focusing on the ways by which people access/use the resources embedded in their relations. This is an instrumental vision of social capital, based on the concept of intentional investment. Actually, some scholars, such as Salvini (2005), counter that in some cases it is possible for actors to obtain social resources due to their own structural positions in the network, without being forced to invest in those resources. For example, Charles Kadushin (2004) proposed the substitution of social capital with the concept of "networked resources," those that are accessible through a specific structural position. Such an approach could help overcome the relevant problem of constructing indicators to measure social capital.

THE MACRO-RELATIONAL APPROACH

A different perspective, the macro-relational approach, evolving out of functionalistic theory, conceives social capital as a collective good consisting of shared values, social cohesion, and trust (Putnam 1993). Here, attention is given to the collective dimension, with social capital considered as a public good, as a social system attribute deriving from an individual relations set and the social actors' cooperative attitude. This mention of a cooperative dimension refers to the preferential range of the systemic approach to social capital.

ROBERT PUTNAM

Spearheading this viewpoint is the work of Robert Putnam' (1993) on the Italian regions' civic traditions (Putnam 1993), where he related the regions' institutional performances to their endowment of social capital, by which he meant "civicness." In Putnam's conceptualization, social capital consists of those features of social life—networks, norms and trust—that enable the participants to act together in a more effective way to pursue shared objectives, thereby increasing the society's efficiency. In this way, social capital becomes a variable capable of supporting a social system's political and economic development, since it facilitates the identification of individual interests with those of the belonging community. In particular, Putnam's concept of generalized trust explains the different institutional performances between the northern regions endowed with greater civicness and therefore efficient political institutions, and the southern regions, which he characterizes with an insufficient civicness that restrains their economic and political development.

Putnam's vision of social capital, in comparison with that of Coleman, shifts from an individual dimension to a collective one, focusing attention on social development and integration dynamics. Even if a reference to social relations still remains, social capital—in its meaning of civicness and trust—refers to the connections between the individual actors. Putnam's perspective, focused on the characteristics of the social capital that is available in a specific social context, provides an interesting interpretive key to modernization processes. However, we must ask if identifying social capital directly with trust, that is, as a political culture characterized by associative and cooperative participation is really useful. Moreover, we must consider that social capital does not always produce favorable outcomes from a collective point of view. Finally, from a methodological point of view, Putnam's measurement of civicness, with its emphasis on the number of associations present in a territory, neglects any analysis of individual social networks.

SOME METHODOLOGICAL ISSUES

The social capital heuristic complexity raises some problems that affect any methodological plan. In the first place, as previously stated, the heuristic complexity of the concept makes it difficult to give a sufficiently precise definition of the term (Chiesi 2003). Another issue affecting a methodological plan is that in the research literature an often-overlapping or intersection occurs between the concepts of social network and social capital. Although they are tightly linked, they also demand a conceptual distinction. Social capital is incorporated into social relations, but it cannot be simply identified with them. While the social networks may be both opportunities and constraints for action, social capital is always productive, because it refers to the resources used by the social actors in order to achieve their interests. Social capital productivity is influenced by social network features, but it also depends on the particular resources activated in those social ties (Piselli 2001).

Moreover, the lack of assent about the definition gave rise to diversified positions about the possibility of empirical measurement of the concept (Chiesi 2003). At the individual actor level (structural level), according to a social capital self-centered vision, it consists of some material and symbolic resources that individuals get from their network of relations. The social capital intrinsic relations model suggests its operating procedures should utilize social network analysis (SNA) techniques (Chiesi 1999). Such analysis can include morphological features (wideness, density); the kind of ties (friendship, neighborhood); the material and symbolic contents of the relation; and the positive or negative determinants for the actor (Piselli 2001). However, network analysis techniques also present a still not-resolved issue: the accuracy and data reliability provided by the respondents in describing their own network (Chiesi 1999).

On the other hand, Lin (2003) points out some methodological problems at the macro level: the inquiries directed to analyze some social capital dimensions (identified by Putnam as civicness) in many cases join individual indicators at an ecological level to represent situation of a specific area. Such macro vision loses sight of the actors and their possibility of investment and social mobilization of the resources.

STRATEGIES OF MEASUREMENT OF SOCIAL CAPITAL

The lack of assent about the definition has given rise to diversified approaches in measuring social capital, and made difficult any comparison of different empirical studies.

The Anglo-Saxon approach, followed in countries such as the United Kingdom (Harper and Kelly 2003; Babb 2005; National Statistics 2001, 2001-2002), United States (Hudson and Chapman 2002), and Australia (Australian Bureau of Statistics 2004; Stone 2001), follows Putnam's theory in focusing on the macro-relational level, in which social capital is meant as civicness. This vision attributes to social capital a strategic role in order to promote societal development. Concern about social capital in the global age has led the governments of these countries to encourage numerous surveys about social capital, usually measured through traditional indicators, such as the number of associations present in a particular context.

At the global level, the governments and the global institutions such as the World Bank try to develop a conceptual framework for measuring social capital for use in national statistical programs.

Lin (2003) points out a methodological problem at the macro level in that the indicators used in these surveys sometimes do not measure social capital but rather its outcomes (e.g., the number of volunteer associations). Furthermore, these inquiries join individual indicators at the ecological level in order to represent specific area situations. Such macro visions do not consider the actors, their possibility of investment, and social mobilization of the resources. Among the many Italian studies carried out through traditional survey methods, it is important to stress that the best use of the SNA techniques in Italy concern the study of social capital (Mutti 1998; Andreotti and Barbieri 2003). Even so, in some cases the use of SNA reflects mainly descriptive intent. The construction of an explanatory model of the social capital phenomenon is instead the goal pursued by Dutch scholars such as Tom Snijders and Martin Van der Gaag, who developed a critical reflection about measurement strategies and introduced innovative statistical models. To give an account of the complexity and the multi-dimensional nature of social capital, and anchoring their empirical strategy within a solid theoretical framework, they constructed a model of causal explanation of the phenomenon that also contained some predictive values.

Referring to Lin's theory of the social resources, these Dutch scholars developed a critical reflection on the possibility of building a measurement of social capital focused on social resources (Van der Gaag and Snijders 2003; Van der Gaag and Snijders 2004; Van der Gaag, Snijders and Flap 2004). This perspective refers to the micro-relational idea about social capital, and measures the concept through SNA techniques. In this approach the indicators of social capital are the aforementioned morphological social network features (measures such as the network wideness, density, etc.); the kind of ties (e.g. friendship); the content of the relation; the possibility for the actor to access people collocated in different professional positions, able to offer different kind of social resources (e.g. information for finding a new job).

The Dutch scholars used three methodological measurements: the "Name Generator/Interpreter," the "Position Generator," and the "Resource Generator." The Name Generator consisted of a list of names, provided by respondents that represented the members of their own social relations networks. Its value lay in its capacity to provide detailed information about these networks and the social capital of the respondents, while its weakness is the time and expenses to investigate its manifestations.

The authors thus gave greater attention to the Position Generator, which was a specially constructed list giving the prestige ranking of professional positions (e.g., lawyer, doctor, etc.) within the social network to whom an individual would have access, thereby measuring the level of available social resources (Van der Gaag, Snijders and Flap 2004). Comparing instrumental actions to get resources and expressive actions to maintain resources (Lin 2001), the Dutch scholars stress that the Position Generator is the better means to study instrumental actions.

Snijders (1999) developed another measurement tool, the "Resource Generator," to overcome some limitations of the other techniques yet retain their advantages. This advance in the measurement of social capital focuses on the resources embedded in social relations. It aims to verify access to specific kinds of social resources, such as prestige/education, political/financial skills, personal skills; and personal support (Van der Gaag, Snijders and Flap 2004).

In comparing the results from three measurement tools, it appears that the Position Generator data are the most useful for general studies of social capital and for instrumental actions in particular (Van der Gaag, Snijders and Flap 2004).

This brief review, by definition, is not exhaustive, and so the measurement of social capital remains open to further elaboration, including its study by other means as well. As we have stressed, the concept of social capital evades a rigid definition, and must therefore be analyzed and interpreted according to the social actors and their social networks (Piselli 2001). In addition, the complexity of the concept raises some different problems both at theoretical and methodological levels. Among the different empirical strategies of measurement carried out at the international level though, the Dutch approach appears to have the most promising predictive value (Milella 2007).

The heuristic complexity of the social capital concept demands that social scientists continue to make further efforts on its theorization and to develop other valid indicators for its empirical measurement.

Bibliography

Andreotti, Alberta, and Paolo Barbieri. 2003. "Reti e Capitale Sociale." *Inchiesta* 139.

Australian Bureau of Statistics. 2004. "Measuring Social Capital. An Australian Framework and Indicators." http://www.abs.gov.au.

Babb, P. 2005. "Measurement of Social Capital in the UK" http://www.statistics.gov.uk/socialcapital/downloads/Social_capital_measurement_UK_2005.pdf.

Bagnasco Arnaldo, Fortunata Piselli, Alessandro Pizzorno and Carlo Trigilia. 2001. Il *Capitale Sociale: Istruzioni per l'Uso*, Bologna: Il Mulino.

Bourdieu, Pierre. 1980. "Le Capital Social, Notes Provisoires." *Actes de la Recherche en Sciences Sociales* 31:2-3.

Chiesi, Antonio M. 2003. "Problemi di Rilevazione Empirica del Capitale Sociale." Inchiesta 139:86-97.

—. 1999. *L'Analisi dei Reticoli*, Milano: Franco Angeli.

Coleman, James S. 1990. *Foundations of Social Theory*, Cambridge, MA: The Belknap Press of Harvard University Press.

Granovetter, Mark. 1974. *Getting a Job*. Cambridge, MA: Harvard University Press.

Harper, R. and M. Kelly. 2003. "Measuring Social Capital in the United Kingdom." http://www.statistics.gov.uk/socialcapital/downloads/harmonisation_steve_5.pdf.

Hudson, L. and C. Chapman. 2002. "The Measurement of Social Capital in the United States." Paper prepared for OECD-ONS Conference on Social Capital Measurement, London, September 26-27.

Kadushin, Charles. 2004. "Too Much Investment in Social Capital?" *Social Networks* 26:75-90.

Lin, Nan. 2001. Social Capital. *A Theory of Social Structure and Action*, Cambridge, UK: Cambridge University Press.

—. 2003. "Capitale Sociale: Paradigmi Concorrenti e Loro Validazione Concettuale ed Empirica." *Inchiesta* 139:5-16.

Loury, Glenn C. 1977. "A Dynamic Theory of Racial Income Differences." Pp. 153-186, in *Women, Minorities, and Employment Discrimination*, edited by P.A. Wallace and A.M. LeMond. Lanham, MD: Lexington Books.

Milella, Stefania. 2007. "Il Capitale Sociale: Analisi Comparata delle Strategie di Misurazione." Pp. 203-229 in *Analisi delle Reti Sociali. Teorie, Metodi, Applicazioni*, edited by Andrea Salvini. Milano: Franco Angeli.

Mutti, Antonio. 1998. *Capitale Sociale e Sviluppo, La Fiducia Come Risorsa*, Bologna: Il Mulino.

National Statistics. 2001 "Social Capital: A Review of Literature." http://www.statistics.gov.uk/socialcapital/downloads/soccaplitreview.pdf.

National Statistics. 2001-02. "Social Capital Matrix of Surveys." http://www.statistics.gov.uk/socialcapital/downloads/soccapmatrix.pdf.

Piselli, Fortunata. 2001. "Capitale Sociale: Un Concetto Situazionale e Dinamico." Pp. 47-75 in *Il Capitale Sociale: Istruzioni per l'Uso*, edited by Arnaldo Bagnasco, Fortunata Piselli, Alessandro Pizzorno and Carlo Trigilia. Bologna: Il Mulino.

Putnam, Robert. 1993. *Making Democracy Work*. Princeton, NJ: Princeton University Press.

Salvini, Andrea. 2005. *L'Analisi delle Reti Sociali: Risorse e Meccanismi*. Pisa: Edizioni Plus.

Stone, Wendy. 2001. *Measuring Social Capital*. Research Paper N.24. Australian Institute of Family Studies.

Van der Gaag, Martin, and Tom A.B. Snijders. 2003. *A Comparison of Measures for Individual Social Capital*. ICS, Free University Amsterdam, University of Groningen.

—. 2004. *The Resource Generator: Social Capital Quantification with Concrete Items*. ICS, Free University Amsterdam, University of Groningen.

Van der Gaag Martin, Tom A.B. Snijders, and Henk Flap. 2004. *Position Generator Measures and their Relationship to Other Social Capital Measures*. ICS, Free University Amsterdam, University of Groningen, Utrecht University.

"And Yet It Moves!" — Civil Society in Southern Italy

FERDINANDO SPINA
University of Salento

The concept of social exclusion refers to an inability to exercise the social rights of citizenship, including the right to a decent standard of living. In this sense, social exclusion is synonymous with poverty, deprivation, social distance, marginalization, and inadequate integration (Silver 2006). In southern Italy, or the *Mezzogiorno*, a widespread condition of social exclusion is prevalent. Therefore, it is hard for southern Italians to feel a sense of community. It seems difficult to go beyond what Banfield (1958) called *amoral familism*, an endemic, enduring, cultural syndrome. The civic virtues, which are predominant in the northern Italian regions, are a world away from the southern Italian regions. Do they really not exist, or are they just hidden? This is no small question, neither for Italy nor for the European Union.

To answer this question, I would like to go on a two-part trip: a descent into social hell and then an ascent to social purgatory. This journey takes place in the south of contemporary Italy as this paper examines the way in which communities destroy and recreate their connections, and in which they destroy and create themselves again. My goal is to understand if a civil society that addresses the State is able to build a new sense of community.

I will first describe the disadvantaged situation in southern Italy, with its low social capital indicators and relevant loss of social trust. Then I will discuss theories and research about the social capital perspective, and underline the importance of the civil society idea in the creation of community, especially referring to Jürgen Habermas' work. Finally, I will illustrate the *traces of community* present in a protest movement initiated three years ago in the region of Puglia in southeastern Italy against the building of a huge gas plant, suggesting that one can consider this movement as a good example of southern Italian civil society. I wish to use this case study toward an understanding of whether or not this movement helped to create or to maintain in some way the local community.

THE DISADVANTAGED SITUATION OF SOUTHERN ITALY

According to the National Institute of Statistics (ISTAT), Italy seems yet "not to be capable of looking beyond the individual spheres and therefore to have a poor inclination towards forming a system" (2006:2). In truth, due to its heritage Italy is characterized by a variety of subjects, behaviors, and situations. There is general risk of disaffiliation, according to French sociologist Robert Castel (2000; 2003). Disaffiliation is the rupture of social bonds, caused by non-integration through work and non-integration into a social and family network. As Castel stressed, disaffiliation is a social process that can involve risks of social exclusion and feelings of insecurity about the future.

The double rupture of the two most important sources of solidarity, family and work, afflicts Italy generally, because of the fragility of the protective regulations of the welfare state. This risk today concerns not only marginal groups but also the middle class, creating a prevailing sense of uncertainty, precariousness, and distrust (Ranci 2002). For instance, a recent European survey highlighted a disturbing result: Italy (along with Bulgaria) has the highest proportion of people who feel left out of society. At the same time, Italians have little trust in their political institutions: nearly 70 percent of people have no faith in any political institutions (Eurobarometer 2007).

More specifically, the vulnerable areas of Italy are concentrated especially in the southern region. In briefly outlining the extent of social exclusion in this area, I must refer first to poverty and income inequality. Income-related inequalities are greater in Italy than in the main European countries: The Gini coefficient for Italy is nearly 36, which is higher than the European Union average of 29, but lower than the 40.8 value found in the United States (United Nations Development Programme 2006). However, southern Italy has the highest inequality of incomes inside family groups. Generally, the income of families that live in the southern regions is equal to about three quarters of the income of families living in northern Italy (ISTAT 2006). Two thirds of families without any member receiving a salary live in the *Mezzogiorn*. Thus, all indicators show that southern Italy suffers the greatest economic disadvantage.

Inequality of income and common poverty results from unequal participation in the labor market. The Italian annual average unemployment rate was 6.8 percent in 2006, but was 12.2 percent in the southern regions (ISTAT 2006). However, we must remember that this value addresses only the people looking for work. Not included are people who refused to search for employment. They are concentrated in the female component of the southern regions and among the younger age groups. Inactive workers, persons who are not classified as employed or unemployed, are 46.6 percent in the *Mezzogiorno*. This statistic suggests their considerable lack of trust for their future and for their own capacity.

Concerning the type of employment, *precarious jobs*[1] are more common in the south while in the north there are more opportunities for standard jobs, both in quantity (more vacancies) and in quality (better contracts and income). Consequently, the southern jobless reduce their job expectations. Another problem that raises vulnerability is the low value placed on human capital, which is a new impediment for interpersonal trust. Complicating matters is the widespread phenomenon of people who are overqualified in employment, due both to the inadequacy of the educational system and to the weakness of demand for qualified work. As CENSIS (2006) noted, social mobility seems to be downward, going to a lower step of the social pyramid. Of course, this means that young southern Italians are forced to migrate to northern Italy, breaking their social primary connections with families and friends. "Only in Italy, one finds lower employment rates and higher unemployment rates for young university graduates compared to the corresponding European values" (ISTAT 2005:9).

Lack of space prevents any discussion on such related crucial problems as crime or illegal work. However, the above data seem to confirm the hypothesis about a widespread risk of disaffiliation. Both the uncertain economic-working conditions (poverty, unemployment, illegal work, atypical jobs) and the break of generalized trust (strong inequality, family crisis, low social mobility) contribute towards an increased risk of social exclusion and marginality. Faced with this intricate framework, one has to avoid any reductionism in considering reasons and solutions. From an historical point of view, southern Italy has a contradictory modernization (Barbagallo 1994); above all, its development has been driven and established from the outside. The literature regarding the *Southern Question*, that is, the persistent gap between the northern and southern regions of the country, suggests that underdevelopment in southern Italy

---

[1] In Italy a *precarious job* is a job with a non-standard and contingent contract of employment (fixed term contract, temporary work with or without a fixed-term, part-time contract, temporary employment, and seasonal). Usually, its meaning is negative.

is due not only to its economic background but also to its cultural background (Toscano 2004). Leading intellectuals such as Francesco Saverio Nitti, Gaetano Salvemini and Antonio Gramsci maintained that the main problem is the lack of self-determination, a poor civic culture, and an indifference to the common good. Sociologically, we can identify the issue as a lack of non-economical networks, trust, and moral values.

Interestingly, the *Mezzogiorno* has been the place from which influential field studies generated the cultural theory of economic development and democracy, notably by Edward Banfield and Robert Putnam. Banfield's thesis of *amoral familism* is well known: the backwardness of communities in southern Italy is explained by "the inability of the villagers to act together for their common good or, indeed, for any end transcending the immediate, material interest of the nuclear family" (1958:10). Banfield refers to an *ethos* that is centered on family, an *ethos* that is dysfunctional for creating and maintaining social networks and community relations, even friendship relations. As a result, amoral familism impedes the possibility of a larger solidarity, of associations, charity, even justice.

It is extremely important to note that Banfield's *amoral familism* bears a striking resemblance to his culture of poverty hypothesis, roundly rejected by most U.S. social scientists. My aim in this paper is not to discuss either of his theories. However, when we remove the fatalism and anthropological determinism from his thesis about southern Italy, we still have information about the influence of a communitarian culture on the continuation or change of social and economic conditions. This is a key point in explaining the failure of State intervention (public works, infrastructure, credit subsidies, tax advantages, massive investments) in southern Italy. The government's disregard for the maintenance or support of community ties is the main reason for this failure. Moreover, the negation of people's autonomous capacity, self-awareness, and identity is a further crucial item in Banfield's cultural argument. Since southern Italians are "prisoners of their family-centered *ethos*" (Banfield 1958:163), the possibility for improvement can only come from *outside*, for instance, central government, the European Union, or multinational corporations. Alessandro Pizzorno (1966) laid out Banfield's inconsistency in understanding actors' behaviors, and suggested that the problem of local communities in the *Mezzogiorno* is wider: it depends on their historical marginality. They are peripheral to the modernization process and its values, and this marginality may avoid the possibility of generating autonomous progress but it also produces disruption of the community's identity.

An intellectual genealogy (Roux 2003) exists between the work of Edward Banfield, regarding some political and cultural assumptions as its incorrigible ethnocentrism, and Robert Putnam's *Making Democracy Work: Civic Traditions in Modern Italy* (1993). The study by Putnam gave a large empirical basis not only to the *Southern Question* but also to theories of social and economic development. Putnam's thesis suggests that social mechanisms of regulation, especially the institutional performance, work well not only by virtue of the State or the market. They also work better, with a greater performance, if within a strong social context, full of associations, trust and civicness. Civicness is a shared moral attitude which involves respecting social norms and pursuing collective actions to obtain a common good. In Putnam's notion of civic community, civicness and social capital are the same. Social capital here refers to three features of social life, networks, norms and trust, which enable participants to function more effectively in pursuing a common goal, something that is really the opposite of Banfield's *amoral familism* (Bagnasco 2004). Reaffirming Banfield's position, the study of Robert Putnam shows that social capital is an arid resource in southern Italian regions. Here, according to him, for centuries horizontal ties of solidarity were destroyed. This impeded any true civic virtue from developing or regional governments from functioning well. We are at the beginning of a *longue durée* process that is hard still to scratch. Moreover, with great pessimism, Putnam considers the unfortunate destiny of the *Mezzogiorno* to be similar to that of developing country:

> Without norms of reciprocity and networks of civic engagement the Hobbesian outcome of the *Mezzogiorno* [southern Italy] — amoral familism, clientelism, lawlessness, ineffective government and economic stagnation — seems likelier than successful democratization and economic development. Palermo may represent the future of Moscow (1993:183).

A recent survey updates and analyses thoroughly Putnam's study and confirms its results (Cartocci 2007). Comparing the new research with the old one, we find that duality of the North/South in Italy still remains the same (see Figures 1 and 2).

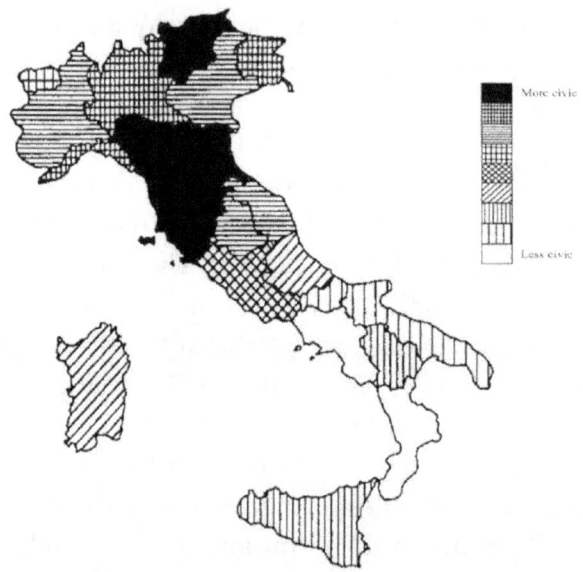

FIGURE 1: *Civic Community in Italian Regions (Putnam 1993)*

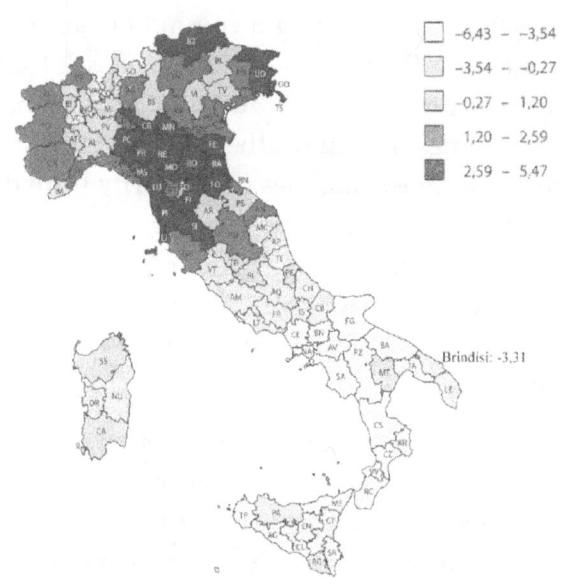

FIGURE 2: *Social Capital Index in Italian Provinces 25 Years after Putnam (Cartocci 2007)*

In summary, the macroeconomic data show how in the *Mezzogiorno*, more than elsewhere in Italy, there is a serious risk of social exclusion. To complete this descriptive framework, so far based on quantitative research, let me refer to some qualitative research that tracked discourse in a local newspaper over a two-year period about social and economical problems in the southern region of Puglia (Spina 2007). Its results confirm the situation described above. The most important value in life was "work" but nobody knew how to get it or how to maintain it. Workers who had lost their jobs stated that they felt themselves to be "ghost workers." Their comments recall Richard Sennett's metaphor (2006) of "the spectre of uselessness," the rapid devaluation of professional experience and identity and greater social exclusion. In the face of globalization, enterprises knew what they needed to survive (research, quality, innovation, and marketing) but they didn't know how to get it. Finally, the most impressive finding was the lack of social trust and the fragmentation of society. Nobody trusted anybody and everybody was at the same time accuser and accused. As a journalist wrote, it is a big "greasy pole" in which no one can make the grade. To paraphrase Piotr Sztompka (1995), trust is the missing resource of southern Italian society.

What are the explanations of this condition that come from southern people themselves rather from than our theoretical commentary? This research showed that everyone thought that the solution was to promote more dialogue to produce a renewed effort to build cohesion as well as go beyond conflicts. Surprisingly, they believed that the means through which this mutual acknowledgement was possible is politics. They hoped not only for new formal legal procedures, but also for a new institutional place to build respect, responsibility, competence, and reciprocity.

SOCIAL CAPITAL, CIVIL SOCIETY, AND DEMOCRACY

Research like that of Banfield or Putnam is quite helpful in describing a complex social reality, such as the *Mezzogiorno*. It provides middle-range theoretical explanations but nevertheless leaves us doubtful about these analytic explanations for social phenomena. Moreover, the most critical element of cultural theory is its emphasis on a familistic and not a cooperative ethos. In this way, one can generalize about individual behaviors and geographic areas that are different (Viesti 2003). Studies such as Banfield's exclude any possibilities of reform and a change for the better, and ignore use of the sociological imagination to consider some other answers and actions.

To go beyond the conclusive pessimism and doom about poverty in the region, I prefer a different approach. The fact is, the lack of social trust and relations, *à la* Putnam on the lack of civic community, produces from the inside the demand for a new *political* community. This, though, differs from the social capital perspective, which is centered on networks within and between communities, but ignores the institutional structure within which these networks are embedded, particularly the role of the State. Discourses from actors of the civil society open new perspectives and put forward some of most frequent criticisms not only of Putnam's idea of democracy but also about ambiguity of the social capital concept.

First, concerning determinism and causality, the more fundamental problem with Putnam's argument is its teleology, or logical circularity: "As a property of communities and nations rather than individuals, social capital is simultaneously a cause and an effect" (Portes 1998:19). Second, negative social capital also exists, as when a strong sense of community causes exclusion of outsiders and control on individual freedoms. In his account of a secret society, Georg Simmel (1950) warned against the exclusiveness of a closed community. Actually, Putnam (2000) distinguished between *bonding social capital* and *bridging social capital*. Last, we must consider the "anti-political prejudice" (Bagnasco 2004:238) and also the volunteers and horizontal associations that help characterize and explain civil society. According to Sidney Tarrow, the role and the character of the State are external to the Putnam model: "The lack of state agency in the book is one of the major flaws of his explanatory model" (1996:395). Pizzorno (1966) offered the same opinion on Banfield. Others studies confirm the relationship between democracy and social capital (Paxton 2002). Moreover, to reduce democratic relations between civil society and State only to associational networks reveals a conservative political attitude: it is the *maternelle* of the theory of civil society (Cohen 2001).

In contrast, we must look at the reciprocal effect of democratic institutions on associations. The place of this relationship is the public sphere:

> The closely related concepts of civil society and public sphere developed in the early modern era to refer to capacities for social self-organization and influence over the state . . . Located in civil society, communication in the public sphere may address the state or may seek to influence civil society and even private life directly (Calhoun 2001:1897).

In this perspective, the seminal work of Jürgen Habermas is an indispensable resource (Habermas 1991; 1996; 1998). Refusing the current relevance of the Hegelian idea of civil society as "bourgeois society" (*bürgerliche Gesellschaft*), Habermas gives a broad definition of it:

> Civil society is composed of those more or less spontaneously emergent associations, organizations, and movements that, attuned to how societal problems resonate in the private life spheres, distill and transmit such reactions in amplified form to the public sphere. The core of civil society comprises a network of associations that institutionalizes problem-solving discourses on questions of general interest inside the framework of organized public spheres (1996:367).

Furthermore, he warns about the uselessness of a more profound explanation. Rather, it is important to understand that the features of social structure to secure a modern differentiated civil society are plurality, publicity, privacy and legality, according to Jean Cohen and Andrew Arato (1992). Next, public sphere is the space in which to achieve the public use of reason:

> The public sphere can best be described as a network for communicating information and points of view (i.e., opinions expressing affirmative or negative attitudes) . . . The public sphere distinguishes itself through a communication structure that is related to a third feature of communicative action: it refers neither to the functions nor to the contents of everyday communication but to the social space generated in communicative action (Habermas 1996:360).

Concerning the Habermasian conceptualization, we must highlight that the formal criteria of communicative praxis, the institutional rules and procedures, are fundamental to obtain a rational outcome from the public sphere. However, fundamental rights do not further a stronger civil society; its enhancement can happen only within itself. Habermas, in agreement with Cohen and Arato (1992), designates this process as *dual orientation*, because actors in public sphere:

> with their programs . . . directly influence the political system, but at the same time they are also reflexively concerned with revitalizing and enlarging civil society and the public sphere as well as with confirming their own identities and capacities to act (1996:370).

Can such as civil society create direct communities with "a high degree of personal intimacy, emotional depth, moral commitment, social cohesion, and continuity in time," referring to the Robert Nisbet's classical definition (1993:47)? Replying to the communitarians' claim for more civic virtue, more communal spirit, and a stronger sense of solidarity, Habermas considers it not only unrealistic, but also problematic, because:

> it places too little confidence in the integrating force of law and too much confidence in the universalistic potential of the prepolitical bonds of informal communities. Law is the only medium through which a solidarity with strangers can be secured in complex societies (1998:441).

This is a key issue in contemporary multicultural society. Therefore, the trust in the legitimacy of the Constitution and rational communicative process secure the solidarity and the social inclusion beyond cultural differences. When this precious trust is threatened in some way, associations, communities, and actors of civil society react, creating new social movements, local or global, and increasing the quality of rational-critical discourses.

FROM PROTEST TO A NEW SENSE OF COMMUNITY: THE BRINDISI CASE

The influential theory of Jürgen Habermas raised an intense debate among scholars, particularly the critical question posed by his approach in the way that public discourses can determine the community life. Looking at a local protest against a huge plant, I will address some aspects of this issue.

In 2001, British Gas Italia S.p.A. (today Brindisi LNG S.p.A.) asked for Italian government authorization to build an 8 billion-cubic-meter LNG (Liquefied Natural Gas) terminal in the southern Italian port of Brindisi, a region of Puglia. In 2002, during two "Conferenze dei Servizi" (an administrative procedure that draws together various public bodies), local administrations and the Ministry of the Environment accepted the project. Next, the Ministry of Economic Development authorized for a British investment in Italy totaling about 540 million Euros.

However, in 2004, large popular demonstrations occurred, followed by a formal protest by the Brindisi Provincial Council that unanimously declared itself against the plant. One year later, the council began its legal battle. First, it filed an *Action for Failure to Fulfill Obligations* to the European Commission against the Italian State, accusing it of violation of EU environmental law in its authorization of the project. Second, it sent a detailed report to the Brindisi prosecutor charging illegal behaviors in connection with the approval process. Finally, it tried to stop construction of the plant through an administrative legal procedure. Nevertheless, construction work on the plant continued.

More recently, the European Commission's Environment Directorate-General issued a document denouncing the serious negligence in not following correct procedure for a regular Environmental Impact Assessment, and complaining that no consultation with the population of Brindisi, as recommended, ever took place. Finally, the new Italian Council of Ministers decided to reopen the permission process, following EU Commission guidelines. In March 2007, Italian police arrested the port's former mayor who supported the project and three managers of British Gas group's Italian unit as part of a corruption investigation.

The local opposition movement insists that the choice to locate the facility in the center of the city port was not properly and fairly evaluated, since nearby are massive high-risk chemical facilities. Further danger from the LNG terminal comes from its close proximity to three power plants producing 20 percent of the nation's energy. As a result of improper evaluation, local residents claim the right to a preventive Environmental Impact Assessment procedure. Lastly, residents believe the project is inconsistent with traditional port activities such as tourism, cruising, and its fishing industry and that it conflicts with an extensive plan to re-appropriate the city's waterfront, following the successful example of Barcelona (with the same project team).

Within a conventional perspective of the NIMBY syndrome generating local opposition movements, we see the usual and reductive dichotomies between the rational/public interest on the one hand, and the irrational/local interest on the other. In spite of this reductive view, let me outline the point related to legal legitimacy. The process to authorize the project had a formal legal ratification, although investigators discovered a secret agreement between English managers of Brindisi LNG and major investors based in a Caribbean island. Significantly, no public discourse about the project occurred in local institutional assemblies or in national public opinion polls. A search in the national press on these issues reveals that they appeared in print only in 2005, two years after the authorization of such a huge facility. This lack of pre-approval discourse represents a serious crisis of legitimacy in its strong Weberian sense. As such, politicians could not provide any rational or moral justification to their constituents. Even more disturbing, such a reality makes it impossible to create social integration through law and institutions, according to Habermasian theory.

Even though Brindisi and its district may have low social capital indicators as shown in Figure 2, this crisis of legitimacy generated local opposition and galvanized a supposed lack of community into a *new sense* of community, leading to several significant results. First, moving beyond the usual partisanship and hostility among political parties that characterizes the Italian political system, local left- and right-wing groups coalesced and acted together for a common goal. Second, in the conflict between economic goals and post-materialistic values, the government hoped that the LNG terminal would spur economic growth, but the affected community recovered its traditional identity (or recreated its own imagined identity) which it defended by opposing external blackmail and threats, such as the risk of unemployment. Third, the citizens' insistence on not being treated as a colony and their protest against this government/company project became a moment of genuine self-determination beyond the tired and trite democratic praxis. The group gatherings, sit-ins, webzines, and other activities enabled them to lay claim to extending their participatory rights in terms of responsibility for risk-taking decisions.

These seemingly utopian virtues found in some recent sociological perspectives (for instance, theory of risk society, theory of recognition, and theory of social movements) are usually ascribed to more democratic, civil, and active communities. In this instance, a community not falling into that description rose to that level because it found a single voice for a common cause.

CONCLUSION

Of course, in this case there were inert moments of conflicts with bureaucracy, private interests, strategic and instrumental ends that clashed and interacted with the aforementioned virtues. At this time, we don't know the final outcome of the movement. More generally as regards the disaffiliation level of southern society, we admit that protest cannot itself create better economic conditions or employment opportunities. What is needed is further research into communicative structures and administrative power within social networks. What is clear, though, is that civil society may not be flourishing in this part of Italy, but it is not dying either.

Italian writer Giorgio Manganelli once argued that Italians seemed not interested in the idea of a fair society, and that because they live in a society comprised of "mostly weak people and only a few powerful individuals, Italy is a society of accomplices" (2007:84). However, the

Brindisi case reminds us we should not underestimate the human spirit. Indeed, there are moments when the weak will work together against becoming accomplices of power, their actions instead making them feel like a community of free people. Perhaps the inspiring message here is that not losing hope is "the greatest contribution we all can make to the future establishment of, if not civil society, then at least a more civil one" (Seligman 1992:206).

References

Bagnasco. Arnaldo. 2004. "Trust and Social Capital." Pp. 230-239 in *Blackwell Companion to Political Sociology*, edited by Kate Nash and Alan Scott. Oxford: Blackwell Publishing.

Banfield, Edward C. 1958. *The Moral Basis of a Backward Society*, Glencoe, IL: the Free Press.

Barbagallo, Francesco. 1994. *La Modernità Squilibrata del Mezzogiorno d'Italia*. Torino: Einaudi.

Castel, Robert. 2000. "The Roads to Disaffiliation: Insecure Work and Vulnerable Relationships." *International Journal of Urban and Regional Research* 24:519-535.

——. [1995] 2003. *From Manual Workers to Wage Laborers: Transformation of the Social Question*. New Brunswick, NJ: Transaction Publishers.

Calhoun, Craig. 2001. "Civil Society/Public Sphere: History of the Concept." Pp. 1897-1903 in *International Encyclopedia of the Social & Behavioral Sciences*, edited by Neil J. Smelser and Paul B. Baltes. Oxford, UK: Elsevier.

Cartocci, Roberto. 2007. *Mappe del Tesoro. Atlante del Capitale Sociale in Italia*. Bologna: Il Mulino.

CENSIS. 2006. *Quarantesimo Rapporto sulla Situazione Sociale del Paese 2006*. Milano: Franco Angeli.

Cohen, Jean, and Arato, Andrew. 1992. *Civil Society and Political Theory*. Cambridge, MA: MIT Press.

Cohen, Jean. 2001. "Pour une Démocratie en Mouvement : Lectures Critiques de la Société Civile. Entretien avec Jean Cohen." *Raisons Politiques* 3:139-160.

Eurobarometer. 2007. *European Social Reality*. 273. Brussels: EU Directorate General Communication.

Habermas, Jürgen. [1962] 1991. *The Structural Transformation of the Bourgeois Public Sphere: An Inquiry into a Category of Bourgeois Society*. Cambridge MA: MIT Press.

——. [1992] 1996. *Between Facts and Norms: Contributions to a Discourse Theory of Law and Democracy*. Cambridge MA: MIT Press.

——. 1998. "Reply to Symposium Participants, Benjamin N. Cardozo School of Law." Pp. 381-452 in *Habermas on Law and Democracy: Critical Exchanges*, edited by Michael Rosenfeld, and Andrew Arato. Berkeley: University of California Press.

ISTAT (National Institute of Statistics). 2006. *Annual Report: The Situation of Italy in 2005. Summary*. Roma: ISTAT. http://www.istat.it/english/annualreport.html. Retrieved October 31, 2007.

Manganelli, Giorgio. [1982] 2007. *Mammifero Italiano*. Milano: Adelphi.

Nisbet, Robert A. [1966] 1993. *The Sociological Tradition*. New Brunswick, NJ: Transaction Publishers.

Paxton, Pamela. 2002. "Social Capital and Democracy: An Interdependent Relationship." *American Sociological Review* 67:254-277.

Pizzorno, Alessandro. 1966. "Amoral Familism and Historical Marginality." *International Review of Community Development* 15:55-66.

Portes, Alejandro. 1998. "Social Capital: Its Origins and Applications in Modern Sociology." *Annual Review of Sociology* 24:1-24.

Putnam, Robert D., with Robert Leonardi and Raffaella Y. Nanetti. 1993. *Making Democracy Work: Civic Traditions in Modern Italy*. Princeton: Princeton University Press.

—. 2000. *Bowling Alone: The Collapse and Revival of American Community*. New York: Simon & Schuster.

Ranci, Costanzo. 2002. *Le Nuove Disuguaglianze Sociali in Italia*. Bologna: Il Mulino.

Roux, Christophe. 2003. "En Attendant Putnam: La 'Culture de Défiance' Italienne dans la Science Politique Américaine de l'Après-Guerre: l'Oeuvre d'Edward C. Banfield." *Revue Internationale de Politique Comparée*, 10:463-476.

Seligman, Adam. 1992. *The Idea of Civil Society*. Princeton: Princeton University Press.

Sennett, Richard. 2006. *The Culture of the New Capitalism*. New Haven: Yale University Press.

Simmel, Georg. [1908] 1950. "The Secret and the Secret Society" Pp. 307-376 in *The Sociology of Georg Simmel*, edited and translated by Kurt H. Wolff. Glencoe, IL: The Free Press.

Silver, Hilary. 2006. "Social Exclusion." Pp. 4411-4413 in *The Blackwell Encyclopedia of Sociology*, edited by George Ritzer. Oxford: Blackwell Publishing.

Spina, Ferdinando. 2007. "Lavoro, Precarietà, Declino: Rappresentazioni Sociali dalla Comunità Salentina." Pp. 231-254 in *Periferie Flessibili* edited by Mariano Longo. Lecce: Pensa.

Sztompka, Piotr. 1995. "Trust: the Missing Resource of Post-Communist Society." Mimeo. Krakow, Poland: Institute of Sociology, Jagiellonian University.

Tarrow, Sidney. 1996. "Making Social Science Work across Space and Time: A Critical Reflection on Robert Putnam's Making Democracy Work." *The American Political Science Review* 90:389-397.

Toscano, Mario Aldo. 2004. *Sul Sud: Materiali per lo Studio della Cultura e Dei Beni Culturali*. Milano-Pontedera: Jaca Book-Il Grandevetro.

United Nations Development Program. 2006. *Human Development Report*. New York: UNDP.

Viesti, Gianfranco. 2003. *Abolire il Mezzogiorno*. Roma-Bari: Laterza.

PART TWO
Community and Isolation

Social Networks and Insecurity

SIMONE GABBRIELLINI
University of Pisa

An MIT professor, Edward Rosenthal (2005), recently published a book in which he calls this era the "era of choice." Human beings have many more possibilities of choice now than in the past, and this fact deeply impacts on our lives. However, he says, too many choices can generate a process of "choosing inversion," with too many choices sometimes meaning no choice at all.

Rosenthal cites many psychological studies that underline this fact. For example, Kalakota and Robinson (Rosenthal 2005) studied the impact of the increasing number of channels on cable television on people's satisfaction, and discovered that above a critical point, there was no difference in having 500 or 1500 channels. Also, Barry Schwartz (2003) demonstrated that having too many choices makes decision processes harder. Sociologists know that the decision-making processes are often hard, prompting many people to rely on shortcuts to solve them. In social networks, those shortcuts can be "opinion leaders."

Katz and Lazarsfeld (1955), analyzing the U.S. presidential election campaign in 1940, developed a well-known model of social influence, called the "two-step flow." Since extended to many other research areas, this model consists of a process in which opinion leaders play a vitally important role for the community. According to the model, people's responses are mediated through their social relationships, and since not all are equal in the network, some play a more active role than others. These people are the opinion leaders, people who, in comparison to the average person, use the mass media more, mix more across social classes, and see themselves and are seen by others as influential on specific topics. This is not a question of timing, as opinion leaders do not necessarily "come first." They do have a relational prominence though, and the two-step flow model tells us something about the relational structure of the network.

Until some years ago we didn't have a theoretical model to justify the presence of opinion leaders in social groups. We know from Milgram's experiment (1969), on average we can reach a random person on earth in just six passages (often called "six degrees of separation"). Since 1959, network analysis researchers have used the Erdos and Renyi uniform random graph model (see Figure 1).

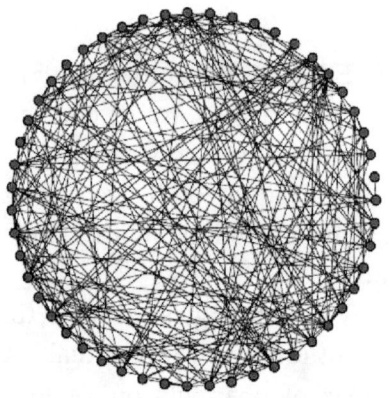

FIGURE 1. *The Random Network*

In this model each node, which represents either a person or an organization, connects randomly to other nodes in the graph, and each node has the same probability to be chosen as the others. This model illustrates the six passages length between people. However, it is based on an unrealistic assumption (Barabasi 2002; Buchanan 2003). If the connections are random, two friends of mine have the same probability of being friends with each others as do a Wall Street broker and a farmer in south Italy. This is, obviously, not the society we live in. Technically speaking, the clustering coefficient of the Erdos and Renyi model is low compared to the one found in real social networks.

Mark Granovetter (1973) offered a seminal contribution to the field of network analysis with the intuition of the strength of weak ties. His theoretical model of society is simple but powerful: each of us live embedded in different but small, dense clusters of people and each cluster has weak ties to other clusters. In other words, in each cluster a person knows well the other members of the cluster, but also knows, even superficially, someone who belongs to a different cluster (See Figure 2).

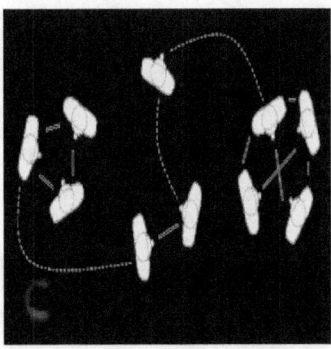

FIGURE 2. *The Granovetter Hypothesis*

Watts and Strogatz (1998) offered a mathematical model that formalizes Granovetter's hypothesis. This Small World model emphasizes the two recurrent properties of social networks: high-density clusters and short path lengths. The important discovery made by Watts and Strogatz is that you don't need to connect a whole network randomly to have the six degrees of separation effect. It is sufficient to add only a few connections at random in an ordered graph to have a so-called "small world." Yet even this model has something missing. In the suggested small world networks, every node on average has the same degree, the same number of connections. However, we know that opinion leaders are something more than the rest of the nodes in the network.

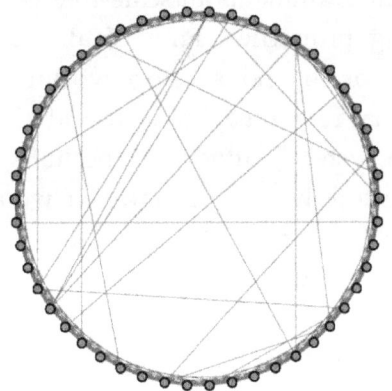

FIGURE 3. *The Small World Network*

Laszlo Barabasi (2002), in studying the Internet network, discovered a particular structure that he called "scale-free." The Internet network structure consists of a few well-connected nodes and many smaller and less-connected nodes (see Figure 4). Approximating the degree distribution of this kind of network is power law, a well-known concept in physics. This model of a few super-connected nodes and many poorly connected ones enables us theoretically to forecast the presence of hubs in networks, and at the same time simulate the mechanism underneath the evolution of such networks, (Barabasi called this mechanism "preferential attachment.")

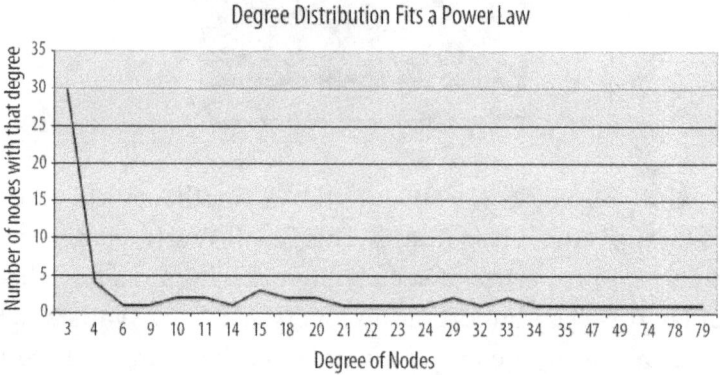

FIGURE 4. *The Scale-Free network*

Are we all in scale-free networks? Many researchers tell us that the answer is yes, that we live in small world networks and often in those small world networks there are some hubs, so that the nodes are not all equal.

Why it is important to think about scale-free networks? One reason is their many interesting properties. First of all, scale-free networks are robust; even if some of the nodes stop working, the network won't collapse. However, what researchers have found about these structures is that they are weak to systemic attacks. If the hubs are under attack, the entire network is affected. It doesn't matter if we are talking about the diffusion of a virus or the spread of a new idea; hubs play a key role in determining the success of the diffusion (Barabasi 2002; Buchanan 2003; Gladwell 2002).

So we can say that small world networks and, even more, scale-free networks do follow the leaders, in the sense that the spreading of information in such topologies accelerates through the topology structure itself. If leaders like an innovation, many members will join the innovation. Otherwise, no one will make the switch.

This mediated mechanism brings us back to an empowered version of the two-step flow model hypothesized by Katz and Lazarsfeld (1955). We have a central node and peripheral nodes, people joined by strong or weak ties, a few people who act as opinion leaders and a larger part of the community who simply follow the leaders. Now, that model has a relational foundation in terms of social network analysis.

Could this theoretical background help us to face terrorism attacks? Or, even better, could it help prevent them?

> The importance of SNA [social network analysis] in fighting the war on terrorism was recognized even before the attacks of September 11, 2001 . . . [M]odern war is *netwar*, a lower-intensity battle by terrorists, criminals, and extremists with a networked organizational structure. These networked structures are often leaderless and able to attack more quickly (Ressler 2006:3).

This author concludes that we need new approaches to combat a network-based criminal organization. In fact, after 9/11 social network experts in academia began to explore the terrorist networks, with the first attempt to map the al Qaeda network made by Valdis Krebs. Each of the nodes in this network is two steps from all the others, making the information flow extremely efficient. Another great center for application of network analysis is the CASOS at Carnegie Mellon University, in which the main issue is to use SNA and agent-based modeling to destabilize simulated terrorist networks (Ressler 2006:4).

We must be aware of the fact that while there is much work in collecting data to draw a social network graph to represent terrorist networks, there is much less work in developing a theoretical model of such a network evolution. The problem Ressler underlines is that, even if this methodological and epistemological point of view can help us as a new tool and as a new way to conceptualize reality, researchers still miss some aspects:

- A deeper knowledge of the subject, because the result of the network analysis should be interpreted in a coherent frame, founded in the vast literature about terrorism;
- How networks recruit participants;
- Why people wish to join terrorist networks.

We can then say that this kind of knowledge about social structure does help us to understand network behavior. Even if we cannot answer the question "why?," we can still try to answer to the question "who?." The causal process that explains the relation between structure and actors is not one way, but circular. We can model the effect that a certain structure has on people's behavior, but at the same time we must take into account, at a micro level, the actor's motivations and beliefs. This circular model will also help us to explain the Ressler issues about why someone chooses to join a terrorist network. Network knowledge can help us to develop models to understand more completely the complex world of social groups, but only if we use it not from a strictly structural point of view, but in a wider epistemological perspective.

References

Barabasi, Lazslo. 2002. *Linked: The New Science of Networks*. New York: Perseus.

Buchanan, Marc. 2003. *Nexus*. New York: W.W. Norton & Company.

Gladwell, Malcolm. 2002. *The Tipping Point*. Boston: Back Bay Books.

Granovetter, Marc. 1973. "The Strength of Weak Ties." *American Journal of Sociology* 78(6):1360-1380.

Katz, Elihu and Paul F. Lazarsfeld. 1955. *Personal Influence*. New York: Free Press.

Ressler, Steve. 2006. "Social Network Analysis." *Homeland Security Affairs Journal* II(2):1-10.

Rosenthal, Edward. 2005. *The Era of Choice*. Cambridge, MA: MIT Press.

Schwartz, Barry. 2003. *The Paradox of Choice: Why More Is Less*. New York: Ecco HarperCollins.

Travers, Jeffrey and Stanley Milgram. 1969. "An Experimental Study of the Small World Problem." *Sociometry* 32(4):425-443.

Watts, Duncan J. and Steven H. Strogatz. 1998. "Collective Dynamics of 'Small-World' Networks." *Nature* 393:440-442.

Why Does the Glass Ceiling Still Exist?

RITA BIANCHERI
University of Pisa

The many social changes that occurred in recent years have also had an effect on female participation in the labor market, both in quantitative terms (increasing their presence) and on a qualitative level (many sectors once exclusively male dominated opening up more and more for women). However, this opening up has in many cases simply represented a public extension of duties carried out within the private sphere, delegating in the various professional fields those competences considered female. Viewed as the bearers of expressivity, reciprocity, and empathy, women often found themselves assigned to value-laden roles as caretaker in the workplace.

Talcott Parsons' functionalist analysis of the family (Parsons, 1955), gave a strong positive attribution to the power aspects of rationality and efficiency and negative connotations to emotional dependence and passivity. This hierarchy and role division still sets the evaluation parameters of female professional performance and has repercussions both on the ways of fitting into the work force as well as on wages. It also places limits on careers. Two case studies—that of women in the judicial system sector and of women in university teaching posts—confirm the continuation of this stereotype and its influence in determining the horizontal and vertical gender segregation in the workplace.

What are the reasons behind the continuation of these inequalities? A first consideration is the fact that, although a significant number of women have gone to work in Italy in the past few years, no corresponding changes have occurred in the functions carried out by the family. No equalization in the distribution of household chores, childcare and general family welfare has taken place, as residual values remain about the role of the family. No adequate fiscal measures to help parents emerge either, mainly because of the prevailing idea that the responsibility of social reproduction is almost exclusively the duty of the family and only marginally that of the State.

An important indicator of this dissonance is the fertility rate which presently in Italy has dropped to 1.3, resulting in negative population growth. This may well be a consequence of a disadvantaged female presence in a socio-institutional context, and in particular in the structure of the labor market. The welfare and cultural models that dominate severely limit the opportunities for individuals with respect to the family. What prevails is what Pierre Bourdieu (1988) defines as the masculine supremacy prevalent in the political sphere, as well as in the labor market and in family relationships.

The norms and values that define role expectations and social politics also determine the modalities of female participation. The stronger are the ties, the greater is the degree of acceptability of their working and integration in the work force, which thereby improves the possibility of achieving one's life expectations. Education plays an important role and so does the continuity of work experience. Not surprisingly then, interventions and measures that act on the differentiated and unequal access for men and women to social, economical and political resources contribute significantly to changes in dominant cultural models.

Comparative analysis shows that in European countries the different occupational realities are influenced by the complex dynamics of these factors. They result from multiple elements that intertwine and integrate among themselves. Even if the increase in women working in the public sphere becomes universally more consistent, the rhythms and modes are different. Various indicators show local peculiarities that result from the interaction of all these variables that cause differences not only in terms of participation but also in occupational typology, wages and access potential to decisional posts.

The case of Italy easily demonstrates that norms are not enough and safeguarding rights only works if society realizes that the gender discriminations still present are a real deficit to democracy and, as a consequence, develop strategies and adequate measures to promote concretely equal opportunities for everyone.

Since women have difficulty in organizing their lives, they require structures and services to aid them in caring for their families and maintaining a professional career. Policies for flexible work schedules, changes in cultural priorities, and a shared family workload—together with recognition of the social value of reproduction—all constitute important factors in this regard.

THE ROLE OF THE EUROPEAN UNION

On the basis of a gender gap widely demonstrated by statistical data and extensive research (see Figure 1), the EU dedicated the year 2007 to these themes. Such a predilection evolved from the 1990s when the theme of a work-life balance became a fundamental objective. It was included in many community political agendas and became an important element in various international contexts for intervention to achieve gender mainstreaming in all sectors. However, as illustrated by passage in Italy of law n° 53/2000, legislation that represents a significant change in the Italian regulations system, such laws may languish because of a lack of widespread implementation.

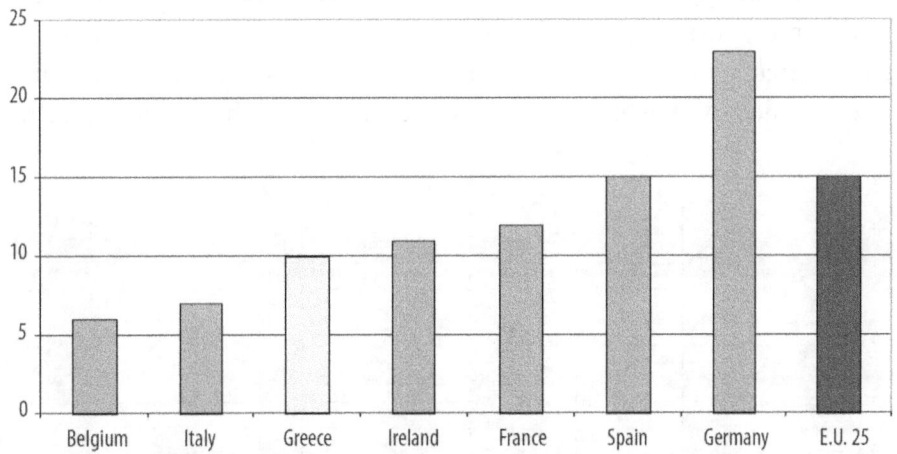

FIGURE 1. *Gender pay gap in some European countries, by percent*
Source: Eurostat, LFS, 2004

To obtain a greater equilibrium between family life and professional work, laws promoting gender equality must become part of everyday culture and common use, both in the public and family environments. The theme of conciliation—requiring an integrated system of enterprise, political organizations and local policies more respondent to individual needs—must primarily focus on personal necessities and needs. Further, this approach must be placed within a wider perspective to become an element of innovation in the labor market and in the whole of society.

What are the obstacles that prevent elimination of the famous glass ceiling? Evidence shows that this is heavily connected to the traditional structure of the family that continues to give an ideological and practical weight to the status quo, as well illustrated by Manuela Naldini and Chiara Saraceno (2007). It constitutes a resistance field that still influences in an important way the choices in women's lives. In fact, even a positive development such as *flextime* (flexible work hours) often forces women to plan carefully their organization of home/work responsibilities and their time management, unlike men who are more removed from such concerns and more focused on their careers.

THE ITALIAN SITUATION

The Italian scene regarding gender asymmetries still persisting in the workplace, particularly with regard to the presence of women in managerial positions (see Figure 2), is relatively similar throughout most sectors of the labor market. Studies reveal that women are notably absent as regards careers and access to higher positions of responsibility, even if the levels of education are often above those of men (Biancheri 2006a, 2006b).

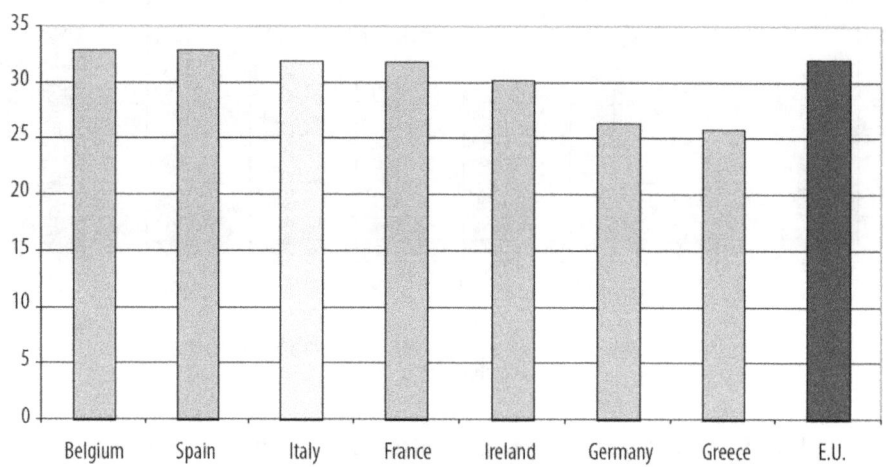

FIGURE 2. *Business women in some European countries, by percent*
Source: Eurostat, LFS, 2004

Because educational achievement typically does not correspond to adequate levels of progress in careers and in salaries, substantial criticism addresses this reality. The Lisbon objective[1] to increase both the female

---

[1] The Lisbon Strategy, also known as the Lisbon Agenda or Lisbon Process, is an action and development plan for the European Union. Its aim is to make the EU "the most dynamic and competitive knowledge-based economy in the wordl capable of sustainable economic growth with more and better jobs and greater social cohesion, and respect for the environment by 2010" set against the background of productivity in the EU being below that of the US. It was set out by the European Council in Lisbon on March 2000. See: http://ec.europa.eu/growthandjobs/pdf/kok_report_en.pdf

labor participation rate and the percentage of women in managerial positions by 60 percent by the year 2010 seems unattainable in Italy. This is especially true when applied to specific occupations (see Figure 3).

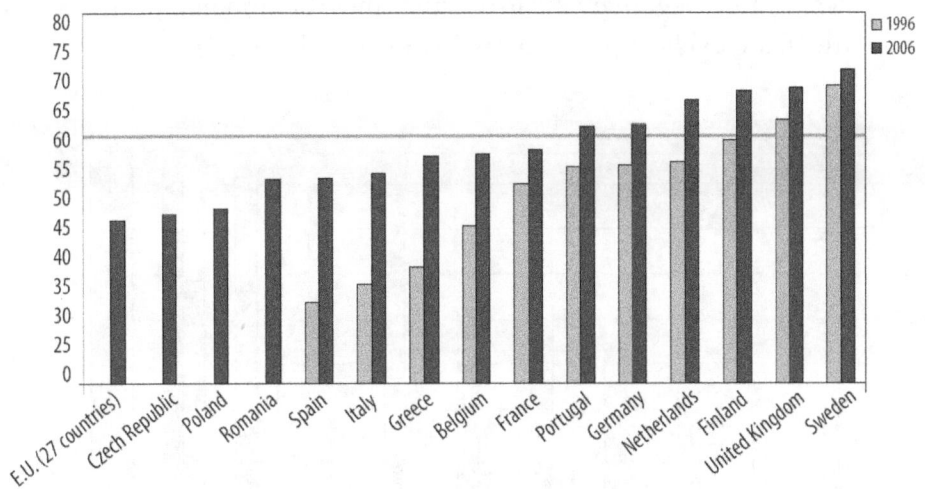

FIGURE 3. *Employment rate in Europe*
Source: Eurostat, LFS, 2004

The female professional presence in the judicial system has significantly increased because access is through examinations. These reduce gender discrimination, given their reliance on the amount of knowledge demonstrated, and so give women an equal opportunity. Even though this process enables women to pursue professional careers in this field, the judicial system still favors male access to the high-ranking positions: out of 440 such slots, men hold 419 and women only 21 (5 percent). On the next tier down for high-ranking places, men hold 672 of the available 726 positions and women hold the remaining 54 (7 percent).

Research data (Biancheri 2006b) shows that this consistent low number of women is not justified by the fact that women have only just quite recently gone into the judicial system. On the contrary, it is at the moment when women magistrates—working in the field for many years and acquiring enough experience for eligibility for elevation in their careers—suddenly become aware of gender-specific obstacles. Even those who succeed in gaining a promotion often encounter gender segregation in such functions as care services inside and outside the family.

Research studies (ISTAT 2000; Biancheri 2008) further show that the limited access to decision-taking positions also results from implicit and informal factors that play a critical role in evaluating capabilities. Such judgments—whether based on assumptions, presumptions, biases, or ignorance—affect women's professional opportunities and, since they are more likely to be negative or patronizing, they help maintain the power structure on all levels of public participation (see Figure 4).

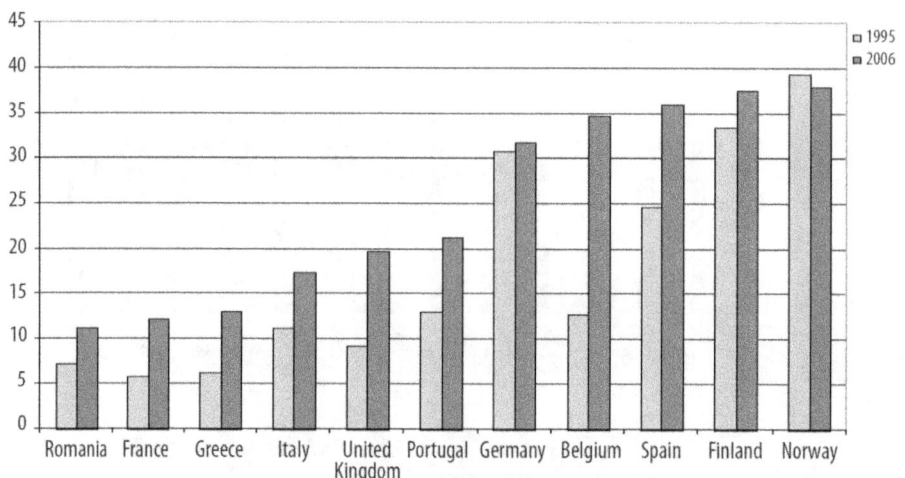

FIGURE 4. *Women in decision making. National Parliaments, by percent*
Source: ISTAT, www.istat.it

Just as the criticism and the disadvantages of gender still play an important role regarding women in the judicial system, so too do they exist in the careers of women university professors, although some differences do exist. In the academic world women represent a minority that is concentrated at the lowest level of university career (see Figure 5).

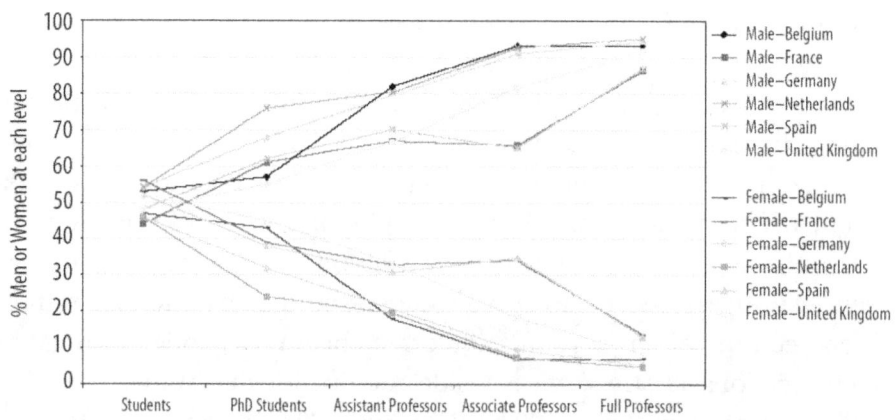

FIGURE 5. *Women in academic positions*
Source: European Commission, 2000

In addition, many women researchers are now beyond the preferred age range to compete for professional faculty positions and so are most likely destined to remain as researchers until they retire (see Figure 6).

% WOMEN	FULL PROFESSOR		ASSOCIATE PROFESSOR		RESEARCHER	
	PISA	ITALY	PISA	ITALY	PISA	ITALY
1997	7.8%	11.4%	21.0%	26.1%	38.1%	39.6%
1998	7.9%	11.4%	21.1%	26.1%	37.9%	39.5%
1999	8.0%	11.6%	21.6%	26.4%	40.8%	41.3%
2000	9.9%	13.3%	24.2%	27.7%	40.9%	41.6%
2001	11.1%	14.6%	26.8%	29.8%	42.4%	42.7%
2001	12.5%	15.6%	28.7%	30.8%	42.8%	43.4%
2003	13.1%	16.0%	29.1%	31.2%	42.8%	43.4%
2004	13.6%	16.4%	29.2%	31.4%	42.2%	43.8%

FIGURE 6. *Women in academic positions at the University of Pisa*
Source: Biancheri ©2006

For women in the university or judicial professions, their difficulties in career advancement are obvious in their disproportionate numbers in places of high-ranking decision making, which further contribute to their invisibility, as well as their inability to change the system since so few are in the positions of power to do so.

With mostly men in decision-making positions promoting mostly men to better positions of authority and responsibility, the vertical gender segregation remains intact. This phenomenon exists in virtually all professions and different organizational contexts. This problem continues despite the steady increase in female labor force participation, despite improved economic recognition, and despite opportunities for professional growth and education. Even though more women than in the past work in jobs previously considered only for men, most face a real barrier in their upward mobility.

Recent female biographies reveal changes among women with high levels of education, particularly in their conception of work. Their instrumental goal of self-fulfillment through work and earned income has been achieved. Notwithstanding these changes, however, they sense a need of what must still be done, understanding that the transversality of the problems goes back to the whole system of social organization.

Many women, in fact, are forced to accept work roles that are less satisfying partly because persisting cultural models reinforce the dominant family typology, as well as gender stereotypes and prejudices. Not only are these modern anomalies of thought not yet eradicated, but also a prevailing structure of male dominance still exists. Furthermore, the presence of informal but highly effective male networks helps perpetuate favored status for access to a career and to places of power. The community strategies discussed at the beginning of this paper may help to reduce the gender gap and shorten the distances among the many different countries that make up the European Union.

References

Biancheri, Rita. 1998. "Associazionismo Femminile." *La Società Civile in Italia. VI° Rapporto sull'Associazionismo Sociale,* edited by IREF. Roma: Edizioni lavoro.

——. 2000a. *Il Pubblico delle Donne, Associazionismo e Partecipazione Femminile*. Pisa: Ets.

——. 2000b. "L'Associazionismo Femminile." *L'Impronta Civica. VII° Rapporto sull' Associazionismo Sociale,* edited by IREF. Roma: Edizioni lavoro.

——. 2003. *Donne nel Sindacato: Rappresentanza e Pari Opportunità*. Roma: Edup.

——. ed. 2005a. *Progetto Libra 2003. Partecipazione Equilibrata delle Donne e Degli Uomini nel Processo Decisionale: Esperienza della Provincia di Lucca*. Lucca: Tommasi.

——. 2005b. "Study of Each Country: Italy, The Case of Lucca." *Participation of Women and Men in Decision-making,* edited by AA.VV. Barcellona: Diputaciò de Barcelona.

——. 2005c. "Nuove Identità Gemminili e Partecipazione Sociale: Il Contesto Toscano e la Provincia di Livorno," in *Sul Filo della Scrittura,* edited by AA.VV. Pisa: Plus.

——. 2006a. "Donne e Sindacato: I Risultati di Una Ricerca."*Sociologia e Ricerca Sociale* 79:107-123.

——. 2006b. "Mercato del Lavoro, Famiglia e Politica Sociologica: Un'Analisi Sociologica delle Carriere Femminili." *Lavoro e diritto*, pp. 580-61.

——. 2006c "Barriere Invisibili. Primo Monitoraggio delle Carriere Femminili nell'Ateneo Pisano," No.17, Pisa. Available on line http://www.unipi.it/athenet/17/art5.htm.

——. 2007b. "Differenze di Genere: Aspetti Sociologici." *Da Esculapio a Igea: Un Approccio di Genere alla Salute,* edited by Rita Biancheri and Liliana Dell'Osso. Pisa: Plus.

——. 2008. *La Dimensione di Genere nel Lavoro: Scelte o Vincoli nel Quotidiano Femminile*. Pisa, Plus.

Bourdieu, Pierre. 1998. *Il Dominio Maschile*. Milan: Feltrinelli.

Eurostat. 2004. *Labour Force Survey*. Available at www.eurostat.ec.europa.eu.

European Commission. 2000. *Science Policies in the European Union: Promoting Excellence through Mainstreaming Gender Equality*. Available at http://cordis.europa.eu/pub/improving/docs/g_wo_etan_en_199901.pdf.

ISTAT. 2000. *Donne all'Università*. Bologna: Il Mulino.

ISTAT, www.istat.it.

Naldini, Manuela and Chiara Saraceno. 2007. *Sociologia della Famiglia*. Bologna: Il Mulino.

Parsons, Talcott, and Robert Bales. 1955. *Family, Socialization, and Interaction Process*. Glencoe, IL: Free Press.

Communities and Social Change: Pasolini's Works as Sociological Sources

LUCA CARBONE
University of Salento

I am grateful to give my contribution to this publication for many reasons. First, this is the country of Lester Ward, the author of *Dynamic Sociology* (1883), which was the first scientific treatise prior to those by Ferdinand Tönnies and Émile Durkheim. This is also the country of Albion Small, first director of the Department of Sociology of the University of Chicago as well as founder and promoter of *The American Journal of Sociology*, one of the leading journals in the world about the development of sociology.

This is the land where Robert Park, Ernest Burgess, and many other researchers founded and developed the Chicago School and its human ecology approach; and, with a little bit of humor, I would add that it is here that Talcott Parsons gave a crucial impulse to the foundation of a great sociological tradition. As you may know, in his masterpiece *The Structure of Social Action*, he stated that three European authors — Durkheim, Pareto, and Weber — had been the most important authors of world sociology, and since then, excluding Pareto, they have become our "founding fathers".

Second, my mentor in the field of sociology, was the late professor Gianni Giannotti, who, in the 1960s and 1970s, was one of the most passionate and rigorous scholars of American sociology in Italy. He improved his knowledge of sociology in the United States, visiting the country several times when he worked on international research projects for the Agnelli Foundation and he became a friend and co-worker of Prof. Norman Birnbaum. I think that, still today, his book *Lo Sviluppo della Teoria Sociale negli Stati Uniti*, and the earlier work, *La Scienza della Cultura*, are relevant as introductions to American social thought. Of course, my knowledge cannot be compared to his wide knowledge, but this article was written in memory of the man and his work.

The third reason is this opportunity to bring the theoretical work of Pier Paolo Pasolini and its topicality to your attention. Pasolini's works include collected papers, films, leading articles, interviews, poems, correspondence, reviews, and theatrical plays. These rich and wide-ranging, as well as intertwined, works deserve an in-depth analysis. Strangely enough, for many and complex reasons, his work has not received due recognition even in Italy, with a few exceptions, but I believe that it will soon become topical again. Although I am truly grateful to Franco Cassano for his relevant and topical book *Il Pensiero Meridiano* (1996) which raised my curiosity for Pasolini's thought, I think that he was too quick in stating that "the epistemological secret of Pasolini's work as a whole" lay in the author's biography, marked by the experience of feeling guilty about his "innocent" homosexuality. This is an existential oxymoron that Pasolini duplicated again and again in all aspects of his work as non-dialectic contradictions. I do not know if it is possible to take into consideration only one key point in Pasolini's work, but I believe that his "presentation" of communities and their change is one of note and so it is the theme of my paper.

THE CONTRIBUTION OF ALBION SMALL

Let me begin with some lines by Albion W. Small, one of the founding fathers of American sociology, that appeared in the first pages of the first issue of *The American Journal of Sociology* (1895), as I think that they may have some methodological relevance:

> ... [N]o scholars in the world are more sagacious than those in the United States about the subordination of all special knowledge to larger relations. Nowhere are the representatives of special sciences less restricted by the contents of their particular material. Nowhere are scholars more anxious to generalize their special knowledge by coordinating it with knowledge of other portions or phases of reality (13).

He elaborated on this view, writing in March 1900:

> Nothing more sharply distinguishes the sociologists, as a class, from the specialists whose fragmentary programs promise nothing conclusive, than the explicit aim of sociology to reach knowledge which shall have a setting for all details of fact about human associations, in a complete view of human associations as a whole (638).

Such statements belong to a modernist vision, to the epoch of "great (meta) narrations," ones that post-modernist scholars criticize and reject. Similarly, we know as well that the growth of sub-disciplinary specializations makes it hard to achieve a global insight of social processes. However, following Norbert Elias (1988) among others, I firmly think that sociologists cannot renounce their claim to inheritance of searching (not superimposing) "societary wholeness."

Moreover, the very risk that Small commented on continues to grow:

> No knowledge is trivial that helps to complete the whole system of knowledge, yet untold energies are wasted in the name of science upon minutiae that are morally certain to remain so unrelated to the developing organon of knowledge about society that they are, and will remain, in effect trifles (1900:645-646).

In these words we may feel the spirit of the "constructor." More often than not, we lack this spirit in our own routine work. Relatedly, Small offered another piece of advice: " . . . [T]he aim of science should be to show the meaning of familiar things, not to construct a kingdom for itself in which, if familiar things are admitted, they are obscured under an impenetrable disguise of artificial expression (1895:14). Even if Small kept in mind the practical goal to involve the "man of affairs" as a reader of sociological issues, his statement is relevant to counterbalance the trend of overusing too abstractly formulated models in the theoretical field, regardless of the "reflexive" *experience* of social complexity.

CLASSICAL APPROACHES TO THE STUDY OF COMMUNITY

Sociologists know that the concept of *community* has always been one of the main issues in the sociological tradition. In an interesting and stimulating overview on community studies, Steven Brint (2001) discussed two relevant but different traditions in the history of sociology: the work by Tönnies, *Gemeinschaft und Gesellschaft* (1887), and the work by Durkheim, *The Division of Labor in Society* (1893). In spite of the influential view of Pitirim Sorokin (1889-1968), I agree with both Werner Cahnman (1973) and Brint in thinking that deep differences exist between the two approaches, although Brint thinks that Durkheim's tradition is more important than that of Tönnies, and Cahnman thought just the opposite. On the other hand, I disagree with Brint as to the relevance of Tönnies' theory and its fortune in sociological research. Stating that "only Durkheim's disaggregated approach has led to a solid record of scientific accomplishment" and by contrast, stating that "the aggregated approach of Tönnies became bogged down in a conflict of and debunking portraits of communities and has largely failed to yield valuable scientific generalizations" is simply too dichotomous (2001). His prejudicial romanticizing of community *against* society is an extremely trivial misinterpretation of Tönnies' seminal work.

Even in his preface Tönnies rejected any identification with romantic thought. He wrote: "My opinion has never been the same as that of Romantic authors; before them the past shines, lit up by poetry" (1963:31-34). Moreover, in his historical reconstruction of the two research approaches, Brint overestimates Durkheim's influence and underestimates that of Tönnies, especially concerning American sociology. Although this topic could itself certainly be the topic for a longer essay, suffice it here to recall what Gianni Giannotti wrote in this respect:

> As Edward A. Shils has pointed out, early American sociology has deeply been influenced by Tönnies' important dichotomy between community (Gemeinschaft) and society (Gesellschaft); so that, the American sociology is still today influenced by it in its most significant paradigms . . . After the success of Parsons' work, Durkheim's influence on American sociology has been overemphasized; anyway, at the University of Chicago during the twenties, Tönnies was more known than Durkheim, and the circulation of Durkheim's books among American social scientists of that epoch could be undoubtedly considered negligible (1976:93-94)).

As Raewyn W. Connell (1997) pointed out in his important essay about the historical creation of the sociological *canon*, "The *Rules* became a must-read classic, for the first time, half a century after it was published." The growing lack of historical understanding is likely to lead to misevaluation. In *Il Pensiero Sociologico* (what we would translate as *The Sociological Thought)*, Franco Crespi (2001:73-75), banished Tönnies, together with Simmel heirs Werner Sombart, Karl Mannheim, and Elias in a short paragraph, whereas he asserted that Durkheim was the founding father of scientific sociology. Nonetheless, it is an historical fact that Tönnies wrote *before* Simmel, and that Sombart was influenced by Tönnies' work. Even so, Durkheim is now considered as one of the founding fathers of the discipline. Nonetheless, at the beginning of the twentieth century, U.S. sociologists were not inclined to recognize him this apical position. Connell notes that:

Platt's (1995) important study of the American reception of Durkheim's *Rules of Sociological Method* . . . shows, by a detailed examination of both textbook references and specialist studies, that Durkheim had only a modest presence in early American sociological thought. He was known as a contemporary, but the *Rules* served mainly as a punching bag for arguments about the importance of the individual (1514).

In brief, if we adopt a *dialogic* [in the Bakhtinian sense of each theoretical work as always the result of many, expressed and/or silent dialogues that an author takes with colleagues, researchers of other disciplines, predecessors etc. approach to our disciplinary traditions (Jedlowski 2003:6)], it is difficult to consider Durkheim as *the* founding father of sociology as a science. This is not the same as saying that his work is unproductive.

Likewise, it is a distortion to accept the mainstream statement applying these two conceptual frameworks to the *same* aspects of community as a social phenomenon. This opinion is deep-rooted. Indeed Sorokin stated, "It is easy to see that Tönnies' *Gemeinschaft* is identical with what Durkheim later styled a group with mechanical solidarity" (Cahnman 1973). This "thesis" has been accepted by most sociologists as evidenced in the many introduction-to-sociology writings (including Italian ones) with few or no variations at all.

I agree with Cahnman when he clearly opines, "Sorokin—to mention only one author for many—is wrong when he asserts that *Gemeinschaft* is identical with "mechanical solidarity" and that merely the terms are reversed" (1973:240). We all know that—by reversing the terms used by Tönnies—Durkheim provided the definition of "mechanical" to gemeinschaft, and of "organic" to gesellschaft.

Four years before the publication of his important book, Durkheim wrote a review of Tönnies' book, in which he accepted the sociological depiction of community, espoused by Tönnies (Cahnman 1973:240-248). Unlike other scholars to follow, he understood that community (gemeinschaft) was not identical with rural village, and wrote, "Although this kind of community is more fully realized in the village than elsewhere, one nevertheless can find it also in the city" (242). Community can develop, not only "in" the city, but just *as* a city. A city can be a community. This is the key point of my paper, with regard to Pasolini's work and I will return to it later. Durkheim does recognize this important aspect in the conception of Tönnies, but just *that* is the "critical point" of his own theory. Continuing the review, he wrote: " . . . but only on condition that the city does not grow beyond certain dimensions and does not grow into the big city of our time" (242).

The difference between the two authors becomes clearer when Durkheim explains the causes of the social-evolutionary shift from mechanical to organic solidarity in the second chapter of his second book, *The Division of Labor in Society* (1999:257-281). As Leo F. Schnore pointed out and Robert Bellah underlined, in this period Durkheim places "primary emphasis to morphological variables in the explanation of social causes" (1959:452). The morphological variables are 1) the number of social units or "the size of society"; and 2) "dynamic" or "moral" density, due to the increase of social ties. Both variables are related to quantities. In order to explain the social shift, Durkheim quotes the most important biologists of his time, Charles Darwin and Ernst Haeckel—and the "struggle for life" (1999:266-268). In his reply to Durkheim, Tönnies opposed this view and objected that "the difference [between gemeinschaft and gesellschaft] is not a simple function of the relative size of these agglomerations" (Cahnman 1973:250), and that social forces are not *merely* biological, that is to say, functional. In Tönnies' conception of community, there was another underlying element, but Durkheim—at that phase in his research—did not recognize its importance.

With regard to this underlying element Cahnman writes, "Mechanical solidarity refers to the external facts of societal restraints; *Gemeinschaft* is derived from the *internal reality* of essential will" (1973:240) (emphasis added).

What's the meaning of this statement? What can we identify as "internal reality" *within* community? Certainly, it is not the coercion of collective conscience. I suppose that the internal element emerges when we compare current conceptions of community with Tönnies' conception. To help us understand, Brint (2001) offers two interesting analytical schemes of community models as shown in Figure 1.

If we carefully consider all of these possible types of community, we may note that the least relevant element is—*time*. What's the temporal range of a community? And what notion of temporality is it?

In Tönnies' conception, gemeinschaft is based on the sacred ties of the living with their ancestors. These ties are intergenerational, and they build a bridge from past to future *throughout* the *social memory* and constitute the *core* of socialization within community. Each member of community is conceived, born, and raised in the light (and constraint) of those sacred ties, in order to perpetuate them. Ancestors belong to the *present* of the community. This social presence of ancestors produces a mnemonic tie with the past which may be intended as one of the "positive" aspects of the *ascription*. Each aspect of community life—including building, trading and so forth—is aimed at celebrating those ties. At the same time, it reinforces the ties with the divine: animals, plants and inorganic matter belong to the divine. This is one of the main themes of Durkheim's last work, *The Elementary Forms of Religious Life* (1973). In Tönnies' view the city is the place where the community as a whole achieves its full potential (1963:79-82). All these aspects that I have sketched above comprise the *local pattern* of community or, in a word, its *identity*.

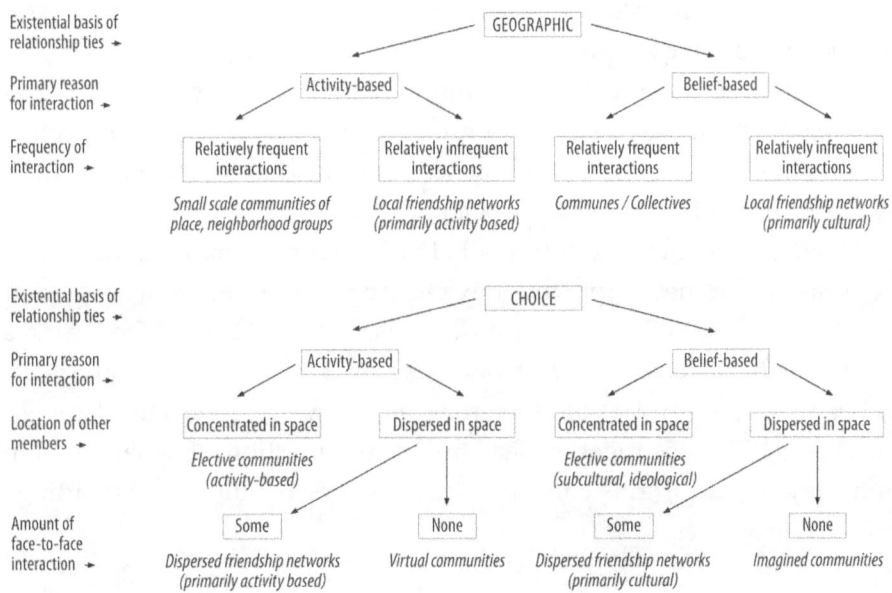

FIGURE 1. *Community Types*

Not until the 1980s did the interconnections between social memory and identity become a central issue in the field of the sociology of memory. As Jeffrey Olick and Joyce Robbins (1998) write, "Memory is a central, if not the central medium through which identities are constituted. Inquiries into identity and memory are . . . related." In their extensive commentary on social memory, they quote a significant passage that seems to reintroduce Tönnies' concept: "Communities . . . have a history—in an important sense are constituted by their past—and for this reason *we can speak of a real community as a "community of memory"* [italics added], one that does not forget its past." Olick and Robbins quote an important scholar like Immanuel Wallerstein asserting, "The temporal dimension of pastness is central and inherent in the concept of peoplehood." Eviatar Zerubavel analyzes "mnemonic socialization" within "mnemonic communities," with regard to the way "we acquire personal and social identities." Memory is the inward tie of community in Tönnies' conceptual system; hence, the "essential will," on which community is based, reveals itself as *memory* (1963:139-142). He also writes that memory is a synonym for "association of ideas," but in my opinion this is a partial definition. What is more topical, in the same part of the chapter, is the fact that Tönnies argues that memory includes and develops from *habit*. Indeed, Paolo Jedlowski concludes his book *Memoria, Esperienza, Modernità* (2002:125-126) by remarking that new research in the sociology of memory focuses on "practices *as* memory, that is, as forms of permanence of the past within the present of a group." "These practices," he explains, "are a system of operational, cognitive, relational habits which constitutes the fabric for continuity of each social group."

Tönnies' statement, "All [social] change can be comprehended only if one grasps the need for the flexible application of concepts to the transitional nature of reality" and Cahnman's observation, "One can read *Gemeinschaft und Gesellschaft* at one time as if it were the analysis of a historical process and at another time as if it were a system of timeless concepts" (1973:105) together lead us to the question of what Pasolini's contributions add to this conceptual framework for the understanding of historical processes.

PASOLINI'S APPROACH TO THE STUDY OF COMMUNITY

Of the thousands of pages, let me draw from just a few of the more relevant passages and begin, first, with how the question of community is more than just a *local* question. "The peasant universe (which comprises urban sub-proletarian cultures, and just until a few years ago, also the working class as a minority) . . . is a transnational universe: that does not recognize even nations" (Pasolini 1975:66). Currently, half of the world's population lives in rural settlements. We may therefore assume that, in many cases, the social ties are community-based in villages and towns of a small or medium size.

Second, Pasolini notes that the scale of time is wider than that of civilization and monotheism. "It is the remainder of a previous society (or of an overlapping of previous societies, all very similar to each other)" (Pasolini 1975:66). It is important to note that all peasant societies are *not*, in fact, *only Catholic*. "There is a continuum among Roman Catholicism, Christianity, Paganism, and primitive religions" (Pasolini 1975:267). Community is based on a perception of sacredness, which is different from what Catholic dogma asserts about the divine: nature itself and its elements are "divine." As Giulo Sapelli (2005:33) asserts, "The current rediscovery of localism is a different matter from the conservation of localism about which Pasolini spoke. Today traditions are invented."

Third, we must debunk the myth of a lost paradise (Bauman 2007c) in order to experience and understand community. "People in this universe did not live a *golden age*, and they were not even involved, if not formally, with *Italietta*. They lived what Chilanti called the *bread age*. That is, they were consumers of extremely essential goods" (Pasolini 1975:66-67). The principles of economic organization within the community, that Karl Polanyi, influenced by Tönnies, has elaborated, are: reciprocity, redistribution and household. On these bases, the rural population lives frugally and often suffers hunger and inequalities in struggling to secure the actual necessities of life. In this social context, the development of a market society is impossible (Polanyi 1974:57-72). In Pasolini's reflection, according to Cassano, we find an anticipation (maybe the roots) of contemporary Italian culture against an unlimited economic growth (Osti 2006). Rethinking the community ties, without building myths on them, is a possible way to participate in the "new war" that the market fights against the community's moral economy (Bauman 2007a:103-107).

Fourth, the identity of community, that is, its *pattern*, lives first of all *within* the bodies, behaviors and "things" of its members. Bodies, behaviors, mother-tongues and things have a form that *returns*, because *that* form is the "visible side" of the pattern, and pattern is the foundation of community. So the shift of pattern produces the change in the form.

> I have said, and I repeat, that acculturation of the "consumer center," has destroyed the various cultures of the Third World (I mean again on a world scale, therefore, I refer also to cultures of the Third World, to which the Italian peasant cultures are profoundly similar): there is only one single cultural model offered to Italians (as well as to all people of the world, after all). Conforming to such a model takes place first of all in the lived, existential experience of people: therefore, in their bodies and

in their behaviours. It is here that values of the new culture of the consumer society are lived, not yet expressed (Pasolini 1975:67).

The growing power of the consumer model is the subject of Bauman's narratives of *liquid modernity*. Bauman quotes, for example, such titles as *I Shop Therefore I Know That I Am* and *The Commercialization of Intimate Life* to remind us of the relevant topic of the *mcdonaldization* of the world (Bauman 2007b:27-33).

Adopting an anthropological point of view, Pasolini uses the comprehensive term "culture" to refer to patterns:

> The culture of a nation is the sum of all [its] (class) cultures: it is the average of them. Hence, it would be abstract if it were not recognizable—or, rather, visible—in the lived and existential experience, and if it had not consequently a practical dimension (1975:57).

> ... culture produces codes ... codes produce behaviour ... behaviour produces a language (1975:59).

Pasolini (1972) examines the language of bodies and things in an essay entitled "Res sunt nomina" (Things are words). This is an ontological theme; its sociological interest lies in the possibility of searching the *meaning* of social life and social change not *primarily* in the conscience of social actors, or in their conscious interactions. Brint (2001) stresses the key point, "My definition [of community] requires only that these [community] relations be based *primarily* on affect, loyalty, shared values, or personal involvement with the lives of others." I would subscribe to Brint's definition of community ties except for his use of the conception of "shared values." Indeed, the notion of shared values as a sociological topic has too many theoretical implications to be dealt with in the narrow space of my paper.

Why do sociologists often have difficulties in recognizing these processes? Perhaps, because they often have not a real existential experience of community life and do not recognize community force, even inertia. This is not a simplistic standpoint. A profound difference exists between a long, unprejudiced experience and its elaboration *within* the social dynamics of the community (as Pasolini experienced them) and a formal theoretical model based on indirect or partial involvement in the community. *Knowledge as experience* (to propose a clumsy translation of Jedlowski's 1994 work, *Il Sapere dell'Esperienza*) makes the difference. In the former case (community as a *reflexive* experience), one may recognize the persistence of community even if it is not a socially dominant form; in the latter (community as a theoretical model), one may not perceive its "presence" and persistence even if its effects are still pervasive. If one takes into consideration what has been stated above, we may understand Pasolini's point of view regarding the possible limits of the sociological approach.

> I lived in Turin for a dozen days. Turin is that city which, for the sociologists, should be like a "Civitas Dei" for the theologians. As in the perfectly utopian "Civitas Dei" all theological hypotheses are realized, so in Turin all sociological hypotheses regarding, in this particular instance, the "quality of life" of people living and operating in a big neo-capitalist city should be realized (Pasolini 1992:540-541).

But something seems to be wrong in the theoretical framework:

> In the real world, everything is infinitely less stiff and adamant than in sociological typologies. There is a point where confusion arises, *always*. Sociologists have some perfect models on hand . . . but no perfect model is ever carried out perfectly. Sociologists may be too projected into the future, and are very little interested in "survivals." Such survivals cause confusion. Therefore, there are existential, immediate, concrete data of "behaviour in behaviour," which are seemingly not "spoken" by sociology (Ibid).

If we take as conceptual background what Paul Connerton (1989) called "mnemonics of the bodies," to which we may add the "mnemonics of things," we may subscribe to what Edward Shils (quoted in Olick and Robbins) affirms about community persistence, "Traditional patterns of belief and conduct . . . are very insistent; they will not wholly release their grip on those who would suspend or abolish them." (1998:129) Pasolini defined as "survivals" what (several years later) Connerton marked as "memory 'incorporated' in bodily practices (as opposed to that 'inscribed' in print, encyclopedias, indexes, etc.)." This aspect of social memory "could be termed inertia." (Ibid)

As an exemplification of what Pasolini anticipated and Connerton reaffirmed, one might consider the socioeconomic development in southern Italy. To understand the difficulty of such development, one has to take into account the confusion caused by the survival of community patterns, incorporated in bodily practices and emotional ties.

If we assume as Small did that sociology is the science of "societary wholeness," the relevance of Pasolini to our understanding of the theme of community becomes apparent.

By adopting literature as a source of sociological knowledge, we may both renovate theoretical concepts and understand social reality in its empirical aspects. That is not a post-modernist argumentation. Indeed, Lester Ward wrote, back in 1902, about the apparent novelty of what we say as contemporary sociologists:

> I have sometimes thought that *more could be extracted from literature than is commonly supposed* [italics added]. If sociologists would go about it in some such way . . . important results could be attained. If the early literature, like that of Greece and Rome, of India, Egypt, Persia, Syria, and China, could be thoroughly sifted for social facts, the labor, though great, would be well repaid. Such writers did not intentionally inform the world as to the industrial, economic, and social condition of the ages and countries in which they lived and wrote, but on every page occur words that are full of meaning for the sociologist who will carefully weigh them and learn what they imply" (1902:641).

I know that our shared vision of the world is based on functionalism; it is marked by an economical and "materialistic" approach to social processes but, without sounding religious, I think that social life is also conditioned by immaterial needs and forces. The social transformation of community depends on the change of the "cultural-bodily" pattern, and not merely on the size of community or on the process of urbanization. As long as the pattern is stable, a community may grow into a city but its social memory, its identity, remains the same. This last assumption makes clear what Pasolini, in a review of the brief stories of the Italian poet Sandro Penna, strikingly writes about social change in Italy (a country "formed" by hundreds of small/medium towns–communities) during fascism and after the Second World War:

> What a wonderful country Italy was during fascism and soon after it! Life was just as we had known it as children, and for twenty or thirty years it would not change. I don't mean in its values—the word value is a bit high and ideological to express what I want to say very simply here—but appearances seemed to possess the gift of eternity: one could passionately believe in rebellion or revolution, because that wonderful thing which was the form of life, would not change. One could feel

himself a hero of change and novelty because he was encouraged and strengthened by his confidence that the city and its people, in their deepest and finest aspect, would not change: *only their economic and cultural condition would rightly improve, but this was nothing compared to the pre-existing truth, which ruled, wonderfully unchangeable, the gestures, glances and body attitudes of a man or a youth* [italics added]. The cities ended in broad avenues, surrounded by houses, small villas or working-class buildings with their "dear awful colours," in the thick countryside: soon beyond the bus or tram terminals there lay stretches of wheat, channels lined by poplars or elders, or those useless wonderful scrubs of robinias and blackberries (1975:179-180).

References

Bauman, Zygmunt. 2007a. *Amore Liquido*. Roma-Bari: Editori Laterza.

——. 2007b. *Homo Consumens*. Gardolo: Edizioni Erickson.

——. 2007c. *Modernità Liquida*. 12th ed. Roma-Bari: Editori Laterza.

Bellah, Robert N. 1959. "Durkheim and History." *American Sociological Review* 24:447-461.

Brint, Steven. 2001. "Gemeinschaft Revisited: A Critique and Reconstruction of the Community Concept." *Sociological Theory* 19:1-23.

Cahnman Werner J. 1968. "Tönnies and Social Change." *Social Force* 47:136-144.

——. 1973. *Ferdinand Tönnies: A New Evaluation*. Leiden: E.J. Brill.

Cassano, Franco. [1996] 2001. *Il Pensiero Meridiano*, 7th ed. Roma-Bari: Editori Laterza.

Connell, Raewyn W. 1997. "Why Is Classical Theory Classical?" *American Journal of Sociology*, 102:1511-1557.

Connerton Paul. 1989. *How Societies Remember*. New York: Cambridge University Press cited in Jeffrey K. Olick and Joyce Robbins. 1998. "Social Memory Studies: From 'Collective Memory' to the Historical Sociology of Mnemonic Practices." *Annual Review of Sociology* 24:105-140.

Crespi, Franco. 2001. *Il Pensiero Sociologico*. Bologna: Il Mulino.

Durkheim, Emile. 1973. *Le forme elementari della vita religiosa: Il Sistema Totemico in Australia*. Roma: Newton Compton.

——. 1999. *La Divisione del Lavoro Sociale*. Milano: Edizioni di Comunità.

Elias, Norbert. 1988. *Coinvolgimento e Distacco: Saggi di Sociologia della Conoscenza*. Bologna: Il Mulino.

Giannotti, Gianni. 1967, *La Scienza della Cultura*. Bologna: Il Mulino.

——. 1976. *Lo Sviluppo della Teoria Sociale negli Stati Uniti*. Manduria: Lacaita.

Jedlowski, Paolo. 1994. *Il Sapere dell'Esperienza*. Milano: Il Saggiatore.

——. [1989] 2002. *Memoria, Esperienza e Modernità: Memorie e Società nel XX secolo*. Milano: Franco Angeli.

——. 2003. *Fogli nella Valigia: Sociologia, Cultura, Vita Quotidiana*. Bologna: Il Mulino.

Olick Jeffrey K., and Joyce Robbins. 1998. "Social Memory Studies: From 'Collective Memory' to the Historical Sociology of Mnemonic Practices." *Annual Review of Sociology* 24:105-140.

Osti, Giorgio. 2006. *Nuovi Asceti: Consumatori, Imprese e Istituzioni di fronte alla Crisi Ambientale*. Bologna: Il Mulino.

Pasolini, Pier Paolo. [1972] 2000. *Empirismo Eretico*, 3rd ed. Milano: Garzanti.

——. 1975. *Scritti Corsari*. Milano: Garzanti.

——. 1992. *I Dialoghi*. Roma: Editori Riuniti.

Polanyi, Karl. 1974. *La Grande Trasformazione*. Torino: Einaudi.

Sapelli, Giulio. 2005. *Modernizzazione senza Sviluppo: Il Capitalismo secondo Pasolini*. Milano: Paravia Bruno Mondadori.

Small Albion W. 1895. "The Era of Sociology." *American Journal of Sociology* 1:1-15.

——. 1900. "The Scope of Sociology." *The Development of Sociological Method* 5:617-647.

Tönnies, Ferdinand. 1963. *Comunità e Società*. Milano, Edizioni di Comunità.

Ward, Lester F. 1902. "Contemporary Sociology II." *American Journal of Sociology* 7:629-658.

Acceptance or Rejection: The Uncertainty and Insecurity of Homosexual Italian Americans

MICHAEL CAROSONE
Brooklyn College, CUNY

The idea for this essay came from my forthcoming book, *The Marginalization of Italian American Writers and Italian American Literature*. I have always been fascinated by how marginalized people live, survive, and thrive, creating their own fulfilled lives, creating their own art, and adding value to their communities and societies, while overcoming adversity. Always feeling like an outcast myself, I am captivated by the perseverance of the non-conformist in any society. As I was researching for the book, I noticed the lack of gay Italian-American writers, and the lack of reference to them. I noticed that their stories were not told, their voices not heard, their existence ignored. Therefore, the purpose of this essay is to bring attention to the uncertainty and insecurity of homosexual Italian Americans in the postmodern world, while also bringing some thought to how such uncertainty and insecurity can be cured. I wish to bring awareness to their ambivalent and quiet battle for attention and acceptance, equality and respect. I want to initiate a discourse on the important and worthy topic that is the lives, struggles, histories, and futures of gay Italian Americans.

THE UNCERTAIN, INSECURE, AND GRIM PRESENT AND FUTURE

Although queer Americans have made great strides, their futures, at times, seem uncertain, insecure, and grim because of the heterosexist society in which they live. Their civil rights continue to be debated and threatened. As for gay Italian Americans, they face discrimination in their everyday lives from the mainstream society, their families, and both communities: the ethnic community and the gay community. As a gay Italian-American man, I have experienced the stereotypes and prejudices associated with being both gay and Italian American, whether by society, my own family, my own ethnic community, or my own gay community.

The editors — Giovanna (Janet) Capone, Denise Nico Leto, and Tommi Avicolli Mecca — of the book *Hey Paesan!: Writing by Lesbians and Gay Men of Italian Descent* (1999:2) write:

> For too long, as lesbians and gay men, we have suffered on dual fronts. We face intense homophobia, silence, and invisibility within our own ethnic community, yet we have found only limited solace within the queer community, where we are all but invisible in gay/lesbian literature. Why is that? While many in the queer community acknowledge Italy as a strong source of culture, most have no awareness of the real history of this country.

The future is as bleak as the present for homosexual Italian Americans unless change occurs in the conservative, traditional, and religious Italian American community. The Italian-American community — with its Roman Catholic history, traditions, prejudices, and conservatism — must accept the fact that Italian-American gay men, lesbians, bisexuals, and transgender people exist, and that they demand attention, respect, and equality. Until acceptance occurs, gay Italian Americans will continue to be rejected by their own ethnic community. And such rejection is not healthy for one's sense of self and ethnic pride. Capone, Leto, and Avicolli further state, "We are also shunned by the Catholic Church, and often develop an awareness about our sexuality steeped in a climate of repression, fear, and homophobia within the family" (1992:2).

As for the gay community, to no fault of its own, it is a group of which many different types of people belong, from many different walks of life. It is unique in that, unlike any other group of people, its members come from every group of people, from every race, religion, class, and culture. Usually, the only thing that homosexuals have in common is that they are attracted to the same sex. Thus, the gay community easily overlooks ethnicity. And lately, with homosexuals fighting for their civil rights, ethnic rights are not a priority. In her essay, "A Divided Life: Being a Lesbian in an Italian American Family," Giovanna Capone (1996:38) writes that her "Italianness is somewhat compromised and rendered invisible" in the gay community of California, where she lives.

THE STEREOTYPES OF (HOMO)SEXUALITY AND ETHNICITY

In the mainstream, heterosexual society, the stereotype for the Italian-American male is a man who is macho, strong, tough, brutish, violent, uneducated, stupid, ignorant, handsome, sexy, and virile, with a big penis and an even bigger sex drive. Thus, Italian-American gay men distance themselves from their ethnic selves because they cannot, and do not want to, fulfill the stereotype of the Italian-American male. They denounce their ethnic halves. They give themselves fully to their homosexual selves because they are more accepted in their homosexual communities; however, they are only accepted as homosexuals, not as ethnic Italian Americans. I have noticed a lack of ethnic pride among gay Italian Americans. Hence, gay Italian-American male writers write about their gay lives, communities, culture, and history, but not about their Italian-American lives, communities, culture, history, and heritage. Such an identity crisis must be solved and corrected by both communities: the gay community and the Italian-American community. Furthermore, such stereotypes are debilitating for both the individuals and the communities.

Even the gay community has created its own stereotype for the Italian-American male. "In the gay media, Italian/Sicilian gay men are commonly depicted as exotic and well-endowed, oversexed and extremely passionate" (Capone et al. 1996:1). In his essay, "Call Me Latin," Tommi Avicolli Mecca (1996:220) asks and answers a question: "Q: Oversexed, well-hung, muscular, macho, working-class, dark, hairy, aggressive, and incredible in bed. What am I? A: An Italian gay male." He explains: "In gay male porno and in the gay male community at large, that's how I'm typecast. Reality doesn't matter. This is what I am to the dominant Anglo gay male culture. A sex machine put on Earth for its pleasure." Avicolli Mecca wants to be acknowledged and valued as more than simply a sex object: "I don't object to being thought of as more passionate and sexual," he writes, "[b]ut I refuse to be invisible in every arena but the bedroom." I agree with him.

(HOMO)SEXUALITY AND ETHNICITY IN LITERATURE

In the mainstream literary world, and in society in general, there exists levels of marginalization within one already marginalized ethnic community: first, all Italian-American writers, regardless of gender, are marginalized; second, Italian-American women writers are marginalized even more because of their gender; and third, queer Italian-American writers are marginalized even further because of their sexual orientation.

I noticed that most of the minimal work published has been written by Italian-American gay women, not gay men. This is because in U.S. society, it is more acceptable to be a gay woman than a gay man. In the male-dominated, male-chauvinistic, sexist, and heterosexist society of the United States, it is considered sexy, titillating to see two women kiss—a heterosexual man's fantasy—but disgusting and sinful to see two men kiss. Italian-American gay women are more accepting of, and comfortable with, their ethnicity; they also deal better with their ethnic stereotypes. As women, lesbians are used to the male chauvinism that gay men are not.

A major, recurring theme in gay Italian-American literature is rejection. Queer Italian-American writers—and their characters—are rejected because they refuse to conform to the traditions, mostly religious, of their families. They feel like outcasts. They are marginalized because they are different. They become alone and lonely. Ironically, in essence, they are treated the same way their immigrant ancestors were treated by the mainstream society when they arrived in America from Italy.

While having a conversation with Giovanna Capone, she informed me that she and the other two editors of *Hey Paesan!* had to self-publish the book in 1999 after many publishers rejected it because, although it was a "good book and a great idea," its topic was "too narrow, too limited, not marketable for a large audience, not going to sell copies." Well, in 2007, eight years later, the three editors are considering a second printing of the book because they still receive requests from hungry and thirsty queer Italian Americans. Obviously, there is an audience for literature by, for, and about gay people of Italian descent.

A movement is occurring: that of gay Italian American literature. It has been happening since the 1980s and 1990s alongside other movements, such as Cultural Studies, Ethnic Studies, Italian American Studies, Queer Studies, and Postcolonial Studies. It has been crawling instead of running, or even walking. But like any infant, gay Italian American literature must learn how to crawl before it learns how to walk. I foresee it maturing into something to be reckoned with.

(HOMO)SEXUALITY AND ETHNICITY IN FILM AND TELEVISION

From 1998 to 2000, I organized film screenings and events for Italian-American filmmakers to showcase their films and screenplays, and for them to talk about their lives as Italian-American filmmakers. Of the many, only one filmmaker was gay. And it is worth noting that his film was the only one that did not deal with ethnicity.

In the summer of 2000, the National Italian American Foundation (NIAF) invited me to its youth retreat to present a seminar on Italian-

American filmmakers. Of course, the discussion included the negative stereotypes of Italian Americans in film and television. To my dismay, many of the participants liked and enjoyed watching *The Sopranos*. It must be stated that of those who liked and watched the television series, most of them were men. Some thought that the acting and writing were just too good not to watch. I do not wish to debate the artistic value of *The Sopranos*. But I want to stress that no other ethnicity is, and would accept being, insulted on television. I do not watch *The Sopranos*, but I read and heard that one of the characters was all of a sudden made gay, and I wonder if making a character gay was simply done for sensational reasons to increase viewership, improve ratings, and tap into the gay community for the very important gay dollar. As a gay man, I am disgusted with the token gay character, and also with my sexuality being exploited by Hollywood, the media, and society. As an Italian-American man, I am disgusted with the representation of the Italian American as *gavone* (or *cafone*), and also with my ethnicity being exploited by Hollywood, the media, and society.

Not many people have seen the independent film *Mambo Italiano* (2003). Although the protagonist of the film is Italian Canadian and not Italian American, I present the film as an example of the conflict between ethnicity and sexuality. Angelo Barberini, the protagonist, is a gay Italian-Canadian man in his early 20s. He is second generation Canadian from Italian immigrant parents. And although he does not struggle with accepting his own homosexuality, he does struggle with "coming out" to his conservative and traditional mother and father. His conflict lies in how to integrate his identity as a gay man with his identity as an ethnic Italian-Canadian man.

THE SOCIOLOGY OF (HOMO)SEXUALITY AND ETHNICITY

On sexuality and ethnicity, Anne-Marie Fortier (2003:1) writes: "it seemed as if they sat uncomfortably alongside each other . . . the gay village and the Little Italy . . . it seemed to me that the very edges of these two worlds met at the intersection of sexuality and ethnicity." Mary Cappello (1996:91) explains that "'sexuality' and 'ethnicity' are neither stable terms nor sites whose contours can be apparently traced. 'Sexuality' and 'ethnicity' can have both everything and nothing to do with one another, just as they might only be truly mutually articulated through other discursive conditions like religious practice and class." Thus, ethnicity and homosexuality can be viewed as mutually exclusive, and when the two interact, they create a conflicted relationship. And it is the conflict that must be resolved in order for a homosexual Italian American to live a healthy and fulfilled life, in which he/she is proud and accepting of both his/her ethnicity and sexuality.

THE PSYCHOLOGY OF (HOMO)SEXUALITY AND ETHNICITY

Psychologists hold that self-concept consists of various parts of the self, including the ethnic self and the gay self. Unfortunately, for many gay Italian Americans, there is a denial and repression of their ethnic selves. The ethnic self is an integral part of the individual because one develops, learns, and individuates by using the rules of one's ethnicity. The denial of the ethnic self leads to low self-esteem and a lack of wholeness in self-concept, which can also lead to self-hate. Recently, psychologists have recognized the importance of providing support through psychotherapy to ethnic homosexuals. Such support helps them to overcome the difficulties of being unaccepted by their ethnic communities, and to realize the significance of combining their ethnic and gay selves.

Teresa Carilli (1996) explains how she felt strangled while growing up as a Sicilian American lesbian. And Giovanna Capone (1996:36) expresses how she "feels torn in half" and "constantly divided." In New York, she feels Italian; in California, she feels like a lesbian; and she thinks "this semi-estrangement is especially painful for those of us raised in close knit, ethnic families."

THE UNCERTAINTY AND INSECURITY OF HOMOSEXUAL ITALIANS

Not only is the future uncertain and insecure for gay Italian Americans, it is uncertain and insecure for gay Italians as well. In October 1980, in Giarre, Italy, two young gay men committed suicide because their love for each other was discovered and ridiculed by their entire village. The first Italian gay association, Arcigay, started in Palermo on December 9, 1980, two months after the suicides.

In his September 2005 article, "An Uproar in Italy Derails Gay Union Hopes," Ian Fisher reported on gay unions in Italy, and wrote: "The two faces of Italy—one increasingly secular and the other still deeply influenced by the church—collided this week in a noisy electoral debate that left one thing clear: Italy, it can safely be said, will not legalize gay marriage anytime soon."

And recently, I read Lou Chibbaro's (2007) article, "Fall of Italian Government Jeopardizes Gay Rights," in which he reports: "Just days after the fall of his fragile, nine-party coalition government, Italian Prime Minister Romano Prodi agreed to reassemble his center-left coalition by demanding that all factions agree to a platform that omits legislation to provide rights to same-sex couples."

On Saturday, May 12, 2007, the John D. Calandra Italian American Institute of Queens College of the City University of New York and the Italian Consulate of New York presented a symposium entitled "The Italian Vote Abroad." The purpose of the symposium was "to revisit the concept of the 'vote abroad.'" It is interesting to note the following information from the symposium: "The unexpected results insofar as the general consensus up to the elections were that Italians abroad were, for the most part, politically conservative."[1] This is why gay Italian Americans—and gay Italians—continue to be neglected and continue to fight for their rights.

CONCLUSION: ACCEPTANCE INSTEAD OF REJECTION

William Faulkner wrote, "Some things you must always be unable to bear—injustice and outrage and dishonor and shame—just refuse to bear them." I can no longer bear being rejected, marginalized, ignored, silenced, and invisible. No one should have to. And as a gay Italian-American man I don't want to, whether in my ethnic community or my gay community, or in society in general.

Unless the Italian-American community acknowledges and accepts its gay members, and unless the gay community acknowledges and accepts its Italian-American ethnic members, nothing will change for the better, and homosexual Italian Americans will continue to lose pieces of their identities by denouncing parts of their identities.

I think that it is time that we do some self-analysis, and ask ourselves why we are the way we are and what needs to change. We need to change the ways in which we categorize, label, and divide ourselves for the benefit of a few and for the misery of many. We need to change our languages, symbols, and signs so that all people are accepted. The best ingredient for a recipe of change is hope. We need to be hopeful that the world will change for the better—even though, at times, change seems impossible.

---

[1] Taken from the announcement for the symposium.

AFTERWORD

I hated being me practically my entire life. I hated being Italian American practically my entire life. I hated the negative stereotypes associated with being Italian American; I did not want to admit that I was American of Italian descent because of such negative stereotypes and images. As a young child, I wanted to change my last name to "Carson," or something else "non-Italian." I was embarrassed and ashamed of who I was and where I came from. My identity was in a crisis, and it would not be until many years later—in my adulthood—after reading much about Italian Americans, written by Italian Americans, that my identity crisis would come to an end. Literature has amazing powers that can change the lives of the readers; literature saved my life.

When I was a young child in elementary school—I cannot remember the exact age—I had a difficult time relating to the other students. I knew that I did not "fit in." I was not the only American of Italian descent, but I was one of the few in a school with mostly Jewish-American and Irish-American children. And of course, I befriended the other three to five children who were also Italian American. We formed a close bond.

Later in life, I would come to realize that my ethnicity was not the only aspect of my life that marginalized me, and made me not "fit in." As a homosexual male, my sexual orientation also marginalized me, and made me feel like an outcast, made me feel less than human. And it must be stated, and known, that with its conservative and traditional ways of thinking, the Italian-American community—my own community—has not always been accepting and understanding of my sexual orientation. Ironically, one marginalized community marginalizes—even minimizes and oppresses—another marginalized community.

References

Capone, Giovanna. 1996. "A Divided Life: Being a Lesbian in an Italian American Family." Pp. 29-49 in *Fuori: Essays by Italian/American Lesbians and Gays*, edited by Anthony Julian Tamburri. West Lafayette, IN: Bordighera Press.

Capone, Giovanna, Denise Nico Leto, and Tommi Avicolli Mecca, eds. 1999. *Hey Peasan!: Writing by Lesbians and Gay Men of Italian Descent*. Oakland, CA: Three Guineas Press.

Cappello, Mary. 1996. "Nothing to Confess: A Lesbian in Italian America." Pp. 89-108 in *Fuori: Essays by Italian/American Lesbians and Gays*, edited by Anthony Julian Tamburri. West Lafayette, IN: Bordighera Press.

Carilli, Teresa. 1996. "Strangled." Pp. 50-59 in *Fuori: Essays by Italian/American Lesbians and Gays*, edited by Anthony Julian Tamburri. West Lafayette, IN: Bordighera Press.

Carosone, Michael. Forthcoming. *The Marginalization of Italian American Writers and Italian American Literature*.

Chibbaro, Lou. 2007. "Fall of Italian Government Jeopardizes Gay Rights." *Southern Voice*. 2 March. Retrieved May 2007. http://www.sovo.com/2007/3-2/news/worldnews/6589.

Fisher, Ian. 2005. "An Uproar in Italy Derails Gay Union Hopes." *International Herald Tribune*. 17 September. Retrieved May 2007. http://www.iht.com/articles/2005/09/16/news/rome.

Fortier, Anne-Marie. 2003. "Outside/In? Notes on Sexuality, Ethnicity, and the Dialects of Identification." Department of Sociology, Lancaster University, Lancaster, United Kingdom. 28 November. Retrieved May 2007. http://www.comp.lancs.ac.uk/sociology/papers/Fortier-Outside-In.

"Italian Vote Abroad: A Symposium." The John D. Calandra Italian American Institute of Queens College of the City University of New York and the Italian Consulate of New York. 12 May 2007.

Mambo Italiano. 2003. Dir. Émile Gaudreault. Screenplay by Gaudreault and Steve Galluccio. Based on the play by Steve Galluccio. Canada: Cinemaginaire, Inc.

Mecca, Tommi Avicolli. 1999. "Call Me Latin." Pp. 220-229 in *Hey Peasan!: Writing by Lesbians and Gay Men of Italian Descent*, edited by Giovanna Capone, Denise Nico Leto, and Tommi Avicolli Mecca. Oakland, CA: Three Guineas Press.

Tamburri, Anthony Julian, ed. 1996. *Fuori: Essays by Italian/American Lesbians and Gays*. West Lafayette, IN: Bordighera Press.

Some Aspects of Social and Spatial Inequalities in Megacities

SONIA PAONE
University of Pisa

This paper contributes to the discussion about the process of dualization in megacities in the developing world. The same process that created megacities, often connected with globalization, has produced new spatial forms and new inequalities and exclusions.

FROM GLOBAL CITIES TO MEGACITIES

In recent years, cities have experienced a period of profound and intense technological, social, economic and cultural transformations, with strong impact on living conditions. In particular, economic changes, connected with the globalization process, have produced a new role for major cities that requires them to become more and more involved in the co-ordination of processes and managerial activities.

Saskia Sassen introduced the term *global city* in her book *The Global City* (1991) to refer to the core capitalist cities of the planet: New York, London, Tokyo and Los Angeles. She pointed to the emergence of these global cities as important nodes of economic organization on the world economic stage and described them as:

> strategic sites for the management of the global economy and the production of the most advanced services and financial operations that have become key inputs for that work of managing global economic operations (Sassen 2006:34).

The dynamic of geographical dispersal and simultaneous integration of economic activities of global firms necessitated the centralization of their strategic corporate functions (management, coordination, servicing, financing). However, these centralized functions become so complex that corporations outsource them to specialized information-intensive firms in such areas as accounting, legal, public relations, programming, and telecommunications (Sassen 2001). In the global economy, urban space serves as command points in the expansion of capitalist globalization. The global economy is organized around command and control centers that coordinate, innovate, and manage the activities of networks of other firms for such advanced services as finance, real estate, consulting, legal services, advertising, design, public relations, and security.

As command and control centers of the global economy, global cities, says Sassen:

> now function in four new ways: first, as highly concentrated command points in the organization of the world economy; second, as key locations for finance and for specialized service firms, which have replaced manufacturing as the leading economic sectors; third, as sites of production, including the production of innovations, in these leading industries; and fourth, as markets for the products and innovations produced (Sassen 1991:3-4).

Manuel Castells has often written about this connection between globalization and cities. His analysis recognizes the role that urban space has assumed in the command of the global economy but also describes the global city as a process rather than a place. Castell's point of view is that the global city is a network of power and economy based on a structure of axes and nodes:

> The global city is not a place, but a process — a process by which centres of production and consumption of advanced services, and their ancillary service local societies, are connected in a global network, while simultaneously downplaying the linkages with their hinterlands, on the basis of information flows (Castells 1996:386).

Sassen noted that there are also regional global cities which structurally resemble one another. Manuel Castells and others refer to these as *megacities*, the product of an emerging new global economy, strictly connected with the growing of the informational society, helping to create this new spatial form. Megacities are vast concentrations of 10 million people or more, and resources cut off from local populations but centrally connected to globally integrated markets:

> Megacities articulate the global economy, link up the informational networks, and concentrate the world's power. But they are also the depositories of all these segments of the population who fight to survive,

as well as of those groups who want to make visible their derelictions, so that they will not die ignored in areas bypassed by communication networks (Castells 1996:380).

Megacities are nodes for both the world and the region. "They are connected externally to global networks and to segments of their own countries, while internally disconnecting local populations that are functionally unnecessary or socially disruptive" (Castells 1996:380).

THE DUAL CITY

Global cities are places of great opportunity and wealth, but they are also places of disadvantage, misery and segregation. This is particularly evident in the megacities of the developing world where "the new techno-economic model is characterized by its productive dynamism and by the way it excludes large territorial and social sectors" and where "within the same metropolitan system there exist the most highly valued and the most degraded functions, the social groups that produce information contrasting with the excluded social groups and people in a marginalized state" (Castells and Borja 1997:38). Megacities can be centers of the global economy even though only a small portion of their population enjoys this affluence. A substantial number of the populace consists of excluded social groups that live in poverty.

Castells describes such a polarized city where opulence and poverty coexist as a *dual city*:

> By dual city, I understand an urban system socially and spatially polarized between high value-making groups and functions on the one hand and devalued social groups and downgraded spaces on the other hand. This polarization induces increasing integration of the social and spatial core of the urban system, at the same time that it fragments devalued spaces and groups, and threatens them with social irrelevance (Castells 1999:27).

DUALIZATION AND POVERTY: THE SLUMS

About 47 percent of the world's population lived in urban areas in 2001. In 2008, their numbers were approximately 3.3 billion people, half of the Earth's population. By 2030, the world urban population is expected to swell to almost 5 billion (United Nations Population Fund 2007). Cities are growing by 60 million per year, but 90 percent of the increase in world population is occurring in the urban areas of less-developed regions, such as Asia and Africa, where annual urban population growth is projected to be 2.4 percent: "The accumulated urban growth of these two regions during the whole span of history will be duplicated in a single generation" (see Figure 1). UN projections are that the rural population will grow slowly at just 0.2 percent per year and will remain nearly stable at about 3.2 billion.

FIGURE 1. *Estimated Urban Populations by City Size*

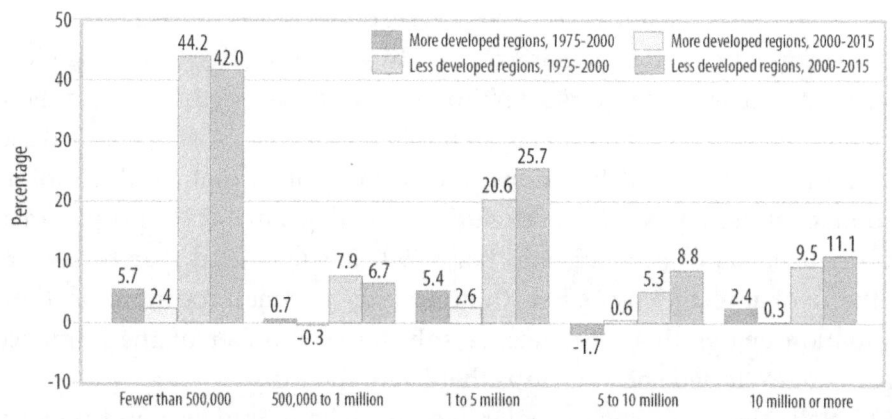

Source: United Nations Human Settlements Programme. 2003.
The Challenge of Slums: Global Report on Human Settlements. London: Earthscan Publications.

All this data lead to the result that urbanization is an enduring trend for the future. As a consequence, the number and size of megacities worldwide will increase. In 1975, there were only 5 megacities but in 2000, they totalled 19 (see Figure 2). Expected to increase further to 23 by 2015, most are located in the southern hemisphere. Unfortunately, this growing urbanization has not been accompanied by adequate economic growth in many developing countries. Consequently, 32 percent of world's urban population lives in slums (Davis 2004, 2006; UN-Habitat 2003).

FIGURE 2. *World Megacities, Population in Millions*

1975		2000		2015 PROJECTED	
Tokyo	19.8	Tokyo	26.4	Tokyo	26.4
New York	15.9	Mexico City	18.1	Mumbai	26.1
Shanghai	11.4	Mumbai	18.1	Lagos	23.2
Mexico City	11.2	Sao Paolo	17.8	Dhaka	21.1
Sao Paolo	10	Shanghai	17	Sao Paolo	20.4
		New York	16.6	Karachi	19.2
		Lagos	13.4	Mexico City	19.2
		Los Angeles	13.1	New York	17.4
		Kolkata	12.9	Jakarta	17.3
		Buenos Aires	12.6	Kolkata	17.3
		Dhaka	12.3	Delhi	16.8
		Karachi	11.8	Metro Manila	14.8
		Delhi	11.7	Shanghai	14.6
		Jakarta	11	Los Angeles	14.1
		Osaka	11	Buenos Aires	14.1
		Metro Manila	10.9	Cairo	13.8
		Beijing	10.8	Istanbul	12.5
		Rio de	10.6	Beijing	12.3
		Cairo	10.6	Rio de Janeiro	11.9
				Osaka	11
				Tianjin	10.7
				Hyderabad	10.5
				Bangkok	10.1

Source: *State of the World Population 2001* Chapter 3, UNFPA.

The term "slum" describes a wide range of low-income settlements and types of housing, including those that could be upgraded. Terms in other languages include *barrios, tugurios, favelas, bidonvilles, gecikondus* and *kampungs*. According to UN-Habitat, a "slum household" is a group of individuals living under the same roof in an urban area who lack one or more of the following:
- Access to improved water;
- Access to improved sanitation;
- Security of tenure (documentation to prove secure tenure status or protection from evictions);
- Durability of housing (a permanent and adequate structure in a non-hazardous location);
- Sufficient living area (not more than two people sharing the same room).

According to the UN report, *State of the World Population 2007*, more than 90 per cent of slum dwellers live in the developing world. The greatest concentration of slum dwellers is in South-Central Asia, followed by East Asia, sub-Saharan Africa, and Latin America (see Figures 3 and 4).

FIGURE 3. *Slum Population by Region, 2001*

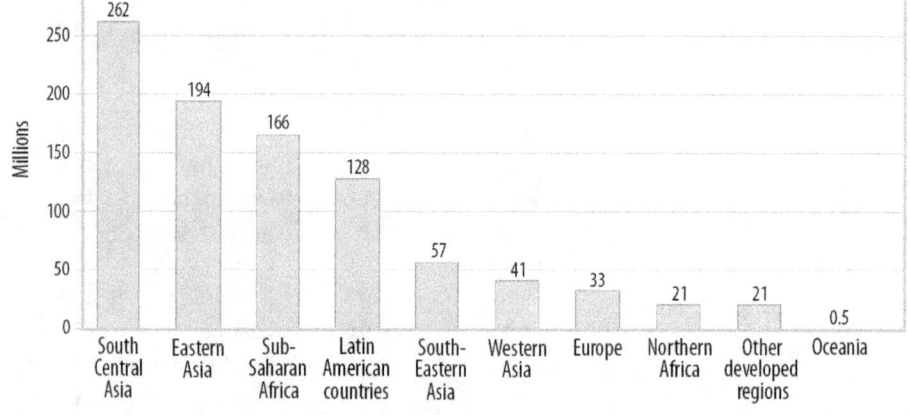

Source: *The Challenge of Slums*

FIGURE 4. *Proportion of Slum Dwellers in Urban Populations by Region, 2001*

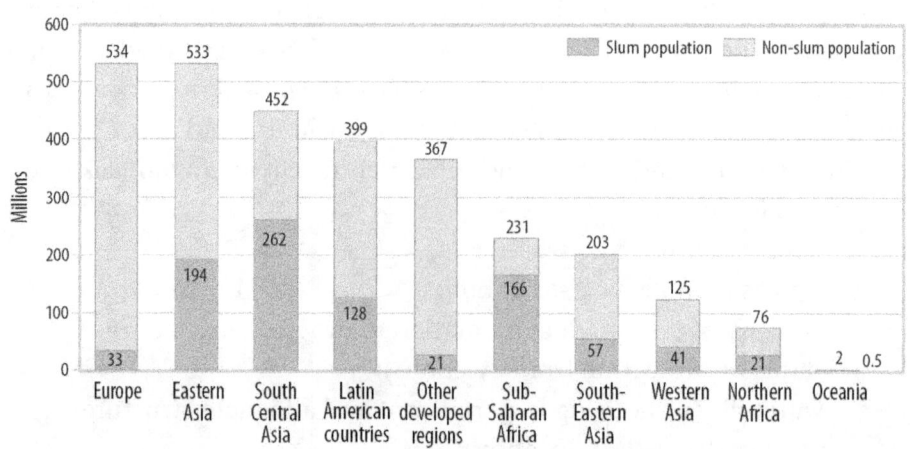

Source: *The Challenge of Slums*

China and India together have 37 per cent of the world's slums. In some areas, such as the sub-Saharan African area, urbanization is synonymous with slum growth. In this region almost three quarters of the urban population lives in slums, while in South Asia the rate is 56 per cent. Countries with the highest percentage of slum dwellers are Ethiopia (99.4 percent), Chad (99.4 percent), Afghanistan (98.5 percent), and Nepal (92 percent). The five great metropolises in South Asia (Karachi, Mumbai, Delhi, Kolkata, and Dhaka) contain a combined total of 15,000 distinct slum communities constituting a population of 20 million (Momentum 2006:26). Within these megacities, the world's largest slum neighborhoods—lacking clean drinking water and adequate sanitation—are Orangi Township in Karachi, Pakistan; Dharavi, in Mumbai, India; Soweto in South Africa; and Kibera in Nairobi, Kenya, each with more than 1 million residents (Momentum, 2006:27).

Dharavi is the largest slum in Asia. A city within a city located in the heart of Mumbai, it is a seemingly unending extension of cramped huts, open sewers, and narrow dirty streets. Its poor drainage systems make it particularly vulnerable to flooding during the rainy season. It has garbage pits, no sanitation, dirty water, and legally does not exist (Momentum, 2006:27).

Another example is Kibera in Kenya that is the largest slum in Africa. It is home to nearly 1 million people and is spread over 2 square kilometers. Sanitation is the biggest problem: the whole area shares 600 pit latrines. Health services are minimal, and over half Kenya's urban dwellers are HIV positive or have AIDS. Epidemics can easily break out. Kebira is just one of Nairobi's 200 slums, housing over half the city's 3.5 million people (Momentum 2006:27).

For the United Nations in the next 30 years, the number of slum dwellers worldwide will increase to 2 billion if no countermeasures are taken to change the situation (UN-Habitat 2003). It is clear that urgent efforts are needed to reduce urban poverty and inequalities in megacities. For this to happen, it is important to propose a new deal that puts basic human rights at the center of all interventions.

References

Amin Ash, and Nigel Thrift. 2002. *Cities: Reimaging the Urban*. Cambridge: Polity Press.
Castells, Manuel, and Jordi Borja. 1997. *Local and Global: Management of Cities in Information Age*. London: Earthscan.

Castells, Manuel. 1996. *The Rise of the Network Society*. Oxford, UK: Blackwell.

Castells, Manuel. 1999. "The Informational City is a Dual City: Can It Be Reversed?" Pp. 25-42 in *High Technology and Low-Income Communities*, edited by Donald A. Schön, Bish Sanyal, and William J. Mitchell. Cambridge, MA: MIT Press.

Davis, Mike. 2004. "The Urbanization of Empire, Megacities and Laws of Chaos." *Social Text* 22(4):9-15.

——. 2006. *The Planet of Slums*, London: Verso.

"Megaslums." Accessed March 5, 2007 http://www.momentum-mag.org/200607/200607-article02.pdf.

Mollenkopf, John, and Manuel Castells. 1991. *Dual City: Restructuring New York*. New York: Russell Sage Foundation.

Neuwirth, Robert. 2005. *Shadow Cities: A Billion Squatters: A New Urban World*. New York: Routledge.

Parker, Simon. 2004. *Urban Theory and the Urban Experience: Encountering the City*. London: Routledge.

Petrillo, Agostino. 2006. *Villaggi, Città, Megalopoli*. Roma: Carocci.

Sassen, Saskia. 1999. *Whose City Is It? Globalization and the Formation of New Claims*, Pp. 177-194 in *Cities and Citizenship*, edited by James Holston. Durham, NC: Duke University Press.

——. [1991] 2001. *The Global City: New York, London, Tokyo*. Princeton, NJ: Princeton University Press.

——. 2006. *Cities in a World Economy*, 3rd ed. Thousand Oaks, CA: Pine Forge Press.

UN-Habitat. 2006. *State of the World Cities 2006-2007*. London: Earthscan.

United Nations Human Settlements Programme. 2003. *Challenge of Slums: Global Report on Human Settlements*. London: Earthscan Publications.

United Nations Population Fund. 2007. *State of World Population: Unleashing the Potential of Urban Growth*. Accessible at http://www.unfpa.org/swp/2007/.

United Nations Population Division. 2005. *World Population Prospects: The 2004 Revision*. New York: Department of Economic and Social Affairs, Population Division, United Nations.

United Nations Population Fund. 2001. *The State of World Population 2001: Footprints and Milestones: Population and Environmental Change*. New York: United Nations Population Fund.

Worldwatch Institute. 2007. *State of the World 2007: Our Urban Future*. Washington, DC: Worldwatch Institute.

The Adaptation of Old vs. New Immigrants: Italians and Mexicans in Perspective

SUSANNA TARDI
William Paterson University

Over the past forty years, significant changes have occurred in U.S. immigration patterns. The new immigrants have increased both the nation's racial and ethnic diversity. Some white ethnics who immigrated during the first and second waves of immigration ask, "Why can't they be like us?" Why can't the assimilation experience of the new immigrants be like that of earlier immigrants? To address those questions, this paper focuses on the structural and cultural factors that influenced the process of societal adaptation of two select U.S. immigrant groups: Italians ("old" immigrants) and Mexicans ("new" immigrants). The extent to which traditional and contemporary models of assimilation adequately explain the process of societal adaptation is assessed.

Numerous studies have attempted to provide general comparisons regarding the assimilation process of "old" (first wave: 1850-1880, English, Irish, German, French, Scandinavian people; second wave: 1880-1920, Italian, Greek, Polish, Russian, and other Eastern European people) versus "new" (early 21st century) immigrants. According to profile data contained in the 2006 *Yearbook of Immigration Statistics*, new immigrants are predominantly non-white people of color from Asia and Latin America, by and large have relatives or family already living in the U.S., and as whole are more geographically dispersed than old immigrants.

COMPARATIVE REASONS FOR MIGRATION

The vast majority of Italians and Mexicans migrated to the United States for economic reasons—"bread and work." The period of peak migration of Italians (1880-1920) corresponded to mass movement of southern Italian peasants who increasingly found daily subsistence in Italy untenable due to sharp declines in the citrus and wine agricultural industries. Similarly, Mexico has had a long history of its citizens looking to improve their economic situation, first by occupying and working land that eventually became U.S. border-states, and since the late nineteenth century by moving to the U.S. to take advantage of better job opportunities.

MIGRATION PATTERNS

Many Italians initially intended to come to the United States on a temporary basis ("shuttle migration"), just long enough to earn enough money to return to their homelands and families. Males typically immigrated first, without the support of other family members and—in the early years of immigration—without an established ethnic community to assist them. Ethnic communities (enclaves) developed as an increasing number of these immigrants elected to stay and live in proximity to their countrymen. These ethnic enclaves shifted the pattern of Italian immigrant movement to a *chain migration*, a sequential flow of immigrants to an area previously settled by family, relatives, or friends. Italian immigration, like most European immigration patterns to the U.S., peaked and ebbed.

Mexican immigration also exhibits a chain migration pattern. An early stage of "male only" Mexican immigration quickly evolved into family migration, but with a pattern of temporarily leaving some children behind with relatives until their parents could establish a stable home environment in the United States. Most Mexican immigrants rely on family networks in established Mexican communities in the United States to assist in housing, job location, and emotional support. Mexican immigration has been larger and more continuous than other groups because Mexico shares a border with the U.S.

SOCIOECONOMIC STATUS

Southern Italian immigrants were predominantly uneducated and unskilled. Many Italian immigrant men took jobs in manual blue-collar occupations such as construction or on the docks, partly due to a cultural preference for outdoor work. The explosion of industrialization in the early 1900s helped in their structural assimilation by boosting blue-collar job opportunities. Increasingly, Italian immigrant women began to appear in female-dominated work environments such as garment industry factories.

Today Italian Americans have, for the most part, become structurally assimilated in terms of occupation, income, and education. According to the 2000 Census, 80 percent of Italian Americans are in executive, administrative, managerial, professional, technical and sales occupations (Milione 2000:426). Studies by Karl Bonutti indicate that Italian Americans have incomes above the national average (1989:73). By the 1990 Census, Italian Americans 25 to 35 years old had achieved educational parity with the broader U.S. population.

Mexican immigrants, in contrast, have had less success and occupy considerably lower levels of occupation, income, and education attainment than the population at large. Only 14.4 percent of Mexican Americans are working in management, professional, and related occupations as compared to 38.9 percent of whites (U.S. Bureau of the Census 2006: Table 10.2). Furthermore, 33 percent of Mexican-American families earned less than $25,000 as compared to 14 percent of whites (U.S. Census Bureau 2006: Tables 13.1 and 13.2). In 2006, 46.9 percent of Mexican Americans had an educational attainment less than a high school diploma, in comparison with only 9.5 percent of the non-Hispanic whites (U.S. Census Bureau 2006: Tables 6.1 and 6.2).

Mexican Americans experience discrimination within a dual occupational system that results in their typically securing only lower-status jobs. According to Joachim Reimann (1998:2), the dominant Anglo perception is that Mexican Americans seeking jobs are not career focused but family focused, leading to a presumption that they therefore lack motivation in the workplace. However, Reimann's research indicates that neither men nor women who strongly value family lack or even show less career focus. In contrast, he found that women who are most committed to family are simultaneously the most invested in their careers. This is yet another indication of how stereotypes of the dominant group present real impediments to the social mobility of the minority group.

FAMILISM

The family has long been the major source of identity and power for Italians. Nuclear family households and extended family relationships generally characterize the traditional Italian family in Italy and the United States. The familial pattern of authority was patriarchal, but the mother had an important role within the household as the "center of life." With passing generations and upward mobility, husband/wife relationships tended to become more egalitarian or democratic.

Traditional Italian core culture, as typically found in immigrant households, displayed 1) traditional extended family relationships; 2) primacy of the family over the individual and all social institutions; 3) formal education viewed as a "luxury for the rich"; 4) Catholicism de-emphasizing Catholic doctrine; and 5) political mistrust. The cohesiveness of the Italian family served as its major source of refuge from societal exploitation and discrimination. The strong work ethic valued by Italian families eventually provided them with unity and power in the labor market. However, the Italian family served as a doubled-edged sword regarding the social integration of Italians. The strong value for residential propinquity (the need/desire to live not with, but close to, extended family members), and the value for interdependence rather than independence, restricted the social mobility of many second and third generation Italian Americans. Accordingly, suburbanization for Italian Americans commonly involved a two-generation move (second-generation Italian Americans and their first-generation parents). The Italian family has undergone transitions from the first to the fourth generation because its very survival rested on its ability to become more flexible.

Similar to the Italians, most Mexican families have nuclear households, extended family relationships, and are moving more toward egalitarian/democratic husband/wife relationships (Keefe and Padilla 1987). Among Italian and Mexican immigrants, family is paramount. In both cultures, familial interdependence is valued over individuality (an "American" value). Traditionally, in both groups, the success of the individual is judged by the contributions made to the family. Maintaining close relationships with extended family members is also important in both groups. For Mexicans, facilitating these relationships are two conditions that did not exist for Italians: the spatial proximity of the Mexican border and instant communication thanks to technological advances.

LANGUAGE

Most current Mexican immigrants, like past Italian immigrants, come to the U.S. with an English language barrier; they neither speak nor understand English. For Italian immigrants, communication with those in the dominant culture often occurred through their American-born, bilingual children (the second generation). Second generation Italian-Americans were often known as "children in the generation of conflict." They were marginalized, caught in the middle of the divergent norms and values of their Italian parents and those of the dominant culture in the U.S.

For Italians, by the third generation the Italian language is predominantly lost, partly because the parents of the second generations used the Italian language as a private means of communication with adults, rather than a key factor for maintaining Italian culture. Second-generation Italian Americans put great emphasis on making their children fluent in the English language. They wanted them to speak English without any trace of an Italian accent to avoid the overt prejudice and discrimination they themselves had experienced.

Mexican parents want their children to be bilingual. According to David Gutierrez (1995:36), maintenance of the Spanish language is an "oppositional strategy" for Mexicans. Two factors aiding native language retention among new immigrants are the civil rights movement and globalization. The U.S. civil rights movement resulted in a heightened awareness of racial and ethnic prejudice and discrimination, and laid the foundation for acceptance of language pluralism. Globalization has also made the dominant culture more receptive to bilingualism. The "acceptability" of bilingualism by the dominant culture, and the desire of the Mexicans for their children to be fluent in English yet preserve the language component of their Mexican culture, increases the likelihood that future generations will become fluent bilinguals. Their fluency in English and ability to communicate in Spanish may significantly influence their adaptation because of the relationship between language and identity. Research consistently indicates that there is a greater likelihood for biracial children to adopt a non-white identity if they speak a language other than English in the home (Zhou and Bankston 1998; Portes and Rumbaut 2001).

NATIONALISM

Most Italians immigrants were predisposed to assimilation. While many initially left Italy with the intention of returning, they eventually bought into the "American Dream" and remained in the United States. Italians valued familism but without nationalistic ties, perceiving respect for Italian culture as separate from respect for the country. Their ethnic identity did not extend far beyond the villages in which they lived. The Italian provinces, particularly in the *Mezzogiorno* (the areas south and east of Rome) were characterized by regionalism, not nationalism. When the Italian peasants fought against the Bourbons, they did so not for nationalism, but as a means of protecting the family from government oppression. The unification of Italy only furthered the gap between the somewhat more affluent and cosmopolitan northern Italians and the southern peasants of the *Mezzogiorno*.

Mexican immigrants appear less predisposed to assimilation. Their distrust for government is based upon its inability to provide economic growth opportunities for its own people, especially those in the lower classes. They strongly value a combination of familism *and* nationalism (love and loyalty for their mother country). This factor, combined with Spanish language maintenance and the spatial proximity of Mexico could impede assimilation. Thus, although both emigrated voluntarily, Italian and Mexican immigrants represent ethnic groups differently predisposed to assimilation.

RACIAL FORMATION

Most Americans perceived Italian immigrants as inferior to other Europeans because of their physical traits (i.e. darker skin and low foreheads). Arriving during a period when racial ideologies were widespread in the U.S., they were stereotyped and racialized as "non-white." They were characterized as dark skinned, swarthy, low browed, unintelligent and criminals. By the third generation, Italians "became" white, but they never defined themselves as anything other than white. Matthew Jacobson (1998) identified two factors that influenced the non-white to white status change of the Irish, Italians and Jews: their intentional maintenance of social distance from blacks and black migration patterns within the U.S. that facilitated the delineation of the black/white color divide. By the late 1920s, the last great wave of European immigration ended. The post-World War II era provided for the economic integration of European immigrants, reducing the fear that the mainstream society previously experienced (Foner 2000).

It must be noted, however, that the dominant group's acceptance of Italians as "white" did not mean that prejudice and discrimination ended. Instead, covert discrimination became a substitute for overt discrimination. The Italian-American community still remains at odds on the issue of discrimination. Italian Americans are conflicted in their attitudes regarding their position in U.S. society. Some Italian Americans revel in achieving a respected status associated with occupation, education, and income. They have realized the "American Dream" and strongly associate themselves with mainstream or upper echelon Americans. Other Italian

Americans see themselves in an ongoing fight to gain legitimacy and respect; they are vocal in campaigning against Italian defamation and discrimination and emphasize the cultural accomplishments and contributions of their ethnic group. Some observers cite this lack of a unified vision as a reason for the relative political ineffectiveness of Italian Americans as group.

For Mexican immigrants, their racial-ethnic history is a complicated one. Spanish conquest of Mexico resulted in a stratified society. At the top were the Spaniards (born in Spain) and *Peninsulares* (Spaniards born in Mexico) who owned the land, ran the government, and maintained a strong alliance with the Catholic Church. In the middle were the *mestizos*, the racial and ethnic groups resulting from intermarriages between Spaniards and indigenous people. At the bottom of the hierarchy were the indigenous groups and enslaved African Americans. The majority of present-day Mexicans are *mestizos*.

Preceding Anglo colonization, Mexicans had established settlements and missions throughout the western and southwestern United States. However, in 1834 these missions were taken over by the U.S. government. In this period (the Golden Age of the Ranchos), the U.S. government gave huge land grants to only a few wealthy Mexican ranchers, resulting in an internal, Mexican (Chicano) class system comprised of three groups: the elite class consisting of wealthy ranchers, mission farmers, and government administrators; a middle class *(mestizos)* consisting of small farmers and ranchers; and a lower class of predominantly Indians who served as manual laborers (Maldonado 1997). During the Mexican-American War (1846-1848), Anglos perceived and portrayed Mexicans and settlers of Mexican descent as lazy, corrupt, cowardly, and unable to manage land; an inferior race unworthy of equality. By relegating Mexicans to an inferior status (as it had in the case of Native Americans), Anglos thereby justified their control of the land over this categorized "race."

In the 2000 Census, although respondents could claim more than one racial classification, the only categories provided were: "White," "Black," "Asian," "some other group," "American Indian and Alaska Native," and "Native Hawaiian or other Pacific Islander." In both the 1990 and 2000 Census, approximately 97 percent of those identifying as "some other race" were of Spanish/Hispanic/Latino origin (Anderson and Feinberg 1999, U.S. Bureau of the Census 2001). In reality, "some Latinos view themselves and are seen by others as white, some as *mestizo*, and a few as black" (Lee and Bean 2004:223), despite a prevailing assumption that people of color self-identify and coalesce around a simplistic racial grouping.

Presently, mainstream Americans see Mexicans as people of color and generally classify them as "Hispanics" or "Latinos." However, the category "Hispanic" has little sociological relevance; it is not a meaningful racial or ethnic category since it throws together individuals who are culturally, socially and economically diverse (Cubans, Dominicans, Mexicans, Peruvians, Puerto Ricans etc.) Politically, this arbitrary categorization may be useful because the divergent groups constitute greater political strength in combination than they do as separate groups with individual identities. As long as the issues at stake are not perceived as threatening to the individual groups, this political "alliance" will undoubtedly continue.

However, political alliances should not be misconstrued as racial-ethnic entities. Mexicans may choose to self identify and perceive of themselves as "white," but in reality, most are people of color and, as such, are subjected to discrimination by the dominant group. Historically, race has been loosely based on physical differences; the more prominent and pervasive the physicalities on individual and group levels, the more difficult ethnic adjustment is likely to be. The core culture may make exceptions regarding the "one drop rule" (identifying Asians, for example, as more on the "white" side of the color line rather than the black side), but in general, its historical societal impact cannot be ignored. Typically, exceptions are not due to social consciousness, but to guilt and/or social class interests.

STRUCTURAL CONDITIONS

At the time of peak Italian immigration, the social structure of the U.S. was much different than that found by more recent Mexican immigrants. The Italians entered a country with a rapidly growing economy, ample job opportunities for those who wanted to work, and a cultural expectation that immigrants would integrate into society, adopt the language, and "become American." World War II initially endangered the acceptance of Italians living in the U.S. because of fears about their loyalty to Italy rather than the United States. However, the significant participation of Italian Americans in fighting in Europe to protect the U.S. was a mechanism that allowed Italians to prove their patriotism; they were becoming "Americans."

Mexicans face both a much more competitive society in terms of job opportunities and uncertain economic growth, and a more pluralistic society that is more conscious of diversity and civil rights. This cultural backdrop evolved through: 1) the election of John Fitzgerald Kennedy as the first non-WASP president of the U.S.; 2) the civil rights movement, which increased racial awareness, particularly regarding Hispanics, Asians and Native Americans, and 3) the social and political power exerted by women. With a transformed American "landscape," today's immigrants encounter many different conditions than did the first and second wave of white immigrants.

Sociologists agree that structural conditions within the host society can influence both the nature and trajectory of the immigrant assimilation process and the immigrant experience. For example, educational attainment is crucial for second-generation social adjustment and mobility and profoundly affects the trajectory and speed of the assimilation path. Yet, the availability of quality, affordable education to new, young, adolescent Mexican-American immigrants is, at best, uncertain. When we include other structural and cultural factors as forces influencing the adaptation process—such as social capital, intra-group conflict, discrimination, peer identification and affiliation, and parental pressure—a truly bewildering array of outcome scenarios can be envisioned.

THEORETICAL PERSPECTIVES ON RACE, ETHNICITY AND ASSIMILATION

In attempting to facilitate an understanding of the assimilation process, social scientists have often confounded the concepts of race and ethnicity. Although perceived by many to be synonymous, in reality the two are separate concepts even though we must examine them simultaneously to understand the social, economic and political consequences on the group or the individual. Ethnicity refers to one's national heritage. Race is a social construct based on physicalities (e.g., skin color, nasal width, hair texture, eye shape, etc.). Historically, racial and ethnic boundaries in the United States have been fluid, as demonstrated by race becoming for the Irish, Italians and Jews an achieved, rather than an ascribed status (Gans 1979, Alba 1990, Waters 1990, Perlmann and Waldinger 1997). Yet the dominant group once used race to impede, or even block, the assimilation of these groups through "racialization" (the treatment of an ethnic group as a racial minority). Even today, a dominant group may still use race as a means to protect and defend privilege.

Assimilation, the process through which immigrant groups become integrated into the dominant culture, originally meant that no significant cultural or structural difference existed between the minority group and the dominant (core) group. However, more recent discussions of assimilation refer to the extent to which the minority group is integrated into the core culture. Assimilation is no longer an "all or nothing" process. A number of theoretical models now explain ethnic group integration and assimilation. According to classic or traditional assimilation, over time immigrant groups become more similar in norms and values of the dominant society (Gordon 1964). This assimilation involves "straight line" acculturation—the longer the immigrant group is in the dominant society, the more similar those group members become to that society. This model falls short in explaining the American experience because: 1) as a one-dimensional and unidirectional model, it presumes a desire on the part of those assimilating to identify with the dominant culture and surrender the culture of their country of origin; 2) it ignores the power differential that exists among groups and the propensity of the dominant core culture to limit access of others; and 3) it does not focus on the importance of cultural and structural conditions (an issue first noted by William Newman in 1973). Some ethnic groups are less equipped for ethnic adjustment because of the cultural conditions, "cultural baggage" (norms, values and behavioral patterns immigrants bring with them from their country of origin), and/or the structural conditions (circumstances they encounter upon entering the U.S., such as economic opportunity, resource availability, type and degree of discrimination encountered, etc.).

Classic assimilation theory did not adequately account for the fact that cultural differentiation was still evident among European ethnic groups despite significant structural assimilation. As a result, a new concept known as "symbolic ethnicity" was incorporated into the assimilation model (Gans 1979, Alba 1990, Waters 1990). Symbolic ethnicity is evidenced in the celebration of ethnic holidays and in having a preference for particular ethnic foods. Symbolic ethnicity is in marked contrast to *ethnic consciousness*, which is imbued by deep-seated cultural norms and values. The assimilation perspective also failed to explain the process of adjustment for African Americans and the more-recently arrived Asians and Latinos. Consequently, another modification of assimilation theory, "segmented assimilation," developed. According to Alejandro Portes and Min Zhou (1993), segmented assimilation provides for variant paths of assimilation based upon social capital, country of origin, settlement area, social class, and education. Possible outcomes include: 1) upward social mobility due to high levels of human capital and favorable reception by the dominant group; 2) downward social mobility due to limited resources, lack of stable employment, prolonged residence in inner city ghettos, and an inability to provide for their children's education: and 3) limited assimilation in which immigrant parents support their children's educational attainment, but simultaneously maintain traditional cultural values which may in turn limit the acculturation of their children.

An alternative perspective to the assimilation perspective focuses on ethnic competition that occurs when discrimination places an individual from a minority group in a disadvantaged position. Structural conditions in the host society, such as ethnic competition along racial and ethnic lines, contribute to the formation of an ethnic identity among second generation Mexicans and their descendants (Portes 1984; Alba 1990; de la Garza et al.1996). Ethnic consciousness is enhanced through antagonism resulting from discrimination. Ono (2002) provides an explanation for inconsistencies in research findings regarding socioeconomic status and ethnic consciousness. According to Ono, intra-ethnic competition for socioeconomic status could be achieved in the absence of ethnic competition and discrimination. Interethnic socioeconomic competition may result in higher socioeconomic achievement and heightened ethnic awareness in the absence of discrimination and subsequent ethnic competitiveness. While Roger Waldinger and Mehdi Bozorgmehr (1996) identified competition for low status jobs between persons of Mexican origin and blacks, Ono suggests that discrimination may be a better indicator of ethnic competition than socioeconomic status.

CONCLUSION

The comparative immigrant experiences of Italians and Mexicans are notable both because of their similarities and differences. Both Italian and Mexican immigrants were, by and large, poor, uneducated, and unskilled with similar perspectives on the role and importance of family. Yet the assimilation trajectories and outcomes of both groups were markedly different. Italians adopted many aspects of the dominant core U.S. culture. Mexicans, however, retained much of their distinct nationalistic and cultural identity and became part of an increasingly diverse mosaic that is the hallmark of current U.S. culture. External factors, such as the availability of job opportunities, the competition for resources, and economic growth have had a profound impact on both Italian and Mexican societal adaptation. Other factors, such as the growth of recognized civil rights and diversity, are relatively new and pose unique structural conditions for today's immigrants. However, the individual effects and intersection of class and race cannot be ignored. Mexican Americans are likely to encounter more long-term opposition than did Italian Americans. Recognition of the complex interplay of forces that influence assimilation and the variability of assimilation outcomes has led sociologists to propose more flexible frameworks for explaining different assimilation trajectories. The segmented assimilation perspective explains the multiple paths Mexicans have recently taken and are likely to continue to take in their adaptation to U.S. society. Segmented assimilation's greatest strength seems to lie in its flexibility to explain assimilation outcomes after the fact. It is less useful is predicting future assimilation outcomes.

It is interesting to note that, while sociological literature contains much discussion about assimilation mechanisms that seek to explain how smaller groups integrate into a larger group whole, we find much less on describing the characteristics of the larger group into which the smaller groups integrate, and identifying any changes the larger group experiences by virtue of that integration. Early studies of assimilation suggested a melting pot concept and, in doing so, implied that the larger group is a monolithic, homogeneous entity that retains its identity while, at the same time, absorbing smaller groups. One can also theorize other mechanisms in which the larger group is influenced by the integration of smaller groups—a process combining both assimilation and mutation. On the other side of the spectrum, the theory of segmented assimilation explains the process in which smaller groups become part of a whole while, at the same time, retaining characteristics of their individual identities. The United States has never been a melting pot. Perhaps, if the larger group is really a mosaic of individual group identities and the concept of whole is more legal than social in nature, then "segmented assimilation" is not assimilation at all, but continued mutation of the larger heterogeneous group.

References

Alba, Richard D. 1990. *Ethnic Identity: The Transformation of White America*. New Haven: Yale University Press.

—. 2000. "Assimilation," Pp. 41-44 in *The Italian Experience: An Encyclopedia*, edited by Salvatore J. LaGumina, Frank J. Caaioli, Salvatore Primeggia, and Joseph A. Varacalli. New York: Garland.

Anderson, M. J. and S. E. Feinberg. 1999, Who Counts? The Politics of Census-Taking in Contemporary America. New York: Russell Sage Foundation.

Bonutti, Karl. 1989. "Economic Characteristics of Italian Americans," Pp. 62-79 in *Italians in the '80s: A Socio-Demographic Profile*, edited by Graziano Batistella. New York: Center for Migration Studies.

de la Garza, Rodolfo., Angelo. Falcon and F. Chris Garcia. 1996. "Will the Real Americans Stand Up: Anglo and Mexican-American Support of Core American Political Values," *American Journal of Political Science* 40:335-351.

Foner, Nancy. 2000. *From Ellis Island to JFK: New York's Two Great Waves of Immigration*. New Haven, CT/New York: Yale University Press/Russell Sage Foundation.

Gans, Herbert J. 1979. "Symbolic Ethnicity: The Future of Ethnic Groups and Culture in America." *Ethnic and Racial Studies* 2:1-20.

Gordon, Milton M. 1964. *Assimilation in American Life: The Role of Race, Religion, and National Origins*. New York: Oxford University Press.

Gutierrez, David G. 1995. *Mexican Americans, Mexican Immigrants and the Politics of Ethnicity*. Berkeley: University of California Press.

Jacobson. Matthew. 1998. *Whiteness of a Different Color: European Immigrants and the Alchemy of Race*. Cambridge, MA: Harvard University Press.

Keefe, Susan E., and Amado M. Padilla. 1987. *Chicano Ethnicity*. Albuquerque: University of New Mexico Press.

Lee, Jennifer, and Frank D. Bean. 2004. "America's Changing Color Lines: Segmented Assimilation and Its Variants." *The Annals of the American Academy of Political and Social Science* 530:74-96.

Maldonado, Lionel A. 1997. "Mexicans in the American System: A Common Density." Pp. 267-282 in *Ethnicity in the United States: An Institutional Approach*, edited by William Velez. Bayside, NY: General Hall.

Milione, Vincenzo. 2000. "Occupations, Present Day," Pp. 425-427 in *The Italian American Experience: An Encyclopedia*, edited by Salvatore J. LaGumina, Frank J. Cavaioli, Salvatore Primegga, and Joseph A. Varacalli. New York: Garland.

Newman, William M. 1973. *American Pluralism: A Study of Minority Groups and Social Theory*. New York: Harper and Row.

Omni, Michae,l and Howard Winant. 1994. *Racial Formation in the United States*, 2nd ed., New York: Routledge.

Ono, Hiromi, 2002, "Assimilation, Ethnic Competition, and Ethnic Identities of U.S.-Born Persons of Mexican Origin," *International Migration Review*, 36(3):726-745.

Perlman, Joel, and Roger Waldinger, 1997, "Second Generation Decline? Children of Immigrants, Past Present—A Reconsideration." *International Migration Review* 31(4):893-922.

Portes, Alejandro, and Min Zhou. 1993. "The New Second Generation: Segmented Assimilation and Its Variants." *The Annals of the American Academy of Political and Social Sciences* 530:74-96.

Portes, Alejandro, and Ruben G. Rumbaut. 2001. *Legacies: The Story of the Immigrant Second Generation*. Los Angeles: University of California Press.

Reimann, Joachim, 1998, "Mexican Americans Value in the Workplace: Correcting Misconceptions." *People at Work* 1:2.

Rumbaut, Reuben G. 1994. "The Crucible Within: Ethnic Identity, Self-esteem, and Segmented Assimilation Among Children of Immigrants." *International Migration Review* 28(4):748-794.

U.S. Census Bureau. 2008. *Statistical Abstract of the United States: 2008*. Washington, DC.

———. 2006. *Current Population Survey*, Annual Social and Economic Supplement, Ethnicity and Ancestry Statistics Branch, Population Division.

U.S. Department of Homeland Security. 2007. *2006 Yearbook of Immigration Statistics*. Washington, DC: Office of Immigration Statistics.

Waldinger, Roger, and Mehdi Bozorgmehr. 1996. *Ethnic Los Angeles*. New York: Russell Sage Foundation.

Waters, Mary. 1990. *Ethnic Options: Choosing Identities in America*. Berkeley: University of California Press.

Zhou, Min, and Carl L. Bankston III. 1998. *Growing Up American: How Vietnamese Children Adapt to Life in the United States*. New York: Russell Sage Foundation.

PART THREE
Identity and Culture

Flexibility and Memory: Individuals and Society in the Age of Risk

MARIA GRAZIA RICCI
University of Pisa

The difficulties encountered by the current generation of young adults in the construction of their own way through life, and of their "place" and identity in society, serve to measure the change in contemporary western societies, and in Italian society in particular. In the 50 years separating this generation from the oldest living generation (that of their grandparents), the redefinition of economic and social models has created an apparently unbridgeable gap between the values, customs and behaviors of the two groups. The experiences of the young do not seem comparable to those of their elders, and consequently their future seems radically unpredictable. The political, social and existential experience handed down through the successive generations of a single community, together with the memory and the social practices connected to it, appear inadequate compared with the profound alterations that globalization has brought to the lives of every individual.

This paper discusses how the link between the concepts of insecurity and memory characterizes individual and collective identity in contemporary society. The wider backdrop for this discussion is the notion of modernity, defined in the dual sense of a historical and social development (affecting institutions and practices) and a program (capable of generating theories for its interpretation). The pairing of flexibility (which is at the center of a densely-packed constellation of analogous terms such as ambiguity, precariousness, insecurity, risk, mobility and instability) and memory (encompassing a sense of the past, present practices, and future projects) expresses the ambiguity of accounts of advanced modernity.

LIBERATION AND DISCIPLINE

Peter Wagner (1994) identified modernity's double soul in the concepts of liberation and discipline, two representations of modernity co-existing since the term's origin. Marx and Weber, as authoritative observers of modernity, contributed to the construction of both these images, emphasizing one or the other aspect of modernity (all that is solid melts into air or the progressive steel cage), and described its irreducibly double nature. When the historical process of extension of freedom breaks the material and symbolic confines of the traditional world, the perception of the uncontrollability or unintelligibility of social mechanisms becomes evident. This perception forms an important backdrop, if not the basis, for all of the crises of modernity, which until now, resolved themselves in a "re-embedding" of individuals in a new social order: a new program implemented through a new formalization of conventionalized and homogenized practices. As Eghigian, Killen, and Leuenberger (2007:2) write, "At the middle of the twentieth century, political parties, states, and the human sciences, too, shared a common belief: that societies and human beings could be known, changed and managed." There was a widespread enthusiasm for public projects, ranging from urban renewal to macroeconomic planning, and important achievements were expected of governments and public institutions. The "age of extremes," as Eric Hobsbawm (1994) named it, was caught up in a zeal for experimentation and pragmatic social reforms for which social knowledge and research practices were mutually responsible.

Public policies were enacted in concert with re-examination of such topics as individuality, identity, personhood and subjectivity (Giddens 1991; Gergen 1991; Taylor 1989; Foucault 1988; Hacking 1995). The social sciences were swept up in the political construction, destruction and reconstruction of twentieth-century societies in a historically novel way. Individuals became sites for public projects, not families, social classes or organizations, and at the same time were encouraged to treat their own lives as projects to be fulfilled (Eighigian et al. 2007).

The project's ambiguity rested in the dual meaning intrinsic to the term *modernity*, which refers either to the construction of spaces of individual and collective autonomy — to the expansion of subjectivity — or to the need for order and control. The great historical transformations, which gave rise to modernity and accompanied its development, defined by Berman (1982) as "the experience of modernity," can be described as an itinerary punctuated by successive dissolutions and consolidations, by processes of uprooting and re-rooting of individuals.

But the principal transformation of modernity, which produced the social configuration defined as "organized modernity" (Wagner 1994) — the practices and institutions that the inhabitants of western democracies, still share — seems to have lost its vitality and its progressive impulse. It is to this crisis to which students of post-modernity refer when they speak of the "end of modernity." Some of the changes in the practices and institutions of western societies that occurred in the past two decades thus appear as a breaking away from roots and a reopening of the mechanisms of "disembedding."

THE UNEASINESS OF MODERNITY

Organized modernity comprises changeable relationships between individual and social identities and the configurations of society; such relationships accompany its birth, temporary consolidation and crisis. The security of all social life in the welfare state permitted individuals to manage themselves flexibly, to begin to "play" with their own roles, to interpret them and to use them to their own advantage, in particular in the weakest categories — that of the always excluded.

Through part-time work, women have been able to be both in and out of the work force, choosing to develop their talents or to take care of their children or elders without losing sight of their own professional self-realization. The young have enjoyed the certainty of the academic curriculum and the clarity of professional outlets; the older generation has benefited from an exit from the world of work, both protected by legislation and financially guaranteed. As Hoffmann-Axthelm (1992:206) wrote, "The modern navigation taught us to establish our own position and thereafter to determine direction, . . . in the same way the modern individual was required to hold good as the focal point of all activities in practical life from which all the societal techniques at his or her disposal could be instituted." However, with the weakening of the protective net of an existing life plan and its predictable outcomes, modern subjectivity generated chronic incongruity of references and models, shaken by the necessity of choosing in the present, while denied the possibility of "investing" in the future. Subjectivity cannot withstand such a situation, and individual lives therefore seem radically precarious (Sennett 1998).

Capitalism continues to power modern life, but in a different form. The central focus shifts from the economy and productive processes to society and the social processes of relations, cohesion and integration; from "heavy commodities to symbolic goods, from markets, factories as real places to non-place locations, from machines to software" (Stehr 2001:ix). The double face of the liberation from the constraints of organized modernity reveals itself; an increasingly fragile social order is the other aspect of the precariousness of individual lives. Contemporary societies became fragile because of their decreasing governability. We can observe this in the remarkable loss of authority of social institutions, undermined both by individuals' growing ability to assert and claim their own rights and by the decline of their own sense of responsibility (Sennett 1976).

The unequal extension of the capacity to act by collective and individual actors in modern society increases the risk for significant segments of society. Furthermore, an accumulation of unanticipated outcomes of purposeful action by small organizations or groups or individuals can result in considerable danger for societal stability and there are serious difficulties in regulating and controlling such risks (Beck 1988). The real problem now is the imbalance between individual and collective capacities to act. The growth of individualities, of knowledge and consciousness related to it, paradoxically produce greater uncertainty and contingency rather than resolution to social problems (Giddens 1990).

Present-day societies become increasingly vulnerable entities. Such vulnerability stems from social conduct as well as from the deployment of artefacts designed to stabilize, routinize and delimit social action. This managed complexity of modern society creates novel risks. Society is a vulnerable system: its infrastructures and technological regimes are subject to accidents as a result of fortuitous or unanticipated human action; to extreme natural events that may undermine the taken-for-granted routines of everyday life; and to deliberate sabotages. However, "Society is vulnerable because—prompted by profound disagreement about its very fabric and legitimacy—large or small groups of individuals are determined to negate it"(Stehr 2001:4).

Until a few decades ago, human life was mostly based on a limited and unchanging set of relationships, often carried out face to face. New technologies now make it possible to sustain relationships—either directly or indirectly—with an expanding range of people. "In many respects," states Kenneth Gergen, "we are reaching what may be viewed as a state of social saturation" (1991:3). With the intensifying saturation of culture, however, traditional patterns of relationships change as well as previous assumptions about the self, both symptoms of a new culture in the making.

FROM SELF TO SELVES

If early modernity invested in the construction of the new identity of the citizen and in the maintenance of social, political and economic stability, late modernity appears to have abandoned the stability of the individual together with the rigidity of social roles. The turn towards an increasing individuality and individualism, as seen in the great variety of lifestyles and projects, corresponds to a multiplicity of incoherent and disconnected relationships inviting individuals to play a variety of roles (Elster 1985). The multiplication of identities and roles can be interpreted not only as a condition of individual self-realization (be yourself!) but also as an expression of the fragmentation of identity and the fragility of individuals for whom collective identification is rendered both difficult and precarious by a plurality of voices vying for the right to reality, to be accepted as legitimate expressions of the true and the good (Gilligan 1982).

Cultural life in the twentieth century has been dominated by two major vocabularies of the self. We have inherited a largely nineteenth-century, romanticist view of the self, one that attributes to each person characteristics of personal depth: passion, soul, creativity, and moral fiber. This vocabulary is essential to the formation of deeply committed relationships, dedicated friendships, and life purposes. For modernists the chief characteristic of the self resides not in the domain of depth, but rather in our ability to reason—in our beliefs, opinions, and conscious intentions. In the modernist idiom, normal persons are predictable, honest, and sincere. Modernists believe in educational systems, a stable family life, and moral training (Flanagan and Oksenberg Rorty 1990). Kenneth Gergen argues:

> Yet both the romantic and the modern beliefs about the self are falling into disuse, and the social arrangements that they support are eroding. This is largely a result of the forces of social saturation. Emerging technologies saturate us with the voices of humankind—both harmonious and alien. As we absorb their varied rhymes and reasons, they become part of us and we of them. Social saturation furnishes us with a multiplicity of incoherent and unrelated languages of the self (1991:6).

The decline of an integrated symbolic universe projects individuals into worlds of meaning whose definitions of reality are not only diverse, but often profoundly incompatible. If individual identity and the sense of subjectivity can no longer be inscribed in a single system, and use a shared definition of reality (Berger and Luckmann 1967), they cease to be perceived as destiny to become instead "choice" and "construction" of the subject. The individuals' horizon of choice therefore becomes ever more open and fluid and they can imagine themselves to be "protagonists of diverse biographies" independent of their own capacity to realize them. The complexity of modern society produces not only a general flattening out of culture, that one-dimensionality analyzed by the Frankfurt School (Marcuse 1964), but also a multiplication of cultural codes and models (Melucci 1991).

THE CONSEQUENCES FOR PEOPLE

The fulcrum of modern identity revolved around fundamental choices for the individual: occupation, role in the public sphere, and position within the family. Identity in the late modern period, however, seems to be defined in a space without strong ties or places in which to lay down one's experiences in a continuous search for social recognition. In the first case, clear identities emerged through investment in the educational system, the exaltation of a stable family life, and a fixed and socially recognized system of work roles. In the second, individuals exist in a continuous state of construction and reconstruction (Sennett 1998; Gergen 1991).

The precariousness of individual careers is not exclusively the product of contemporary society. On the contrary, it has always accompanied changes in human existence such as colonialization, exodus, migration, conflict, or major social unrest, albeit with different degrees of visibility. A clear indicator of epochs of "crisis" is the collective perception of a twilight moment created because the old order has been cast adrift, while the new one is not yet visible. On the individual level, this is seen in a loss of one's bearings and great unease (Rosaldo 1989; Colley 1998; Boym 2001).

During the last century, the quantity and velocity of change definitively did away with the age-old accumulation of traditions on which the mechanism of social reproduction had been based in the past. Traditional cultures respect the past, and attribute great importance to symbols and practices that enclose and perpetuate the experience of whole generations, but, with the advent of modernity, the reinterpretation and clarification of social practices takes on a radically different character. They are constantly being altered—often in a substantial way—by single individual actions, in such a way that the routine transformation of the activities of daily life lose their intrinsic link with the past.

In all cultures, social practices are normally modified in the light of relevant discoveries but it is only with modernity that the revision of conventions—assuming a reflective character—becomes a radical phenomenon that pervades the very basis of reproduction of the system itself (Melucci 1991; Giddens 1991).

The fractures between generations that followed one another throughout the twentieth century provide a clear measure of the change. The U.S. anthropologist Margaret Mead (1970) used this "generational fracture" to focus perceptively on the origins of modification of cultural transmission and of the groups which transmit knowledge.

In the past, the continuity of culture and the incorporation of innovations depended on the success of the traditional system of cultural transmission through which the young learned to replicate the world of their elders. Modernity innovated by creating an environment adaptive to change. It developed a new model of society—the nation—of whose values universal public education has been the engine of this cultural transmission. The current situation bears witness to the profound fracture created by the decline of these values. The difficulty adults have in transmitting models of behavior suitable for the present—a group of stable and shared values, a credible program for society, and a collective memory—finds a clear counterpart in an apparent lack of receptiveness on the part of the young. As a consequence, the younger generation seems to perceive reality by means of shock and superficial stimuli, rather than through experience gradually digested over time. This manner of perceiving reality favors the sense of social extraneousness and anomie, which we currently encounter in many areas and levels of social interaction (Simmel 1919; Jedlowski 1994).

THE PAST AS A FOREIGN COUNTRY

Precisely for these reasons, memory has become one of the central elements in the debate on modernity. What sort of memory we assume that it is possible to construct and transmit today, to whom, and by what means, have thus become unavoidable questions. Reflection on the existence of a "duty of memory" (Kattan 2002), or on the pedagogical task of transmitting events that have a particular symbolic value or occupy a central position in the history of a community in the effort to maintain (by means of a heritage of common values) the specificity of the group or the society, has taken on a new importance.

The narrative of the everyday, together with the discourse of official history, confirms to us our belonging both to a selected group and to a wider society. These constitute the raw materials that allow us to make sense of what we do and to represent it; to conserve the past by reformulating it in a way that responds to the actual needs of individual or group identity. Memory works by selecting and filtering those traces of the past which respond more closely to the project which informs them. Halbwachs (1980) refers to this aspect of the distinction between collective and social memory: the former is the clear perception of the past, while the latter constitutes the vague background that lies on the periphery of subjective awareness, taking the form of a general sense of familiarity but without the power to transform itself into tradition. However, what may today seem to have been forgotten, because it belongs to the memory of a minority or losing group, may reappear tomorrow in different circumstances to respond to different needs because, as F. C. Bartlett (1977) maintains, the work of remembering is nothing more than "an effort after meaning," the work of adapting to the world and to its constantly changing demands. This "effort after meaning" aims to find meaning that agrees with the present needs of individuals and the groups to which they belong and to reduce disorientation with respect to perceived complexity and novelty.

If, in the fragmentation of generational continuity, Bartlett and Halbwachs had already perceived the decline of an absolute past, in the sense of shared and reiterated memory, Benjamin (1970) would perceive the radical side of the profound break that took place. In the modern era, collective memory is no longer a product renewed through tradition, but an accumulation of ruins, a collection of quotations, of fragments of the past which acquire strength only in the suggestive power of the images they evoke. Arendt (1973) would further argue that the richness of the past is never definitively lost in the chance destruction caused by the "wings of the angel of history," although she recognized that each generation's reconstruction of what preceded it is uncertain and changeable.

The transmission of the past, always carried out by new individuals, represents a line of continuity as well as of dispersal of the inheritance of thought, practices and objects that each generation seeks to hand over to the next one. It encompasses not only the memory of what has been, but also the uncertainty of what will be passed on. Therefore collective memory possesses a composite and plural nature that no longer implies homogeneity and coercion, but instead openness to new configurations and combinations of the individual memories that constitute it. The contemporary individual can identify with diverse and dissonant memories and recognize him/herself in many "places" (Namer 1987), while belonging to none of these.

We hand down a series of practices, of "places" of history: the basic elements of a collective identity that, in large part, are shaped by mechanisms of erosion, of forgetting, of invention (Nora 1989). Awareness of the difficulty in the construction of meaning, of the uncertainty upon which contemporary society reproduces itself, has triggered a dual process. On the one hand, there is the cult of preservation, of origins, and a general sense of nostalgia and, on the other, contempt for tradition, the perception of the obsolescence of the heritage of the past, and a widespread cultural amnesia.

The generations "in charge" are responsible for the past and perpetuate it to the extent to which they see themselves as heirs to it. Evading this duty is not a crime in that it does not have a moral aspect. It does, however, indicate that the relationship between single individuals and the community to which they belong has become more distant, that the borders of identity are crumbling, and that the sense of extraneousness has become a constituent part of the lives of individuals.

A WORLD OF FOREIGNERS

In the world of everyday life, defined by Alfred Schütz (1979:182) as the ensemble of knowledge that is taken for granted and that directs individual action, our history as individuals is played out in a reality which, for the most part, is perceived as already given. On the other hand, if this common store of knowledge did not exist, we would not be able to understand our environment nor would we be able to locate persons and objects within a structure of meaning. The assumptions accepted and universally shared by a community are constructed collectively in a myriad of microrelationships. These relationships lay the foundations of a past that cannot be avoided if one wishes to comprehend the present.

The reality and the reliability of the human world are based primarily on the fact that we are surrounded by things that are more permanent than the activity that produced them, and also potentially more permanent than the lives of their creators (Arendt, 2004:67-68). The ancient *polis* — as a physical ordering of a territory, but also as a way of organizing individuals—guaranteed its citizens an identity and the continuity of their individual histories by giving them roots and recognition within a wider shared history. In the same way, the factory or the office or whatever other physical place of work, with its practices, organization, symbolic dimension and placement within the social imagination, represented for modern subjects the "space of appearances" in the broadest sense of the term: the space of public recognition, the origin of citizenship, and a deeper rooting of identity.

The large-scale abolition of work, activated by a profound destructuring, a radical dematerialization, and an irreversible shattering of the link between practices, objects and individuals has opened up a new era of nomadism. This, in the words of Zygmunt Bauman (1998:103), is "tourism" for the strong and "vagabondage" for the weak. The former move around because the (global) world within their grasp is attractive, the latter because the (local) world within their reach is inhospitable.

We are all in movement, whether through choice or not, even when physically we stay put. The deep sense of belonging to a place, a group, or a culture is increasingly no longer a viable option. The fact of staying put in one place, of being "locals" no longer leads to a particular sense of rootedness. Even the reality in which we are immersed, and the lasting existence of the whole social world, continue to be founded on the awareness of the continuity of the external world, of the presence of others and on shared memory (Augé 1998).

The problem we must confront is that of a social dynamic that produces not integrated members of the community but foreigners. Today's speed of social change is without doubt the constant factor reflected in the general mechanism of transmission across generations and in the construction of identity. The difficulty in transmitting a social model (values, norms, customs, and rituals but also jobs, practices, and institutions) undermines the ties joining one generation to the next. The latter becomes fragile because its components identify only weakly with the culture of the community, which it perceives as distant, and in which individuals feel that they are occupying a marginal position.

The loss of the social centrality of many of the institutions of organized modernity (of the nation-state, the family, and work as we have known it) has contributed to the undermining of the stability of the entire network of human relations and of the individual's trust in such a network. Since not only the construction of identity, but also its preservation, have become problematic, young people may perceive the most reasonable strategy to be that of avoiding any long-term undertaking, of not tying themselves to any one place, of not assuming responsibility for anything or anyone. If it is impossible to control the future, one may refuse to attempt to do so and simultaneously renounce all responsibility for the consequences of one's actions in the present (Sennett 1976).

We are living in interstitial times. Modern societies are becoming an indeterminate social configuration. Their indeterminacy is the result of human action, but not of deliberate human design. They emerge as adaptations to the persistent but evolving needs and changing circumstances of human conduct. Among the most significant transformations in circumstances that face human conduct is the continuous enlargement of human action, including an extension of its limit to growth (Stehr 2001:2).

Increased individualism does imply an uncoupling from certain collective obligations and constraints, and the distinct possibility that the role of the stranger becomes less 'strange' for more and more individuals. Every experience of life seems to carry along with it a portion of history which seems difficult to integrate with the others in the construction of a well-rounded identity.

If we agree with Christopher Lasch (1984) that the meaning of identity concerns either persons or things, it is easy to recognize that, in late modernity, both have lost their solidity, that is, their own definition and continuity. In the case of persons, the possibility of laying down an authentic sense of self—one's own memory—has been lost. A world constructed of solid objects replaced by objects constructed for immediate obsolescence represents a real problem, if in no other sense than that of environmental equilibrium. What future social impact will these rootless lives ("throwaways" as Bauman (2004) calls them) have? What can they transmit? What kind of society can they project for those who will come after them if the past really becomes a "foreign country?"

References

Arendt, Hannah. 1958. *The Human Condition*. Chicago: The University of Chicago Press.
—. 1973. *Men in Dark Times*. Harmondsworth: Penguin.
Augé, Marc. [1994] 1998. *A Sense for the Other: The Timeliness and Relevance of Anthropology*. Stanford, CA: Stanford University Press.
Bauman, Zygmunt. 1998. *Globalization: The Human Consequences*. Oxford, UK: Blackwell.
—. 2004. *Wasted Lives. Modernity and its Outcasts*. Cambridge, UK: Polity Press.

Bartlett, Frederic C. [1932] 1977. *Remembering: A Study in Experimental and Social Psychology.* Cambridge, UK: Cambridge University Press.

Beck, Ulrich. [1986] 1988. *Risk Society: Towards a New Modernity.* London: Sage.

Benjamin, Walter. [1955] 1970. *Illuminations.* London: Cape.

Berger, Peter L. and Thomas Luckmann, 1967. *The Social Construction of Reality: A Treatise in the Sociology of Knowledge.* London: Penguin.

Berman, Marshall. 1982. *All That is Solid Melts into Air: The Experience of Modernity.* New York: Simon and Schuster.

Boym, Svetlana. 2001. *The Future of Nostalgia.* New York: Basic Books.

Colley, Ann C. 1998. *Nostalgia and Recollection in Victorian Culture.* Basingstoke, UK: Macmillan.

Eghigian Greg, Andreas Killen, and Christine Leuenberger, eds. 2007. *Introduction: The Self as Project: Politics and the Human Sciences in the Twentieth Century.* OSIRIS, 22:1-25.

Flanagan, Owen, and Amelie Oksenberg Rorty, eds. 1990. *Identities, Character, and Morality: Essays in Moral Psychology.* Cambridge, MA: MIT Press.

Elster Jon. 1985. *The Multiple Self.* Cambridge, UK: Cambridge University Press.

Gergen, Kenneth J. 1991. *The Saturated Self: Dilemmas of Identity in Contemporary Life.* New York: Basic Books.

Giddens, Anthony. 1991. *Modernity and Self-Identity. Self and Society in the Late Modern Age.* Cambridge, UK: Polity Press.

Giddens, Anthony. 1990. *The Consequences of Modernity.* Cambridge, UK: Polity Press.

Gilligan, Carol. 1982. *In a Different Voice: Psychological Theory and Women's Development.* Cambridge, MA: Harvard University Press.

Hacking, Ian. 1995. *Rewriting the Soul: Multiple Personalities and the Sciences of Memory.* Princeton, NJ: Princeton University Press.

Halbwachs, Maurice. [1950] 1980. *The Collective Memory.* New York: Harper & Row.

Hobsbawm, Eric. 1994. *The Age of Extremes: The Short Twentieth Century 1914-1991.* London: Abacus.

Hoffmann-Axthelm, Dieter. 1992. "Identities and Realities. The End of the Philosophical Immigration Officer." Pp. 196-217 in *Modernity and Identity,* edited by Scott Lash and Jonathan Friedman. New York: Wiley-Blackwell.

Jedlowski, Paolo. 1994. *Il Sapere dell'Esperienza.* Milano: Il Saggiatore.

Kattan, Emmanuel. 2002. *Penser le Dévoir de Memoire.* Paris: P.U.F.

Lasch, Christopher. 1984. *The Minimal Self: Psychic Survival in Troubled Times.* New York: Norton.

Lash, Scott and Jonathan Friedman, eds. 1992. *Modernity and Identity.* New York: Wiley-Blackwell.

Marcuse, Herbert. 1964. *One-Dimensional Man: Studies in the Ideology of Advanced Industrial Society.* Boston: Beacon Press.

Mead, Margaret. 1970. *Culture and Commitment: A Study of the Generation Gap.* New York: Doubleday.

Melucci, Alberto. 1991. *Il Gioco dell'io: Il Cambiamento del sé in una Società Globale.* Milano: Feltrinelli.

Namer, Gerard. 1987. *Mémoire et Société.* Paris: Klincksieck.

Nora, Pierre. 1989. "Between Memory and History: Les Lieux de Mémoire." *Representations* 26:7-25.

Rosaldo, Renato. 1989. "Imperialist Nostalgia." *Representations* 26:107-122.

Sennett, Richard. 1998. *The Corrosion of Character.* New York: Norton.

Sennett, Richard. [1976] 1986. *The Fall of Public Man.* London: Faber.

Simmel, Georg. 1919. *Philosophische Kultur: Gesammelte Essays.* Leipzig: Klinkhardt.

Stehr, Nico. 2001. *The Fragility of Modern Society: Knowledge and Risk in the Information Age.* London: Sage.

Taylor, Charles. 1989. *Sources of the Self: The Making of Modern Identity.* Cambridge, MA: Harvard University Press.

Wagner, Peter. 1994. *A Sociology of Modernity: Liberty and Discipline.* London: Routledge.

Weber, Max. [1920] 1970. *The Protestant Ethic and the Spirit of Capitalism.* London: Unwin University Books.

Preserving Italian American History and Culture: Great Resources in Search of an Audience

DOMINIC CANDELORO
Italian Cultural Center at Casa Italia, Stone Park, Illinois

Direct memory of the grand saga of Italian migration to the United States, the Little Italys that they built, the family-based culture that they kept, their broken English, their political radicalism, their brand of religion, and their dreams have almost disappeared on both sides of the Atlantic. On the other hand, the 2000 U.S. Census identified a sizable population claiming Italian ancestry. The top ten states in population are: New York (3,254,298), New Jersey (1,590,225), Pennsylvania (1,547,470), California (1,533,599), Florida (1,147,946), Massachusetts (918,838), Illinois (739,284), Ohio (720,847), Connecticut (652,016), and Michigan (484,486). Four states have more than 15 percent of their population with Italian ancestry: Rhode Island (19.7 percent), Connecticut (18.6 percent), New Jersey (16.8 percent), and New York (16.4 percent). The national estimated population of Italian Americans varies from the Census total of 16 million (5.6 percent of the total U.S. population) to 25 or 30 million cited by such organizations as the National Italian American Foundation and the Sons of Italy.[1]

Despite the numbers, Italians have had plenty of time to assimilate. It has been six generations since the beginning of mass migration, three generations since the end of World War II, and a good two generations since the bulk of post-war migration. The exogamy rate of Italian Americans is estimated at 70 percent. To what extent can/will this changed ethnic group preserve its history and culture?[2]

---

[1] U.S. Census web data on Italians in the U.S. is at http://factfinder.census.gov/servlet/SAFFIteratedFacts?_event=&geo_id=01000US&_geoContext=01000US&_street=&_county=&_cityTown=&_state=&_zip=&_lang=en&_sse=on&ActiveGeoDiv=&_useEV=&pctxt=fph&pgsl=010&_submenuId=factsheet_2&ds_name=DEC_2000_SAFF&_ci_nbr=543&qr_name=DEC_2000_SAFF_A1010&reg=DEC_2000_SAFF_A1010 percent3A543&_keyword=&_industry=

[2] Richard D. Alba. 1985. *Italian Americans, Into the Twilight of Ethnicity*. Englewood Cliffs: Prentice-Hall.

FOUNDING FATHERS OF ITALIAN AMERICAN STUDIES

The history and sociology of Italian immigrants has been covered rather extensively since 1900. A few highlights will suffice to illustrate. The most prodigious researcher in the field was Giovanni Schiavo, who produced a dozen fact-filled volumes detailing the exploits of Italian explorers, clergy, and businessmen.[3] He also developed a detailed profile of Chicago's Italians in the 1920s, as well as several attacks on the Mafia myth. Leonard Covello, New York City's first Italian-American high school principal, conducted a sociological survey of the Italian-American school child (second generation) that has served as a baseline for subsequent researchers.[4] Rudolph Vecoli (1964) used his study of Chicago Italians to challenge Oscar Handlin's standard interpretation of immigration as a monolithically "uprooting" experience that led to fast assimilation.[5] Vecoli, who subsequently became Director of the Immigration Research Center at the University of Minnesota and a world leader in the field, reported strong evidence of cultural retention over the generations.[6]

Another milestone publication, *WOP! A Documentary History of Anti-Italian Discrimination*, appeared in 1973. The author, Salvatore LaGumina, went on to make many contributions to Italian American studies capped off by *Italian American Experience: An Encyclopedia* (2000), for which he was the lead editor along with Frank J. Cavaioli, Salvatore Primeggia, and Joseph A. Varacalli. The mostly forgotten Italian-American involvement with socialism, labor organizing, and U.S. left wing movements was documented in *The Lost World of Italian-American Radicalism* (2003), edited by Philip Cannistraro and Gerald Meyer. Published to engender pride among a mass audience is Leon Radomile's *Heritage Italian-American Style Bilingual* (2nd edition, 2003). Even from this quick survey, it is clear that a respectable body of information about the Italian-American experience exists and is available to the curious. It is also evident that much work remains to be done in collecting additional historical materials, especially from the post-World War II migration. Advanced technology will allow

---

[3] Giovanni Schiavo. 1954. *Four Centuries of Italian-American History*. New York: Vigo.

[4] 1920s dissertation by Leonard Covello, *The Social Background of the Italo-American School Child: A Study of the Southern Italian Family Mores and Their Effect on the School Situation in Italy and America*, edited by Francesco Cordasco (New York, 1972).

[5] Oscar Handlin. 1951. *The Uprooted*. New York: Little, Brown, 1951.

[6] Rudolph Vecoli. 1964. "Contadini in Chicago: A Critique of The Uprooted." *The Journal of American History* 51:404-417.

additional tools for collection and interpretation of data.

AMERICAN ITALIAN HISTORICAL ASSOCIATION (AIHA)

Several notable cultural organizations continuously engage in production of informative studies about Italian Americans. The American Italian Historical Association, founded in 1967 by Vecoli, Leonard Covello, LaGumina and others, has published over 30 volumes of its proceedings containing almost 500 articles in about 6,000 pages by researchers in Italian American studies.[7] The Association has nurtured the careers of hundreds of academics focused on various aspects of Italian Americana. Its 40 annual conferences since 1967 have attracted scholars from Italy, Canada, and Australia. AIHA is a major force for the production and dissemination of cultural studies with an Italian-American theme.[8] For example, the West Coast membership of AIHA produced *Una Storia Segreta*, a powerful and well-documented exhibit/website and book on the mistreatment of Italian Americans in California after the 1941 Pearl Harbor attack.[9]

PURSUING OUR ITALIAN NAMES TOGETHER (POINT)

An organization with even more members than AIHA and with the ability to use new research tools to penetrate into the family life of the millions of Italians who immigrated to the U.S. is POINT. (www.point-pointers.net/home.html) This organization of genealogists recently claimed 28 chapters across the nation with myriad publications, websites, and conferences. New trends in genealogy push the researchers to go beyond the simple recitation of lineage to focus on aspects of social history and this should have a beneficial impact on the preservation and dissemination of historical patterns that will be of interest to a larger public. Two other important genealogical resources include Grace Olivo's *Comunes of Italy* and Jenny Floro-Khalaf's italianancestry.com/.

The New Jersey Italian and Italian American Heritage Commission is a government-funded institution that seeks to strengthen the cultural identity of Italians and Italian Americans through public education programs that

---

[7] See the history of AIHA by Frank J. Cavaioli, "The American Italian Historical Association at the Millennium" (2002). Available on the web at www.aihaweb.org/AIHAhistory.htm.

[8] Visit www.aihaweb.org.

[9] Lawrence Di Stasi, ed. 2001. *Una Storia Segreta: The Secret History of Italian American Evacuation and Internment During World War II*. New York: Heyday Books.

preserve and promote an accurate, non-stereotyped understanding of the contributions and accomplishments of people of Italian heritage. Founded in 2002, the Commission focuses on introducing Italian/Italian-American materials into school and university curricula around the state.[10]

REPOSITORIES

Italian Americans have been preserving the primary sources of their history—papers, letters, newspapers, photographs, parish records—in several notable repositories. The Immigrant History Research Center has collected materials from Italians in addition to those of the full range of immigrants to the U.S. Much of the collection is available online at www.ihrc.umn.edu/.

A project of the Scalabrini Fathers, the Center for Migration Studies (CMS) was established in 1964. Though it has many holdings related to Italian Americans and the American Italian Historical Association, its focus is on migration as an international, global phenomenon. CMS publishes the *International Migration Review*, as well as books and monographs, and sponsors conferences on international migration and immigration and refugee policy issues. Its catalogue is available online at www.cmsny.org/.

Another Scalabrini institution, the Centro Studi Emigrazione Roma, was led for many years by Gianfausto Rosoli, an emigration historian and scholar. The library contains over 35,000 books, 200 periodicals, article reprints, dissertations, and conference papers, as well as photographic archives on Italian emigration worldwide. The archives of the Scalabrini Fathers also provide rich documentation on a personal and parish-level of Italian-American communities.

Headed by Nicholas Ciotola, the Italian American Collection is a part of the Senator John Heinz History Center and the Historical Society of Western Pennsylvania in Pittsburgh. The Collection was started in 1990 and has extensive holdings of archival materials, artifacts, oral histories, and photographs related to Western Pennsylvania Italians. Its mission also includes public programming, exhibits, and publication (see www.pghhistory.org/wpaitalians.asp).

One of the results of the NEH "Italians in Chicago Project 1978-1981" was the establishment of the Italian American Collection in the Special Collections Department of the Richard J. Daley Library at the University

---

[10] Visit njitalia.nj.gov/.

of Illinois in Chicago. It contains thousands of items including photos, documents, memorabilia, films, audiotapes, and oral history transcripts as well as materials relating to the career of Congressman Frank Annunzio. The Jane Addams Hull House Collection in the same library also has many materials relating to Italian immigrants (see www.uic.edu/depts/lib/specialcoll/).

The Museo ItaloAmericano, located at the Fort Mason Center in San Francisco, focuses on art as the window to Italian and Italian-American culture. Since its founding in 1978, the Museo ItaloAmericano has collected, researched, and displayed art works of Italian and Italian-American artists. Its other programs emphasize Italian language and films rather than Italian-American culture (www.museoitaloamericano.org).

Notable private collectors of Italian Americana include Ernesto Milani of Cuggiono, who has a vast collection of memorabilia from midwestern and western settlements of Italian immigrants;[11] and Paul Porcelli who has amassed thousands of photographs from over 300 separate Italian-American religious festivals.[12] While the number of festivals has declined from 3,000 in the 1920s, the strong survival of 300 into the twenty-first century is testimony to the residual strength of Italian religiosity and ethnicity. These festivals also remind us that the lives of immigrants and their descendants consisted of much more than the deprivation and alienation that are the hallmarks of the migration process. On another note, Jerome Krase of Brooklyn College has created another remarkable collection of images of Italian-American urban spaces.[13]

As even this cursory review of archival repositories indicates, students of the Italian American past have ample resources to construct and reconstruct their history.

LITERARY RESOURCES

While it is impossible to do a complete survey of Italian American literature in the present context, it appears clear that there is a substantial body of creative published materials of varying quality that portrays the

---

[11] Milani asserts that it is easier to find archeological remains of the ancient Romans than it is to find letters and documents relating to the Italian American diaspora in the early twentieth century.

[12] Porcelli is working on a book entitled "When the Saints Come Marching Out," drawing from his attending and photographing more than 240 of the 300 Italian saint processions in the U.S.

[13] For example, see http://academic.brooklyn.cuny.edu/soc/semiotics/v1n1/p6.html.

Italian American heritage. Literature, of course, speaks to subjective matters, feelings, and attitudes that might be difficult to capture in historical chronologies. Here again, Italian immigrants and their children have provided a remarkable window to their inner narratives. If perhaps not as prolific or as popular as the literary achievements of Jewish or African American ethnics, Italian-American creative writers have passed on a respectable body of literature to their second, third, and fourth generation descendants.

To name just a few from the early generations, Pascal D'Angelo's *Son of Italy* (1924) was an early autobiography that won literary praise for some of the nation's top scholars. Pietro di Donato's *Christ in Concrete (1939)*, was a masterpiece and a national best seller. Jerre Mangione's numerous non-fiction books about Italy and Italian Americans included *Monte Allegro* (1943), an authentic depiction of an extended Sicilian family in Little Italy in Rochester, New York, and *La Storia: Five Centuries of the Italian American Experience* (1993). John Fante's *The Saga of Arturo Bandini* series, including *Ask the Dust* (1939), *Dago Red* (1940), *Full of Life* (1952), and *The Brotherhood of the Grape* (1977) attracted the attention of literary scholars on both sides of the Atlantic. Though a distinguished classical scholar/poet/teacher, Joseph Tusiani's autobiographical poems and those celebrating Italian-American heroes in *Gente Mia* (1978) touch on the full range of both positive and negative experiences and emotions sustained by generations of Italian immigrants to the U.S.

Since the late 1970s women writers like Helen Barolini's *Umbertina* (1979) and *The Dream Book* (1985), an anthology of Italian-American women writers, have flourished. *From the Margin* (1991) by Anthony Julian Tamburri, Fred L. Gardaphè, and Paolo A. Giordano, packaged past and contemporary Italian-American writers in an anthology that was well-received, sometimes becoming the textbook for college courses on Italian American literature. This same trio, with seed money from the Fondazione Giovanni Agnelli, founded *Voices in Italian Americana (VIA)*. *The Bibliography of the Italian American Book* (2000) by Fred Gardaphè and James Periconi documents and annotates the burst of creativity that marked the 1980s and 1990s. The majority of the new writers were women. In fact, the Italian American Writers Association has a database of 2,700 works of literature by Italian Americans online at http://www.iawa.net/database.htm. A recent anthology, *The Italian American Reader*, edited by Bill Tonelli, features samplings from 68 contemporary masters.

Tamburri, Gardaphè, and Giordano (all of whom currently hold influential academic positions) also founded Bordighera Press in 1989, originally to publish *VIA*, but soon branched out and have since published hundreds of titles of creative writing by and about Italian Americans. When combined with the publications of the older (1978) Canadian-based Guernica Editions, the number of published books on the topic has risen exponentially.

Other resources for the study of Italian American literature include Fernando Alfonsi's anthology, *Poeti Italo-Americani e Italo-Canadesi* (1994), and the forthcoming English version of *Italoamericana*, originally published in Italian by Mondadori Press in 2005, and now being translated by Robert Oppedisano, the director of Fordham University Press. The collection includes some of the earliest Italian-American writings, from 1880 to 1943 by a wide variety of Italian-American writers, performers, artists, and composers.

Despite the quantity of books published, the number of books about Italian Americans that have reached the best seller lists is rather small. Di Donato's *Christ in Concrete, The Godfather* (1969), and other writings of Mario Puzo, Gay Talese's *Honor Thy Father* (1971) and *Unto the Sons* (1992) are among the exceptions that prove the rule. Two recent popular women authors who consistently produce best-selling fiction about Italian-American characters are Adiana Trigiani (*Big Stone Gap* series, etc.) and Lisa Scottoline, a mystery writer whose main characters are Italian-American women from Philadelphia.

Clearly, Italian Americans have written more than enough books, articles, poems and essays to keep their descendants amply informed for generations to come. The challenge lies in the priorities of the descendants. Will they have the time or the inclination to delve into this treasure trove?

SCHOLARLY JOURNALS

Italian Americana is a historical, cultural and literary journal founded in 1982 by Ernest Falbo and Richard Gambino, and edited for many years by Bruno Arcudi of SUNY Buffalo. His successor was Carol Bonomo Albright at the University of Rhode Island. From 1994 to 2003, the poetry editor was Dana Gioia, who later became head of the National Endowment for the Arts.

Two other scholarly journals which have collected significant studies on Italian American culture are *AltreItalie* and the *Italian American Review*.

AltreItalie calls itself an "International Review of Studies on the People of Italian Origin in the World." A publication of Fondazione Giovanni Agnelli in Torino, it first appeared in 1987. Edited chiefly by Maddalena Tirabassi, the publication is truly global in focus and, not surprisingly, multilingual. In recent years, *AltreItalie* has evolved into a web publication with extensive search capabilities (http://www.altreitalie.org/). *IAR* began as a project of the Italian American History Society (1992), then went to the Verazzano Institute at Mercy College, and finally moved into the John D. Calandra Institute of the City University of New York, Queens College, in 1996. The semi-annual journal is focused on the social science approach to the study of Italian American culture. Its editors in recent years included Philip Cannistraro and Vincenzo Milione.

STEREOTYPES IN POPULAR CULTURE CREATED BY THE MASS MEDIA

The most dominant part of American culture is mass media. For many Italian Americans, the portrayal of Italian Americans in film and television is the most important issue facing their ethnic group. Mass media thrives on easy stereotypes of all their subjects. The Mafia/gangster stereotype has dominated the film industry since the origin of moving pictures. Fascination with the "outlaw," along with the indisputable flair of the flamboyant Capone-types, has made far more money for Hollywood than the gangsters themselves were ever able to accumulate from their underworld enterprises. Moreover, "Godfather I" and "Godfather II" and TV's "Sopranos" are artistically among the very best that the culture has produced. The profit motive and compelling artistry (often by Italian Americans) have emblazoned this negative stereotype on Italian Americans, four generations after most of the real gangsters have left the scene. Even a recent children's movie, "Shark Tail," featured Luca, Lino and Frankie as Italian gangster sharks. Other films like "Marty," "Vendetta," "Uncle Nino," "Miracle Match," and even "A Bronx Tale," provide a more balanced image of Italian Americans, but they have been much less successful and much less numerous than the gangster movie (see also www.stereotypethis.com).

RECENT DOCUMENTARIES

Based on the scholarship of AIHA members and others, in recent years numerous independent filmmakers have produced documentaries with at least some small impact on Italian-American audiences. Perhaps more important, these documentaries have preserved important aspects of Italian American culture in the accessible DVD format. To promote awareness of these documentaries, I present the following examples: Gia Amella's "And They Came to Chicago," Michael DiLauro's "Prisoners Among Us," Peter Miller's "The Legend of Sacco and Vanzetti," Paul Budline's "Anti-Italianism: Discrimination and Defamation in the History of Italian Americans" (which features Joe Piscopo and Tony Lo Bianco reflecting gangster stereotypes in the movies), Stephanie Longo's "Watch the Pallino," Heather Hartley's "I Linciati: Lynching of Italians in America," Joseph Raben's "Italian Americans and Federal Hill," Veronica Diaferia's, "Closing Time: Storia di un Negozio," Alexandra Corbin and Susan Morosoli's "The Italian Gardens of South Brooklyn," Paul Reitano and Terrence Sacchi's "Dyker Lights," David Katz' "The Kings of Christmas," Tony DeNonno's "Heaven Touches Brooklyn in July," Alex Halpern's "Nine Good Teeth" Don McGlynn's "Louis Prima: The Wildest!" Basile Sallustio's "My Brother, My Sister, Sold for a Fistful of Lire," Edward Landler and Brad Byer's "I Build the Towers," Joseph Cultrera's "Hand of God," Camilla Calamandrei's "Prisoners in Paradise," and Abigail Honor's "Saints and Sinners." Additional information about each of these productions, can, of course, be obtained using search engines on the Internet.

MUSEUM EXHIBITS

Museum exhibits are an important means of disseminating information about the Italian-American past. While most Italian American communities are capable of assembling photos, documents, and memorabilia, only a few have done so in a professional way. Perhaps the most impressive is in Pittsburgh. Located on the fourth floor of the Senator Heinz History Center, the Italian American Special Collections gallery is the museum's permanent display of museum artifacts collected from the Italian-American community. Artifacts on display include food and wine-making equipment, saint statues used in religious processions, tools used by Italian-American craftsmen, and works by Italian-American artists. Nick Ciotola, the curator, has also collected oral histories and archives for the institution (http://www.pghhistory.org).

While Philip Cannistraro's 2002 exhibit, "The Italians of New York: Five Centuries of Struggle and Achievement," (2002) was only a temporary event, elements of it can be found as a virtual exhibit at http://qcpages.qc.edu/calandra/museum/index.html. Led by Joseph Scelsa, the Italian American Museum, affiliated with CUNY, has a presence on the web and it purchased several buildings in New York's Little Italy for conversion into a bricks-and-mortar museum.

Chicago boasts the Italians in Chicago Historic Photo Exhibit at the Italian Cultural Center/Casa Italia in Stone Park. It is a permanent version of the exhibit created by the original NEH Italians in Chicago Project, directed by this author. Though the formal archives for this exhibit remain at the University of Illinois-Chicago, the library of the Italian Cultural Center is building an online database of its published and archival holdings accessible at ItalCulturalCenter on the LibraryThing.com website.

Funded in large part by sports mogul Jerry Colangelo, the National Italian American Sports Hall of Fame is located on Taylor Street in the heart of Chicago's Little Italy. Using hi-tech graphics and sports memorabilia, the museum takes an exciting, nostalgic look at sports heroes and the sense of pride and identity that their success on the field gave to Italian Americans in their quest for acceptance and social mobility (http://www.niashf.org/).

Recently mounted in the Colorado Historical Society is Alisa Zahller's "Italians in Denver" exhibition. Surprisingly, the Colorado population into the 1920s was 20 percent Italian American. Though the exhibit will be closed by the publication date of this volume, its basic elements are captured in its catalogue and the community is working to find a permanent home for the exhibition. The voluminous archives collected in preparation for the exhibit are part of the Colorado Historical Society's permanent collection.

The previously mentioned Museo ItaloAmericano in San Francisco focuses mainly on art, but has in the past featured historical exhibitions on such topics as the life story of Domenico Ghiardelli.

New Orleans is the home of Piazza D'Italia which is adjacent to the American Italian Renaissance Foundation Museum and Library. Inspired by Joseph Maselli, the institution maintains a colorful and dramatic exhibit on the Italians (mostly Sicilians) in New Orleans. Many of the holdings of the museum are published in *Images of America: Italians in New Orleans* edited by Joseph Maselli, The Library contains the papers of the pioneering Italian American researcher Giovanni Schiavo (http://www.airf.org/).

PROSPECTS OF PERPETUAL PROFESSORSHIPS

Most attractive to Italian-American academics is the dream that donors from the community will partner with major universities to create permanently-endowed professorships of Italian American studies. The idea that a university endowment would provide a tenured professor a full-time opportunity to research, write and teach about the Italian-American experience is the dream of our field. Some progress has been made in that direction, but until a dozen or so major universities have such an arrangement in place, the dream will not be complete.

The current situation is fluid. There is no definitive list of endowed programs, several are in formation and they often have different structures. The list compiled by Anthony Tamburri recently on i-Italy is as follows: the Charles and Joan Alberto Italian Studies Institute, the Joseph M. and Geraldine C. La Motta Chair in Italian Studies, and the Valente Family Italian Studies Library (with a collection of Italian books second to none) all at Seton Hall University; the Casa Italiana Zerilli-Marimò, home of the Department of Italian Studies at New York University; the Joseph and Elda Coccia Institute for the Italian Experience in America at Montclair State University; and the George L. Graziadio Center for Italian Studies and Chair of Italian Studies at California State University in Long Beach.

Elements of UNICO and the Sons of Italy often make alliances that include named sponsors. A tireless advocate of endowed Italian American studies at major universities is Frank Cannata, a longtime leader in the UNICO organization. One of his accomplishments was the creation of the Aldo DeDominicis Graduate Fellowship in Italian-American History at the University of Connecticut.

The Italian American program at John Carroll University in the Cleveland area seems well established. At NYU the Tira al Segno group supports some Italian American programming. The Italian American Cultural Center's Dr. Frank A. Franco Library is on the campus of Alvernia College in Reading, Pennsylvania.

When dealing with endowments, there are several caveats. First is the "Dante Ogre." Italian-American donors and the university administrations often fail to make a distinction between Italian American studies and Italian studies or conveniently blur the differences. Because the study of Dante and the Renaissance has higher credibility in academic circles than the study of immigrants and their communities, donations collected for the purpose of advancing Italian American studies often end up serving the research and teaching of Italian studies. And often the professors appointed to an Italian American chair are really Italianists

The second caveat is that arrangements that apparently endowed professorships can sometimes be a way for universities to manipulate budget lines with no real net gains for the cause. That is, they get the endowment to pay for expenses of services that the university was already providing.

HISTORIC NEWSPAPERS AND OTHER PUBLICATIONS

Italian American culture has produced hundreds of Italian language and English publications that help us chart their fortunes.[14] Some general publications like *Il Progresso Italo-Americano* had long runs. IHRC, CMS, CSER, the Archivio Centrale dello Stato in Rome, and other repositories contain the copies of newspapers and other publications produced and consumed by Italian immigrants and their children.

Many others were advocacy publications pushing socialism, philosophical anarchy, religion, etc. While World War II brought an end to many Italian language periodicals, Italian-English and mostly English publications still serve the Italian-American community into the fourth and fifth generations after major immigration. (A partial list can be found at http://www.ccsu.edu/italian/giornali_italoamericani.htm.) Among the more important publications that can be used to study post-World War II Italian American culture are: *Fra Noi* (Chicago, monthly, 1960–present), *L'Italo-Americano* (Los Angeles, weekly, 1908–present, at www.italoamericano.com/), *Italian Tribune* (Newark, NJ, weekly, 1931–present, at www.ItalianTribune.com); *America Oggi* (NJ, daily, 1988–present). *Fra Noi* began as a Scalabrini publication but became secular two decades ago. *L'Italo Americano* is currently a Scalabrini publication. *America Oggi* was begun by staff members of *Il Progresso Italo Americano* when that paper ceased publication in 1988. It is the only daily newspaper and it maintains a sophisticated and detailed website.

Among the publications taking up the brief traditions of lifestyle magazines like *IA* and *Identity* of the late 1970s are *Primo* and *Amici*.

---

[14] For a full discussion of the subject see Pietro Russo. 1972. "La Stampa Periodica Italo-Americana," in *Gli Italiani negli Stati Uniti: L'Emigrazione e l'Opera degli Italiani negli Stati Uniti*. Edited by Rudolph J. Vecoli et al., and subsequent works by the same author.

Among other contemporary publications are: *Italian American Digest* (New Orleans) and *Voce* (Las Vegas).

When it comes to newspapers, we see, again, that the dedicated reader of Italian would have little trouble finding abundant information and ideas about Italian immigrants in America and their descendants.

PRESENCE ON THE WEB

The general public is the target audience for "Milestones" created by Salvatore La Gumina and John Marino for the National Italian American Foundation.[15] It presents a detailed chronology of important achievements, often little known, of Italians in the United States from 1492 to the present. For the past 10 years H-ItAm has provided some 400 scholars and activists a forum and a network for the academic (though not always) discussion of issues touching on Italian Americans. A part of H-Net, sponsored by Michigan State University, H-ItAm is among the 100 listservs for humanities scholars that have revolutionized subject matter communication among academics. The H-ItAm website contains a searchable archive of more than 50,000 Items. Another affiliate of H-Net is H-Italy which focuses exclusively on the history of Italy. Italian Americans in Seattle and St. Louis have especially sophisticated web portals.[16]

Led by Anthony Julian Tamburri, Dean of Calandra Institute, and Ottorino Cappelli, University "L'Orientale," Naples (among others), i-Italy was launched in late 2007. A new generation entity, beyond listservs and web pages, i-Italy is an interactive blog-based magazine that features "public intellectuals" exploring the new realities of Italian-American ethnicity and identity in the twenty-first century, i-Italy has attracted as its writers some of the top scholars and writers in the US.

The place where the American public gets up close and personal with "authentic Italians" is not the library or the Web or even the movies. It's at the *Festa Italiana*.

OSIA lists 448 Italian festivals held in 35 states and the District of Columbia between February and December 2008.[17] The leaders are New York (91), New Jersey (70), Pennsylvania (66), Illinois (33), Massachusetts (32), California (30), Connecticut (22), Ohio (22), and Rhode Island (13).

---

[15] http://www.niaf.org/milestones/index.asp
[16] Visit http://beta.italiaseattle.com/ and http://www.italystl.com/
[17] http://www.osia.org/public/pdf/2008_festival_directory.pdf

That adds up to something like 5 million attendees annually (equal to the migration of Italian immigrants to America). The message that these events convey to Italian Americans about themselves, and to the general public about the "Italian" sense of food, fun, entertainment, religiosity, and patriotism, is enormous. The largest *Festa Italiana*, in Milwaukee, offers a full range of activities including *Opera Lirica* and extensive historic photo displays. Smaller fests confine themselves to standard Italian-American foods and 1950s Italian-named entertainers. That the festivals engage the volunteer work and energy of so many is a tribute to their continuing sense of Italian identity. These events are fundraisers that appeal to the masses. On the other hand, it is annoying to many Italian-American public intellectuals that so many Italian ethnics put so much energy into an activity with so little payoff for the preservation of anything beyond the most superficial.

CONCLUSION

Many primary sources exist for documenting Italian-American experiences, with many opportunities for capturing more. Institutions collect and preserve them, and people and entities are willing and able to research and disseminate the results.

However, is there a market for Italian American studies? In this third millennium, with all of our preoccupation with problems like terrorism, global warming, the explosion of information on the Internet, and our fascination with sports and dozens of other interests that compete for our attention, do we have the energy and will to preserve and disseminate this small page in world history? Can Italian American studies survive in an academic climate that seems to value diversity of race, gender, and class only as it emanates from disadvantaged minorities? Are we (Italians, Americans, and Italo-Americans) sufficiently interested in this material because of what it tells us about ourselves and our respective countries? Or, as we move toward a global culture, will we satisfy ourselves with the one-dimensional stereotype of the poor, hard-working immigrants whose Italian-American children and American grandchildren moved up in the world and whose Italian names and memories dissolved into the American melting pot?

Italian-American organizations that protest against mafia stereotyping, promote religious festivals, and celebrate Columbus Day will always be there. Italian business, cultural, and governmental entities, which can benefit from an Italian-American identity no matter how superficial, will always be present.

Perhaps the best hope for the preservation of Italian American culture is the National Italian American Foundation (www.naif.org). Established in the ethnic caldron of the 1970s by politically savvy Washington leaders, NIAF modeled itself as a lobby group and formed an Italian-American Congressional Caucus. Presidents and candidates for president always attend its banquets. NIAF eventually was able to tap the resources of the powerful and wealthy, using both old and new methods of fundraising. A recipient of Charity Navigator's highest rating, NIAF proudly proclaims that it is the "only national Italian organization to receive this coveted designation." And though it has matured into a reliable source of funds for the cultural projects of academics (including this author and the conference from which this book emanates), media makers, and language educators, NIAF still has its work cut out for it. Its challenge is to keep the attention of the Italian-American elite, to increase its revenue base, and to maximize its grant awards that preserve and disseminate Italian American culture as well as the Italian language and the civilization that produced it. That's a tall order.

The future of the Italian American past will be determined by the current generation of organizational leaders and academic leaders. Will they step up to the plate, form an alliance, and support a state-of-the-art approach to cultural conservation? Or will they continue to go their separate ways—the academics writing books that only other academics will see and the organizations sponsoring banquet after banquet to fight diseases and award $1000 scholarships to bright high school students? We may know the definitive answer to this question within the next decade.

Local Development, Cultural Identity and Popular Culture in Peripheral Areas

ANGELO SALENTO
University of Salento

In Europe, in past and present times, many events have given rise to concerns about the creation of national and sub-national identities. The Yugoslav wars, for example, represented an extraordinary instance of the extent to which the claim to an identity can degenerate into a violent impulse towards "purification." The rhetoric of identity—as in the case of the request by some in the Catholic Church hierarchy to ratify *ex lege* the recognition of the "Christian roots" of Europe—often proves to be inclined towards the logic of conflict, which certainly does not help achieve the goal of world peace desired by the Western democratic tradition.

The theoretical reconstructions of the concept of identity have undoubtedly embodied this type of concern. The idea of *identity* has been reconstructed as a kind of "loose cannon," as a semantic device, which is likely, intrinsically, to "slide" and "degenerate."

According to these assumptions, one could assert, as the Italian anthropologist Francesco Remotti suggests, to be *against identity* (Remotti 1996). However, this term (we could say, its conditions of use) has several meanings, and some of them are definitely different from each other. If one wanted to find a semantic nucleus, which is common to all uses of the term *identity* (at the collective level, excluding the individual psychological dimension)[1], it would certainly be generic and anodyne: every attempt to build a symbolic boundary produces an identity (without any possible clarification of the rigidity and permeability of the boundary, or of the ways in which the boundary itself is protected). Building a boundary is an activity in which we all are constantly and inescapably

---

[1] The word identity is not part of the "traditional" terminology of social sciences. Mainly unknown to the classical authors of sociological works, this word spread during the social movements in the 1970s, first in the United States, and later in Europe. In that period the word identity started to indicate a process of collective self-recognition.

engaged, in a more or less conscious way. If humans are biologically "incomplete" beings who need to complement themselves *culturally* (Geertz 1973), the construction of a cultural identity—the cognitive construction of one's own peculiarity—is an inescapable need.

If identity may become "the fundamental, determining, obsessive need" (Remotti 1996:59) to overcome diversity, the term *identity* may indicate practices which have little or nothing to do with the denial of diversity. Following the suggestion provided by Italian sociologist Alessandro Pizzorno, no meaning of the word *identity* should be taken for granted. On the contrary, the phenomena to which it refers should be examined at any time and according to the circumstances (Pizzorno 2007). In other words, one should not wonder if the problem is to side *in favor of* or *against* identity, but rather, which kind of identity should be supported. Which definitions of self should one privilege, and—above all—for which purpose?

IDENTITY AND CULTURAL AUTONOMY: PERSPECTIVES FOR SOUTHERN ITALY

The social construction of identity probably has little to do with the reduction of possible alternatives, for it seems aimed at *searching* possible alternatives within a social scenario, marked by the spreading of a "global" identity. This paper seeks to pinpoint some of the conditions necessary (and sufficient) to avoid this kind of social process, thus causing the risk of degeneration.

This process is observable in some regional and sub-regional contexts in southern Italy. Here, for about a decade now, social discourses have been characterized by references to *identities*: the identity of the local population, the identity of the territory, the identity of places, etc. Accompanying the increase in references to identity has been a growing attention towards the cultural heritage of the so-called "tradition," usually referred to as the generic term of *popular culture*.

This increasing emphasis on popular culture is a complex phenomenon. Certainly not related to only one aim, its exaltation in fact often has economic aims, or is intended to maximize consensus for local policy-makers. Nonetheless, the production of identity, through the lure and manipulation of the so-called traditional cultures, is one of the main "strategies" of a trend oriented towards reappraising the prospects of social development in southern Italy, a locale that some consider as "backward." To accept this arguable generalization, one must make some assumptions concerning the so-called *Southern question,* particularly regarding the still-ongoing political and intellectual debate on the situation of southern Italy that began early in the twentieth century.

According to a view held by some U.S. functionalists, the economic and social underdevelopment of southern Italy is due to a cultural deficit among its population. For example, U.S. political scientist Edward Banfield (whose "culture of poverty" arguments are rejected by most U.S. social scientists) argued that the "economic backwardness" of southern Italy resulted from its propensity for so-called *amoral familism.* In fact, Banfield claimed that southern Italians tended to behave opportunistically to obtain benefits for their families, neglecting their civic responsibilities and the common interests (Banfield 1958).

A second interpretation suggested that the backwardness of southern Italy was due to the late development of the industrialization process in this area, compared with that of Italy's northern regions. This belief, popular in Italy until the 1980s, justified industrial investment policies that created some productive areas (particularly in the steel and chemical sectors), ones now going through a crisis (see Graziani 2000).

Finally, according to another interpretation, the backwardness of southern Italy was due to two completely different factors. First of all, it was a consequence of the exclusion of the southern regions from the process of economic, cultural and social integration in Italy ever since national unification. Secondly, this weak economic condition was aggravated by the attempt to impose a development model completely alien to the *Mezzogiorno*'s history. In other words, southern Italy and its population were *denied* their specificity, their dignity. Instead, they were reduced to a mere *object* of politics, or rather—as scholars in the tradition of cultural studies would pose it, using a term by Foucault—to an object of *governmentality.* Carlo Levi first proposed this interpretation in his popular work, *Christ Stopped at Eboli* (1945). However, it remained a minority idea until the 1990s, when it became widely acknowledged within the social sciences in Italy.

According to the Apulian sociologist Franco Cassano, the essential problem of the *Mezzogiorno* was not its inability to follow the development models of industrialized countries. On the contrary, it was due to the unfounded belief that the *Mezzogiorno* could follow them, thus ignoring its own specificity, and its own potential. Hence, Cassano and many other Italian social scientists propose "to give back dignity to the

South as an *author* of the thought, to bring to an end a period in which the South has been thought of by others" (Cassano 1996:10). In other words, the only workable development for southern Italy is to focus on the material and cultural resources of its territory and its people. Reconstructing and revitalizing its past can overcome obscurity and marginality by bringing to light events and circumstances previously neglected by national history and historicism.

Through this perspective, it can easily be understood that the construction of an identity can become an important resource for groups who compete for material and symbolic resources, by emphasizing traditional local culture. At the moment, this approach to recoup local specificity appears facilitated by some typical characteristics of the postmodern economy and aesthetics, in particular, by the commercial exploitation of *difference, specificity,* and *typicality* (see Rifkin 2000).

THE CASE OF SALENTO

Salento, a province in southeastern Italy, is a useful illustration of some of the characteristics of this phenomenon. Since the early 1990s, there have been many cultural movements aimed at re-establishing the heritage of the so-called *popular culture*, or repertoires of knowledge related either to material culture, or to forms of popular art and music. Within just a few years, Salento gained cultural interest, leading not only to an exponential rise in the number of tourists, but also to a representation (and self-representation) of its social fabric. These results are stimulating an unprecedented economic growth as well as a social and cultural dynamism. Both Salento's inhabitants and a wider public see the new cultural image as evidence that popular culture may represent an extraordinary "archive" of potential. Despite the dissatisfaction with many "post-national" paradigms circulating in current debates, this potential from the past can be tapped in the present for a better future. Thus, popular culture seems, in this case, to be a nexus for a new construction of identity, a repertoire of specificity that characterizes a territory and its population.

Several objections, however, rise up against the enthusiasm produced by this renaissance based on neo-community and identity issues.

First of all, it should be remembered that the rediscovery of popular culture is linked, in some ways, to its economic exploitation. A characteristic element of mass consumption in postmodern society is the attraction created by specificity, by peculiarity, by local typicality (Jameson 1991). If this assumption is true, the construction of an identity based on traditional culture could be induced and governed by the need to make profits. In this view, identity and community would be mere products of the cultural industry, doomed to be put on sale. Numerous European social scientists—such as Benjamin, Horkheimer, Adorno, and Morin—have highlighted this risk in their well-known analyses. In the case of Salento, debates on identity are clearly connected to "territorial marketing" and tourist promotion strategies. This process might lead to gradually construct an identity mainly based on expectations of the *leisure* market.

Secondly, local politicians often use popular culture as a way to promote their own visibility. For example, organizing events involving traditional music has become, in just a few years, a real trend for local politicians, who try to gain consensus this way. Quite often, the interest of political actors does not correspond with the promotion of social and economic development. On the contrary, it tends to hinder changes, to entrench a system of privileges, to affirm a hierarchy. In other words, it damages the identity that it declares to be protecting.

A well-built relation between the production of identity and social development can be only created when the values of identity are deep-rooted and shared. Otherwise, any strategic promotion of alleged local identities is nothing but a mystification, an *identity drift*, with detrimental effects both for social development and identity itself. The promotion of extemporary "identities" produces disorientation and leads towards development patterns alien to *genius loci*. Conversely, a development process founded on the centrality of the place, requires "a strong self-identification of the community that has settled, which takes possession of its own territory, identifying itself in the territory's history, environmental balance, cultural, economic, aesthetic and organizational values, in a growth process through the promotion of internal qualities" (Magnaghi 1994:33).

Alongside the risk of an instrumental use of popular culture, either for economic or political ends, there could also be a local, uncooperative attitude and a degeneration of identity. A repeated and ostentatious celebration of one's own specificity can actually create an enhancement of identity, including a perception of one's own "superiority," which is both unfounded and dangerous. Even though the risk of confrontational degeneration could be ignored, there is no doubt that the aspects discussed above could lead to an uncooperative attitude on a cultural level, thus causing regression.

How can we minimize these risks? Under what conditions does a process of construction of identity fail to cause an uncooperative attitude and repression of otherness? Helpful in clarifying this concept is the keyword *reflectivity*, which refers to the ability of social actors to have an "external" view of their own practices and their representations (see Bourdieu 1992). Usually, this is a task that scholars carry out in theoretical analyses. Since research "looks backward" and life "looks forward," social actors seldom have the opportunity to look at their practices and their representations. However, a culturally mature social context (and this not only refers to the education level) allows for observation and discussion of the practices generated within it.

Hence, in a certain sense, *reflectivity* is *deconstruction*. It constantly involves going back over the stages of the construction of identity; learning "not to take identity seriously"; learning not to forget its historical and artificial character. In short, it is about *understanding* identity, not experiencing it blindly "from within," but constructing it consciously, with a detached view, ready to challenge it and to consider it as an open, never-ending process. If a social context envisions a cultural sphere, active and open to challenges, with an authoritative and democratic political leadership, it has a good chance of using its own cultural identity, even by restoring traditional repertoires, as a resource for—and not as an obstacle to—social and economic development.

With about one million inhabitants, Salento functions in a sub-regional context, in which there are valuable instruments of cultural production facilitating an acceptable level of reflexivity. About 30,000 students are enrolled in the local university in Salento. Three city newspapers and five local broadcast networks constantly develop debates on local culture, on the production of identity, and on the use of popular culture. Certainly, in many instances, the rhetorical (and sometimes instrumental) use of these terms prevails. But the qualitative level of the discussion is usually satisfactory, because the subjects involved are often cultural operators, artists, and university professors. In other words, these are representatives of cultural elites who reject the strictly economic and political uses of the cultural products and of the concept of identity. Therefore, in the public sphere of Salento, the possibility exists for the creation of a good level of awareness concerning the scope, limits and risks of the celebration of local identity.

THE RESULTS OF AN EMPIRICAL STUDY

In August 2006, together with a group of six young scholars and two photographers[2], I conducted some exploratory research on the opinions and motivations of the audience at the most important ethno-musical festival in Salento (called "Notte della Taranta"), which attracts around 100,000 spectators each year, many of them coming from other Italian regions. About 150 interviews were carried out, which were then subjected to a qualitative analysis. The research aimed at assessing the capability of the audience to observe the event that it was witnessing. In other words, the analysis was aimed at understanding if the audience had an *external* and *critical* perception of the ethno-musical products and their celebration.

For about ten years, this festival has been intensely discussed (in TV programs, newspapers, universities, etc.) by cultural operators, artists, intellectuals and representatives of the political class. The often polemical stances concern two main themes. The first one refers to the meaning of tradition and its "normative" value. Some people assert that, starting from a "reified" concept of popular culture, a conservative—and possibly exegetic—attitude should be kept also in artistic performances. Starting from a processional and evolutionary conception of culture, other people argue that changes and "contaminations" of the ethnological heritage are acceptable and desirable. The second one refers to the risks of "exploitation" of popular culture, by means of its public use, especially by the political class.

The results of this research were encouraging. Most of the people interviewed perceived the event to be a great celebration, in which the reference to tradition enabled them to create a social tie, founded on the recognition of differences, on an inclusive, albeit temporary, community afflatus. Almost all interviewees had a decidedly aware cultural interest in the objective value of the music that they were listening to, and expressed criticism. Almost all of them immediately recognized the universal value of the peculiarity of local cultures and did not accept that there could be either a hierarchy of values or any local enhancement. Only a small minority of people attributed a parochial value to the celebration of traditional cultures, and considered it as evidence of the cultural primacy of one's own community.

---

[2] This research, which I coordinated, involved five graduate students in Sociology (Cosimo Botrugno, Marta Melgiovanni, Adriana Puliti, Federico Renna, Daniela Stabile), one graduate student in Cultural Heritage (Alessandra Guareschi) and two photographers (Paolo Benegiamo and Pierluigi Luceri).

The most common element in the interviewees' statements was the expectation of *authenticity*. Sometimes, they considered this element as negative, criticizing the expectations of authenticity attributed to the celebrations of ethno-musical heritage. They saw this element as essentially inconceivable, since it is a generally expressive mode. The semantics of authenticity, one could argue, are a mixture of rather different expectations because, actually, everyone expresses it using different terms and references (and more often than not, denies its foundations). Some people interpret authenticity as a "return to the past," others as a projection of the past to the future, and still others as a "link with the territory."

For many people, authenticity corresponds to the appreciation of the specific culture of local communities, in this way expressing their need for *cultural autonomy,* and their desire for a "repossession" of endangered forms and modes of expression. In many cases, the desire for celebration is expressed through popular music, as well as through other symbolic elements, such as "local wine." People perceive that they can abandon the commercial and consumerist movers of daily life and sociality. Accordingly, many of the interviewees expressed particular enthusiasm for an "authentic" celebration. For example, Marilena, a 58-year-old employee, stated:

> I am glad, because this is like a flush of youth, I mean, things are very old and all is very young at the same time. . . . People are happy to participate in it and, also, to enjoy it. There is a mixture of things, and this is pleasant.

Similarly, Ferdinando, a 24-year-old worker said:

> I like it, because it is a feast. There is *pizzica* playing [an ethno-musical genre of Salento]. I hoped to enjoy myself, as I did, to listen to music, good music, both to dance to and to listen to. I like people in Salento, I like their way of living and appreciating the things they have. Here there are a lot of these things, and they try to safeguard them . . . People are very fond of music, and then they drink to enjoy themselves and socialize.

Many of those interviewed clearly expressed their belief that the revival involved a relevant dimension of economic exploitation of the ethno-musical heritage. However, this was not always a radical criticism; it was often a risk evoked as a side effect of a phenomenon, but appreciated anyway. For example, Marco, a 34-year-old train driver, affirmed:

Like all other things that emerge as a result of tradition and culture, then inevitably business comes into play, and in that case nobody renounces money. At first, the culture, the music of the place, the food you eat are good, real. Then, a lot of people arrive, and a lot of money circulates, and the product is then commercialized.

In general, the particular festiveness of the social encounter was associated with the characteristics of the place (often referred to as an image of nativeness, of deep "rootedness in history"), and with influences linked to "culture" and to "tradition." These elements seemed to provide the encounter with a particular force, and a particular ability to generate social ties, albeit temporarily. In other words, it was not an ordinary feast, but a "qualified" feast, with particularly intense connotations.

Within the movers of the public, any attempt to identify the predominance of a "cultural" and esthetical interest or the attraction exerted by the feast and by sociality would be really arbitrary. On the contrary, what can be affirmed is that in the statements provided by those interviewed, sometimes we noticed the emergence of a cognitive link between the ethno-musical revival and elements—treated in a detached and critical way—of the tourist image of Salento. Other times there was a prevalence of a more "controlled" attitude and an explicit—even though generic—reference to elements deriving from demographic and ethnographic studies.

Generally speaking, the findings that emerged from this research show that the users of cultural traditions do not consider traditions and identity in terms of "absolute" differences. On the contrary, they seem to appreciate the perspective of recognition and comparison of differences and of peculiarities which are *plural* and *imperfect*, porous and overlapping with each other. In fact, the enjoyment of the feast is often accompanied by a detached or even critical attitude; the spectator believes to be experiencing a profit-oriented event.

If the main risks of the processes of the production of identity lie in the exploitation of traditions and in the trend towards closure and regression, the attitude of the public is certainly reassuring. The public does not see the celebration of traditions naively, and does not regard local identity as a cultural primacy of their community. Instead, there exists the desire to interpret the celebration of ethnological assets as a chance of acknowledgement, openness, and pluralism—or, rather, as a "feast of differences."

Although it was a limited study, the conclusions of this research are encouraging, because they suggest a way to achieve *cultural autonomy*.

This path offers simpler and more pleasant ways to know not only oneself but also others, putting aside the social passions that Georg Simmel held to be linked to *dispossession*: jealousy, envy and spite.

The unification of the world has not yet been accomplished. Perhaps, the Promethean project of assimilation of the world under the dominion of technology and market is still far from its catastrophic implementation. In the interstices of the globalized world there is still room to engage in dialogue and cultural autonomy. What we will become continues to be the child of what we want to become, and no social change is beyond our control.

References

Banfield, Edward C. 1950. *The Moral Basis of a Backward Society*. Glencoe, IL: The Free Press.

Bourdieu, Pierre. 1992. *An Invitation to Reflexive Sociology*. Chicago: University of Chicago Press.

Cassano, Franco. 1996. *Il Pensiero Meridiano*. Roma-Bari: Laterza.

Geertz, Clifford. 2000. *The Interpretation of Cultures*. New York: Basic Books.

Graziani, Augusto. 2000. *Lo Sviluppo dell'Economia Italiana: Dalla Ricostruzione alla Moneta Europea*. Torino: Bollati Boringhieri.

Jameson, Fredric. 1991. *Postmodernism, or The Cultural Logic of Late Capitalism*. Durham, NC: Duke University Press.

Magnaghi, Alberto. 1994. *Il Territorio dell'Abitare. Lo Sviluppo Locale Come Alternativa Strategica*. Milano: Franco Angeli.

Pizzorno, Alessandro. 2007. *Il Velo della Diversità. Studi Su Razionalità e Riconoscimento*. Milano: Feltrinelli.

Remotti, Francesco. 1996. *Contro l'Identità*. Roma-Bari: Laterza.

Rifkin, Jeremy. 2000. *The Age of Access: The New Culture of Hypercapitalism Where All of Life Is a Paid-for Experience*. New York: J.P. Tarcher/Putnam.

The Use of Cultural Heritage in Italy and in the United States

SARAH SICILIANO
University of Salento

What are today the historical meanings and functions of cultural heritage in the public sphere? What is the "use" of cultural heritage in Italy and in the United States, and what is its role in Italian and American culture? How, and to what extent, are Italy and the U.S. investing in their cultural heritage? To offer some insight into these questions, this paper examines cultural heritage as a narrative milieu, a space where several subjects constantly act and interact in time and space. As Michel de Certeau claims, "Imposed knowledge and symbolism are manipulated by those using them without having contributed to their creation," requiring the re-experienced cultural heritage to change and become a new "story" in order to continue through time (de Certeau 2005:67). What is the meaning of such usage other than, as de Certau says, the degree to which its user and how the product itself are assimilated? In the use of cultural heritage, the Italian and American models—although extremely valuable and interesting—both show some criticalities. This paper aims to outline several strategies for an appreciation of the cultural heritage in Italy and the United States, individuate their limits, and suggest a possible alternative scenario.

THE ITALIAN MODEL

With its artistic and historical heritage, Italy holds first rank in the world for tourist appeal. Italy lists 41 of the 830 UNESCO cultural heritage sites scattered among 138 countries, making it the country with the highest percentage.[1] We must, however, consider what makes Italian

---

[1] Based on the Convention Concerning the Protection of the World Cultural and Natural Heritage adopted in 1972, UNESCO selected 830 sites (644 cultural heritage sites, 162 natural sites, and 24

cultural heritage unique, as we cannot simply reduce it to a list of threatened areas or masterpieces to be defended and preserved. Instead, the uniqueness of Italian cultural heritage rests in an enormously rich continuum linking the masterpieces to the connective tissue of the hosting territory. Italy's appellation of "open-air museum" is a consequence of the awareness that Italian museums do not just casually gather collections of works of art, but "are born in, and nurtured by the very territory that generated them" (Settis 2005:74). As a consequence, the homeland perception of every Italian is shaped by classical culture, archeology, art, architecture, literature, music, and even landscapes and traditions. Museum collections reflect the history of the hosting places and territory, because every work belongs to this extensive interweaving in which it is set. This Italian peculiarity (so different from what happens at the J. Paul Getty Museum, or at the Metropolitan Museum, or at the Louvre, to cite just a few international museums), generates a unique perspective; it is the thread connecting the works exhibited in museums, kept in churches, in the streets, and linking towns and landscapes, that mainly determines the quantity and the quality of our cultural heritage.

The genetic code of the Italian model resides in this very perspective: in the appreciation of cultural heritage, born from a solidly rooted need for tutelage. Article IX of the Italian constitution reads, "The Republic promotes cultural development and scientific and technical research . . . It safeguards natural beauty and the historical and artistic heritage of the nation."[2] The fact that this article is among the first 12 articles of the Italian constitution under the section "Fundamental Principles" (a fact with very few analogies with constitutions of other countries) is of extreme relevance. As the former Italian President Carlo Azeglio Ciampi said, it is "an important indication of the *mission* of our country, of a way of thinking, and a way of life" (Ciampi 2003). Our Constitution, he continued, states that tutelage "must be understood not as passive protection, but in an active sense, that is, in function of the citizens' culture, it must make our heritage enjoyable by all." Thus, President Ciampi reminded us that Italian national identity is based on Italians' awareness of being keepers of a unique cultural heritage, a heritage that is, mainly, our costume (that is, our custom). "This is the Italian way of experiencing reality, giving it

---

mixed sites).

[2] This and all the following translations to English are mine.

significance, representing it, and, finally, communicating it.

Yet, Italy has so far been unable to develop its enormous potential. Beyond declarations, wishful thinking, and a few rare cases, Italy seems incapable of transforming its own cities from places to contemplate into growth opportunities for those regions. Italy does not yet know how to convert its own traditions into a role that could/should be offered by communication. Cultural heritage, in fact, exists not only for its expressive contents, but also (and mainly) in the very moment of its action and communication, that is, in its reception. Cultural heritage includes "social relations," for it exists in a larger context, where it encounters negative experiences (resistances, obstacles, sometimes oppositions), but also promises opportunities, successes, and acquisition of good practices (Toscano 2003). The more the community is able to give sense to cultural heritage, the more the latter reinforces the community's bonds.

Such an abundant European (and Italian in particular) cultural heritage finds its historical origin in the imprinting of a sapiential culture, where the culture producers worked for the court and therefore had to comply with the tastes and requests of their patrons. In the relationship between a rich patron and a cultivated protégé, the nobles bestowed support, friendship and protection on the literati or artists, who in turn provided advice, support and assistance through their works, offered to their patrons as a status acquisition. Intellectuals, sculptors, and artists have always been part of the retinue of the powerful. So ensconced, they could elaborate a universally acknowledged historical, political, and ethical influence. In Italy, therefore, cultural heritage assumed the historical function of representing power and/or the powerful in the eyes of their subjects. Historically, then, culture was not just a set of goods produced for mere pleasure or education, but also as a demonstration of authority and power to tame and govern the masses.

In the Italian tradition, cultural heritage was essentially an *instrumentum regni*: Romans built theaters and amphitheatres—monumental showplaces—as privileged means for imperial propaganda and a tangible display of power. Through them, Rome sought to become the cultural heart of the empire. These buildings were to be built only in those cities that Rome selected as centers of self-representation. In ancient Rome, although theatrical performances were held on the occasion of religious celebrations or funereal ceremonies, their sacred dimension was of secondary importance. Those performances were primarily intended as a *ludus*, an entertainment. The same was true with amphitheatres and their gladiatorial games, *venationes* (hunting enactments or fights between men and beasts), and, sometimes, *naumachie* (naval battles). In Rome, the organization of public displays at the State's expense was a political choice, originating from (and representing) the need for power. Admission was free and open to everybody.

As ancient Roman leaders knew, sapiential culture should not be limited to the dissemination and teaching of the inherent values of cultural heritage, and it should not be secluded in its ivory tower, considering conservation as an absolute value. This perspective could nurture a sense of death, and such a sense would plunge everyday life into a "sacred knowledge" by which everyday life would be, at the same time, merged with, and shattered by it.

On the other hand, the sacred dimension that culture acquired in Italy (finding its roots as early as in the pre-unification Italian States) determined a cultural and legal practice for the preservation and defense of cultural heritage.[3] Public provisions for art and culture preservation are an Italian distinctive feature: Italy was a model, in Europe at first and worldwide afterwards. To represent the idea of art preservation in its original context, Salvatore Settis cited an historical anecdote of the kingdom of Naples. Charles VII of Bourbon wore a Roman ring found in the excavations of Pompeii during his visit. The excavation had started under his order in 1748, with the goal of bestowing prestige to the royal family. When Charles VII moved to Naples in 1759 to become the new Spanish King, he handed over the kingdom of Naples to his son, Ferdinand. On this occasion, Charles VII also left to Ferdinand his ring because "it belongs to the king of Naples, not to the king of Spain." Today, that very ring is at the National Archeological Museum in Naples (Settis 2005:272).

If preservation and managing do not become components of a single process based on knowledge and promoting the appreciation and enjoyment of the country's artistic legacy, how can we optimize the precious inheritance of the "Italian model"? The subdivision and overlapping of national and regional competency is a criticality of Italy as a system, threatening Italian cultural heritage (it is quite difficult to define clearly who is competent to deal with what). That is why, in Italy, cultural

---

[3] Concerning the Italian tradition on preservation, see Settis 2005, especially pp. 199-205 and pp. 271-286 where Settis outlines the milestones of tutelage in Italy, from to pre-unification States to the present day.

heritage preservation remains confined to the protection of its original form for its enjoyment by a small circle of estimators. In so doing, however, cultural heritage risks becoming completely self-referential.

Centochiodi, a recent film by the Italian director Ermanno Olmi, shows, that "Although they are necessary, books do not speak by themselves [I libri, pur necessari, non parlano da soli]" (Olmi, opening epigraph). Olmi tells the story of a young university professor teaching history of religions at the University of Bologna. Rich, handsome, at the top of his career, the young professor rebels against "a world made out of paper" where books become more important than the message they carry or than those to whom they are addressed. He therefore decides to change his life with an extreme act: he nails to the floor and to the desks the valuable manuscripts of the library of the University of Bologna, and he gets rid of all his wealth to seek refuge, on the run, on the banks of the river Po. Here he is born to a new life, living in simplicity, in communion with the local people, recovering "to be saved" the values that give meaning to life. The police eventually find this "new Christ" and arrest him. In front of the police officer, a modern Pontius Pilate, the former professor declares that he is *definitely accountable but not guilty*, because *all the books of the world are not worth a good coffee with a friend*.

The message of *Centochiodi* is that books, if they don't become the embodiment of life, if they are kept on a shelf as if on a pedestal, and are considered more important than the message they carry, then they are mere objects, firmly nailed to an useless knowledge. Similarly, if cultural heritage is held captive by its own sacred aura, if it is unable to emancipate and actualize reproduction, meeting the needs of its audience in the given circumstances, is nothing but self-referential[4]. The everyday use of books as a form of cultural heritage must be through their continuation in the use of words. Using one of the foundations of structuralism—Saussure's distinction between *langue* (a system of signs and social abstractions) and *parole* (a sound and individual act)—English philosopher Gilbert Ryle compares *langue* to capital, and words to the operations the capital makes possible. In case of the use (and, therefore, of the consumer), it is necessary to transform the words in the books into actions, translate cultural heritage into everyday life. Any kind of communication involves a commitment, and, therefore, imposes not only

---

[4] On the aura of the work of art, see Benjamin 2000.

a behavior of substance, but also a relational one (Ryle 1968:109-116).

As a result, Italians are neither always able to consider cultural heritage as a potential actor in a new standard of development, nor to look at it as an opportunity for social and economic expansion along with the social and civil growth of the community, and thus a tool for urban upgrading. Even when good projects are realized, they typically lack a unifying, common policy. Italian institutions find it difficult (if not impossible) to understand the actual potential of their extraordinary cultural heritage. Its potentiality does not necessarily lie in the capacity of attracting tourism. Instead, if correctly managed, Italian cultural and artistic heritage, would allow the transformation of the territory from a resource into a product. In so doing, our territory would become an identifiable subject, it would develop an identity of its own and, by creating a network for supporting the national territorial system, it would become a reference point for generating wealth. In other words, cultural heritage assumes a *hub* function. In computer science, a *hub* is the sorting fulcrum of the network. In this form, cultural heritage could attract and manage resources, knowledge, and competences beyond the strictly cultural ones. From these we must begin proposing, planning, building, and disseminating products and services on a local, national, and international scale.

THE U.S. MODEL

Unlike Italy, the United States cannot claim a rich cultural and artistic heritage. UNESCO lists "only" 20 U.S. sites out of a total of 830 world heritage sites. Famous U.S. museums exhibit mainly contemporary works of art, or objects that seldom illustrate the story of their territory. However, these museums are true cultural incubators because Americans learn how to manage their economic resources, investing in culture as a vehicle for development. It is often necessary to acquire original works of art that, although not necessarily historically bound to the territory, are able to interact with it. There are plenty of resources. Sometimes, American museums exhibit stolen works of art, objects of legal contention with the countries from where they have been illegally exported. A good example is the extravagant Getty Center in Malibu, California (an architectural copy of the Villa dei Papiri in Ercolano, Italy), which hosts some of the most important exhibits of Greek, Roman, and Etruscan antiquities in the U.S. For years, the Getty Museum legally purchased works of art stolen from Italy and Greece. With Marion True, former director of the Getty Museum, on trial in a Rome court, Francesco Rutelli, Italian minister for "Beni e Attività Culturali," tried to recover 52 Italian works of art illegally exported. After a long negotiation, Michael Brand, present director of the Getty Museum, and Minister Rutelli signed an agreement on December 31, 2007, for returning 40 Italian works of art.

Among the remaining Italian works of art in the Getty Museum catalog, the "Venus Morgantina"—a statue sculpted in Sicily in the fifth century B.C. (2,400 years ago) and purchased by the Getty Museum in 1988 for $18 million—will be returned in 2010 to be displayed in series of exhibitions. According to a joint note of the Italian ministry for "Beni e Attività Culturali" and of the Getty Trust, the fate of bronze statue known as "Victorious Youth" (attributed to Lysippos and depicting a young victorious athlete) found in Italy in 1964 and "purchased" by the Getty Museum in 1977, depended on the resolution of the legal controversy. As an exchange for these restitutions, the Italian government signed a collaboration agreement with the Getty Museum, providing for loans of important works of art, joint exhibitions and projects for research, conservation and restoration (de Luca). How, though, can we interpret these developments?

Kwame Anthony Appiah, a Princeton University professor of philosophy, recently wrote that since cultural heritage belongs to the history of humankind, their exhibition in important international museums is right and proper (Appiah 2006). Many important museums are "globalized" and thus now attract a large number of visitors. Some of the most famous museums in the world became multi-millionaire enterprises by adopting management techniques and strategies acknowledging culture as an instrument for economical guidance. This consequence corroborates Appiah's viewpoint, but it also implies the decontextualization of works of art and the loss of their histories. This is a typical characteristic of "liquid modernity," marked by the central role of consumption action.

How, then, can the better management of cultural heritage in the U.S. possibly have a high economic return? It is surely not with museum earnings. Although museums did become multinational repositories of culture, their maintenance mainly depends on charity and their investments in stocks and bonds. In the U.S., culture produces a remarkable tourist flow and, as a consequence, enriches the territory. The induced economy that culture produces is, therefore, an indirect one. No museum in the world is self-sufficient. Museums only meet 30 percent of their expenses by direct returns (tickets, merchandising, refreshment sales, etc.). Funds for the remaining 70 percent either come from the State (as in the case of the Louvre in Paris), or from private donors thanks to a charity system enhanced by substantial tax benefits. The latter is the case of the Getty Center in Malibu, where donors' funds provide capital for stock investments. In 2006, this investment policy, initiated by Paul Getty in order to guarantee the survival of the museum bearing his name, earned the museum $275,275,000 against its expenses of $293,568,000.[5]

Settis locates the "financial secret" of U.S. museums not, as commonly believed, in their being private institutions, but in the practice of investing charitable donations in the stock market. The U.S. museum system is not profit oriented. In fact, U.S. museums are *non-profit* institutions; their activities generate losses, not profits, and they can only work when they have a strong capital base behind them. Accordingly, this "American model" is unworkable in Italy, where the system is totally different and the private sector participates only when a profit can be realized, thereby rendering the American practice inapplicable (Settis 2005:42).

Evidence of this contrast can be found in the international mobilization of the directors of the most important museums of the world against the provisions on cultural heritage privatization provided for in the Italian Financial Act of 2002, an event that received universal media attention. Meeting in New York, these directors drafted a resolution against this Italian legislation that entrusted to the private sector "the whole management of the service for the public enjoyment of cultural heritage." Although sharing the desire for greater autonomy for Italian museums, the directors argued "Although American museums are mainly private, and not public institutions, they are neither managed as private enterprises, nor entrusted—completely or partially—to private enterprises, and are managed in a completely *non-profit* regime." Therefore, they urged the Italian government to assume its responsibilities and "move with the due prudence before transferring museum management to private enterprises" (*Il Giornale dell'Arte* 2001:1).

Although good foreign practices can serve as models, these cannot be simply imported "as they are" without recognizing that they must be

---

[5] Data from Foundation Center. Knowledge to build on http://foundationcenter.org. Retrieved August 27, 2007. Also, see Settis 2005, p. 75.

applied in a different context. What Italy could do, following the "American model," is to encourage donations by means of attractive tax benefits. The Getty Museum's experience exemplifies this model. As Settis (himself one of its directors) explained, it evolved into a complex system of research, education, and preservation institutes thanks to a successful policy of investments. In a brief span of time, the Getty Museum managed to increase its initial patrimony of $750 million to $7 billion, notwithstanding the purchase of the new place, and of several paintings, books, and archive material" (Il Giornale dell'Arte 2002:1, 8-10).

We must analyze the "structure museum" in the U.S. from the perspective of a long-lasting cultural model, born in a social system based—as Tocqueville described—on democracy. Today, Tocqueville still can provide useful hints to help our understanding of the differences between the European and American models, including their diversities of cultural life. The liberal American Dream that Tocqueville analyzed is today still a cultural norm, even though Tocqueville belongs to another era. Gordon Wood reminds us that, as Joyce Appleby recently showed, the generation that dominated American life in the 1830s popularized the concept of American identity, of American modernization, and of American generosity, one that is still so powerful and popular that it is virtually impossible to deconstruct (Wood 2001).

The influence the institution of democracy had on the U.S. cultural model is of significance here, as Tocqueville explained:

> The Anglo-Americans settled in a state of civilization, upon that territory which their descendants occupy; they had not to begin to learn, and it was sufficient for them not to forget . . . Education has taught them the utility of instruction, and has enabled them to transmit that instruction to their posterity. In the United States society has no infancy, but it is born in man's estate (Tocqueville I:316).

> When men living in a democratic state of society are enlightened, they readily discover that they are confined and fixed by any limits which force them to accept their present fortune. They all therefore conceive the idea of increasing it (Tocqueville II:38).

This ideal condition encouraged the formation of a frame of mind nurturing a market (and a breed of consumers) for cultural products. This is also the reason why U.S. cultural producers deal directly with the public. Democracy made possible the percolation of humanities in the industrial classes and, vice versa, of the industrial spirit in the literary production and in literary tastes. In Europe, however, the survival of cultural producers depended on aristocratic patronage. Tocqueville's analysis shows that Americans devote more attention to practical sciences than to theory. Very few devote themselves to purely theoretical aspects of human sciences, unless the theory is functional to practical application. Industrial classes are not particularly refined or sophisticated, and are easily satisfied. The case of aristocracies, where readers are few and more demanding, is entirely different. The democratization of culture put culture through an industrial process that perverted its nature, changing its function and its expressive formats. This is why the cultural product increases its value through quantity, rather than quality, through novelty rather than tradition. Tocqueville used the example of an artisan who

> strives to invent methods which may enable him not only to work better, but more quickly and more cheaply; or, if he cannot succeed in that, to diminish the intrinsic qualities of the thing he makes, without rendering it wholly unfit for the use for which it is intended. When none but the wealthy had watches, they were almost all very good ones: few are now made which are worth much, but everybody has one in his pocket. Thus the democratic principle not only tends to direct the human mind to the useful arts, but it induces the artisan to produce with great rapidity many imperfect commodities, and the consumer to content himself with these commodities (Tocqueville, II:50).

For this reason, in the U.S., along with an increase in competition and productivity, the unit value of goods tends to decrease. Becoming entrepreneurs is easier in the U.S. than in Europe, because, paradoxically, U.S. entrepreneurs have a high rate of failure.[6] In the same way, cultural heritage is linked to market issues, involving both the economic value of cultural heritage in the U.S. and its management by marketing principles.

A POSSIBLE SOLUTION

The Italian and the U.S. cultural models both show important criticalities with negative (although different) outcomes. However, if we examine the specific crystallizations of these two rigid models, something

---

[6] For a recent analysis of U.S. society, see Parrillo 2007. Moving from historical and sociological research on the U.S, Parrillo confutes the stereotypes and the wrong knowledge sedimented in the *opinio communis*.

new emerges. Jeremy Rifkin—a modern counterpart to Tocqueville—suggests in his new book—bearing the provocative title *The European Dream*—a scenario that may offer a way out from the dead end.

Beginning his analysis in European cultural, scientific, and artistic history, Rifkin points out that, while Europe promotes sustainable development, social integration, and collective responsibility, the United States favors individual wealth, unlimited economic growth, and the protection of private interest. According to Rifkin, a new dream is spreading through the world: the European Dream. This is the idea of an innovative new super-nation, centered on community, on the acceptance of cultural diversities, and on the concept of sustainable development. In this perspective, it would be possible to integrate individual free will with a community-oriented sense of responsibility. Rifkin sees Europe as an immense open-air laboratory, where everyone wants to be connected to a global network without, at the same time, losing the sense of a cultural and local identity.

Such is the aim of *Europedia*, an experience of interactive public communication established to celebrate the 50th anniversary of the European Community. *Europedia* is a "gymnasium" for active and creative citizenship, where it is possible to explore and try the idea of a languages-united Europe via the sensitivity of the new media, in real and virtual situations. Real spaces in the piazzas of Rome, Turin, and Lecce hosted interactive video and installations of interaction design to offer a direct, instantaneous story of their construction, without leaving any space to imagination so to give the visitor the impression of a direct physical experience. The virtual public space of the Internet allows registered users to tell their own stories of the places they know, live in, or visit. Thus, participants generate a shared treasure providing sense and significance to a Europe in constant evolution built by its citizens from below, and not imposed from above (http://www.europedia.it, Retrieved September 3, 2007).

To Europeans, liberty is not synonymous with autonomy. The meaning of liberty resides, instead, in the social network. For Europeans, to desire the quality of life in the present time means to live in a sustainable connection with the land, and, therefore, to grant the needs of present generations without compromising those of future generations. In such a context, the appreciation of cultural heritage becomes a fundamental asset, linking economic growth to the dynamic balance of the environment, and social cohesion.

It would appear that cultural heritage must break free from the two reference models (the Italian and the American), in order to be reborn. If we apply Rifkin's operational modality to cultural heritage, we can see culture as a "reservoir of interferences" (to use an expression of the Italian sociologist Alberto Abruzzese) that belongs to experiential culture, a milieu of critical action rather than of critical thinking. In other words, culture is not the product of the values of stability and continuity of modernity with its social, political, religious, ethical, legal, esthetical, technological, and media traditions dictating *critical thought,* but rather, it is a context comprised of experiences dropped in the consumption dynamics of the cultural industry (*critical action*) (Abruzzese 2003:128). The concept of culture as "reservoir of interferences" is increasingly fueled by everyday life and consumptions, and allows the consumer to inhabit the process and to participate in it. The same concept is not limited to visual contemplation, but also involves a direct knowledge and experience of the cultural object, plunging into the citizens' lives, rather than the latter into the process, thus recalling the need to transform the resource into a product. Beginning this transformation process, therefore, must coincide from the moment the potential visitors or "non-visitors" leave their homes. We cannot/must not exclude the sociodemographic reality that, although not a consumer of the cultural product, the public may be involved if duly stimulated.

The territory should be the hub of a network capable of producing value, attracting knowledge, and shaping a wide range of cultural competences (i.e., not only limited to the cultural sector, but to its related sectors as well). This is exactly what the Rete delle Città Strategiche (RECE) is trying to do. RECS is an initiative of the mayor of Florence, Leonardo Domenici, that attracted the participation of 21 Italian municipalities and the attention of many European ones (including Monaco, Birmingham, Prague, Edinburgh, Stockholm, and Bremen). The RECE aim is to unite the municipalities who adopt the "Piano Strategico" as an innovative instrument for the governance of territorial development processes by connecting the social actors with the political ones, choosing governance goals, initiating shared processes for territorial transformation, and attracting local investors to compete at a supra-local level. Above all, the "Piano Strategico" plans and recommends possible long-term scenarios for cities, understood in this broader sense of shared, participatory values.

On January 18, 2008, Tuscany became the first region in Italy to pass a law on participative development methods for its territory. This grassroots participation in territory planning is a democratic procedure allowing citizens to know, evaluate, and comment on the choices at an early, pre-decision stage. By thinking collectively about territory and sharing the needs for the public good, citizens turn from a mere audience into active protagonists. Thus, the creation of a network not only contributes to a sharing of knowledge, but also allows a relational exchange. This relational perspective, thanks to the activation of a set of cross-actions favoring a full-scale economy, is able to obtain satisfactory results with a minimum waste of resources. If our goal as Italians is to be increasingly competitive with other reference systems, we must think according to an interaction perspective and emerge as an integrated system.

Experiential culture is an instrument that can enhance our heritage. This does not imply either the destruction of identity or of the historical and cultural integrity of places through harmful interventions, but it does not suggest embalming the heritage either. Imagine, for example, an ancient piazza, historically, a meeting point or a place devoted to sharing experiences. Why, therefore, it should be "defended" from, say, a concert? Was it not in an empty Piazza della Signoria in Florence that the Neptune fountain was vandalized in 2005? Such destruction never happened when the piazza hosted public concerts. Historical piazzas, like any other place needing to "stay alive," must accept modern social usage. A piazza, kept as a museum for self-exhibition, risks a frozen fate.

How, then, should the U.S. and Italy look at culture and cultural heritage? If we adopt Rifkin's point of view, we can look at cultural heritage as at a narrative milieu. A constant "invention of everyday life" intrinsically belongs to every cultural heritage. Not unlike the social ones, cultural heritage codes "are constantly modified by their users into metaphors and ellipsis of their poaching" (de Certeau 2005:19). Moving from this condition of "poachers," the use of cultural heritage allows the recycling of cultural heritage and, therefore, its reconstruction in a new set of experiences. Cultural heritage then becomes a dynamic organism, always ready to reinvent itself under the solicitation of interferences, hints, and external good practices. In such a process, however, a culture of appreciation must coexist with a culture of safeguard. Together, appreciation and safeguard will respond to the new needs of contemporary life, thus increasing knowledge opportunities.

The awareness of cultural heritage, from a plain collection of knowledge, becomes an internalization of meanings, fusion/confusion, definition/redefinition, and birth/rebirth through use and consumption (de Certeau 2001:14). In the process of construction and deconstruction, reproduction becomes an autonomous entity, a subject of social interaction, a carrier of significance.[7] This significance can produce wealth, relational networks, and sustainable development. Representation forms of cultural heritage may change, but their substance cannot. A good example is the "White night" phenomenon, an experience born in Berlin in 1997 (although the first real "White night" was in Paris twinning with Rome in 2002) and repeated every year since.

The "White night" is a collective experience permitting an experience and view of the city with different eyes. For this special event, the city stays open all the night long from evening to morning. Night, obscurity, and everything that symbolically "darkens" melt along unusual paths, marked by lights and sounds not only as a symbolic opening, but as a reality. At the same time, various events (art, music, performances, solidarity, sports, shopping), and a variety of activities target a diverse public. The phenomenon of the "White night" spread worldwide to many locales of various sizes. In particular, small municipalities adapted the "White night" to their own size and specificity.

For example, Melpignano di Lecce, Italy, hosts the internationally renowned "notte della taranta," presenting literary meetings, art exhibitions, theatre performances, and concerts utilizing electronic music and reggae rhythms revisited through "tarantismo" sonorities. The "notte della taranta," now a "glocal" event, a local event on an international scale (the event is broadcast live and worldwide on Puglia Channel), revives the myth of "tarantismo" that has characterized Salento since the middle ages. According to this myth, the rhythm of the "pizzica" had therapeutic effect on the victim of the bite of the "taranta" (a big black poisonous spider, whose bite provokes a convulsive illness, similar to epilepsy). Thus, dancing to the rhythm of the tambourine was a moment of liberation from internal conflicts and anguish. Through dance, it was possible to get rid of the daily difficulties of a poor life, marked by work

---

[7] On the relationship of author and public, see in particular Barthes 1977; Foucault 1979, pp. 141-60; Tota 2003, especially pp. 21-24.

in the fields and by the repression of sexual instincts. The risks connected to the translation of "tarantismo" in a modern key and its inclusion in the media, lead to an important question: has the "tarantismo" become a political instrument for the assertion of our real or supposed authenticity and authority? As the Frankfurt School claims, only by analyzing phenomena in their entirety, by having a complete perception of facts, by becoming aware of the risk of commercialization and spectacularization of culture, and by developing a clear critique of each of its parts, will we be able to analyze mass society, and to understand what must be done to overcome culture commercialization.

In everyday reality, we must appropriate cultural heritage, learn how to translate/transform it into action, dwell in it, and live it. Of course, everyone will do it in different ways because each person's history is different, and so is each one's reference context. Also, the application of Rifkin's perception to the use of cultural heritage is not without difficulties, weaknesses, sometimes even hypocrisies. It is an ambitious and long-term project that rightly Rifkin defined as "a dream," expressing his desire for its further debate. What is important is offering humanity a new and daring vision of the future, matching the challenge of a "glocal" society bringing together every locale's cultural identity so that the former experiences the latter.

References

Abruzzese, Alberto, 2003. *Voce: Critica* in: *Lessico della Comunicazione*, Roma: Meltemi.

Appiah, Kwame Anthony. 2006. *Cosmopolitanism: Ethics in a World of Strangers*. New York: W.W. Norton & Co.

Barthes, Roland. 1977. *Image Music Text*, Glasgow: Fontana-Collins.

Benjamin, Walter. [1955] 2000. *L'Opera d'Arte nell'Epoca della sua Riproducibilità Tecnica*, Torino: Einaudi.

Ciampi, Carlo Azeglio. 2003. "Benemeriti della Cultura e dell'Arte," Palazzo del Quirinale, Rome. http://www.quirinale.it. Retrieved August 24, 2007.

de Certeau, Michel. [1990] 2005. *L'Invenzione del Quotidiano*, Roma: Edizioni Lavoro.

De Luca, Maria Novella. 2007. "Accordo Fatto con il Getty Museum: Torna la Venere, il Lisippo Ancora No." *La Repubblica*, 2 agosto.

Foucault, Michel. [1969] 1979. "What is an Author?" in *Textual Strategies*, edited by Josui. V. Harari. Ithaca, NY: Cornell.

Il Giornale dell'Arte. 2001. "Appello dei Direttori dei Più Grandi Musei del Mondo contro le Norme sui Beni Culturali Contenute nella Finanziaria 2002." November, p. 1.

—. 2002. "Battaglie senza Eroi." November, pp. 1. 8-10.

Olmi, Ermanno. 2007. *Centochiodi*. Mikado, 2007.

Parrillo, Vincent N. 2007. *Diversità in America*, Milano: Franco Angeli.

Rifkin, Jeremy. [2004] 2005. *Il Sogno Europeo. Come l'Europa Ha Creato una Nuova Visione del Futuro che*

Sta Lentamente Eclissando il Sogno Americano, Milano: Oscar Mondadori.

Ryle, Gilbert. 1968. *Use, Usage and Meaning*. Pp. 109-116, in *The Theory of Meaning*, edited by G.H.R. Parkinson. Oxford: Oxford University Press.

Settis, Salvatore. 2005. *Battaglie senza Eroi: I Beni Culturali tra Instituzioni e Profitto*, Milano: Mondadori Electa.

de Tocqueville, Alexis. [1835:I-1840:II] 1994. *Democracy in America*. New York: Alfred Knopf.

Toscano, Mario Aldo. 2003. "Per una Sociologia dei Beni Culturali." *Sociologia e Ricerca Sociale* 71:1-37 (ora anche in: Sul Sud. Materiali per lo studio della cultura e dei Beni culturali, Milano-Pontedera: Jaca Book/Il Grandevetro.

Tota, Anna Lisa. 2003. *Sociologie dell'arte: Dal Museo Tradizionale all'Arte Multimediale*, Roma: Carocci, in part. pp. 21-24.

Wood, Gordon S. 2001, "Tocqueville's Lesson: Democracy in America. *The New York Review of Books* 48(8): May 17.

Globalization and Negotiated Global Awareness: Whither Individualization?

INO ROSSI
St. John's University

Ulrich Beck, Wolfgang Bonss, and Christopher Lau (2003) deal with globalization in the context of risk society and second modernity, focusing, in particular, on the twin processes of 'globalization' and 'individualization.' This work locates the origins of the second modernity in the 1960s and characterizes it as constituted by three processes.

First, a *multiplicity of boundaries* emerged between social spheres, between nature and society, between science and superstition, between life and death, between nation-states, between the national and international, between 'us' and 'others.' As a result, many choices of boundaries became possible as well as conflicts over the drawing of boundaries (2003:19). Second, *multiple rationalities* (or multiple claims to knowledge), that is, extra-scientific criteria of knowledge gained recognition and, as a result, many alternative boundaries between the various forms of knowledge as well as between science and politics became possible. Third, because of this socio-cultural fragmentation, a *quasi-subject* emerged. The subject is no longer a master of the environment: the individual does not know to which group he/she belongs and what the boundaries of one's own responsibility are. Yet, the subject must quickly select from among the many choices continuously appearing within a fragmented social environment. The subject can do this only 'reflexively.'

This term goes back to the reflexive theories of the second modernity of Scott Lash, Anthony Giddens, and Ulrich Beck who share some points in common, but also differ in others; I focus on Beck's version. In Beck's opinion, during the first modernity, or the modernity of the industrialization and nation-state, social institutions were stable and clearly delineated; this was the era of 'reflectivity' when the subject could subsume a clearly determinable object with certainty.

With the break of the second modernity, characterized by cultural uncertainties and multiplicity of boundaries (a point on which postmodernists concur), a "reflexive" realization emerged that mastery of the environment is impossible. Individual and institutional decisions presuppose that new boundaries have been redrawn, but these are fictive boundaries that are treated as if they were true for practical purposes. [*We have here fictive social relations and a fictive social structure.*] The subject is left only with a 'reflexive' capability, capable only of immediate, quick, autonomous, and indeterminate reflexes, given the continuous pressure to make new and quick decisions under conditions of socio-cultural fragmentation. Like a *bricoleur a' la* Levi-Strauss, the subject is continuously combining new alliances and construing activities without time or even the possibility of being reflective. [*We have here an a-cognitive combinatorics.*]

Since social institutions no longer have any firm boundaries, the subject faces a multiplicity of inclusionary and exclusionary practices, a multiplicity of ways in which things can be bounded together: hence, the subject's knowledge can only be probabilistic and possibilistic (Beck, et al. 2003:23). The subject can no longer be understood as an autonomous subject, but only in terms of networks and interaction. What is for one individual the setting up of boundaries, for another individual can be an overstepping of boundaries [*relativization of social structure*]. "Individualization" deepens asymmetries and increases impossibilities for another individual [*chaotic social structure*]. Since the subject no longer knows the boundaries of individual responsibility, ethical dilemmas can be only collectively decided on an arbitrary basis [*collective ethical relativism*].

The new "quasi-subject" that replaced the stable and unchanging subject of the first modernity is a fictive decision-maker and the author of one's own biography. The new 'reflexive subject' is both the result as well as the producer of its own network and situation; one is both a sovereign and prisoner of one's own decisions and the decisions of others. "Subjectivity is a product of self-selected networks, which are developed, through self-organization, into spheres that enable self-expression, and reinforce it through public recognition. Both the self and the public develop in tandem" (Beck et al. 2003:25-26). [*We have here a co-constitutiveness of the '(reflexive) subject' and 'the public' through self-organizing networks!*] There is more to come: the self and the public are blurred: "The subject becomes part of a self-selected network which allows connection and communication, but also makes it the object of choices and decisions of others. The subject is no longer the planner and ruler of its own life, guided by pre-given principles. [*Here the overarching influence of neoliberal ideology is momentarily forgotten*!!] On the contrary, the subject is transformed into a constitutive part of a context that determines its subjectivity and within which it exercises joint decision-making power. [*How can a context of blurred relations be a determining co-constitutive power of the subjectivity? In what sense can blurred relations have a self-organizing power and how can they be co-decision makers with the subject when the subject is itself part of the self-selected network?*] Beck makes another leap. "Quasi-subjectivity, thus, describes a situation of socially constructed autonomy that is understood and experienced as such" (p. 26). [*Subjectivity is reduced to or made a part of self-constructed, blurred and ever changing social relations. We have a total relativization of the subjectivity and of the social structure! How can a 'reflexive' subjectivity experience a 'socially constructed autonomy"?*] At this point, one is tempted to ask whether we can find anybody who thinks that Beck's fragmented and blurred social reality helps explain the determined leadership, ideology, and strategies of al Qaeda and other terrorist groups. [For an essay on this topic see Knorr's essay in Rossi 2007.]

Earlier, Beck—together with E. Beck-Gernsheim (2002)—introduced the *deus ex machina* of the "self-culture" seemingly to fill the vacuum left by the relativized subjectivity and atomized social structure. But these two authors extend their relativizing discourse also to the notion of culture. Self-culture is nothing more than "the adventurous search of the many for a 'life' of their own" (p. 42). [*How is this conceivable, if there are no longer autonomous or "reflective" subjects?*] Beck & Beck-Gernsheim explain that "self-culture is unpredictable both for oneself and for others." [*Hence not much guidance and certainty is introduced by the concept of 'self-culture.'*] This *deus ex machina* is conceived as some sort of a third sector that differs from politics and economics, "a self-authorizing, self-referential sphere," "an autonomous logic of self-organization distinct from the other two" [namely, the political and economic institutions] (p. 43). "Self-culture means detraditionalization, release from pre-given certainties and supports. Your life becomes in principle a risky venture" (p. 50). "With the emergence of a self-culture, it is rather a lack of social structures which establishes itself as the basic feature of the social structure . . . the image develops of an ambivalent society without social structures" (p 51).

[*One has difficulty seeing how any kind of self-organizing logic is possible in a fragmented society that lacks clearly definable social structures!*]

Cut off from clearly delineated social institutions—family, ethnicity, class—the individual finds oneself in an existential uncertainty (p. 210). [*This seems to contradict the notion of a self-organizing logic!*] I don't think that Beck can produce constructive concepts after he has introduced 'individualization' that equates quasi-subjectivity with the atomization of social structure. The old concept of identity—together with class, family, ethnic group, and state—have been 'zombied' by Beck. Can his theorizing save his own concept of 'individualization" from a 'zombie' status?

THEORETICAL AND EMPIRICAL CRITIQUES

In a recent work I have shown, among other things, that Beck's notion of second modernity is based on a 'straw-man' definition of nation-state and first modernization (Rossi 2008). His notion of first modernity and related clarity of scientific criteria and institutional boundaries ignores the abundant literature on anomie, alienation, and the disruptive consequences of colonialism on local institutions. [For an example of such critique, see Rossi 2008: last chapter.] A sharp distinction between first and second modernity is based on a lack of understanding of sociological research. More importantly, recent historical trends amply document that, far from blurring national and ethnic boundaries, globalization is fueling strong nationalisms, ethnic struggles and religious extremisms: socio-cultural boundaries have been demarcated with a new vigor.

The three co-authors of the 2003 article also misunderstand the Levi-Straussian combinatorics to which they refer, when they explain the dynamics of the 'quasi-subject'. In fact, the 'salvage mind' of aboriginal people operates according to the rules of a concrete logic, a logic that produces systematic classifications of animal species and social groups (Levi-Strauss 1966; Rossi 1974, 1982).

It is telling that our three authors announced fifteen research projects to empirically determine the extent of epistemological uncertainty, social ambiguities and the political economy of uncertainty. None of these three authors have replied to my inquiry about their research findings nor have I seen any such findings published.

Meanwhile, empirical refutations of Beck's notion of individualization have begun to appear on the basis of European surveys and "World Value Surveys"—the latter been conducted in 80 percent of the world's countries. Metka Mencin Ceplak (2006) reports that 60 percent of the Slovenian youth placed at the top of their ranks "health, friendship, family and a secure family life, freedom and independence and global peace," and, at the same time, they expressed a "relatively high degree of optimism about the future" (Ceplak 2006:294).

Reliance on the family and optimism about the future are consistent with other self-expressive orientations of people amply documented in the adult population of post-industrial societies by the World Values Surveys (http://www.worldvaluessurvey.com/). (See Inglehart and Welzel 2005:2).

This massive cross-national survey data show that "rising levels of existential security and autonomy" lead people to emphasize self-expression, individual liberty, individual autonomy, freedom of expression, and civil and political liberties that constitute democracy. "In short, socio-economic modernization brings the objective capabilities that enable people to base their lives on autonomous choices" (Inglehart and Welzel 2005:2-3).

> Never before in history have the masses experienced levels of existential security comparable with those that have emerged in postindustrial societies . . . This unprecedented high degree of existential security enables people to focus increasingly on goals beyond immediate survival (pp. 28, 45, 56).

Let us examine a few other European studies that have dealt in an explicit way with Beck's theses. Chtouris et al. (2006) conducted structured interviews with a random sample of 353 young Greeks ranging from ages 15 to 29 and found that

> . . . education is viewed by Greek young respondents as the most important means for social and professional integration. *Family* proves to be of almost equal importance for Greek young people. Their social capital consists of family, relatives and friends (p. 307).

These authors explicitly state that their findings are at odds with Beck's individualization and uncertainty thesis.

> In contrast to some observations that emphasize both individualization of the risk and reflexivity and in response to the pressure exercised on young people for more labor flexibility and more geographical and professional mobility, the case of Greek youth demonstrates a strong form of family solidarity (p. 319).

A more direct test of Beck's theory is provided by Paul de Beer (2007), who begins by citing studies that show that the Netherlands is one of the most liberal, progressive and post-modernist countries. He conceptualizes "individualization" as a combination of three trends: detraditionalization, emancipation, and heterogenization. *Detraditionalization* means the decreasing adherence of individuals to traditional institutions as measured by membership in the nuclear family, churches, trade unions and political parties. *Emancipation* means the lessening of the influence of social groups and institutions on the attitudes of individuals, as measured by any decrease or increase of predictability of people's attitudes and behaviors on the basis of their 'objective characteristics (sex, age, marital status, religious affiliation, and level of education). *Heterogenization* indicates individual attitudes and behavior, resulting in a greater *freedom of choice* in four major life events: the choice of university studies, the choice of a job, the decision to marry, and the age of giving birth to a first child. These indicators were measured at two different times, in data collected in the 1970s and 1980s and in data collected from 2000 to 2002, by the Dutch Social and Cultural Planning Office on the cultural changes in the Netherlands. Only the detraditionalization trend found support in the data and not the emancipation and heterogenization trends.

This empirical test of Beck's theory is significant for at least three reasons: first, it makes use of a precise and quantified measure of individualization; second, the theory is tested with a population from an advanced and progressive country; third, the data are from a random sample of the total population rather than just the youth.

Mark Banks (2006) examined the activities of Manchester's entrepreneurs who worked in cultural industries and found that these entrepreneurs shared an abundance of collective memories and experiences that were "cultivated through a historical immersion in Manchester's various social, political and cultural 'scenes.'" The data suggested "that localities may not only provide cultural entrepreneurs with economic advantages and/or aesthetic inspiration (as is conventionally argued), but might potentially act as a framework for the articulation of moral-political and social values in the course of cultural work" (p. 466). The authors conclude, "These cultural entrepreneurs are pursuing careers underpinned by a diverse assemblage of motives and moral principles, and, as such, contrast markedly with the desocialized drones distinctive to the fatalist critique" (p. 467).

We could go on citing survey data from the United States. Suffice a reference. On the basis of a careful analysis of survey data on American culture, Baker (2004) concluded that " . . . the evidence shows overwhelmingly that America has not lost its traditional values, that the nation compares favorably with most other societies, and that the culture war is largely a myth" (Baker 2004). Various interviews conducted as part of the World Value Survey project provide clear socio-cultural configurations of Confucianist, Islamic, Hindu, Israeli, Vietnamese, ex-communist, Latin-American countries that are based on the responses of people. We could refer also to the contemporary strong nationalistic tendencies in Russia, China, India, Iran and other countries of the world, and similarly to the strong ethnic revivals and struggles provoked, among other forces, by the impact of globalization. These political events add additional weight to the world survey data that is at odds with Beck's theses on the fragmentation of traditional institutions, the resulting uncertainty of the individual, and the atomization of social structure.

THE DIALECTIC NEGOTIATION OF GLOBAL AWARENESS
AND MULTIPLE IDENTITIES

Our review of the empirical counter-evidence to Beck's theses shows the need for a more convincing interpretive framework. Globalization literature is filled with controversies on the issue of socio-cultural identity in our global age: some authors have argued or documented the fragmenting impact of globalization on cultural identities, while others have argued for the homogenizing impact of globalization of world's cultures, such as the "coca colonization" (Hannerz 1992) and McDonaldization (Ritzer 1993) of the world. Still, others have spoken about 'indigenization" [or the expression of the global in local forms] and about "creolization" [or the creation of new cultural forms via the selective assimilation of external cultural elements by local cultures that gives new meanings to external cultural elements] (Cohen and Kennedy 2000).

In a previous article published in this series of volumes derived from meetings of Italian and Italian-American sociologists, and indefatigably edited by Mario A. Toscano and Vincent N. Parrillo, I provided a framework to analyze the global on the basis of a cross-tabulation of the local, national and international levels of concerns on the one hand, and the prevalence of the cultural or political or economic principle of social organization, on the other (see Table 1).

TABLE 1
The Threefold Articulation of the Global

SOCIETAL CONCERNS	PRINCIPLES OF SOCIAL ORGANIZATION		
	Cultural	Political	Economic
Local (Ethnic, Religious)	1	2	3
National	2	1	3
International	3	2	1

1=Most dominant principle of social organization   3=Least dominant principle of social organization
⎯⎯⎯► =Primary integrating process   ◄-------- =Secondary integrating process

Source: Modified from Ino Rossi, "Nationalism and Social Identity," pp. 101-111 in *Millennium Haze: Comparative Inquiries about Society, State and Community*, edited by Mario A. Toscano and Vincent N. Parrillo. Milan: Franco Angeli, 2000.

From that framework I subsequently derived three types of identities (ethnic, national, and global) that prevail respectively at the local, national, and international levels of societal concerns (Table 2).

TABLE 2
Dominant Structures and Related Identity at Three Levels of Societal Concerns

SOCIETAL CONCERNS	DOMINANT STRUCTURE & [IDENTITY]		
	Cultural	Political	Economic
Local	1	2	3
	Cultural institutions [Ethnic identity]		
National	2	1	3
		Political institutions [National identity]	
International	3	2	1
			IGOs [Global awareness]

1=Most dominant social institution and [identity type]   3=Least dominant social institution and [identity type]
⎯⎯⎯► =Primary integrating process   ◄-------- =Secondary integrating process

Source: Reconceptualized and retitled from Ino Rossi, ed. *Frontiers of Globalization Research*, New York: Springer, 2007, p. 5.

Strong cross-cultural evidence on the co-presence of these three types of identities in contemporary societies is provided by the surveys of 80 percent of world societies by the already mentioned World Value Surveys project. Traditional civilization cores and national experiences persist while modern values, first, and post-modern values, next, are selectively adopted respectively in the industrial and post-industrial phases of development (Inglehart and Baker 2000; Inglehart and Welzel 2005).

The first two cells of Table 1 point to the dominance of particularism. The orientation toward modern and post-modern values (as world societies move respectively to the industrial and post-industrial stages of development) is one component of "global awareness." What the other components and what is the relationship among ethnic identity, national identity and global awareness? The third cell includes also principles of world culture (universalism, individualism, voluntaristic authority, rational progress, and world citizenship) (Boli and Thomas 1997), as well as the ideology of neo-liberal globalization. The principles of world culture operate at the supranational level of the intergovernmental organizations (IGOs), like the World Bank, IMF, WTO, etc. Neo-liberalism is the overarching ideology of global capitalism.

It is immediately evident that the three levels of identity are far from being in a relationship of peaceful coexistence. For lack of space, I briefly discuss the relation between certain components of the first two levels on the one hand, and of the third level on the other hand, to show how a negotiated 'global awareness' is dialectically generated by the three levels of the global architecture.

At the international level, economic neoliberalism [with its de-culturing, de-humanizing and disempowering qualities] imposes itself on all countries as the only universally valid formula for economic development and a democratic way of life. This is the *thesis* moment of the dialectics of globalization or the confrontational instantiation of the global on the national and local (for a discussion of this point see Rossi 2007, chapter one). Such a confrontation produces counter-distantiations at the national and local levels of societal concerns: this is the *antithetical* moment of dialectical globalization. This counter-distantiating thrust leads to the re-inventing of cultural traditions and movements toward alternative (and democratic) forms of globalization: these counter-movements coalesce into the *dynamic synthesis or the ongoing construction of a pluralistic* globalization and multiple identities. I refer to this ongoing synthesis with the term "global awareness" because of its inchoate and fluid nature (for a more detailed discussion, see chapter one in Rossi 2007).

From this perspective, globalization does not produce a fragmentation of social institutions (and individual uncertainty a la Beck), but a confrontation of institutions that finds a resolution through an interaction among the *three layers of the global architecture*: (a) deeply anchored and enduring national and civilizational heritages [particularism]; (b) a cultural orientation toward modern values and then postmodern values, as a result of respectively the industrial and post-industrial phase of development [this is a layer of cross-national commonalities that builds on top of traditional civilizational values]; (c) principles and structures of world governance where the need arises for intercivilizationally-sensitive institutions and a heightened sense of global awareness. I focused in this paper on the fact that neo-liberalism is imposed as a universally valid ideology on the rest of the world (Schirato and Webb 2003), whereas in reality it is at the service of nationalistic purposes (Alexander in Rossi 2007). This is the reason why the "confrontational global" spurs nationalist and ethnic reactions as well as a revival and reinterpretation of related forms of identities.

In conclusion, a heightened creativity and not a demise of subjectivity is the outcome of global dynamics. The new dialectic trajectory follows this path: confrontation of the global → ethnic and nationalistic reactions → negotiated global awareness → intercultural competence → multicultural performance → cosmopolitan personality or "transnational identity" (Beck 2005:93) or "radical discovery of the other" (Beck 2005:285).

However, the last stage of this dialectic trajectory must be understood in a positive and dynamic sense, which is much at variance with Beck's conceptualizations. For Beck, the old ontological distinction between "us" and "them" is replaced by an inclusive distinction of us and them, and by a "dual locatedness for all." "Both culturally and politically, people experience and live out apparently contradictory identities and loyalties, without this being experienced as contradictory either in a person's own mind or in others' expectations" (p. 36).

This sybillic conceptualization is a consequence of Beck's theory of second modernity and related atomization and individualization of social structure. The old ontological distinction between "us and them" was made possible by fixed and clear boundaries that, according to Beck, were present in the first modernity. On the contrary, with the second modernity "the boundaries separating us from others are no longer blocked and obscured by ontological differences but have become transparent" (Beck 2006:8). Hence, "differences, contrasts and boundaries must be fixed and defined in an awareness of the sameness in principle of the others . . . Cosmopolitanization, thus understood, comprises the development of multiple loyalties as well as the increase in diverse transformational forms of life" (Beck 2006:9).

How are these processes possible if, in the second modernity, clear cultural boundaries have disappeared and social structure has become atomized, as Beck (2003) told us? Actually, Beck subsequently admitted that boundaries have not disappeared, but have become transparent so that multiple identities and "transnational identity, culture and statehood" become possible (2005:93). In 2006, Beck asserted that cosmopolitanism entails "a recognition of cosmopolitan differences" and "the principle that local, national, ethnic, religious and cosmopolitan cultures and traditions interpenetrate, interconnect and intermingle" (Beck 2006:7). The explanation of these apparently slippery statements lies in the other principle of cosmopolitanism, namely in "the impossibility of living in a world society without borders and the resulting compulsion to redraw old boundaries and rebuild old walls" (Ibid.).

Finally, we re-encounter the same notion found in Beck's earlier writings, the arbitrary and 'reflexively" drawing of new boundaries that are treated, for practical reasons, as if they were real. This 'enduring' perspective of Beck explains why reconstructed cosmopolitanism is the place where different cultures intermingle and share in the sameness of differences. Three clarifications are necessary to make sense of Beck's perspective: a) social boundaries do not became transparent but are redrawn in an arbitrary and 'reflexive' way; b) cosmopolitanism becomes a 'reflexive' re- construction where cultures interpenetrate and intermingle because their differences have become blurred; c) as a result, the sameness of cosmopolitanism is the sameness of differences that are blurred (and fictitious) reconstructions of what in the first modernity were (deemed to be) objective differences. We still need a more convincing explanation of how "dual locatedness" is related to the sameness of the others. Let me forego a much more thorough critique of this fictitious cosmopolitanism and the related fragmentation of social relations (see Albrow's critique of this notion in Rossi 2007) to outline briefly a definition of cosmopolitanism that is based on "lived through" (as opposed to 'blurred away') conflicts of cultural, economic, and political nature. The massive intrusion of the instantiating global (*thesis*) produces a sharp awareness and reformulation of inter-societal differences and rights to self-preservation (*antithesis moment*), and finally, the realization that the sharper those differences are, the clearer the commonalities become. Some sort of "sameness" (at a higher level) emerges from sharp differences (at the confrontational level): (*this is a constructive and ongoing synthesis*). Let me explain.

The historical record is full of beneficial inter-civilizational influences and, even in our days, we can benefit from each other's cultural uniquenesses and strengths; for one thing, we can appreciate and learn from certain characteristics of cultures different from ours (*complementarities of cultural differences*). At the same time, we realize that some countries have natural resources and others have technological resources; hence, countries need to complement each other's strengths (*complementarity of different resources*). We realize also that we must negotiate and compromise with other nations because we compete for the same strategic resources and world influence (*interdependence deriving from the need to negotiate over opposing needs and goals*).

As much as the reality of "differences" remains entrenched in world politics, then as much it must remain the analytical propeller of cosmopolitan inclusiveness or global awareness. Truly, global awareness is pluralistic in nature and global identities (if and when we really reach the level of 'identification') are pluralistic also. But this is not just a juxtaposition or "dual locatedness" a' la Beck. Plurality of resources and needs are the engines that generate the awareness of inevitable complementarities and interdependence. Much more than from an intermingling of cultures and interests, cosmopolitanism is based on a common humanity and a common survival need (*sameness*), the need of complementing each other's *different* strengths and of negotiating over *competing* interests and *mutually opposing* ambitions. [The alternative would be hegemony and unilateral militarism.] Hence, *sameness* (awareness of a common humanity and a common survival need) derives from the sharp realization of *differences*. Instead of an "awareness of the sameness in principle of the others" (Beck), we have an awareness of the complementarity and interdependence generated by differences. In this sense 'difference' will and must remain the continuing propeller of our global communalities and the collective chance for survival.

References

Albrow, Martin. 2007. "Situating Global Social Relations." Pp. 317- 332 in *Frontiers of Globalization Research*, edited by Ino Rossi. New York: Springer.

Alexander, Jeffrey C. 2007. "Globalization as Collective Representation: The New Dream of a Cosmopolitan Civil Sphere." Pp. 371-382 in Rossi, *Frontiers of Globalization Research*.

Baker, Wayne E. 2004. *America's Crisis of Values: Reality and Perception*. Princeton, NJ: Princeton University Press.

Banks, Mark. 2006. "Moral Economy and Cultural Work." *Sociology* 40(3):455–472

Beck, Ulrich. 2005. *Power in the Global Age*. Translated by Kathleen Croos. Malden, MA: Polity Press.

—. 2006. *The Cosmopolitan Vision*. Translated by Ciaran Cronin. Malden, MA: Polity Press.

Beck, Ulrich, Wolfgang Bonss, and Christopher Lau. 2003. "The Theory of Reflexive Modernization: Problematic, Hypotheses and Research Programme." *Theory, Culture and Society* 20(2):1-33.

Beck, Ulrich, and Elisabeth Beck-Gernsheim. 2002. *Individualization: Institutionalized Individualism and its Social and Political Consequences*. London: Sage.

Beck, Ulrich, and Johannes Willms. 2004. *Conversations with Ulrich Beck*. Malden, MA: Polity Press.

Boli, J., and G. M. Thomas. 1997. "World Culture in World Polity: A Century of International Non-Governmental Organization." *American Sociological Review* 62(12):171-190.

Ceplak, Metka Mencin. 2006. "Values of Young People in Slovenia: The search for Personal Security." *Young* 14(4):291–308.

Chtouris, Sotiris, Anastasia Zissi, Efstratios Papanis, and Konstantinos Rontos. 2006. "The State of Youth in Contemporary Greece." *Young* 14(4):309-322.

Cohen, Robin, and Paul Kennedy. 2000. *Global Sociology*. New York: New York University Press.

De Beer, Paul. 2007. "How Individualized are the Dutch?" *Current Sociology* 55(3):389–413.

Knorr Cetina, Karin. 2007. "Microglobalization." Pp. 65-91 in Rossi, *Frontiers of Globalization Research*.

Hannerz, Ulf. 1992. *Cultural Complexity: Studies in the Social Organization of Meaning*. New York: Columbia University Press.

Inglehart, Ronald, and Wayne E. Baker. 2000. "Modernization, Cultural Change and the Persistence of Traditional Values." *American Sociological Review* 65 (February):19-51.

Inglehart, Ronald ,and Christian Welzel. 2005. *Modernization, Cultural Change and Democracy: The Human Development Sequence*. New York: Cambridge University Press.

Levi-Strauss, Claude. 1966. *The Salvage Mind*. Translated by John Weightman. Chicago: University of Chicago Press.

Ritzer, George. 1993. *The McDonaldization of Society: An Investigation into the Changing Character of Social Life*. Thousand Oaks, CA: Pine Forge Press.

Rossi, Ino, ed . 1974. *The Unconscious in Culture: The Structuralism of Claude Levi-Strauss in Perspective*. New York: Dutton.

—, ed. 1982. The *Logic of Culture: Advances in Structural Theory and Method*. South Hadley, MA: J. F. Bergin.

—. 2007/2008. *Frontiers of Globalization Research*, edited by Ino Rossi. Hardcover and paperback edition (with updates). New York: Springer.

Schirato, Tony, and Jen Webb. 2003. *Understanding Globalization*. Thousands Oaks, CA: Sage Publications.

Toscano, Mario A., and Vincent N. Parrillo, eds. 2000. *The Millennium Haze: Comparative Inquiries about Society, State and Community*. Milan: Franco Angeli.

"World Values Surveys," network of social scientists coordinated by the World Values Association http://www.worldvaluessurvey.com/.

The Maintenance of a Commons

CHRISTINE ZINNI
State University of New York at Buffalo

Globalization, along with the development of communication technologies, and new economies have advanced a conceptual change and fundamental restructuring of economic and social relationships across time and geographic space(s). As currently conceptualized in the capitalist marketplace, "connectivity" (through virtual space) and "access" (rather than ownership) to goods and services are key metaphors of the global age. As such they are intricately related to modern ideas about security and risk.[1]

At the same moment the virtues of "connectivity" in virtual space are promulgated, the rhetoric of *disaster capitalism* has furthered a paradigm shift in our thinking about physical and social space. As Naomi Klein (2007) emphasizes, *disaster capitalism* has put forth a vision of a "ruthlessly divided world," one that promotes the privatization and enclosure of physical space and threatens the very idea of a public sphere and the workings of civil society. According to this new world view, average citizens are no longer deemed capable of managing their own security and/or risk. Moreover, security is not for everyone as "conflict, disaster-related functions, and the building and/or (re)building of public infrastructures are performed by corporations at a profit" (p. 50). Needless to say, the potential long-range consequences of this shift are disturbing. Along with creating a polarized world of winners and losers, the rhetoric of disaster capitalism distances individuals from their natural environment and calls into question the democratic notion of equal access. Most

---

[1] See Jeremy Rifkin, *The Age of Access* (New York: Putnam, 2000) for an extended discussion of these issues. Rifkin argues the shift from a market economy to a new global "network' economy involves a marginalization of physical property and ascendance of intellectual property. Not inconsistent with Klein's assertions about disaster capitalism, Rifkin points to the privatization of physical property by corporations, the proliferation of gated communities, the growing gulf between rich and poor, and erosion of individual rights.

important, as Klein asserts, disaster capitalism "replaces the core function of government and local citizens with its own profitable enterprises . . . Creating a state within a state, "this corporate shadowstate has been built almost exclusively with public resources . . . yet the vast infrastructure is all privately owned and controlled. The citizens who funded it have absolutely no claim to a parallel economy or its resources. (pp. 50-51)"[2]

This paper asks the reader to consider the modern thrust towards *disaster capitalism*, the corporate privatization and enclosure of space and attendant ideas of security and risk in light of civil society and the longstanding efforts of everyday people(s) to maintain a "commons." Through examination of the socio-spatial elements of a "Little Italy" created by a group of immigrant stonecutters and their families from the Abruzzo region of Italy, the paper will highlight how the maintenance of their commons served to reinforce democratic principles, contribute to the ongoing security of individuals, and bolster the health and well-being of several communities-at-large. On yet another level, consideration of the histories of the stonecutters illumines some of the ways in which changing ideas of security and risk are related to shifts in capitalism. As Jerome Krase argues:

> Little Italies [sic] are important places to study not only because they are venues for assimilation and acculturation but because the "spatial" idea also is a powerful force in Italian, Italian-American and American culture and society. It is critical to not only consider the places where Italians demographically dominate(d), but where Italians live as minorities, where they once lived, and where they never lived at all. Actual and virtual spaces help us understand the Italian American past, present and future (1997:104).

---

[2] As Klein asserts, "Disasters themselves are making new markets [. . .] and have morphed into what is best understood as disaster capitalism—a complex in which all conflict and disaster related functions, can be performed by corporations at a profit. Arguing *disaster capitalism* is a direct byproduct of a free market economy, she explains: Every time a new crisis hits "the fear and disorientation that follow are harnessed for radical social and economic shock therapy. The end result is the same kind of unapologetic partition between the included and the excluded, the protected and the damned, that is on display in Baghdad. From "Disaster Capitalism: The New Economy of Catastrophe" in the October 2007 issue of *Harpers Magazine* 31(1889):47-58. See also Jeremy Scahill's work, *Blackwater* (2007), on how the corporatization of security usurps the function of the state and threatens the working of civil society. Viewed from a somewhat different angle, Walter W. Powell examines the growing divide between winners and losers in "The Capitalist Firm in the 21st Century" in *Working in America* (3rd edition) edited by Amy Wharton (New York: McGraw Hill, 2005), pp. 80-94.

My arguments on this subject evolved out of oral history research conducted in western New York and the Abruzzo region of Italy over the course of eight years. What started out as documentation of the feast of Saint Rocco, the patron saint of the stonecutters in the village of Hulberton, New York, became in effect an extended study of the vernacular architecture and textile constructions of three generations of Alfedenesi stonecutters and their families. This research comprised part of my dissertation work which, in turn, became the basis of a traveling multimedia exhibition entitled *Writings in Stone and Textiles*. Composed of archival documents and interviews with ten families in western New York and Italy, the study revealed that Alfedenesi stonecutters had a long history of transnational migrations traveling *oltremontane* (over the mountains) as well as over *oltremare* (across the sea) to work in stone quarries, on public projects, bridges and roads, monuments as well as numerous civic and religious structures on several different continents.

For the most part, the labors of Italian *artigiani* or artisans were subsumed in *meta* histories that focus on the genius of architecture and/or city planning and its design. While many of the public structures shaped by the hands of immigrant artisans became associated with the glory, enduring permanence and/or security of civic governments, religious institutions and/or the nation state, my research reveals the actual lives of Alfedenesi stonecutters contained some of the same elements experienced by a global labor force today: mobility, contingency, insecurity and high elements of physical risk.

Embarking on this documentary journey of the stonecutters' lives and work before 9/11, this paper not only tracks changes in the meaning of security through the stonecutters' histories, but reflects the ethnographer's own experience of changes in the meaning(s) of security and risk in today's world.[3] Viewed through the lens of *disaster capitalism*, the counter discursive space/place of the stonecutters' commons is wide indeed!

---

[3] For more on my approach to the subject, see the early work of Michael Bakhtin as well as the writings of Dennis Tedlock, Michael Frisch, and Alessandro Portelli on the dialogical aspects of oral history work. My transcription of oral histories in this essay on based in part in Tedlock's work, *The Spoken Word and the Work of Interpretation*. Philadelphia: University of Penn., 1993. My use of the word commons resonates with Roger Lohman's definition of the term as not only a physical, but social space/place for interaction(s) and dialogue. As Lohman asserts, a commons is "a place for talking, listening, seeing and/or being seen; it can be a town square, a building, a home or a public space outside the marketplace and state control." See *The Common*. (San Francisco: Jossey-Bass, 1992), p. 62.

To this end, the first section of this paper examines the maintenance of a commons in light of the larger history of enclosure movements in Italy's *Mezzogiorno*. The second part of the paper looks at the particular migrations of Alfedenesi stonecutters to America and how their creation of space(s) and a "commons" played out in the little Italy they created in western New York. The third section or summary discusses the relevance of commons vis-à-vis *disaster capitalism* and ideas about security and risk in today's world.

RELEVANCE OF THE COMMONS VIS-À-VIS IDEAS OF SECURITY AND RISK

As political economists from Marx to Jeremy Rifkin assert, Enlightenment thinking and the European *enclosure* movements of the sixteenth through eighteenth centuries created a fundamental shift in Europeans' conception of nature and physical space, impacting ideas of security and risk. The natural and man-made disasters of the thirteenth and fourteenth centuries—food shortages, plagues, and wars—led to increased concerns about the ways in which the security of societal groups was tied to nature. With the rise of mercantile capitalism in the fourteenth and fifteenth centuries, ideas about security and risk became ever more bound up with the taming and control of nature, technological progress, the working of machines, and the profit motive. As Rifkin explains in *Biosphere Politics*, the new cosmology of the Enlightenment was compatible with the new technological revolution as it reasoned nature was a giant machine and/or an inert source of raw material and resources for the benefit of humans (1991:27-52). Noting that the Enlightenment world view provided the philosophical justification for Europeans' separation from nature and a basis for changes in distribution of the land, Rifkin asserts that "nowhere was the impact of this new thinking more poignant and directed than in the European *enclosure* movement, a little known social upheaval that had reaching consequences, changing the very basis of human relationship to the environment and society" (p. 37).[4] Conceptualizing nature as a "raw resource" for profit, enclosure movements sent European peasants into enforced exile from their ancestral

---

[4] As Rifkin emphasizes, Bacon's scientific methodology helped set the tone for a new way of thinking about security as it created a philosophical shift in conceptions of humans' relation to the land and physical space. Likening nature to a harlot, Bacon simultaneously sought ways to harness its power. Descartes also promulgated a mechanistic world view: one in which ideas of security and risk were predicated on predictability and control over the forces of nature.

homes and set in motion a mass migration of peasants into European cities from Amsterdam to Rome. The enclosure movements also paved the way for the emergence of the industrial and urban revolutions.

As Rifkin goes on to explain, from the sixteenth through nineteenth centuries, the increased privatization of publicly held land and its enclosure with hedges, ditches or other barrier to the free passage of men and animals was carried on by acts of parliament and licensed by the kings. Prior to this time medieval European agriculture was communally managed with peasants pooling individual holdings and resources. Common pastures were used to graze animals and lands were jointly cultivated. Peasant councils administered the commons, and common decisions were made on crop rotation, planting harvesting, and care of animals, cutting of forests, allocation of water, and use of farm animals and plows.

The longstanding existence of a village commons, and the practice of subsistence agriculture and tending pastureland in common, provided an economic safety net for peasants. Whereas social organization had revolved around the maintenance of commons and bartering of goods and services during feudal times, enclosure movements served to undermine communalism and the distribution of land. In Western Europe and Italy, human labor came to be viewed as a commodity based on its market value. Providing labor for towns during the rise of mercantile capitalism, enclosure movements also set the stage for the idea that security was tied to the interests of nation states rather than local communes.

The impact of the enclosure movements played out somewhat differently across Western Europe—counterbalanced to a great degree by the maintenance of public space and the ability of the peasants and to maintain a social and physical commons. As Roger Lohman argues, something of the emerging differences could be seen in the contrast between sixteenth-century Amsterdam and Rome. As Lohman posits, even to the present day,

> No city in human history is more reflective of the range and diversity of the commons than is Rome (99) . . . even during the Counter Reformation, plays, along with public performances staged on carts or platforms could be seen on the streets of Rome during Catholic feasts and festivals. [In contrast to Amsterdam, where] "there were no museums, villas or gardens open to visitors, the Vatican and public gardens were freely available to all." [Moreover, Rome rose] "to new heights as [it] had become the important center of pilgrimages [118-119].

Along with the social commons maintained with the celebration of Catholic festivals and feasts, the effects of the enclosure movement in the rural parts of southern and south-central areas of Italy and/or the *Mezzogiorno* were mitigated by the existence of publicly held lands and communal rights or *usi civici*. In areas like the mountainous heartland of the Abruzzo, where land was less arable hence less valuable to mercantile capitalists, some pasturelands continued to hold in common. As Leonard Covello asserts *usi civici* provided access to "pasturage, gathering of fire wood, cultivation of land [moreover] the use of communally owned water rights and the principle of collective ownership was considered a sacred privilege and persisted until the most recent times (1967:49-50)." Up until unification of Italy in the 1860's, Church lands were also utilized by the peasants as a commons.[5]

The existence of a social and physical commons supported feelings of *campanilismo* as well as feelings of intimacy felt with the natural world. Peoples of the *Mezzogiorno* resisted, in large part, the nationalism of the Risorgimento based on their connection to individual paese and its people. The performance of culture in the form of religious feasts and festivals and oral traditions reinforced villagers pride in their place of birth as the histories of their families were entwined with that of the village. As Richard D. Alda explains, "The village and its surroundings were something intimate, familiar, where stone, tree and field were connected to this personal sense of history and place (1969:30-31). Rituals performed in the public commons also strengthened mutual bonds and *campanilismo* through devotion to patron saints, the totemic *protectors* of local landscapes and *paesi*. Furthermore, the rise of mutual aid societies served to fill the gap in the economic safety net created by the privatization of church lands in the late eighteen hundreds.[6]

---

[5] I am grateful for talks with Agostino Cerasualo for insights into this subject of usufruct rights. See his unpublished master thesis, "Peasant Movements in Calabria 1943-1953" (University of Illinois at Chicago, 1989). In *The Social Background of the Italo American School Child*, Corvello states, "The *usi civici* and *diritti collettivi or* communal rights are in existence even today in Italy" (49). As Eula asserts in *Between Peasant and Urban Villagers* "municipal officials were thus obliged by law to uphold the distinction between public land and that traditionally held by the church and administered by the municipality. In the years before unification, material benefits distributed within the framework of a traditional society lessened peasant suspicion. The Church held a leading role as benefactor to the poor. Roman law still dictated until 1861, that Church land were also public lands and as such were subject to the legal authority of local municipality [. . .] Central to this position was the principal of *usufruct*, a crucial benefit in the daily life of the peasant"(215-217).

[6] As Briggs asserts in *An Italian Passage*, "Studies of mutual aid societies [served] the core function of security and risk. Chief among the benefits were health, life, and unemployment insurance; education

For the Alfedenesi *artigiani* born in the mountainous heartland of the Abruzzo region of Italy, communalism and cooperative action was perpetuated through guild-like structures and cooperatives based on their work as skilled artisans as well as mutual aid societies under the auspices of the patron saints.[7] Carved into the lintels of stone houses in the center of Alfedena knowledge, signature stonecutter's mallets were incorporated into ancient familial coats-of-arms and marked how knowledge of the artisan's skill was passed down from generation to generation through apprenticeships.

*Stonecutter's mallet and coat-of-arms
above lintel of doorway in Alfedena, Italy*
(Photograph courtesy of the author)

---

for the intellectual, moral and social advancement of the membership and their families, support of the trade and economic interest of members; advancement of local communal interest; maintenance of a social center; and the initiation of producer and consumer cooperatives (1978:24).

[7] Op. cit., Lohman credits medieval artisan guilds' support of the cults of patron saints with furthering communalism and the maintenance of a village commons. Reflecting changes wrought by the enclosure movements, he explains that the "gulf between artisans and mercantile guilds widened in 16 and 17 c. with the rise of merchant entrepreneurs and wage labor" (1992:114).

Along with a plethora of headstones in the local cemetery bearing a stonecutter's mallet, a modern-day statue of a stonecutter in the town's central park notes citizens' collective pride in the skill of the Alfedenesi and identification with the stonecutter's art. Constructed in the 1960s, the plaque underneath the statue commemorates how the stonecutters shaped the *sampietrini* or paving stones that grace Saint Peter's Square as well as many of Rome's other famous *piazze*.

Statue of stonecutter in central park of Alfedena, Italy

It reads:

Ai suoi selciatori
Che migrati alle cave basaltiche dell' Agro Romano
Per secoli squadrarono e modellarono selci cordoli
Pavmentarono e decorarono strade e piazze di Roma
Con alta professionalita ed abnegazione profonda
Alfedena
Orgogliosa e riconoscente
Ad imperitura memoria
Eresse nell'anno 1966

Along with all the visual homages marking the stonecutter's art, a booklet outlining some of the labor demands of Alfedenesi stonecutters documents the formation of a cooperative during the last quarter of the nineteenth century. The cooperative bears the names of several stonecutters who made seasonal sojourns to work in quarries outside Rome and later immigrated to America.

DIASPORA TO AMERICA

Italian stonecutters carried the practice of cooperative action with them in their transnational migrations to America. After working in Greece, some of the Alfedenesi stonecutters found work in Washington DC, others in the granite quarries of Vermont.[8]

As Norma and Virginia Di Laura, the daughter of expert stonecutter Pasquale, explained:

> Our grandfather Ercole Di Laura was a Master stonecutter. Our grandfather and his father (our great grandfather) went to Athens to work on the restoration of the Parthenon and when they got back to Rome. a labor broker told them that they needed skilled stonecutters and stonemasons in America.
>
> Our mother's father went from Alfedena. His name was Pompeii Lombardo. When he got back from his work in Athens, he went directly to Washington, DC to work on a new wing of the Capitol Building.
>
> That was in the 1880s, so it is almost *a hundred* years ago![9]

Passed along by word of mouth, news of available work in quarries of red medina sandstone was also promoted by quarry owner organizations

---

[8] In *Building Little Italy: Philadelphia's Italians before Mass Migration* (Philadelphia: Pennsylvania State University, 1998), Richard Juliani notes how "painters, sculptors, musicians and writers often migrated from city to city until they attained artistic success and financial security." Juliani describes the work of Enrico Causici, a stonecutter who worked on public projects, monuments and carvings for the Capitol building in Washington DC (81)

[9] This quote is taken from an audio taped interview with the DiLaura sisters conducted by folklorist Bob Gates back in 1982. The audio project was funded by the New York Council of the Arts (NYSCA) and organized by Bill Lattin, Orleans County Historian. Almost 25 years later, I videotaped sessions with the Di Lauras and descendants of the immigrant stonecutters. Their testimonies were woven together in the video documentary that I produced, entitled, "The Road from Alfedena," in 2006, that was funded in part by NYSCA and the National Italian Foundation. As indicated earlier, my approach to transcribing and/or "scoring" oral narratives in free verse to accent their paralinguistic features is based on belief that "oral history is poetry and poetry is oral history." See Dennis Tedlock, *The Spoken Word and the Work of Interpretation* (Philadelphia: University of Pennsylvania Press, 1983).

as well as the Stonecutters Journeyman's Association, one of the first trade unions in America.[10] Compelling hundreds of Alfedenesi to migrate to the western part of New York State, quarry work demanded mobility and independence of its workers. As Walter Powell asserts in his study of the new global economy, in this respect workers during the heyday of industrial capitalism shared something in common with white and blue collar workers of today's world. Although wage levels and opportunities have changed, mobility, contingency and flexibility are still required of today's workers (pp. 82, 86).

In the late 1800s, a consortium of powerful owners from New York City developed the sandstone quarries in the region along the western part of the canal. According to a local newspaper published in 1890, 19 quarries employed about 1,800-2,000 men with a payroll of over $75,000. The quarried stone was sold and shipped along the Erie Canal on barges to large cities like Cleveland, Buffalo and New York, and used for paving blocks and curbs along with its use in buildings.

BUILDING EMPIRE BUT NO SECURITY

While a consortium of New York quarry owners cut deals in the halls of power and promoted a utopian vision of a nation fashioned in stone, workers involved in the actual quarry work led a much humbler existence. Like the immigrant stonecutters from Ireland and Poland who came before them, Alfedenesi workers stayed in little huts built by the consortium. Called "nine pins" because the little houses all sat in a row and resembled bowling pins, they were so close to the quarry that blasts would often rock the house. Corroborated by newspaper accounts, oral histories reveal that even with the introduction of new pneumatic machines, the work was backbreaking. With silica embedded on their faces and eyes, the workers' lungs also absorbed the material, leading to TB or other complications. Called "brown lung," "black lung" or "stonecutters' disease," some workers chewed tobacco to absorb the silica dust and

---

[10] Underscoring the role unions played during the early years of industrialization, Stanford M. Jacoby notes how "craft unions facilitated the skilled workers' propensity to move as secretaries furnished reports on condition of trades in the area. [Moreover,] trade unionism helped to curb the foreman's arbitrary exercise of power and give the skilled worker some control over the term of his employment." In "The Way It Was: Factory Labor Before 1915," in *Working in America: Continuity, Conflict and Change*, p. 13.

avoid the disease as best they could. Stonecutters not only worked in quarries but traveled to different sites and large cities to work on the construction of medina sandstone buildings. Along with the risks and mobility involved in their work, there was little job security. As Stanford Jacoby asserts in his study of labor before 1915, "The only worker rights consistently recognized during the course of the day was if a man is dissatisfied, it is his privilege to quit" (2006:13).

A LITTLE HELP FROM NEIGHBORS

For the Alfedenesi who decided to make the area around western New York their home, contingency and risk involved with quarry work was offset by several factors: the creation of small gardens, the ability to live off the land along with the practice of bartering with one another for goods and services, assuaged unstable work conditions. The greatest pride, however, seemed to be the men's ability to shape their own physical or built environment. As in their Italian paesi, reciprocity was the byword. If in need, stonecutters and their families could turn to a communal network of paesani for food, shelter, economic and social support. The skill and creativity of the Alfedenesi men came be seen in the plethora of homes in the region, composed, in part, of medina sandstone. Men often came together on individual construction projects, working together to build interior and exterior parts of houses: porches, fronts, window sills, steps and walkways.

Underscoring how the stonecutter's skill and art/works had been forged in the Old Country and the ways in which remembered "roots" formed the basis of communal efforts and identities, the headstone of stonecutters' graves near the Hulberton quarries display Italian inscriptions. As noted in the oral histories of descendants of stonecutters, it was not unusual for stonecutters to carve headstones for their neighbors and they often did it for free. The cut letters on the grave markers reflect the value the stonecutters placed on manual skill and dignity of work with one's hands: visible signs of the stonecutters' pride in being "builders."[11]

---

[11] See Joseph Sciorra's work on sidewalk altars and shrines for a discussion of the relationship between the pride of craftsmanship, vernacular architecture, polyvocality and the use of space. As Sciorra notes in his study of the building of a Mount Carmel grotto, "Interactions invest the built environment and/or "visual texts" with meaning" (1993). Luisa Del Giudice's brilliant study of the modern "arch villa," Donna Gabaccia, Jerome Krase and Dominic Candeloro's documentations of the urban space of Little Italys take up these issues from somewhat different perspectives in their works.

This pride was evidenced in the private correspondence of Gilda Trivisond, the daughter of expert stonecutter Felix Trivisondoli:

> The immigrants would boast about their ancestors having built Rome and that now they were building America. My father said: "When I came here as a boy, I had never seen so much mud. We had streets of stone where we came from. This was a great place to come to because there was so much that had to be built and so much of it of stone."
>
> This was some advice he gave me about building, "If you build anything, it's best to build of stone."

The lack of security attached to stonecutters' seasonal and itinerant work during the late nineteth and early twentieth centuries was also offset by women's piecework in textiles, and factory work in beaneries and vegetable storage facilities. For their part, women's work on textiles inside the home not only provided gainful employment, but reinforced links to the old country. Like the men who came together to work on projects, immigrant women got together to share recipes, cook and do needlework—creating in effect, a social commons which furthered bonds among the families. Needlework patterns passed down over generations were also shared with newcomers to the circle, their *'mericani* "sisters."

Like the personalized stonework of the men, immigrant women's needlework constituted an active form of remembering, often encoding scripts and patterns from the old country. Virginia and Norma Di Laura recall how their great grandmother fashioned a coverlet which inscribed the date their grandfather Ercole left for America and the date he returned to Italy to convince his family they should all emigrate back to the States.

In this way, the insecurities and risks attached to the Alfedenesi's circumstances in the new world were mitigated by the maintenance of an active commons and diverse forms of writing culture. Artistry and knowledge of materials, patterns, and methods informing the Alfedenesi's creations through the media of stone and textile not only served to map connections across generations of Alfedenesi, but bridge distances between different physical environments—conveying, in so many ways, a sense of continuity and permanency in the midst of great change(s)[12] The oral tradition and "writings" through the media of stone

---

[12] See the works of Michael J. Eula, Robert Orsi, Joseph Sciorra and Louisa Del Giudice for insights

and textile(s) served as a viable means of marking memories—functioning, in effect, as practical, economic, social and spiritual counterweights to the precarious elements of the Alfedenesi immigrant's work lives—and the real fears attached to the experience of being strangers in a strange land. Learned in Alfedena, knowledge of how "to work" stone and/or thread was passed down over generations and intricately tied to knowledge of land and the natural world. Like the *contadini* or peasants who came from diverse parts of the *Mezziogiorno* during the great diaspora of the past two centuries, Alfedenesi *artigiani or* artisans also utilized their experience with subsistence agriculture and animal husbandry to survive. Cooperatives as well as mutual aid societies originally forged in Italy and based on *campanilismo* also helped provide economic and social safety nets.

As in Italy, celebrations in the honor of patron saints served spiritual as well as social purposes. Second generation Alfedenesi Americans were baptized and married in the little church of Saint Rocco, built by immigrant stonecutters in 1907. As the patron saint of contagious diseases, prayers to Saint Roc' served to console the men suffering from the stonecutter's disease and/or silicosis of the lung. Activities devoted to honoring Saint Roc' and Mary were organized in conjunction with the workings of a mutual aid society called the "Loyal Wing" club. Alluding to Alfedena's ancient history and the conferring of its original name of "Aufedena" by Julius Caesar, the title referenced the role of the Alfedenesi in protecting the Romans from the incursion of Hannibal and his troops over the Apennine Mountains back in 1 A.D. Serving to further cement the bonds between the diasporic communities of the Alfedenesi in America to their ancestral homeland in the old country, the activities of the Loyal Wing Club in western New York were supported by membership donations and musical celebrations. As Gilda Trivisond noted, "They had officers, regular meetings social events and performed works of charity. They had special collections for the widows and the needy." Functioning before and after the enactment of social security, meetings held at the club's building in Albion as well as at annual celebrations at Saint Rocco's Church and Saint Mary's Church provided the venue for raising capital. As Trivisond underscores, her father and

---

into the particular ways in which pre-Christian elements were incorporated into religious practices of the Italians, serving in effect as counter discursive sites

other workers were proud of their good fortune to be American, often discussed the virtues of democracy, and even longer history of the country's original inhabitants, the Native Americans.

Mirroring changes in capitalism, the advent of new construction materials like concrete led to the demise of the medina sandstone quarry industry in western New York. By the 1920s large numbers of Alfedenesi stonecutters had joined paesani in large industrial cities like Detroit and Pittsburgh to work in construction and assembly line jobs in the burgeoning auto industry.[13] Like the paesani who chose to settle in western New York, Alfedenesi who migrated to Detroit built a clubhouse for the Loyal Wing society devoted to the sole purpose of meetings and maintaining a commons that recalled roots in the old country. Along with support for local widows and the sick, money was raised to help relatives back in Italy after the ravages of earthquakes and World War II.

Angelo Manella working on restoration of medina sandstone building, Saint Joseph Chapel, Albion New York, 1982
(Photograph courtesy of Orleans Country History Department)

Back in Hulberton, the early death of immigrant stonecutters from silicosis as well as out-migration to larger industrial cities caused Saint Rocco's church to fall into disrepair. Restored in 1960s largely through the efforts of Frank Di Carlo, a stonecutter and at one time the official mayor of Hulberton, an annual festival to celebrate Saint Rocco's feast day was

---

[13] Op cit. As Walter W. Powell tells us, this trend contrasts with advances in the second half of the twentieth century when "employment was no longer associated with mobility and "stable" factory work provided benefits like sick leave, insurance, and paid vacations. Unionism had given rise to increased job security with benefits and pensions for skilled workers after a thirty-year low but job security appears tenuous to many employees as revamping of jobs and organization structures as downsizing and contracts have increased."

organized on the grounds opposite the church. Over the past 30 years, the stone church and festival have served as a temporary autonomous zone (TAZ) or commons for the community-at-large. A team of Saint Rocco's "workers," no longer solely of Italian ancestry, interact in the planning and design of the yearly events surrounding the festival to honor the saint, truly making it a community affair. The "workers" claim that as soon as one festival ends, they are busy with preparations for the next. Relishing the taste of traditional dishes based on recipes from the old country and the sight of bocce tournaments played by Italians from around the region and Canada, during this time numerous Alfedenesi from diasporic communities in Michigan and Pennsylvania make pilgrimages to celebrate mass in Saint Rocco's Church and visit gravesites in Saint Joseph's Cemetery.

For their part, descendants of stonecutters, now scattered in towns and cities across the United States, are engaged in white collar as well as blue-collar work. Although risk is rarely gauged by the amount of physical danger experienced on the job and security has taken on new meanings, changes wrought by globalization and de-industrialization in the later part of the last century continue make the prospect of stable and permanent jobs uncertain. Separated by miles, older descendents of the stonecutters still keep in contact through the auspices of the Loyal Wing Club. The creation of a virtual commons on the Net reinforces bonds for younger generations of Alfedenesi Americans. Buttressed in so many ways by the lived experience of physical/social spaces shaped by their predecessors so many years ago, third, fourth and fifth generations of the stonecutters find a measure of security in actual and virtual "links" to a past grounded in built environments fashioned by the hands of their ancestors.

CONCLUSION: SECURITY AND RISK IN TODAY'S WORLD

Through consideration of the ways in which elements of security and risk have been managed over the course of several generations of Alfedenesi stonecutters and their families, I have attempted to underscore how their social/economic and spiritual bonds functioned to bridge private and public spheres. I have argued security was enhanced and risks mitigated through everyday interactions and the meanings attached to creative constructions shaped through the media of stone and textile.

The building and maintenance of a commons across time and space stand in stark contrast to the rhetoric and values of *disaster capitalism* in today's global world. Rather than reinforcing commonalties, connectivity, and continuity across generations and physical space(s), *disaster capitalism* effects a historical disconnect through the privatization and enclosure of spaces. The commons shaped by the stonecutters and their families, *enhanced* feelings of security reflected their social and spiritual links to their natural environment and to each other. In contrast, disaster capitalism advances disparities between the rich and the poor, and promotes feelings of uncertainty and insecurity. Furthering the desacralization of nature initiated during the Enlightenment period, disaster capitalism promulgates the idea that nature is simply a resource for humans' use and exploitation. As Klein suggests, disaster capitalism plays not only on the hysteria around natural disaster and man made disasters, but feelings of insecurity, and management of risk. It feeds on hyperbolic rhetoric of unpredictability (and control) of nature, and promotes economic restructuring and reengineering of markets based on crises created by natural disasters such as man-made wars and terrorism.(2007:47-58). In contrast to a commons shaped by individual hands, linked to the natural world, and based on communal skill and *communitas*, disaster capitalism promotes exclusivity and the corporately-owned and controlled use of space(s) and security. This new world vision is a far cry from the ways in which elements of security and risk were managed by groups of immigrants less than half a century ago. If we adhere to this new world vision and the belief that security is no longer within our hands, the disempowerment that follows will not only affect our sense of agency, but alienate us from the very workings of civil society and a commons essential to the furtherance of democratic principles.

Bibliography

Alba, Richard D. 1985. *Into the Twilight of Ethnicity*. Englewood Cliffs, NJ: Prentice Hall.

Banchelard, Gaston. 1969. *Poetics of Space*. Trans. By Etienne Gilson: Boston: Beacon Press.

Briggs, John W. 1978. *An Italian Passage: Immigrants to Three American Cities, 1890-1930*. New Haven. CT: Yale University Press.

Cerasualo, Agostino. 1988. "Peasant Movements in Calabria, 1943-1953." Urbana, IL: University of Illinois, unpublished Master's thesis.

Covello, Leonard. 1967. "The Agriculture System of South Italy." Pp. 34-64 in *The Social Background of the Italo American School Child*, edited by Francesco Cordasco. Ledien: E. J Brill.

Croce, Randy. 2006. *If Stones Could Speak*. Video documentary.

Davis, John A. 1979. "The South, the Risorgimento and the Origins of the Southern Problem." *Gramsci and Italy's Passive Revolution*. London: Croom Helm, 1979.

Defino, Susanna. 2004. "The Toll of Reconciliation: North and South in Post-Unification Italy:

Reconstructing Societies." Pp. 103-117 in *The Aftermath of War in Memory, Identity, and Reconciliation,* edited by Flavia Brizio Skov. Baton Rouge, LA: Bordighera Press.

Del Giudice, Luisa. 1993. "The Arch Villa." Pp. 53-106 in *Studies in Italian Folklore,* edited by Luisa Del Giudice. Logan: Utah State University Press.

Eula, Michael J. 1993. *Between Peasant and Urban Villager: Italian Americans of New Jersey and New York: The Structures of Counter Discourse 1880-1920.* New York: Peter Lang.

Gabaccia, Donna R. 2000. *Italy's Many Diasporas.* Seattle: University of Washington Press.

Hunt, Margaret. 1999. *The Stonecarvers: Master Craftsmen of the Washington Cathedral.* Washington: Smithsonian Institution Press.

Jacoby, Stanford M. 2005. "The Way It Was: Factory Labor Before 1915." Pp. 80-94 in *Working in America: Continuity, Conflict and Change,* 3rd edition, edited by Amy Wharton. New York: McGraw-Hill.

Kirshenblatt-Gimblett, Barbara. 1989. "Objects of Memory: Material Culture as Life Review." Pp. 329-338 in *Folk Group and Folklore Genres,* edited by Elliott Oring. Logan: Utah State University Press.

Klein, Naomi. 2007. "Disaster Capitalism: The New Economy of Catastrophe." *Harper Magazine* 31(1889):47-58.

Krase, Jerome. 1997. "The Spatial Semiotics of Little Italies and Italian Americans." Pp. 98-127 in *Industry, Technology, Labor and the Italian American Communities,* edited by Mario Aste. Staten Island, NY: American Italian Historical Association.

Lohman, Roger. 1992. *The Commons: New Perspectives on Nonprofit Organizations and Voluntary Actions.* San Francisco: Jossey-Bass.

Powell, Walter W. 2005. "The Capitalist Firm in the 21st Century." Pp. 80-94 in *Working in America*: Continuity, Conflict and Change, 3rd edition, edited by Amy Wharton, New York: McGraw-Hill.

Minicuci, Maria, 1982. "Il Disordine Ordinato: L'Orgaizzazione dello Spazio in un Villagio Rurale Calabrese" *Storia dell Citta* 24:93-118.

Parrillo, Vincent N. 2006. *Strangers to these Shores,* 8th ed. Boston: Allyn and Bacon.

Rifkin, Jeremy. 2000. *The Age of Access: The New Culture of Hypercapitalism Where All of Life is a Paid-For Experience.* New York: Putnam.

Sciorra, Joseph. 1993. "Multivocality and Vernacular Architecture: Our Lady of Mount Carmel Grotto." Pp. 203-244 in *Studies in Italian Folklore,* edited by Luisa Del Giudice. Logan: Logan State University Press.

Tedlock, Dennis. 1993. *The Spoken Word and the Work of Interpretation.* Philadelphia: University of Pennsylvania Press.

Yans-McLaughlin, Virginia. 1982. *Family and Community: Italian Immigrants in Buffalo, 1880-1930.* Urbana, IL: University of Illinois Press.

Unless otherwise specified, material in this essay is based on interviews with the following descendants of stonecutters:

Norma and Virginia Di Laura. 1982 Albion, NY, conducted by Robert Gates for the Orleans County History Department.

Norma and Virginia Di Laura. 2002-2006, Albion, NY, conducted by Christine Zinni.

Leno Spada. 2005. Alfedena, Italy, conducted by Christine Zinni.

Gilda Trivisond and niece, Caroline Nenni. 2006. Buffalo, NY, conducted by Christine Zinni.

PART FOUR
Perception and Politics

The Disappearing Italian Expatriate Voter and the Census of Italians Abroad

ROCCO CAPORALE
St. John's University and Institute for Italian-American Studies, NY

In 2001, the Institute for Italian American Studies received a grant from the Province of Salerno to conduct a study of its emigrant population in the world. Again, prior to the April 2006 general elections in Italy, the Institute was asked by various North American candidates belonging to different parties to help analyze the official lists of voters made available to them by the Italian Interior Ministry. A similar request came from the newspaper *America Oggi* to conduct a pre-election research and poll.

On the basis of the experience gained from these projects, several months later we asked and received from the Italian government the pertinent breakdown of all Italian voters listed in the *Anagrafe degli Italiani Residenti all'Estero (AIRE)*. We were thus in a position to extend our analysis to various aspects of what was then considered the final and clean list (*allineata*) of expatriate Italians throughout the world entitled to vote. To conduct accurate research through telephone interviews, we also managed to assemble the telephone numbers of nearly two thirds of the Italian voters in the USA and Canada.

A few months later, with a small grant from a generous sponsor, we selected the State of New Jersey, which has a total Italian voting population of 19,648, and conducted an initial in-depth analysis of voters in that state. Much to our surprise, we discovered that the official AIRE list (so-called "cleaned" or "*allineata*") for that state still contained 17 percent errors, that we proceeded to correct down to an estimated error rate of 3 percent, the *zoccolo duro* beyond which we could not progress on our limited budget.

Since the official *Elenco* of voting Italians abroad comprised 2,614,839 expatriates, we calculated that, had someone wanted to replicate the analysis we conducted for the State of New Jersey, the whole list could be cleaned and brought down to a tolerable error level with an investment of less than $750,000.

Much to our surprise, however, we discovered that in the nearly 20 years since the voting law of 1988 was passed, the Italian government had spent over $150 million, had hired 350 *digitatori* (researchers) precisely to do the job of cleaning the *Elenco* AIRE and that Italian consulates worldwide received permission to hire for that purpose 150 adjuncts, over and above the standard consular personnel. In spite of all this, Italy not only still lacks a sufficiently accurate database of Italians abroad, but, as a result of the government-conducted cleaning drive, nearly half of Italian expatriates were deleted from the voting list altogether.

We interpret this to represent the latest ruse in a long history of devious neglect and second-class treatment with which the country has dealt with its emigrant citizens. Let us remember that the mass emigration exodus from Italy acquired momentum, beginning with Italian unification, and increasingly involved people from the south of Italy. Partly for these reasons, from the very beginning of the great migration, the government of Italy has been tragically ambivalent toward its emigrant citizens.

Confronted with their government's incapacity to provide basic working and subsistence conditions, 26 million Italian emigrants brought about the only major revolution that Italy has ever experienced, as they abandoned the land that could not give them a basic, decent human living. All great nations in the world have lived through a major, historically redeeming, and bloody revolution. Italy never had one, with the exception of the mass migration of its proletarian class during the 19th and 20th centuries, a bloodless and individualistic revolution in typical Italian style.

Italy was secretly pleased with the mass migration of its citizens. It lowered the pressure on its labor market and, ironically, provided Italy with a steady and massive flow of foreign exchange from its disenfranchised expatriates, with which to finance its political life and the emerging industries of the north. In 1916, through the *Banco di Napoli* alone, the equivalent of $15 billion (in today's currency) made its way from its expatriates to Italy. "Good riddance and, please, send money!" would appropriately describe the attitude of the national bureaucracy and political leaders of the time.

It is a little known and hardly appreciated fact that the first politician to grasp the meaning of *"l'altra Italia"* (the other Italy) was Benito Mussolini. His motivation was obviously political and imperialistic, underpinning his ambition to establish abroad a strong fascist following. But it is undeniable that Mussolini was the first and almost only Italian politician to pay serious attention to Italians abroad, giving them a sense of dignity and unity, of belonging to a great nation, whose citizens had spread all over the world out of sheer survival necessity.

It is sufficient to recall that all his famous speeches from the *balcone* of Palazzo Venezia would begin with the typical harangue: *"Camice nere della rivoluzione; Italiani d'oltre i monti e d'oltre i mari; uomini e donne di tutta Italia. Ascoltate!"* . . . *(Black shirts of the Revolution; Italians living beyond the mountains and across the seas; all men and women of Italy. Hear me!)*

And it was he who ideated and built the World Center for Italians in the world, Naples' magnificent complex, *la Mostra d'Oltremare e del Lavoro Italiano nel Mondo*, which the Italian government never used for its original purpose, but later converted first into temporary housing for disaster refugees and more recently into a commercial fairground.

The resumption of mass migration after World War II, rather than stimulating a change in Italy's interest in its emigrant citizens, increased its dependence on their remittances, while the nation made hardly any provision for them. We must give recognition to another right wing politician, and member of the Alleanza Nazionale party, the Hon. Mirko Tremaglia, for espousing the cause of Italian expatriates. From 1912 to 1988, virtually no significant laws or provisions regarding Italians abroad were passed. Yet over the course of 50 years, almost single-handedly, Tremaglia pushed legislation for some form of recognition of the contribution of Italian emigrants.

He succeeded in two major achievements. First, the government granted Italian expatriates the opportunity to *exercise* the right to vote by correspondence and to elect representatives of their home Italian communities from their adopted countries. Until 2001, Italian expatriates *had* the constitutional right to vote but, in reality, had no way of *exercising* it because of the distance from Italy, but primarily because Italy did not even know who, how many and where these expatriates were. As parliamentary representative Almirante put it, Italy was committing *"un vero e proprio genocidio elettorale"* . . . (the equivalent of an electoral genocide). The second and related legal breakthrough made it possible (albeit for a limited length of time) for those emigrants who had lost their Italian citizenship, due to naturalization into the host country, to reacquire it.

On October 27, 1988, the Italian Parliament passed the first law, Legge Tremaglia, n. 470. Rightly entitled *"Anagrafe e Censimento degli Italiani all' estero,"* it established in each Italian *comune* a special register named AIRE (*Anagrafe degli Italiani Residenti all'Estero*) with all the pertinent information on those who had emigrated. The data for the entire country was to be assembled by the Ministry of Interior, which was given a mandate to account for and monitor the entire Italian diaspora and their change of residence, if any, using whatever source could provide *all' indirizzo comunque accertato* (the known or available address).

The law made specific provisions for eliminating an emigrant from the AIRE, if he/she returned to Italy, died, reached 100 years of age, or because of *irreperibilita' presunta* (presumed impossible to contact) in the course of two subsequent censuses. The law also urged consular authorities to do all in their power to ascertain the status of the emigrants, even using information derived from local authorities. This was in 1988!

This census was to take place at the same time as the national census of the residents of Italy and was entrusted to the Foreign Ministry, who was completely responsible for its accuracy. The data to be collected about Italians abroad was to include level of education, occupation, and all other pertinent socioeconomic information. All of this was to be done by mail, using appropriate questionnaires. Consular authorities were encouraged to seek help from local authorities, business enterprises, institutions, associations of Italians, the media, and other means to accomplish this task.

The Ministry and all consular offices were to receive help from ISTAT, the National Institute of Statistics, and were permitted to hire additional personnel in proportion to the size of their territory and the Italian population. At the conclusion of the census, the consular authorities were to send the data back to each of the 8,000+ emigrants' *comuni* of origin for updating, and the Foreign Ministry was to publish a detailed report on the distribution and conditions of Italians abroad.

To pay for this plan, the government allocated 5 billion lire in 1988 and 10 billion lire every year henceforth, plus 2 billion more for the Ministry of Interior. Whatever was not spent in a particular year could be used during the next two years.

The law had three crucial shortcomings: 1) for various reasons, the *comuni* were incapable of serving as the primary source of the needed information on the expatriates; 2) the consulates (and for that matter the Foreign Ministry) did not have the necessary structure to gather *ex novo*, or even to update previously collected data, nor did they have at their disposal competent personnel exclusively allocated to this important task; and 3) the procedure envisioned for the census did not include the adoption of new and updated methodologies of data gathering that would have proven valid, such as use of telephone directories, Internet addresses and membership lists from more than 8,000 associations of Italians abroad and of the *Comites*, all strategies to verify in real time the demographic complexities of the population of Italian expatriates.

In 1991, ISTAT published the results of the first "Census" (however conducted). The identified 5.1 million Italian emigrants residing abroad were distributed thus by continents:

North America	423,374
South America	1,798,088
Central America	13,909
Europe	2,192,411
Australia	587,295
Africa	84,843
Asia	15,827
TOTAL	5,115,747

The communiqué noted that these were all citizens with valid Italian passports and consequently, the thousands of emigrants who had opted for the citizenship in their land of emigration, and thus had temporarily lost their Italian citizenship, were not included.

Then, in 1992, a landmark legislation allowed dual citizenship for all Italians who had acquired another nationality, thereby permitting those Italians who had "lost" their Italian citizenship due to naturalization to reacquire it. As a result, the number of those who registered themselves with the *Anagrafe* (AIRE) increased tenfold (see Table 1). To cite just a small example, in the following year those who requested registration in Canada amounted to 152,000, while over 309,000 did so in the United States.

As the date of the 2000 census approached, the Italian government decided to postpone its own foreign citizen census-taking until 2003, because some additional momentous changes in the law were forthcoming. However, both ministries published interim data on Italians abroad. The Foreign Ministry's report indicated that, as of December 31, 2004, more than 3.4 million expatriate Italians had registered at the various consulates, out of a total of 4,250,000 estimated Italian citizens abroad.

TABLE 1
Number of Italians abroad who registered with AIRE, 1990-2004

YEAR OF AIRE REGISTRATION	NEW REGISTRATIONS
1990	894,638
1991	528,816
1992	132,794
1993	137,942
1994	146,600
1995	107,811
1996	99,268
1997	130,386
1998	110,894
1999	154,005
2000	140,868
2001	187,414
2002	219,459
2003	297,275
2004	155,598
TOTAL REGISTRANTS 1990-2004	3,443,768

Two years later, at April 2006 election time, the number of Italians abroad listed in the AIRE was up to 3,529,809 of which only 2,623,338 had the right to vote.

In the specific case of the *circoscrizione* of North America (US, Canada and Central America), the total number of Italians enlisted in the AIRE—officially listed as 403,596 in February 2006, dropped to 347,000 in April, and by June 30th, 2006, was down further to 192,390, of which only 161,022 were eligible to vote.

This unbelievable play of numbers was due to a swift and drastic pruning operation by the Italian Government: any Italian resident abroad who had not registered, had not answered a notice from the local consulate, or was otherwise untraceable was struck down from the list of voters, without further ado. Thus, the total Italian expatriate community in the world entitled to vote dropped from the official Foreign Ministry count of over 5,000,000 in 2000, to 3,500,000 in 2005 and, as of June 30, 2006, to only 2,632,382.

An extremely interesting aspect of this whole drama is its political underpinning among the Italian political parties. For over 50 years it had been the *Italian political right* that had pushed for a census of, and a vote by, Italian expatriates. The understanding was that most of these nostalgia-filled old-timers and crypto-fascists would vote for the right. This fear may probably explain why the Italian left consistently opposed, with unabashed determination, the proposed legislation in favor of granting the right to vote to Italian expatriates.

The 2006 elections, however, by a fluke of fate made the vote abroad a determining factor in the victory of the left. What happened? For one, while the left presented itself united, the right split into five competing parties. Yet other forces were at play. Latin America oriented itself preferentially away from the left/right division of Italian politics into a more independent voice. The older voters of the United States overwhelmingly sided with the right, as expected, while the younger, post-WWII immigrants of Europe, Canada and Australia gave their preference to the left. The sum total, however, gave the left the 25,000 narrow vote margin to claim victory. Thus by some form of cruel irony, the left became a paladin of the Italian expatriates' vote.

On June 18, 2003, in a scorching criticism of the events of the previous five years, the representatives for foreign affairs of the political left said this about the ways the government of the right had handled the issue.

> "We are extremely worried," they stated, "by the results of a first check of the vote by correspondence . . . we are perplexed by the anomalies and discordances found in the various lists of Italians who are entitled to vote, by the handling of the procedures on the options for the vote abroad and by the scarce information provided our citizens . . . " The complaint stated that according to the Foreign Ministry there were somewhere between 2,916,982 and 3,964,887 Italian nationals abroad, of which only 2,447,787 were adults and eligible to vote. "But . . . " they noted " . . . if we were to rely exclusively on the data provided by the Consular Offices, the voters would come closer to 3,279,972. In addition, however, it must be taken into consideration that of the 2,447,787 Italians abroad listed in the official "*Elenco*" of voters by the Italian Ministry of Interior only 1,608,185 correspond with the data of the Ministry of Foreign Affairs, while the remainder are included only in the AIRE of the 8,000+ Italian Municipalities. From these data we conclude that nearly 50% of the Italians included in the consular lists are excluded from voting and are disenfranchised.

The critics further noted that in the official list there was no indication of the consular jurisdiction for 48,653 entries, that in 527,451 cases there were serious incongruities in the addresses, that would put in jeopardy the delivery of any mail to them, that 8,227 were repeated entries and that 13,191 entries showed such lack of data that it was highly improbable that a letter addressed to them will ever reach them. "In summary," they concluded, "of the 2,447,787 entries only 1,871,344 could be safely reached by the postal service." In a word: the procedure followed until then had been disastrous (*disastrosa*). They urged the government to accelerate the cleaning task and suggested the creation of a single, centralized national AIRE of all Italians abroad not linked to the 8,000+ Italian municipalities (Notiziario NIP–News Italia Press agenzia stampa–N° 2–Anno XI, 5 gennaio 2004).

The government responded by carrying out *Operazione Mailing: missione voto all'estero*. Two million letters were sent out to verify the actual address of the voters and synchronize the entries of the two ministries. Ministro Tremaglia was granted the additional sum of 6 million Euros for this task. Unfortunately, the mailing did not contribute much to the solution. While in November 2004 the difference between the two lists was estimated to amount to 800,000, after the mailing campaign 1,800,000 voters were eliminated.

On February 8, 2006, the Ministry of Interior published in the *Gazzetta Ufficiale* the "*Elenco Aggiornato dei cittadini italiani residenti all'estero*," indicating that as of December 31, 2005, there were 3,520,809 citizens abroad who could vote by correspondence, and that they were distributed as follows:

Europe	2,039,149
South America	885,673
North and Central America	403,597
Africa, Asia, Oceania and Antartides	192,390

In April 2006, the Italian political elections were held. The Ministry of Foreign Affairs announced that (mysteriously!) only 2,699,421 ballots had been sent. The envelopes voted and mailed back to the consulates were 1,135,617, equal to 42.07 percent of the total packages mailed. (In Europe the packages returned were, on average, 38.44 percent, in Latin America 51.81 percent, in North America 37.3 percent, and in Africa/Asia/Oceania 44.12 percent).

After the elections the Institute for Italian-American Studies of New York conducted a telephone survey of a statistically representative sample of voters in the U.S. and Canada to find out whether the electoral ballots had been received. The findings from this survey are illustrated in the following chart with its dramatically self-explanatory data:

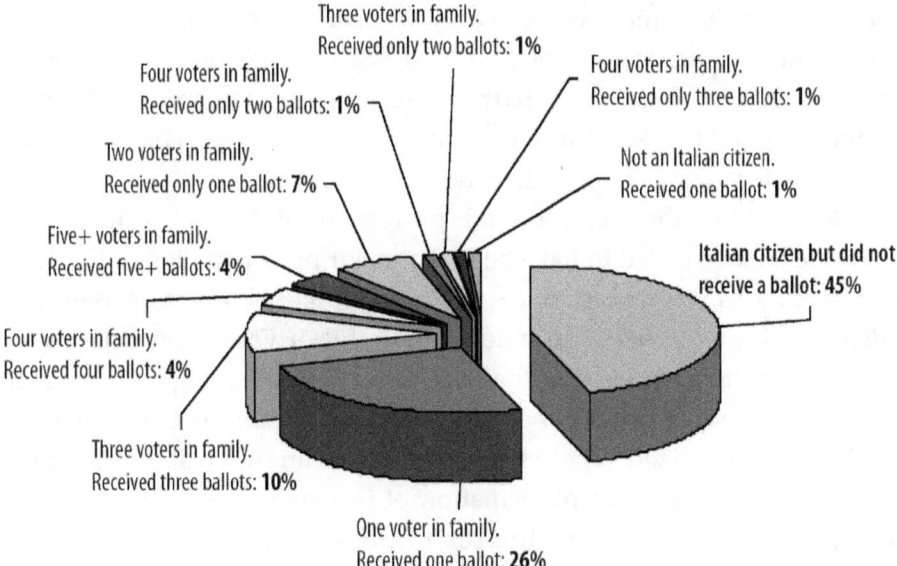

VARIATIONS IN BALLOTS RECEIVED BY ITALIAN FAMILIES IN USA AND CANADA
Source: 2006 Survey by Institute for Italian-American Studies, NY

Finally, when the data distributed by the official Ministry of Interior in its documents on February 28, 2006 and June 30, 2006 were compared, they yielded the following results:

TABLE 2.
Italian Voters listed in USA Consular Jurisdictions in 2006

CONSULAR JURISDICTION	RESIDENT ITALIAN CITIZENS ON FEBRUARY 29, 2006	RESIDENT ITALIAN CITIZENS ON JUNE 30, 2006	DIFFERENCE
Boston	15,429	12,750	-2,679
Chicago	14,510	11,045	-3,465
Detroit	11,528	10,021	-1,507
Philadelphia	20,455	20,506	51
Houston	3,610	3,143	-467
Los Angeles	12,888	11,974	-914
Miami	11,301	11,390	89
New York	80,288	49,750	-30,538
Newark	15,418	11,855	-3,563
San Francisco	9,244	9,118	-126
Washington, DC	4,431	2,860	-1,571
TOTAL USA	199,215	154,412	-44,690

Source: Adapted by Institute for Italian-American Studies from Interior Ministry data.

Having established the Italian government's responsibility for this unbelievable mess, we need to ask: who else is responsible for this rather depressing state of affairs? Much of the confusion and errors illustrated by the above data can be traced to the overlapping and incongruous responsibility of the two Ministries in charge and in competition with each other. At the same time, however, a great deal of responsibility rests on the CGIE (*Consiglio Generale degli Italiani all'Estero*) and on the *Comites*. It was definitely an essential part of their mission to monitor the work conducted by the two Ministries, especially in view of the significant sums of money and personnel involved.

Undoubtedly, the defense and protection of the right to vote of expatriate Italians ought to have been the major preoccupation of the above two institutions. However, since the majority of members of these two bodies had been elected with barely a handful of votes from friends and relatives, it is no surprise that the defense of the voting rights of ALL the electorate was not of prime concern to them, since their own election might thereby be jeopardized. The whole event is in line with Italy's historical lack of interest for greater participation of its expatriates in the life of the nation, even though rarely has this sentiment been openly expressed.

A few months ago, in the course of an interview with a member of the Italian Parliament, a former student of mine, a very liberal political figure, I was stunned to hear her strongly worded objections to the very idea of granting expatriate Italians the right to vote. Shortly thereafter, another member of Parliament, Senator Andrea Pastore, openly proposed a strategy that effectively would preempt and nullify the voting rights of expatriate Italians.

At the same time one must recognize that a significant part of the community of expatriates has consistently shown considerable ignorance, laziness, lack of interest, suspicion and alienation in its relationship with the Italian government and with the electoral process. Here is a concrete example: In the course of cleaning the government data, we called Mr. "Couldntcareless" (pseudonym) of Brooklyn, whose name and address appeared twice in the list, to inform him that he was listed twice in error in the AIRE list. The reply of Mr. "Couldntcareless" was clear and insistent, "Professor, I don't care. Leave it the way it is, even if it is wrong." (Mr. "Couldntcareless," however, in responding to our call for a verifiable telephone number, had unknowingly given us his correct address.)

EPILOGUE

However mystifying, the ballet of conflicting numbers presented in this paper reflects a real but unacceptable situation when we deal with a nation desirous of recognition as one of the most advanced societies in the world.

It can be of little comfort to note that even the USA—proud of its complete and updated list of American citizens abroad who can vote by mail—nevertheless has about one in five of its 5 million citizens abroad unable to make his/her vote count due to delays in mail delivery, failure to receive the ballot, or bureaucratic complexities invariably associated with voting by mail. Whether in Italy or the USA, the procedure of voting by mail needs correcting and perfecting to prevent it from becoming a form of vote suppression.

In the case of Italy, in addition to the shortcomings of voting by correspondence, we find a basic incapacity to correctly list all the voters. When Italian Prime Minister Romano Prodi visited Bahia, Brazil, a few months ago, he was informed that while the total estimated Italian population there was about 10,000, only 1,400 of these were registered with the AIRE.

In the New York Consular area, with a population of nearly 4 million Americans of Italian origin, the Ministry's data indicated that the eligible Italian voters numbered 83,000 in 2006, but the consular database recognized only 65,000 of them, of which only 52,000 received a ballot in the 2006 elections.

To this effect, it is at the same time comforting and dismaying to note that on September 30, 2007, the Italian Ministry of Interior announced that it was *reinstating into the AIRE 400,000 Italian citizens abroad, who had previously been taken off the list in error,* thus raising the total number of Italian citizens abroad with the right to vote to over 3 million! This subdued and nonchalant admission by the Italian Government of its humungous blunder goes only a short way toward repairing the significant damage to its community abroad, because it raises more questions than it answers. The most crucial question is: If, by its own admission, over 400,000 of its citizens abroad (nearly one in seven) were deprived of their right to vote due to government ineptitude in 2006, on what basis can the results of those elections be deemed valid and legitimate?

The next obvious question is: How can we be certain that the governmental error in listing Italians abroad in the AIRE has affected *only 400,000* of them? If, as noted before, by March 6, 2000, more than 3.8

million people had registered at the various consulates out of an estimated total of 4.25 million Italian citizens abroad, what happened to the remaining 800,000 that the Italian Government is still excluding from the AIRE?

The time has come for Italy, wanting recognition as one of the most socially advanced countries in the world, to put a stop to this "electoral genocide," which constitutes a fundamental betrayal of its democratic structure.

References

Cagiano de Azevedo Raimondo 2000. *Le migrazioni internazionali: il cammino di un dibattito.* Torino: G. Giappichelli Editore.

Cariani Giovanni 2004. "Un censimento dimenticato o quasi: la rilevazione dei cittadini italiani all'estero." *Mobilità e trasformazioni strutturali della popolazione, Quaderni del dipartimento per lo Studio delle Società mediterranee n. 28.* Bari: Cacucci Editore.

Cariani Giovanni, Pier Paolo Pace, and Alberto Silvestrini. 2005. *La rilevazione degli italiani all'estero: alcune considerazioni preliminari.* Rome: Istat.

Cortese Aldo, 2004. *Le comunità italiane all'estero all'inizio del XXI secolo,* in *Mobilità e trasformazioni strutturali della popolazione. Quaderni del dipartimento per lo Studio delle Società mediterranee n. 28.* Bari: Cacucci Editore.

Ministero degli Affari Esteri. 2001-2002. *Il Ministero degli Affari Esteri in cifre – Annuario Statistico.* Roma. Anno 2000.

Notiziario NIP – News Italia Press agenzia stampa. Torino: N° 2 – Anno XI, 5 gennaio 2004.

Contadini, Sovversivi, and Electors: Italian-American Radicalism and Municipal Elections in 1940s New York City

MICHELE ROSA-CLOT
University of Pisa

> *"No democracy can endure as long as political minorities are deprived of [the] right to appear on [the] ballot."* — VITO MARCANTONIO

With a few notable exceptions, historians have failed to recognize the variety and diversity of the Italian-American political experience.[1] In the past four decades, Italian Americans have generally been characterized as a "non-ideological, politically apathetic, or conservative" group (Meyer 1996:33). According to this perspective, Italian Americans tended to avoid any interaction with the world of U.S. politics, and when they did interact, they remained either within the logic and structure of party machines, or within the dialectic of Italian fascism and international antifascism. Historians have looked at the active radicalism of Italian Americans as atypical, and at Italian-American radical politicians such as anarchist Carlo Tresca and Fusionist-Laborite Vito Marcantonio, or less famous local politicians like communist councilman Peter V. Cacchione, as exceptional examples of *sovversivi* (Krase 1985).

The twin tendency to political apathy and electoral abstention of the Italian American was an undeniable phenomenon, but, as Italian historian Stefano Luconi stresses, in the last four decades scholars have contributed to underscoring the magnitude of Italian-American disinterest for electoral participation (Luconi 2002:16). The predominant approach toward Italian-American political participation was framed around sociologist Edward C. Banfield's notion of "amoral familism" (Banfield 1958). This was systematically used to describe the Italian-American community, in an effort to explain its lack of political and electoral

---

[1] The most relevant exception is Cannistraro 2003. See also Meyer 1989, and Meyer 1996.

participation. According to this thesis, the centrality of the family led Italian Americans to seek their full realization as a group within their own community rather than in the democratic polity. The set of values thus formed and transmitted within the Italian ethnic group were essentially individualistic and self-centered, and undermined any political participation, especially through large institutional structures such as the political parties.

A number of peculiar characteristics of Italian-American immigration tended to reinforce this approach. Unlike other ethnic minorities, abstention characterized Italian-American political behavior for a long time, and, in particular, that of new immigrants. While the other ethnic group that characterized the new immigration wave between the 1890s and the 1910s—the European Jews—participated actively to electoral dynamics and to machine politics, Italian immigrants exhibited a constant disaffection to the politics, especially those of the Left (Tomasi 1975). Low electoral turnout rates among Italian Americans were also a consequence of a typical aspect of Italian immigration: the conscious resistance to integration. Many Italian immigrants postponed indefinitely the acquisition of U.S. citizenship, a precondition for the right to vote, because they cultivated the hope of going back home after making their fortune in America.[2]

The widespread conviction that Italians reproduced inhibiting behaviors of political involvement within their U.S. community, which were characteristic of the backward rural society from which they came, contributed to reinforcing the thesis of the marginality or apathetic orthodoxy of Italian-American ethnicity in the story of political elections within the United States. This traditional perspective of Italian-American political behavior, however, is not satisfactory. The focus on Italian-American non-political behavior caused historians to neglect the existence of Italian-American radicalism and its contributions. Although the limited dimension of Italian-American political participation is unquestionable and the majority of Italian-American political activity was centered on the traditional parties' machine, sections of the community adopted a different conduct.

---

[2] In New York City, for example, in 1915, Italian-American turnout was of only 15,000 voters, even though the potential electoral force of the community was over half a million (Levine 1966; Sowell 1981; Vecoli 1978; Nelli 1983).

The history of New York City politics between 1936 and 1947 suggests how the traditional interpretation is too restrictive. During this decade, three converging events changed New York politics in an original direction, unbalancing the traditional political equilibrium and giving visibility to an original Italian-American political dimension: the crisis of the Democratic party, the success of radical third parties such as the American Labor Party (ALP) and the American Communist Party (CPUSA – CP), and the adoption in 1936 of a new city charter that substituted the traditional electoral system of the Board of Aldermen (the *Single Member District system*) with proportional representation.

Ethnicity has always been a fundamental component of New York City's politics. As "the Golden Door," "the dollar's Mecca," "the main port of entry for millions of immigrants seeking a better life," New York City saw its political parties create a political system that took into account the delicate dynamics and conflicting interests of the diverse composition of the city (Kessner 1977:10; Bayor 1978:1.) By 1860, when Italians made their appearance in the slums in Spring Street, the immigrant Irish represented 25.4 percent of the white population of New York City and during the following decades, against nativist resistance, the Irish minority took solid control of Tammany – the Democratic Party organization of New York County.

When, in the 1890s, the massive immigration of other ethnic groups (notably the Jews and the Italians) started challenging their political monopoly, the Irish engaged in a systematic policy of exclusion of the newer immigrants from the spaces of politics and administration. This policy, however, had short life; the increasing political weight of the new immigrant population threatened to unbalance the traditional electoral dynamics and prompted a change in the electoral policies and political administration of the public offices. Jews and Italians, traditionally excluded from the favors of New York City's Democratic party, started looking elsewhere to claim their share of political power.[3]

In an attempt to prevent eventual defection to other parties (notably the Republican and the Socialist), in 1902, under its new leader Charles

---

[3] The Republican Party was the first to support an Italian in Congress: for mayor (in both cases Fiorello La Guardia), and for U.S. Senator (Edward Corsi in 1938). The election of Fiorello La Guardia in 1933 was the first major event in the electoral life of Italian-Americans in New York City. His following two mayoral elections and Vito Marcantonio's five successful political ALP candidacies to Congress – from 1939 to 1951 – represented momentous events in the process of political maturation of Italian Americans in the City (McNickle 1993:48).

Francis Murphy, Tammany started giving a number of offices to non-Irish ethnic groups, particularly to Jews.[4] However, nominations of Italian Americans to important political or administrative positions remained irrelevant for a long time. Although since 1860, New York's Italian colony had constantly grown in number, passing from the "little handful of Italians" registered in the census of 1860 to the 391,000 foreign-born Italians recorded in 1920 (one-third of Greater New York's white population and one fourth of the national total of Italian immigrants), Italians were not ethnically represented in the Board of Aldermen—the main administrative assembly of the city (Kessner 1977:14; Miranda and Rossi 1976). The first Italian district leader for Tammany was Albert Marinelli in 1931, and this, only after two Marinelli armed supporters "persuaded" the incumbent (the Irish-American Harry Perry) to step aside (Kessner 1977:14; Miranda and Rossi 1976). Between 1922 and 1942, only four of the 51 elected candidates in the State Senate were of Italian descent and between 1935 and 1936 less than 10 percent of the candidates for the major parties were Italian American (Meyer 1996).

A consistent portion of the Italian-American community's political life remained centered on Tammany Hall (or on other local Democratic organizations like the Madison Club in Brooklyn) as a center for the distribution of political and administrative favors—a power that Tammany enjoyed since the 19th century, and grew even further at the beginning of 1900. Between 1904 and 1934, almost without interruption, the Democratic Party had the control of the mayor's office and of New York City's Board of Aldermen. During these years Tammany systematically took control of the city and of its economic and administrative resources, and, as Krase and LaCerra point out, a large part of the political behavior of both the Italian-American bosses and of the Italian-American electorate was machine-driven because, even though they did not obtain ethnic representation, machine politics offered a wide array of other political advantages (Krase and La Cerra 1991).

Along with Tammany's unstoppable successes, the widespread climate of political and administrative corruption that characterized the Democratic government of the city nurtured a steady anti-Tammany spirit that coalesced at the beginning of the 1930s around the Seabury

---

[4] Starting in 1909, for example, the position of Borough President of Manhattan was usually given to a Jew.

investigations.[5] In 1930, per Governor Franklin Delano Roosevelt's request, the New York State Supreme Court appointed a special investigator—Judge Samuel Seabury, "an austere and imposing fifty-seven-year-old [and] one of the most widely respected personages in New York City"—to probe into the political and administrative scandals or, as the *National Municipal Review* wrote, "in the . . . orgy of misrule" (Allen 1993:242. Mitgang 1962:159; *National Municipal Review* 1936:299). In the summer of 1932, after two years of public investigations, Seabury's public denouncement of "graft and crookedness of every description and in every phase of the city government," gave a serious blow to the political stability of the Democratic Party machine (Shaw 1954:36). After the investigation results were publicized, the resulting public indignation forced Mayor James J. Walker to resign, and triggered a diffused reaction of blame and hostility towards the Democratic party apparatus that was increasingly described, as expressed in an article in the *New York Times*, as "an organization made up of mercenary men bent on making money out of political power" (*The New York Times* 1932:22).

Seabury's investigations represented a judicial and political blow against Tammany, and were the first of the three converging events that changed New York's traditional political patterns. Although the Democratic Party never failed to maintain its preponderant majority in the Board of Aldermen, after the "Seabury scandals," the political signal that New York's electorate expressed in 1933 at the election of an interim mayor to fill Walker's vacancy, shifting in favor of Fusion coalitions and third parties, and demanding political and administrative reform, indicated a clear disappointment.[6] Even if the Democratic candidate John P. O'Brien was easily elected, he fell considerably short of the result Democrats obtained in any other electoral contest in the same year (McNickle 1993:33). In 1933, Tammany Hall lost some of its absolute control over New York's electoral politics.

The second of the three converging events that changed New York's politics, increasing the visibility of an Italian-American radical component, was the political and electoral success of two radical electoral

---

[5] In the first sixteen years of the century (and with only four exceptions) the Democrats were able to obtain the majority of the board of aldermen, and between 1922 and 1937, Tammany maintained its majority over 80%. The Democratic Party lost its majority only in 1902, 1906, 1912, and 1914 (McNickle 1993:48).

[6] At the 1933 election for the interim mayor, the Socialist Party received more than double the ballots cast for the Socialist presidential candidate that year (McNickle 1993:33).

formations, traditionally external to the long-established bipartisan politics: the American Labor Party (ALP) and the Communist Party (CP). From June 1934 onward, the threat of European Nazi-Fascism induced Comintern to instruct the communist parties around the world to form alliances with the socialist parties and, a few months later, the Seventh World Congress of the Comintern in 1935 concretized these policies in the Popular Front. In the U.S. as well as in Europe, communist parties had the opportunity to turn into "a respectable, legitimate political movement" (Kelly 1990:137).

Formally organized on July 16, 1936, the ALP was traditionally described as an essentially Jewish phenomenon. However, several elements show not only how "there existed an avowedly leftist cohort within the Italian-American community" (Meyer 1996:47) that provided local leadership for the ALP and the CP (the chairman of the new party, Luigi Antonini, was an Italian American) (McNickle 1993:48.), but also how Italian Americans had been a significant electoral component of the party (Meyer 1996:47).[7] The ALP tapped into a wide electoral basin mostly comprised of ethnic minorities and cohesive neighborhoods of both Italian Americans and Jewish Americans.[8] ALP's strategy to provide "a line under which Socialists and other radicals and liberals could vote for the New Deal without voting for the Democratic Party" (Waltzer ix, 2) was extremely effective, and against every prediction in its first elections in 1937, the ALP polled 21 percent of the valid votes. Between 1936 and 1950, the ALP polled an average of 15 percent of New York City's candidates for president, senator, and mayor, and frequently polled high percentages for other offices (Waltzer 1977:ix, 2. Meyer 1996:36. *The New York Red Book*. See also *The New York Times* 1945:4; Waltzer 1977:112).

Although the average Italian-American vote for the ALP roughly represented 10 percent of the electoral force of that ethnic group, the Italian vote reached high peaks when an Italian American led the ALP ticket, as in East Harlem, where Vito Marcantonio won six terms as an ALP candidate from 1939 to 1949. Furthermore, when he ran for mayor in 1949, against another Italian American, Democrat Vincent Richard Impellitteri (mayor of

---

[7] Antonini was the vice secretary of the ILGWU, the main union supporting the ALP, and a prominent figure both among Italian Americans and Jews of New York City (Bayor 1978:20-21, 80. McNickle 1993:48).

[8] In particular, the ALP polled good results in East Harlem in connection with the candidacy of Vito Marcantonio: a political union that contributed to create a "positive attraction between the ALP and the Italian-American community" (Meyer 1996:42).

New York between 1950 and 1953), Vito Marcantonio secured the compact vote of East Harlem, and over 30 percent of the vote in other Little Italys (Meyer 1989; Waltzer 1977:41, 143)

In the same period, after New York's communists abandoned the sectarian radicalism of the militant Third Period anti-New Deal politics, the CP began a season of collaboration fusion with the ALP, building a second focus for the electoral attraction of Italian-American radicalism in New York City (Bayor 1978:67, 75. *The New York Times* 1937:10). From 1922 to 1925, the U.S. Communist Party's Italian Bureau—a section of the party formed by first-generation immigrants and others specifically working with the foreign-born—ranged from 138 to 581. By 1938, when the party counted an enrollment of 51,000, the Italian bureau counted between 500 and 800 members (between 1 and 1.5 percent). Among the foreign bureaus of the party, the Italians ranked below the Jews who boasted 4,000 members, but were on par (in terms of registered members) with other major ethnic groups such as the Germans, Russians, and Greeks (Meyer 2003:206).

In 1948, the Italian-American section represented 300, or 3 percent, of Manhattan's 10,000 CP members (Meyer 2003:206) and was able to exert some attraction during public events such as the two parades and a mass rally organized after the invasion of Ethiopia, together with the League against War and Fascism, attended by between 20,000 "Italian and Negro people," according to the *New York Times*, and 50,000 to 75,000, according to the African-American *New York Age* (Meyer 2003:211). Italian-American participation in the Communist Party was also strengthened by the activities of the Garibaldi-American Fraternal Society, the Italian-American section of the International Workers Order (IWO)—a CP affiliated fraternal organization. Membership of the Garibaldi Fraternal Society grew steadily until 1947 when it reached nearly 11,000 members—that is 6 percent of IWO's total membership (Meyer 2003:207). The IWO was known among Italian Americans by its Italian name— Ordine Italiano Internazionale or OOI. The OOI promoted the Communist Party's Italian-language press and other activities connected both to the endorsement of the CP and to other issues specifically directed to the Italian-American community. The many activities that the Garibaldi Society and one of its most dynamic lodges (La Progressiva, active in East Harlem) promoted in New York are a good indicator of the IWO involvement with the Italian-American community. Located in the heart of Marcantonio's El Barrio, La Progressiva had an average of 80 members but could attract several hundreds at its public meetings. The lodge was one of the main electoral supporters for Vito Marcantonio's candidacies and systematically provided legal assistance to Italian Americans in citizenship related cases, weekly political lectures, and a number of neighborhood social activities like open road parties and community picnics. These public initiatives were able to attract from a few hundred to several thousand people (*L'Unità del Popolo* 1940a:1; *L'Unità del Popolo* 1940b:3).

Finally, the communist press specifically addressed to Italian Americans provides an important clue verifying the existence of a radical component of the Italian-American community. Although the Italian American communist press always represented a small percentage of the total Italian-American potential readership, the radical and communist Italian papers circulated in significant numbers: the circulation of *L'Unità del Popolo*, published between 1938 and 1951, reached its zenith in 1940, with approximately 10,000 copies: almost 10 percent of the total volume of Italian-American papers (Meyer 2007).[9]

However, the organization of a third electoral pole around the ALP and the successes of the CP was not possible because of the change in international climate or because of the loss of consensus of the Democratic machine. In 1936, a third critical transformation of New York's electoral structure affected the electoral dynamics of the city. On November 3, 1936, on the wave of the Seabury investigations, and at the peak of a five-year-long anti-Tammany campaign, New York adopted a new charter providing for proportional representation (PR) for the election of its city council. If the foundation of the ALP introduced a disruption of the traditional political relations on the plan of national representation, the transition to an electoral system based on proportional representation was a serious interference at the municipal level.[10]

---

[9] The CP sponsored a number of newspapers aimed at its influential national constituents. Its Italian-American section sponsored *Il Lavoratore* between 1924 and 1931, *L'Unità Operaia* from 1932 and 1938, *L'Unità del Popolo* from 1938 to 1951, and *Unity,* from 1951 to 1961.

[10] With the traditional majority system known as Single Member District System (SMD), every state, county, or city is divided in as many electoral districts as there are representatives to elect. Each district is entitled to one representative only, who is elected by plurality. The candidate winning the plurality of the votes obtains the entire representation for the district. The SMD henceforth gives the winning party a "super representation" and tends to polarize the electoral battle within the two major parties participating in the electoral contest, with hardly any room for the creation of "third parties" or independent candidates. Proportional representation (PR), instead, is based on the idea that every party participating in the elections held at large should be entitled to a percentage of representatives equal to the percentage of the popular votes it has received. For a detailed history of

In 1937 and 1939, the first two city elections with the proportional representation (PR) system showed how the change of electoral laws induced the transformation of the city's political balance. Aside from the previously mentioned success of the ALP enabling it to become the city's second party with 21 percent of the votes, the new city council included substantial minorities that the majority system would otherwise have excluded from representation. (Rosa-Clot 2007:321-322).

With the third PR election in November 1941, the scenario began to change in a way that many observers considered disturbing. Not only, for the first time in New York history were women, a black candidate—Adam Clayton Powell Jr., a Fusion/ALP candidate—and several Laborites elected to the city council, but the newly constituted council listed among its members a communist: Peter V. Cacchione, "natural leader of Brooklyn's Italian-Americans" (*L'Unità del Popolo* 1940c:3) and President of the National Electoral Committee of the Communist Party, was elected in Brooklyn with 48,299 votes. With public opinion increasingly anti-immigrant (and anti-Italian), and anti-Communist, the election of Cacchione, Communist and Italian American, caused a political and cultural trauma.

Immediately after the election, newspapers, politicians, and commentators raised their voices against the "scandal" of a communist's election. The *Brooklyn Eagle*, a stubborn enemy of the La Guardia administration, expressed disappointment in the anti-PR coalition, publishing an editorial entitled "Election of Red to Council Is New Blow to P.R. System," thus codifying the argument that, eventually, led to PR abrogation six years later (*Brooklyn Eagle* 1941). After the third PR election in 1941, an article in *The Political World* read:

> A. Clayton Powell, the Negro, got thousands of votes from the politically ignorant who naturally supposed that they were voting for an Anglo-Saxon, and Peter Cacchione, the Communist, got thousands of votes from Italian Americans whose first thought was racial rather than American (cited in Hermens 1943:n. 27).

The anti-Communist apprehension and the anti-proportionalist propaganda increased to an intolerable level in 1943 with the re-election of Cacchione to the city council and the election of a second communist councilman, Benjamin Davis, a black candidate elected with the votes of a

---

New York's proportionalist experiment, see Rosa-Clot 2007:229-335

surprisingly large majority of the Harlem electorate. From the first abrogation campaign in 1940, a part of the anti-PR propaganda focused on the consideration that PR was giving super-representation to racial, ethnic, and religious minorities. As Ferdinand Hermens, a political science professor at Notre Dame University and an influential anti-PR commentator, explained in 1943, "Another aspect of the 1941 Council elections was the recurrence of 'freaks' on large scale" (Hermens 1943:47). Cacchione and, after 1943, Davis were elected only by virtue of their being "ethnic" and "racial" candidates rather than communists.

The proportionalist coalition responded by publishing an analysis of the vote and studies of the transfers of the Hare system's ballots. For example, as explained in an article in the *National Municipal Review* on December 1943, when six candidates with Italian names or ancestry were defeated, the second choices on their ballots were not redistributed to the remaining Italian candidates, but according to partisan lines instead (*National Municipal Review*, 1943:624.) As a matter of fact, every candidate in the 1941 electoral race carefully avoided emphasizing specific or radical issues to appeal to the largest number of electors. Even communists and "leftist" ALP candidates found a shelter under the ample umbrella of the war with Nazism and of protection of "people's interests." After his election on November 12, 1941, Peter Cacchione issued a soothing statement aimed to console those in the city who were in shock at seeing an Italian communist and a black (Rev. Adam Clayton Powell) enter the city council for the first time in the history of the city. Cacchione repeated, once again, that "[m]y election is a mandate from the people of Brooklyn—and so I consider it—a mandate to continue and intensify my efforts in behalf of the unity of all peoples and forces working for the defense of America" (*L'Unità del Popolo* 1941:1-2; Gerson 1976:109).

In emphasizing that his mandate came from the people of Brooklyn, Cacchione simply stated what was commonly recognized. His vote was only partially based on a communist vote, as it came, instead, from "thousands of ballots cast by Democrats, Republicans, Laborites, veterans, Unionists, and Italian-Americans" (*L'Unità del Popolo* 1941:2). Thanks to the peculiarity of the electoral system and to the knowledge of his neighborhood, Cacchione could analyze in detail his electorate, and could define, with good approximation, the political inclination of his electors. For every one of his 35,000 first choices, Cacchione's staff calculated that he received six first choices from non-Communists. Once the second and third choices were added, calculations showed that the communist vote for Cacchione was roughly 10 percent of his final 48,629 votes (Gerson 1976:110). As Cacchione and his aides concluded, the hard core of his vote came from left wingers, readers of the communist and progressive foreign language press. Many votes "were cast by militant trade unionists, and some from liberal intellectuals," but not necessarily from Italians and communists (Gerson 1976:110).

Notwithstanding the severe anti-PR and anti-Communist criticism that tried to link Cacchione's successes, electoral laws, and ethnic vote, Italian-American ballots were not the primary source for his election. The neighborhood vote for Cacchione was considerable and Cacchione got his most solid vote from Jewish neighborhoods; among white candidates, he obtained the best results in the black neighborhoods. Even though he did not get landslide results in Italian-American neighborhoods, Cacchione drew consistent support from them. However, as Gerson stresses, "As a practical matter . . . his 'ethnic' Italian vote was no greater and in fact less than that of some Italian-American machine candidates" (Gerson 1976:111). Nonetheless, it is important to note how Cacchione was indeed able to secure a reservoir of Italian-American working-class votes, particularly from neighborhoods mainly populated by Italian-American longshoremen and garment workers.

In conclusion, the Italian-American tendency to find parameters of aggregation within the community rather than on external political structures generated in U.S. scholars the perception of Italian Americans as lethargic or non-political. But if the traditional notion of "amoral familism" is indeed helpful in explaining some of the deepest sociological mechanisms of southern Italian *contadini*, it seems largely insufficient to explain Italian-American community political dynamics in their entirety. During the 1930s Italian Americans participated actively in national politics, becoming "a fundamental component of the electoral coalition that elected Franklin Delano Roosevelt in 1932 and helped the Democratic Party to maintain control of the presidency until the election of Dwight Eisenhower in 1952" (Luconi 2002:11; translation mine).

The story of the electoral and militant activity of Italian Americans in New York City between 1936 and 1947 does not fit within traditional descriptive parameters. The electoral conduct of Italian Americans in New York City in the 1930s and 1940s not only demonstrates that charges of political apathy are misleading and inaccurate, but also that an important, although minority, part of the Italian-American community contributed to shaping politically radical issues. The Italian vote did not go only to the Democrats and Republicans, as Ronald Bayor claims in his study on the electoral behavior of New York City's ethnic groups. Italian Americans did not support the ALP or the CP only because of the ethnic identification with La Guardia, Vito Marcantonio, or with the other Italian-American candidates, or because of the incredible amount of activities they sponsored in their neighborhoods. Italian Americans did not vote for Marcantonio only in his fiefdom — East Harlem — but they cast their votes for the ALP and the CP in other Manhattan neighborhoods as well as in the other New York boroughs (Bayor 1978:32).

Despite the facts that, for the first two decades of the 20th century, the radicalism of the more politicized among Italian immigrants was commonly associated with anarchism, and that, historians of Italian-American immigration deemed the execution of Sacco and Vanzetti in 1927 as representing "the end of a road [of Italian-American radicalism] rather than the beginning of one" (Topp 1996:142), the radical stream of the Italian-American community did not turn "apathetic." Furthermore, the Italian-American contribution to the increasing electoral strength of the CP was a real phenomenon and fully visible in the figures in municipal elections held after 1936. Because of the new proportionalist electoral laws, the CP accumulated real electoral strength instead of having it dispersed (and defeated) in various districts. As a matter of fact, in the 1930s, Italian Americans became an important part of public dissent and constituted a small but noteworthy component both of the American Labor Party and of the Communist Party.

The use of proportional representation in New York City favored the emergence of social forces and political subjects that, barely visible under the majority system of representation, disappeared again after 1947 with the abrogation of PR. In the brief interval in between though, they proved to be a structural component of the city and a legitimate part of the U.S. democratic system. The elected Italian-American Laborites and communists — as well as those women and men who joined the city council for the first time in the city's history — were not "invented" by the new electoral system, but were already part of the city's actual political pattern. Proportional representation merely gave them institutional visibility.

In 1975, historian Richard Gambino summed up, "Some Italian labor militants . . . were socialists or anarchists, [however] the vast majority of the transplanted *contadini* cared nothing for ideologies" (Gambino 1975:117). This is true; the majority of these *contadini* shared its political life within Italian community *machine politics*. However, what Gambino and the tradition dismissing Italian Americans as apathetic both underestimate is that the "handful of radicals and socialists" (Glazer and Moynihan 1963:214) was not and was not deemed irrelevant.

References

Allen, Oliver E. 1993. *The Tiger. The Rise and Fall of Tammany Hall*. Reading, MA.: Addison-Wesley.

Banfield, Edward C. 1958. *The Moral Basis of a Backward Society*. Glencoe, IL: Free Press.

Bayor, Ronald H. 1978. *Neighbors in Conflict: The Irish, Germans, Jews, and Italians of New York City, 1929-1941*. Baltimore: The John Hopkins University Press.

Brooklyn Eagle. 1941. "Election of Red to Council Is New Blow to P.R. System." 13 November.

Cannistraro Philip V. and Gerald Meyer, ed. 2003 *The Lost World of Italian-American Radicalism: Politics, Labor, and Culture*. Westport. CT: Praeger.

Gambino, Richard. 1975. *Blood of my Blood: The Dilemma of the Italian Americans*. New York: Anchor Books.

Glazer, Nathan and Patrick Moynihan. 1963. *Beyond the Melting Pot: The Negroes, Puerto Ricans, Jews, Italians and Irish of New York City*, Cambridge: The M.I.T. and Harvard University Press.

Gerson, Simon. 1976. *Pete: The Story of Peter V. Cacchione: New York's First Communist Councilman*. New York: International Publishers.

Hermens, Ferdinand A. 1943. *P.R., Democracy and Good Government*. Terre Haute, IN: University of Notre Dame Press.

Kelly, Robin D. G. 1990. *Hammer and Hoe: Alabama Communists during the Great Depression*. Chapel Hill, NC: University of North Carolina Press.

Kessner, Thomas. 1977. *The Golden Door: Italian and Jewish Immigrant Mobility in New York City, 1880-1915*. New York: Oxford University Press.

Krase, Jerome. 1985. "The Missed Step: Italian Americans and Brooklyn Politics." Pp. 187-198 in *Italians and Irish in America: Proceedings of the Sixteenth Annual Conference of the American Italian Historical Association*, edited by Francis X. Femminella. Staten Island, NY: The American Italian Historical Association.

Krase, Jerome and Charles La Cerra. 1991. *Ethnicity and Machine Politics*. New York: University Press of America.

Levine, Edward M. 1966. *The Irish and Irish Politicians: A Study of Cultural and Social Alienation*. Terre Haute, IN: University of Notre Dame Press.

Luconi, Stefano. 2002. *Little Italies e New Deal: La Coalizione Rooseveltiana e il Voto Italo-Americano a Filadelfia e Pittsburgh*. Milano: Franco Angeli.

Marcantonio, Vito. N.d. Telegram to Hon. Morton Witken, Chairman of the Philadelphia Board of Elections. Vito Marcantonio Papers, Box 4: Electoral Democracy: Contested Elections. New York Public Library, New York.

McNickle, Chris. 1993. *To be Mayor of New York: Ethnic Politics in the City*. New York: Columbia University Press.

Meyer, Gerald. 1989. *Vito Marcantonio: Radical Politician, 1902-1954*. Albany, NY: State University of New York Press.

—. 1996. "The American Labor Party and New York City's Italian American Communities, 1936-1950." Pp. 33-49 in *Industry, Technology, Labor, and The Italian American Communities: Selected*

Essays From the 28th Annual Conference of the American Italian Historical Association in Lowell, Massachusetts, November 11-13, 1995, edited by Mario Aste and others. New York: American Italian Historical Association.

———. 2003. "Italian Americans and the American Communist Party." Pp. 205-227 in Cannistraro, Philip V. and Gerald Meyer, ed. *The Lost World of Italian-American Radicalism: Politics, Labor, and Culture*. Westport, CT: Praeger.

Miranda, Edward J. and Ino J. Rossi. 1976. *New York City's Italians: The Size Residential Distribution and Socio-Economic Characteristics of New York City's Italians*. New York: Italian American Center for Urban Affairs.

Mitgang, Herbert. 1962. *The Man Who Rode the Tiger: The Life and Times of Judge Samuel Seabury*. Philadelphia: J. B. Lippincott Company.

National Municipal Review. 1936. "New York to Vote This Fall." 25:5, p. 299.

———. 1943. "Racial Voting a Minor Factor." 32:12, p. 624.

Nelli, Humbert S. 1983. *From Immigrants to Ethnics: The Italian Americans*. New York: Oxford University Press.

The New York Red Book. 1945. Albany, NY: Williams Press.

The New York Times. 1932. "The Seabury Report." 26 November, p. 22.

———. 1937. "Reds Join Labor in a United Front to Aid La Guardia." 27 September, p. 10.

———. 1945. "Tabulation of the Election Results in New York." 7 November, p. 4.

Rosa-Clot, Michele. 2007. "One Representation under God. Evoluzione del concetto di rappresentanza elettorale e storia della rappresentanza proporzionale negli Stati Uniti d'America." Ph.D. dissertation, Università degli Studi di Pisa, Pisa.

Shaw, Frederick. 1954. *The History of the New York City Legislature*. New York: Columbia University Press.

Sowell, Thomas. 1981. *Ethnic America: A History*. New York: Basic Books.

Tomasi, Silvano M. 1975. *Piety and Power: The Role of the Italian Parishes in the New York Metropolitan Area: 1880-1930*. New York: Center for Migration Studies.

Topp, Michael. 1996. "The Italian-American Left: Transnationalism and the Quest for Unity." Pp. 119-147 in *The Immigrant Left in the United States*, edited by Paul Buhle and Dan Georgakas. Albany: State University of New York Press.

L'Unità del Popolo. 1940a. "1000 persone al Picnic dell'Ordine." 17 August, p. 1.

———. 1940b. "Attività della Loggia 'La Progressiva'." 21 September, p. 3.

———. 1940c. "Un'intervista con Peter Cacchione." 19 October, p. 3.

———. 1941. "Quattro Italo-americani eletti al consiglio municipale di New York." 22 November: 1-2.

Vecoli, Rudolph J. 1978. "The Coming of Age of the Italian Americans: 1945-1974." *Ethnicity* 1:19-147.

Waltzer, Kenneth Alan. 1977. "The American Labor Party: Third Party Politics in the New Deal–Cold War New York, 1936-1954." Ph.D. dissertation, Harvard University, Cambridge, MA.

White Ethnics and White Privilege

KARYN LOSCOCCO
University at Albany, SUNY

The critical study of whiteness has emerged as a key component of the sociological study of race in the United States. The goal is to recognize that white is also a racial category and that membership in it confers privileges denied to people of color. Rather than center analysis of race on the problems that race poses for African Americans and Latinos, for example, scholars investigate the relationship between white advantage and the disadvantages of other racial groups. A central aim—to get people to see whites as a racial group rather than the default category whose race is invisible and unproblematic—is a difficult and important one in the post Civil Rights era. Most whites are unaware that their lives are shaped by race; indeed, they think of people of color, but not themselves, as having a race (Dalton 1995). Embracing ethnic identity, as Italian American and other white ethnic groups do, is far more common. Yet ethnic pride contributes to masking white privilege.

BECOMING WHITE

Many of those whose families have roots in Europe are unaware that their ancestors were not automatically considered white, such is the taken-for-granted nature of their whiteness now. However, the history of European immigration to the United States in the nineteenth and early twentieth centuries is also a history of the social construction of whiteness (e.g., Allen 1994; Roediger 1995). First the Irish and then Italians, Greeks, Jews and other groups from southern, central and eastern Europe were labeled as nonwhite (Ignatiev 1996; Barrett and Roediger 1996; Parrillo 2009). By the 1920s, mainstream scientists promoted the idea that true Americans were white and that "real whites" came from northwestern Europe (Sacks 1994:19).

Racism was a new dimension of antagonism toward newcomers during the wave of immigration that began in the 1880s (Pavalko 1981;

Parrillo 2009). The immigrants and their children were segregated in overcrowded areas of the city, and confined to particular occupations. "Italians, Poles, Greeks and Jews were called derogatory names, attacked by nativist mobs, and derided in the press" (Waters 1996:444). The slur "guinea," used to refer to Italian Americans in the United States until the 1970s, was originally used to disparage African slaves and their descendants (Roediger 1995). In the 1890s the term was transferred to European immigrants, "especially to darker southern Italians (and sometimes to Spanish, Greek, Jewish and Portuguese) immigrants" as part of a more general process to link these immigrants with African Americans rather than with the Northern European laborers who called themselves "white men" (Roediger 1995:656).

Race-based exclusion applied especially to Italians and Jews because they stood out the most on the basis of their large numbers, physical features, ethnic neighborhoods, and distinctive cultural practices (Parrillo 2009). According to Puleo (2007) Italians were lynched more than any other immigrant group, though not nearly as much as African Americans. He also contends that in some parts of the South, the law held that Italians could not attend white schools. The violence and discrimination directed toward southern Italians stemmed from their proximity to African Americans in workplaces and communities, as well as in the public imagination (Puleo 2007:81).

Eventually, the meaning of the category *white* was reframed to include Italians and other southern, central and eastern European groups through a particular set of sociohistorical circumstances (Allen 1994; Barrett and Roediger 1996). There are some differences in the way that the various Euro-origin immigrant groups shed racial oppression by solidifying their status as whites, but World War II played a crucial role in relaxing the tightly held boundaries around the category of white to include them (Sacks 1994).

ETHNIC PRIDE AND THE DENIAL OF WHITE PRIVILEGE

Today, descendants of these immigrant groups often resist the notion that there are advantages that come from being white. They interpret the concept of white privilege to mean that their families have not worked hard to achieve acceptance and success. For so many, the mere notion of racial advantage diminishes the challenges overcome by their ancestors. The case of Italian Americans is particularly interesting, because those who came from southern Italy (80 percent of Italian immigrants) took their place at the very bottom of the socioeconomic hierarchy (Puleo 2007) and for a variety of reasons were slower to achieve success than other immigrant groups (Alba 1985).

The family stories of Italian Americans whose ancestors came to the United States during the great wave of migration tell of tenacious and brave immigrants who left behind the security of culture, and often of family, to eke out a living in a largely hostile U.S. society with little use for them. The arduous journey and the degrading processing at Ellis Island are vividly depicted in *The Golden Door*, a 2007 film by Emanuele Crialese. The movie also shows the patience and hope that sustains these world travelers in search of a better life, if not for themselves, then for future generations. The first American chapter of these family tales often contains poverty, illness and difficult living conditions, because so many Italians from southern Italy came with no marketable skills, limited education, and high rates of illiteracy (Puleo 2007; Parrillo 2009). The children of these immigrants also endured difficult lives, even those born in America. Children would often work when they were very young, contributing to the family income by shining shoes, selling newspapers or helping in family shops — often forgoing or cutting short their own education to do whatever they could to bring in more money for the family.

Still, many of those children, or their children, would learn a skilled trade, get high school diplomas, and even college educations. Many were able to save enough to move out of the inner cities and purchase homes in working class communities. By the 1950s Italians were in the thick of the exodus to American suburbs, marking their arrival in, or their proximity to, the middle class (Alba 1985). Thus within a few generations, it was possible for the families of many Italian immigrants to serve as examples of the American dream fulfilled. These are stories of perseverance in the face of deprivation, surmounting obstacles, and working hard to gain the skills needed to succeed; stories shared by immigrants from all over the world.

Yet the happy ending would not have come so quickly, if at all, were it not for societal acceptance of Italian families as white, even if it sometimes seemed begrudging. Without that all-important claim to whiteness, it would have been extremely difficult to get the vocational training and solid educational foundation that are key elements in the stories. It would have been difficult or impossible to secure the jobs that provided a family wage. Nor would Italian American families have been able to buy homes in the suburbs, a common component of white immigrant success stories made possible by federal housing and loan programs that were denied to African Americans (Sacks 1994). As Sacks argues so persuasively, Italian Americans, like the Jews at the center of her argument, were able to live the American dream because of post-WWII programs, including the generous occupational and educational provisions of the GI Bill. As whites, irrespective of ethnicity, they were beneficiaries "of the biggest and best affirmative action program in the history of our nation" (Sacks 1994:18).

For most European immigrant groups who came to the United States during the Great Migration (1880-1920), the process of becoming American was closely connected to the process of becoming white (Barrett and Roediger 1996). As Sacks (1994) points out, Jews were the first of the immigrant groups from southern and eastern Europe to gain a foothold in the (white) American middle class. Quoting Steinberg (1989:103), she explains that through a quirk of historical timing, Jews' skills and experience fit the needs and opportunities of the economy. It would take Italians longer to get to the middle class, but it was far speedier than would have been possible had they stayed at the bottom of the racial hierarchy with African Americans.

For Italian Americans and other Euro-Americans to acknowledge that we have benefited from our inclusion as whites, to say that we have never been saddled with the depth of oppression dealt to blacks, does not in any way take away from the incredible sacrifice and hard work of our ancestors. It simply means recognizing that we cannot equate our own families' struggles to overcome economic deprivation and negative stereotypes with those of blacks. We cannot judge African Americans as though they have had the same opportunities as white ethnics to construct a better life for future generations.

THE DIFFERENCE BETWEEN ETHNICITY AND RACE

One of the reasons that many white ethnics do not understand their racial privilege is that they equate ethnicity and race. For example, when white students are asked to write about their race, many discuss being "Italian," "Irish," "Russian," "Polish," or "Jewish." However, a major difference between the two concepts is that ethnicity is not relational, while the concept of race derives from a ranking of groups. Ethnicity is the bearer of culture, the repository of our music, holidays, the foods we eat, our sense of family and so on (Dalton 1995:107). One's sense of being Italian does not depend on someone else being Hungarian or Armenian. We do order ethnicities to some extent, but they would exist independent of such ordering.

Once ethnic groups are accepted as white and gain the benefits of the assimilation that accompanies this designation, ethnicity becomes largely symbolic. It becomes an aspect of identity invoked for enjoyment, a function of personal choice with little social cost (Alba 1990; Waters 1990). White ethnicity is optional and situational (Waters 1990); Italian Americans can decide whether, when, and how much they want to "be" Italian. Negative ethnic stereotypes still exist; the automatic connection of Italians to organized crime has been especially hard to erase, for instance (Puleo 2007). However, ethnic stereotypes are of relatively little consequence in a society in which race is such an abiding feature of how social life is organized.

Unlike ethnicity, race is meaningless outside of a relational framework (Dalton 1995). We would not know what it is to be black in the United States without a sense of what it means to be white. The two positions on the racial hierarchy emerged together and have shifted and changed in various ways, but there is always a relationship between them.

Nor is racial identity a function of personal choice in the United States. Chinese American author Gish Jen, from Yonkers, tells a story that illustrates this poignantly. She writes of a day at the playground when her young son was pedaling along happily in his toy car only to be stopped by two older white boys who blocked his way, putting their hands on the hood of his little car and shouting "You're Chinese! You are! You're Chinese!"(Jen 1998:266). The fact that he is also Irish has no relevance in this unsettling encounter. Though his parents may succeed in their goal of raising him to value both facets of his ethnic identity, they cannot escape the fact that his non-white ethnic identity also carries with it a racial position deemed "less than" that of whites.

If race were equivalent to ethnic identity, the differences between racial groups would be of little economic consequence. Yet race continues to rank order people for vitally important things like educational opportunities, jobs and income, loans and housing (e.g. Hacker 2003; Massey and Denton 1998). The legacy of race oppression against African Americans results in a huge gap in wealth between whites and blacks. It is nearly impossible for African Americans to bridge the wealth gulf through earnings because whites, including the groups who did not start out as white, have been passing on financial assets that can provide a family with a social class position well above where they would be based on their own earnings (Shapiro 2004).

THE VESTIGES OF SLAVERY

As European-Americans many of us have fully internalized the importance of the American dream and its central tenet—that we live in a society where all are free to achieve according to their efforts. As whites we do not have to think about race; the racism that gives us advantages is invisible to us. We are rarely reminded of our racial group membership or what it means for our lives. We do not learn that our ancestors self-consciously distinguished themselves from blacks. Yet history shows that they did so with vigor because they learned quickly that there were tremendous advantages to being white (Barrett and Roediger 2008). Children are taught about slavery as a regrettable period in American history, but not about the role of slavery in the social construction of white privilege. Perhaps even our teachers do not understand fully that race would not matter if had not proved a very useful way to divide people and to distribute power and resources (Dalton 1995; Kushnik 1996).

Consider William Foote Whyte's discussion of the clash between the Irish and the Italians in the North End of Boston early in the 20th century. He frames these "race conflicts" as part of a logical process. The newest immigrant group is seen as intruding on the gains made by the group who arrived before them. Italian mistreatment by the Irish is no different from Irish mistreatment by the English (Whyte 1939). This argument highlights an obvious difference between the history of African Americans and that of white immigrant groups. Blacks did not hold a temporary spot at the bottom of the racial and economic pecking order. They were never allowed to "transcend race" and be viewed primarily as just the most recent ethnic group. The definition of white would not be relaxed to include them, greatly limiting their upward mobility.

The permanent newcomer status of blacks facilitated the acceptance and upward mobility of groups like the Italians. When Italians and other European immigrants were pulling themselves up by their bootstraps, they were doing so *as whites*, and with the unrecognized help of blacks. This is an important, but untold part of our family stories. Recognizing the relationship between white advantage and black disadvantage does not suggest that blacks cannot achieve upward mobility and economic success. Indeed, history offers many examples of African American success, and the numbers of families of African ancestry who have achieved the American dream continue to grow. The family stories of African American mobility are just all the more remarkable because the obstacles overcome were so much greater.

As memoirs, news reports and statistical studies show us, even blacks who achieve the American dream do not escape the racial biases that were planted deep within American culture. This is one key difference between Euro-Americans and African-Americans. It brings us back to history and to that "peculiar institution," slavery. Many whites roll their eyes or spout off angrily when the topic of slavery is brought up in the context of current discussion about race. Many descendants of European immigrants equate the situation of African-Americans with their own. They do not understand that the imagery and language, the science and law, needed to mark blacks as less than human were woven into the fabric of society so skillfully and so tightly that strong threads of racism remain, even though the economic institution was abolished. Crediting D. Marvin Jones with the insight, Dalton notes that slavery "served to indelibly link" blackness to inferiority and danger (1995:156). One of the most poignant expressions of being seen as less than human comes from "hip hop generation" author Kevin Powell, writing about the 1995 Million Man March, during which black men gathered in the nation's capital to hear criticism of social policy and a call for renewed activism:

> Many people of various hues and persuasions have suggested to me—and I thought about this on the day of the Million Man March—that because I managed to escape the ghetto, and because I've been to college, and because I'm a 'successful' journalist and a published author, that I have, indeed, made it. I beg to differ. The diversity of black men at the Million Man March made it abundantly clear that status or material achievement did not, and cannot, eradicate—no matter how much we dupe ourselves into believing that it does—a very basic and spiritual need to be regarded *and* treated like a human being. (Powell 1997:222-223)

WHITENESS IN INSECURE TIMES

There *is* evidence that more whites are recognizing themselves as a racial group. Some recognize racial advantage, work at being "race traitors" and study and practice anti-racism (Ignatiev 1995; Kivel 2002; O'Brien 2001). Yet the economic insecurity and fear of terrorism caused by national and global developments seems to lead to an embrace of whiteness that keeps racial hierarchy in place. For instance, affirmative action has become a symbol of loss for many whites, and they mobilize as whites to protect the privilege that they see being eroded. They do so without acknowledging their privilege, however, engaging in color-blind racism, a series of mechanisms through which whites deny racism and its privileges (Bonilla-Silva 2006). This is why the student who said "So what? I'm white! It hasn't ever gotten me anything!" speaks for so many whites, who see their race as more of a disadvantage when they think about it at all.

Perhaps the growing economic inequality and fear that are part of contemporary American life make it harder to consider advantage or acknowledge privilege. Whites preoccupied with their own attempts to gain or hold onto a piece of the ever-shrinking economic pie available to them may not take the time to consider the differences between their own histories and those of people of color. In a tense and frightening world, white people do not want to hear about what they see as "ancient history" or acknowledge (and then grapple with) their white privilege. There are so many other things to worry about.

Yet it is illogical to judge all groups as though they have had (and have now) the same chance to succeed. Imagine a foot race. If the lanes are the same, it makes sense to judge how well people run by how quickly they get to the finish line. Yet if history shows that white ethnics got a "false start," running before blacks were given a chance to get to the starting line, and if there are more and higher hurdles in the lanes assigned to blacks, then it is not surprising that many whites will get to the finish line more quickly. Many whites had a tough race to run, and reached the finish line through hard work and perseverance. Still, we cannot seriously argue that whites are better runners than blacks if African Americans had an even tougher foot race to run.

In a highly competitive capitalist country such as the United States, with its emphasis on individualism, it seems natural to seek explanations for economic outcomes in individual and group behavior. The legal and overt racism of America's past has gone "underground." Thus whites come up with all kinds of other reasons for the well-documented and persistent white-black gap. It's anything *but* racial bias. Whites say they don't "see" color; that they were taught that there is only one race, the human race. They don't talk about race or acknowledge racial difference, all in the name of racial progress.

Race becomes the proverbial "elephant in the room," alive and powerful to people of color, avoided or denied vigorously by whites. As an example of how confusing this is for some white people, I was giving a public talk about race and a white woman came up to me to discuss further what "that woman" near the back of the room had said. I had no idea who she meant and asked her to describe the woman. She hemmed and hawed, trying to describe the woman's clothing, and then I "got it." "Do you mean the black woman who was sitting near the door?" "Yes," the white woman replied, considerably relieved, and then she whispered; "I didn't know if I could *say* that!" The side benefit of white color blindness, even if not actively sought, is that if a person does not see race or knowingly treat others differently because of their race, then she or he cannot be accused of having racial privilege.

It is interesting that one way whites acknowledge their racial identity is in feeling they are under attack for something they were, as one person put it, "just born with." Many well-meaning whites walk on eggshells, trying to keep from being called racist. Why is that label something that whites try to avoid so much that they persuade themselves race is something that cannot be discussed – especially in the company of people of color? Perhaps it is because the accusation might expose the illogic in their constructed personal narratives. As one white man said after listening carefully to my arguments, "My grandparents started with nothing but their labor. If we could do it, I just don't understand why more blacks can't do it too." Perhaps it is because the connections between white ethnic family histories and the family histories of African-Americans have not been told often enough.

To go back to the example of the foot race, in the post-Civil Right era, *more* blacks may get to start the competition at or near the same time as white ethnics, yet the legacy of oppression they carry will slow them down to varying degrees. The hurdles they had to jump were apparent when racism was built into the laws of the country. The vestiges of that system still present hurdles, but many of these are unseen by whites. There are still a disproportionate number of African Americans, even in the 21st century, who will have a hard time catching up because of an inordinate number of extremely difficult obstacles early in the foot race. As Stanley Fish reminds us, blacks "have been subjected first to decades of slavery, and then to decades of second-class citizenship, widespread legal discrimination, economic persecution, educational deprivation, and cultural stigmatization" (1993:130).

We might expect that white ethnics whose ancestors knew the meaning of being degraded and exploited on the basis of appearance and customs would be quicker to acknowledge the privilege of whiteness. Yet sometimes it seems just the opposite. In one classroom discussion of white privilege, a student said, "My parents were immigrants and haven't always had the advantages of being white, so that is probably why I think that people of color aren't really that bad off." We accept the ideology of meritocracy, touted in the American dream, and embraced by immigrants of all skin tones and nations, that success is there for all who are willing to work for it. For families and groups that have achieved success, it is easy to believe. We also somehow convince ourselves that the obstacles our families overcame are not so different from the ones experienced by African Americans. Because success stories are always about individuals and families, we also seek explanations for any lack of success in individual and group behavior and values. To acknowledge the ways that the structure of society causes group disadvantage is to suggest that success is also partly due to structure. That brings us back to the resistance of many white ethnics to arguments that seem to undermine the stories of courage and sacrifice that are integral to their sense of family history.

The hard work of their families was real, and current day feelings of vulnerability are real, but so is racial discrimination. Only by understanding how our past and current lives are intertwined with those of blacks, will more white ethnics see that their whiteness has carried more weight than their ethnicity in American society; that African Americans have had a much more difficult history than white immigrant groups; and that attempts to address the current-day legacy of this different history are vitally important.

References

Alba, Richard M. 1990. *Ethnic Identity: The Transformation of White America*. New Haven, CT: Yale University Press.

Alba, Richard M. 1985. *Italian Americans: Into the Twilight of Ethnicity*. Englewood Cliffs, NJ: Prentice-Hall.

Allen, Theodore. 1994. *The Invention of the White Race: Racial Oppression and Social Control*. London, England: Verso.

Barrett, James E. and David Roediger. 1996. "How White People Became White." Pp. 402-406 in *Critical White Studies: Looking Behind the Mirror*, edited by Richard Delgado and Jean Stefancic. Philadelphia, PA: Temple University Press.

Bonilla-Silva, Eduardo. 2003. *Racism without Racists: Color-Blind Racism and the Persistence of Racial Inequality in the United States*. Lanham, MD: Rowman & Littlefield.

Dalton, Harlon L. 1995. *Racial Healing: Confronting the Fear between Blacks and Whites*. New York: Doubleday.

Fish, Stanley. 1993. "Reverse Racism or How the Pot Got to Call the Kettle Black." *Atlantic Monthly* 272 (November): 128-136.

Hacker, Andrew. 2003. *Two Nations: Black and White, Separate, Hostile, Unequal*. New York: Scribner.

Ignatiev, Noel. 1995. *How The Irish Became White*. New York: Routledge.

——. 1997. "How To Be a Race Traitor: Six Ways to Fight Being White." p. 613 in *Critical White Studies: Looking Behind the Mirror*, edited by Richard Delgado and Jean Stefancic. Philadelphia, PA: Temple University Press.

Jen, Gish. 1998. "An Ethnic Trump." Pp. 265-268 in *Half and Half: Writers on Growing Up Biracial and Bicultural*, edited by C. C. O'Hearn. New York: Pantheon Books.

Kivel, Paul. 2002. *Uprooting Racism: How White People Can Work for Racial Justice*. British Columbia, Canada: New Society Publishers.

Kushnik, Louis. 1996. "The Political Economy of White Racism in the United States." Pp. 48-67 in *Impacts of Racism on White Americans*, 2nd ed. edited by Benjamin P. Bowser and Raymond G. Hunt. Thousand Oaks, CA: Sage.

Massey, Douglas and Nancy Denton. 1998. *American Apartheid: Segregation and the Making of the Underclass*. Cambridge, MA: Harvard University Press.

O'Brien, Eileen. 2001. *Whites Confront Racism: Antiracists and Their Paths to Action*. New York: Rowman & Littlefield.

Parrillo, Vincent N. 2009. *Strangers to These Shores*, 9th ed. Boston, MA: Allyn & Bacon.

Pavalko, Ronald M. 1981. "Racism and the New Immigration: Toward a Reinterpretation of the Experiences of White Ethnics." *Sociology and Social Research* 65:56-77.

Puleo, Stephen. 2007. *The Boston Italians*. Boston: Beacon Press.

Roediger, David. 1995. "Guineas, Wiggers and the Dramas of Racialized Culture." *American Literary History* 7:654-668.

Sacks, Karen Brodkin. 1994. "How Jews Became White." Pp. 78-102 in *Race*, edited by Gregory Steven and Roger Sanjek. New Brunswick, NJ: Rutgers University Press.

Shapiro, Thomas M. 2004. *The Hidden Cost of Being African American: How Wealth Perpetuates Inequality*. New York: Oxford University Press.

Steinberg, Stephen. 1989. *The Ethnic Myth: Race, Ethnicity and Class in America*. Boston, MA: Beacon Press.

Waters, Mary C. 1996. "Optional Ethnicities: For Whites Only?" Pp. 444-454 in *Origins and Destinies: Immigration, Race and Ethnicity in America*, edited by Silvia Pedraza and Ruben G. Rumbaut. Belmont, CA: Wadsworth Publishing Company.

Whyte, William Foote. 1939. "Race Conflicts in the North End of Boston." *The New England Quarterly* 12:623-642.

The More Things Change: Comparing Italians in World War II and Arabs in the War on Terror

PAUL A. MAGRO
Ball State University

In December 1941, the U.S. entered World War II after the Japanese attack on Pearl Harbor. Japan, Germany, and Italy became enemies of the United States, and many Americans soon perceived immigrants from those countries as potential threats to national security. Thousands of U.S. residents of Japanese, German, and Italian descent were declared enemy aliens and had their liberties curtailed, their property seized, and many even relocated to "safe" zones, and in some cases, to internment camps, where they were kept under surveillance as reassurance to the American public that they were no threat.

Some 60 years later, the United States became a target for global terrorists because of its policies and involvement in the Middle East. On September 11, 2001, members of the extremist Islamic group al Qaeda carried out a spectacular series of attacks against the United States. The United States was as stunned as it had been after Pearl Harbor, and subsequent events led to U.S. invasions and occupations in Afghanistan and Iraq in what has since become known as the "Global War on Terror."

How has the United States managed to balance the issue of national security with the treatment of immigrant groups and their families? Were lessons learned in the years since the outbreak of World War II, or is there credence to the adage, "The more things change, the more they remain the same?" To answer this question, I first examine the events of World War II and the issues that affected the Italians living in the United States at that time, followed by a discussion of the terrorist attacks of September 11, 2001, the Global War on Terror, and its effect on the followers of Islam and the people of the Middle East. I then compare these two groups and their respective treatment subsequent to these world events, and conclude with a discussion of the difficulty in making that comparison.

WORLD WAR II

The U.S. formally entered the war subsequent to the Japanese attack on the naval base at Pearl Harbor, Hawaii on December 7, 1941. On December 8, President Roosevelt asked Congress for a declaration of war against Japan, soon followed by those against Italy and Germany. But even before any formal declarations of war, Roosevelt issued proclamations 2525, 2526, and 2527, declaring anyone of Japanese, Italian, or German origin over the age of 14 who had not become a naturalized citizen as an enemy alien. At the same time he invoked the Alien Enemy Act of 1798, which granted the President broad powers to deal with enemy aliens. FBI Director J. Edgar Hoover, however, waited neither for formal declarations of war nor presidential proclamations. Without warrants, the FBI immediately began arresting Italian, Japanese, and German aliens whose names were on previously compiled lists. Hoover later reported that 1,291 Japanese, 857 Germans, and 147 Italians had been arrested during this initial sweep (Report to the Congress 2001[1]).

After the initial arrests by the FBI, hundreds of other Italians were arrested in the first six months of the war. About one-half of those were either released immediately or released on parole, while the other half were interned. In all, over 600,000 Italian born immigrants in the United States were to be declared enemy aliens, and although not all were arrested, most were affected in some way. Of those who were arrested, many were transported to internment camps in Montana, Oklahoma, Tennessee, and Texas. Many families faced financial ruin at the loss of a breadwinner or the freezing of financial assets, and most endured the stigma that occurred with the arrest and internment of a family member (Report to the Congress 2001).

In the days immediately following the attack on Pearl Harbor, Lieutenant General John L. DeWitt, Commander of the Western Defense Command, recommended to the War Department that all enemy aliens be removed from the area between the Pacific Coast and the Sierra Nevada Mountains. What followed was a policy struggle between the War Department, Justice Department, the FBI, and local politicians and officials on exactly what was to be done and how. It also evolved into an

---

[1] Report to the Congress of the United States, A Review of the Restrictions on Persons of Italian Ancestry During World War II, November 2001. Henceforth for the sake of brevity, this citation will be referred to as "Report to the Congress 2001."

archetypical Washington tangled web of varying recommendations, half-truths, and political maneuvering and infighting.

Between December 1941 and March 1942, the government established military zones (later changed and modified several times) in which enemy aliens were restricted or prohibited. These configurations resulted in a mass relocation of Italians by the Justice Department, beginning in February and involving more than 10,000 resident Italian aliens (Congressional Record 1999; Report to the Congress 2001).

A full plan for total internment of Italians and Germans on the west coast was never implemented, although all Japanese from the area were removed from designated zones and relocated in internment camps. In a compromise plan, the War Department granted DeWitt and the Western Defense Command the authority to remove Italians and Germans (including those who were U.S. citizens) whose presence in designated areas were deemed to be dangerous and unacceptable. The Individual Exclusion Program called for those who were declared to be dangerous persons to be relocated on an individual basis according to two criteria: "suspicion of the individual or the sensitivity of the area where he resided" (Report to the Congress 2001).

Finally, on February 19, 1942, President Roosevelt signed Executive Order No. 9066. The order authorized the Secretary of War and designated military commanders to make determinations on who may be included or excluded from prohibited military zones (Executive Order 9066). In all, some 254 people were excluded under this plan.

Arrest, detention, and relocation were not the only issues that Italians encountered. Some 52,000 Italian resident aliens were required to be at home between the hours of 8:00 p.m. and 6:00 a.m., with 354 arrests for curfew violations, most of them in California (Congressional Record 1999; Report to the Congress 2001). Enemy aliens were not allowed to possess firearms, short-wave radios, cameras, flashlights, or other items designated as "instruments of possible espionage and/or sabotage." Restrictions on fishing and the confiscation of fishing boats also greatly affected many Italians, particularly on the west coast, where they dominated the fishing industry.

Procedures were established within the first days of the war that allowed the FBI to obtain search warrants from U.S. Attorneys instead of judges. Again, disagreements occurred in the government regarding citizens' rights and searches, and again a compromise was reached. First, enemy aliens would be given the opportunity to turn in any prohibited contraband, and second, the mere fact of being an enemy alien was deemed sufficient cause for search. Nationwide, authorities searched about 2,900 Italian homes and confiscated contraband from 1,632 people (Congressional Record 1999; Report to the Congress 2001).

By May 1942, the War Department told DeWitt that, although he retained the power to exclude aliens from prohibited zones on an individual basis, no further mass relocation of Germans or Italians would take place. In June, with the relocation of the Japanese complete, DeWitt lifted the exclusions from the restricted zones (Report to the Congress 2001). Finally, on October 12, 1942 (the Columbus Day holiday), in what was apparently a well-timed political move with elections barely a month away, Attorney General Francis Biddle declared that Italians would no longer be considered enemies and announced the lifting of all restrictions (Fox 2004).

In what was perhaps the cruelest irony to this story, over 500,000 Italian Americans were serving in the U.S. military at the time. By the war's end that number would grow to 1.2 million (making Italian Americans the largest ethnic group to have served in the war), many of whom had parents who had been subject to these policies and restrictions (Congressional Record 1999; Prisoners Among Us 2004).

Almost 60 years later, on July 1, 1999, Congressmen Rick Lazio and Eliot Engel introduced their bill H.R. 2442 to the Congress. On November 7, 1999, the *Wartime Violation of Italian American Civil Liberties Act* was signed into law by President William Clinton. The act and its subsequent report address the treatment of Italians and Italian Americans during World War II and the denial of their civil liberties. In part, the act said

> A deliberate policy kept these measures from the public during the war. Even 50 years later much information is still classified, the full story remains unknown to the public, and it has never been acknowledged in any official capacity by the United States Government (Report to the Congress 2001).

9/11 AND THE WAR ON TERROR

Terrorism in the Middle East in the late 20th century began to grow in the attempt to preserve religious sects of the Islamic faith and also in opposition to Israel and the policies of the U.S. Among the terrorist groups that arose was al Qaeda, Arabic for "The Base," which was first formed in violent opposition to the Soviet presence in Afghanistan in the 1980s and originally supported by the United States. Headed by the son of a Saudi oil magnate, Osama bin Laden, al Qaeda considers the U.S. military and political involvement in the Middle East as foreign occupation, and was responsible for several attacks aimed at the U.S. in the 1990s (Hagan 2002; National Commission on Terrorist Attacks Upon the United States 2004). Later, the tragic events of September 11, 2001 killed over 3,000 people, more than the number killed at Pearl Harbor in 1941 (National Commission on Terrorist Attacks Upon the United States 2004).

The War on Terror began when the United States responded with the invasion of Afghanistan in its hunt for bin Laden and al Qaeda, and later with its incursion into Iraq. The United States claimed that Iraqi dictator Saddam Hussein was a threat to the United States and to the world with illegally held weapons of mass destruction and the harboring of al Qaeda members. The people of the United States generally supported the Afghan invasion, but Bush Administration plans to invade Iraq met with mixed support from the beginning. Many more people opposed the inclusion of Iraq in the War on Terror on several grounds, among them the lack of evidence of the presence of weapons of mass destruction or of al Qaeda in Iraq.

It should be noted here that it is not the intent of this paper, nor is it within its scope, to chronicle the events of the war, its morality, or the United States' successes and failures in its planning or execution. However, it is realistic to say that the United States' invasion of Iraq was intended to be a short-term military operation followed by stabilization and establishment of a new Iraqi government. Instead, as of this writing, it remains entangled in a complicated political struggle that has led to a civil war among rival Islamic religious factions. It has taken its toll in economic and political costs as well as in the number of civilian and military casualties of war. It has also led to a resurgence of questions about immigration and national security in what many believe to be xenophobic proportions, not seen since Franklin Roosevelt's issuance of proclamations and executive orders in 1941 and 1942. Undoubtedly, the events of September 11, 2001, and the War on Terror created a fear in the people of the United States. Much of that fear focused on the Islamic religion and on the people of the Middle East, neither of which had previously been of much concern to the majority of Americans.

In 2000, the total number of people in the U.S. of Arab[2] origin was about 1.2 million, a population that had been steadily increasing since 1980. Four months after the 9/11 attacks, the Census Bureau issued a report estimating the number of illegal aliens in the U.S. and indicated that "at least" 58,000 people from the Middle East were undocumented and living in the United States (de la Cruz and Brittingham 2007; U.S. Bureau of the Census 2003).

After 9/11 and the beginning of the War on Terror, several laws, policies, procedures, and orders were passed and implemented as part of the government response to those events. While it is impossible here to list and explain all of them, a discussion of some of the major ones is in order.

Most notable is probably the USA PATRIOT Act (or "United and Strengthening America by Providing Appropriate Tools Required to Intercept and Obstruct Terrorism Act of 2001"), which was signed into law by President Bush in October 2001, just one month after the attacks (Library of Congress 2001). The PATRIOT Act is extensive, providing sweeping changes to existing laws and creating provisions for fighting terrorism. It broadens government powers in surveillance, intelligence gathering within the United States, finding money-laundering operations used for financing terrorism, and finding terrorists entering the country, and it also creates new federal crimes for acts of terrorism.

Under the PATRIOT Act, support of any organization that the Secretary of State designated as a terrorist organization became grounds for deportation. The act also gave the Attorney General the power to detain any person that s/he has reasonable grounds to believe may be engaged in terrorist activity as described in the act (Butterfield 2001). The act passed easily with bipartisan support from Congress, but soon became controversial. Many claimed that the law allowed violations of privacy and stretched governmental powers beyond legal constitutional limits. Among the complaints were that the inclusion of domestic terrorism in the act allowed harassment and surveillance of the government's political opponents or those who criticized the government; that records of ordinary citizens such as business documents, library borrowing, or other private records could be freely scrutinized by the

---

[2] The U.S. Bureau of the Census considers "Arab" origin to be those with ancestry originating in several Middle Eastern and North African countries. Similar to the way the term "Hispanic" is used, it is assumed that while there are strong commonalities held between these "Arab" countries, there are cultural and other differences as well.

government; and that allowing the government to conduct searches and then seek warrants for them later would effect sweeping changes in the way all search warrants would be executed in the United States. The government countered by saying that many of the procedures pre-dated the PATRIOT Act and the law only facilitated their use against terrorism, and that sufficient checks had been instituted to prevent civil liberties abuses (U.S. Department of Justice 2007).

Several other Department of Justice (DOJ) directives sought to enhance national security. One of them allowed for the monitoring of attorney-client communications (Greenya 2003). In its Voluntary Interview Program, the DOJ compiled a list of some 8,000 young men from countries with "al Qaeda presences" to be interviewed for informational purposes to aid in helping to catch terrorists or to help thwart potential terrorist attacks. Many of them were later placed in deportation proceedings as a result of these interviews. A series of special registration requirements were also created for those coming from nations with ties to al Qaeda, again resulting in several deportations

A result of these laws and directives has been both the deportation and the detention of many people of Arab origin. It is difficult to know, however, exactly how many people have been affected. Citing national security reasons, government information has not always been forthcoming, and since the events and investigations are ongoing, it is difficult to know what the outcomes will be (Greenya 2003; Tumlin 2004).

In the weeks following the 9/11 attacks, a public backlash in the U.S. arose against Muslims and Arabs. In 2000 a total of 28 hate crime incidents reported against them occurred, and in 2001 that number increased to 481. Incidents included at least 3 murders plus numerous beatings, assaults, vandalism, arson, and direct threats (U.S. Department of Justice 2003). The aftermath of September 11 took an emotional toll on Muslims and Arab Americans as well. Many were afraid to wear traditional clothing or display any outward signs of their faith or ethnic background, and many reported staying home for weeks or even months at a time, fearful of carrying out normal activities. Many had been interviewed by the FBI or other federal agencies, and refused to report hate crimes and other incidents because of fear of becoming entangled in immigration problems or of being deported (Wessler 2002).

How do these two chapters in American History compare to each other? I turn to that examination next.

COMPARISONS

By the late nineteenth century, a combination of natural disasters, crop failures, and widespread disease outbreaks coupled with the problems of a struggling new government made life in Italy difficult for many. Especially hard hit were the peasants in the south of Italy and Sicily, which spurred a mass emigration of farmers, peasants and laborers to other lands, much of it to the United States (Library of Congress 2007).

Most of the Italians who came worked at low-paying and physically demanding jobs. Most came with little money, little command of English, little education, and few job skills. They were different from Americans in culture, religion, and physical appearance. Much of the American response to their coming was hostile, and many Americans saw them as dirty, criminal, and clannish, unable and unwilling to assimilate into American culture (Library of Congress 2007).

Most of the Arab/Middle Eastern people who have come to the United States, however, have been better prepared for their migration. On the whole, Middle Easterners have come with higher levels of education, better and more marketable job skills, and, while not always affluent, most have not endured the levels of poverty that their Italian counterparts once did. As with the Italians, the societal response has not always been friendly. They, too, were seen as different from Americans in culture, religion, and physical appearance, which seemed strange to Americans. Many also were seen through the media stereotypes of the rich oil sultan or the crazed terrorist, even before the events of 9/11. Arabs, however, have tended to mix much more freely in U.S. society than did the Italian immigrants. With more education and better job skills, the Arabic people work and attend school side-by-side with Americans to a much greater degree than did the Italians.

The Catholicism of the Italian immigrants was also seen differently in the U.S. than the Islamic religion of most Arabs. This is not to say that anti-Catholic sentiment did not exist, for certainly it did. But while discrimination and anti-Catholic sentiment existed into the twentieth century, it was on the wane by 1941 and Catholicism was a better-known and established religion by that time. In 2001, however, Americans still knew relatively little about Islam, and to a great extent it is still seen as different, strange, and outside the American mainstream. With proclamations by terrorists of a holy war against all non-Muslims, Islam and factions of Islam embroiled in a civil war in Iraq, the religion is also seen by many Americans as a direct cause of the events of 9/11 and the current War on Terror. Without a solid knowledge of the tenets of mainstream Islamic belief, Islam is seen as a point of contention between Americans and the Arabic people who have settled here.

Although the Japanese attack on Pearl Harbor was a surprise, the knowledge that the United States would probably enter the war at some point was not. America had closely watched the events in Germany and Japan—and Italy's alliance with them—in the 1930s, and America's entry into the war seemed to be inevitable at some point. The attack on Pearl Harbor only facilitated what both the Roosevelt administration and the American people had already seen coming. By the mid-1930s plans were underway for both U.S. entry into battle, as well as for domestic defense. In 1936, FBI director Hoover ordered the collection of information for anyone with the potential to become an enemy of the United States. By 1939, Hoover had not only amassed a great deal of information, he had also arranged his lists both alphabetically and geographically, indicating the anticipation of arrest and/or relocation. In 1940, Congress also passed the Alien Registration Act which required the registration of all aliens with the Immigration and Naturalization Service (Report to the Congress 2001).

In 2001, most people of the United States were as surprised by the 9/11 attacks as they had been by the attack on Pearl Harbor 60 years before. And although there had been many warning signs throughout the 1990s that an attack of these proportions was possible, most Americans were caught off guard. According to the 9/11 Commission, the "9/11 attacks were a shock, [but] they should not have come as a surprise" (National Commission on Terrorist Attacks Upon the United States 2004). In its final report the commission members wrote

> We do not believe leaders understood the gravity of the threat. The terrorist danger from Bin Laden and al Qaeda was not a major topic for policy debate among the public, the media, or in the Congress. Indeed, it barely came up during the 2000 presidential campaign (National Commission on Terrorist Attacks Upon the United States 2004).

There have been no prohibited zones established and no mass relocations in the War on Terror as there were in World War II with Roosevelt's issuance of Executive Order 9066. Neither have there been any curfews, restrictions on what property one is able to own, nor any occupational restrictions. Perhaps most importantly, there have been no mass declarations of any ethnic group as enemy aliens as there was with Proclamations 2525, 2526, and 2527. Is that because the United States learned from the lessons of the past? Yes, but that is only part of the answer.

Culturally, the people of the United States in 1941 were more inclined to be antipathetic toward the racial and ethnic minorities of the time. It had been less than 20 years since nativist sentiment shut down the great waves of immigrants and restricted immigration with quota laws. The country had not yet been through the civil rights era and had not yet been acclimated to the idea of free and equal treatment for all that the civil rights movement would later usher in. Neither had the Supreme Court revolution of the 1960s yet occurred, which saw sweeping changes in the guarantee of due process that was intended to protect people from the actions of government.

The succeeding generation came of age and went through those two events in their formative years. But they saw the events of World War II as history, not as part of their experiences. Since the brunt of the war restrictions were placed on the Japanese and only to a lesser extent the Italians and Germans, it was the treatment of the Japanese that came to the forefront for them and they were largely unaware of restrictions on Italians and Germans. In 1988, for example, the United States officially acknowledged the injustices that occurred in the internment of the Japanese, and formally apologized and made monetary reparations for them, with no mention of the treatment of the Italians or Germans. Still, the post-war generations were abhorred by what they were taught about the Japanese treatment, and a declaration of all Arabic and Islamic non-citizens as enemies of the United States in the War on Terror would probably not have been tolerated to the same degree as it had been during World War II. But it is only partly correct to say that the United States had "learned its lesson," for although the treatment of the Arabs and Muslims does not entirely parallel the treatment of the Japanese, Italians, and Germans of World War II, some of it is eerily similar.

Certainly the right to privacy has been at issue in both events. Just as J. Edgar Hoover compiled lists of potential enemies prior to the start of World War II, the Department of Justice compiled lists of young men to be interviewed as part of its Volunteer Interview Program. And while that program did not result in detention based on ethnic background, it did result in deportation for many and for arrests in others.

Just as the risk assessment in the lists that were compiled by the FBI in World War II were based on membership/support of ethnic organizations, one provision in The PATRIOT Act gives the Secretary of State power to deport anyone who supports an organization designated as a terrorist organization. Perhaps most striking is that one of the provisions of the PATRIOT Act gives the government the power to search and to seek a warrant after the fact, reminiscent of the compromise that was reached in 1942 stating that the mere fact that anyone who had been declared an enemy alien was cause for search.

While there has been no wholesale detention of those residing inside the United States, the government began interning captured members of al Qaeda and the Taliban in 2001 immediately after the 9/11 attacks. According to published reports, some 775 detainees have been held at Guantanamo and, as of 2006, some 450 have been released or were scheduled to be released. The remaining detainees may be held indefinitely (Dedman 2006).

The Bush administration has been highly criticized in its treatment of detainees for not only the abuse of power in holding detainees illegally, but for allegations of mistreatment and torture as well. While the detainees being held at the military base at Guantanamo Bay in Cuba have received most of the attention, charges of illegal detention and torture or abuse have been leveled at several locations. A *New York Times* editorial, for example, criticized the government for abuses at Abu Ghraib prison in Iraq, Bagram Air Base in Afghanistan, and "other, secret locations run by the intelligence agencies." The editorial also charged that "These are not isolated incidents, but part of a tightly linked global detention system with no accountability in law" (*New York Times* 2005).

The entire story of the arrest and treatment of detainees may not be entirely known for years, if at all. Citing national security concerns, the government and the military have not been forthcoming with information. The government has argued that the suspension of rights has always occurred in times of war and that the detainees are not members of a national army and therefore not subject to the Geneva Convention. But it should also be noted that there has been no formal declaration of war against a sovereign nation. Because of the nature of the war, the legality of the holding and treatment of the detainees may, indeed, change the rules of the treatment of prisoners in future conflicts. The arrest and detention of the designated "enemy combatants" is not comparable in many ways to the detentions of World War II. Yet even with national security a legitimate concern, it still brings to mind the plight of the Italians, Germans, and Japanese in that era.

The War on Terror and national security concerns has had several consequences on immigration practices and policies that were not present in World War II, when there was virtually no immigration to the U.S. Today, national security has become inextricably entangled with issues of immigration, both legal and illegal, and in fact, the War on Terror has shaped American immigration policy since 9/11. Many of those who have committed terrorist acts against the U.S. have also been guilty of immigration fraud. Several had entered on visas, including student visas, temporary visas, and tourist visas (Camarota 2002; Kephart 2005).

CONCLUSION

A comparison of the treatment of two different immigrant groups in two different wars across a span of some 60 years must necessarily come with a few caveats. We are first of all hampered in two obvious ways. First is the legitimate issue of national security. No matter what one's view is on the War on Terror, the fact remains that the United States is involved, and that given that involvement, the United States has enemies and those enemies still seek vulnerabilities to attack. Whether information that has been classified was done so for security reasons or as a cover-up, only future historians may some day be able to tell. We are also hampered by the nature of government bureaucracy itself. Different agencies with different authority at different times, coupled with the vagaries of individuals and the mountains of documents produced by government, makes sorting through it all a monumental task that may only, at best, give a partial picture of true events.

We must also be cognizant of the fact that temporal comparisons are not always possible, and when they are possible, they are not always fair. We are given the luxury of hindsight today when examining the sociohistoric context of the past; we are also given the disadvantage that the events of today are still unfolding and have not yet come to their conclusion. We can only see the past through the lens of the present, but that may not be adequate enough to see, experience, and feel the same things that those going through those events saw, felt, and experienced at the time.

Yet the adage that those who fail to learn from the mistakes of the past are bound to repeat them is also relevant here. The world is a much different place today than it was in 1941, but the fears of the people that were generated by two different attacks on them are the same. It is the cultural and governmental response to those fears that leads us to question what has been learned in the interim. Time will be the ultimate judge of what has changed, how much has changed, and what has not changed between 1941 and today. But in the meantime, it behooves us to come to the conclusion that the more things change, the more they remain the same.

References

Butterfield, Jeanne. 2001. "What Does the Patriot Act Mean for Immigrants?" Washington, D.C.: American Immigration Law Foundation.

Camarota, Steven A. 2002. "The Open Door: How Militant Islamic Terrorists Entered and Remained in the United States, 1993-2001." Washington, D.C.: Center for Immigration Studies, Center Paper 21. http://www.cis.org/articles/index.html. Retrieved April 2007.

Congressional Record, U.S. House of Representatives. November 10, 1999, pp. 11904-11910. Washington, D.C., U.S. Library of Congress, http://thomas.loc.gov. Retrieved April 2007.

Dedman, Bill. 2006. "In Limbo: Cases are Few against Gitmo Detainees." MSNBC October 24, 2006. http://www.msnbc.msn.com/id/15361740/. Retrieved May 2007.

de la Cruz, G. Patricia and Angela Brittingham. 2003. "Arab Population: 2000." U.S. Census Bureau, Census 2000 Brief. http://www.census.gov/prod/2003pubs/c2kbr-23.pdf. Retrieved April 2007.

Doyle, Charles. 2002. "The USA Patriot Act: A Sketch." Library of Congress. http://thomas.loc.gov/cgi-bin/bdquery/z?d107:h.r.03162. Retrieved April 2007.

Executive Order 9066. http://www.ourdocuments.gov. Retrieved April 2007.

Fox, Stephen. 2004. "Uncovering the Myths of Italian American Relocation." *Prisoners Among Us website* at http://www.prisonersamongus.com/. Retrieved April 2007.

Greenya, John. 2003. "Immigration Law in Post-9/11 America." *Washington Lawyer*. August, 2003. Washington, D.C.: DC Bar Association.

Hagan, Frank E. 2002. *Criminology*. Belmont, CA: Wadsworth.

Kephart, Janice L. 2005. "Immigration and Terrorism: Moving Beyond the 9/11 Staff Report on Terrorist Travel." Washington, D.C.: Center for Immigration Studies, Center Paper 21. http://www.cis.org/articles/index.html. Retrieved April 2007.

Library of Congress. 2001. H.R. 3162 Public Law No: 107-56. http://thomas.loc.gov/cgibin/bdquery/z?d107:h.r.03162: Retrieved April 2007.

Library of Congress. 2007. *Italian Immigration*. http://memory.loc.gov/learn/features/immig/al/italian3.html. Retrieved April, 2007.

National Commission on Terrorist Attacks Upon the United States (9/11 Commission). 2004. Final Report. http://www.9-11commission.gov. Retrieved April 2007.

New York Times. 2005. "Un-American by Any Name." Editorial June 5, 2005. *Prisoners Among Us*. 2005. Documentary Film by Michael Angelo DiLauro. Scranton, PA: Michaelangelo Productions.

Report to the Congress of the United States. "A Review of the Restrictions on Persons of Italian Ancestry During World War II." November 2001. Washington, D.C.: U.S. Department of Justice.

Tumlin, Karen C. 2004. "Suspect First: How Terrorism Policy Is Reshaping Immigration Policy." *California Law Review*. 92:4.

U.S. Census Bureau. 1993. *We the Americans: Foreign Born*. Washington, D.C.: U.S. Department of Commerce.

U.S. Census Bureau. 2003. Current Population Survey, Annual Social and Economic Supplement, 2003.

U.S. Department of Justice. 2003. "National Crime Victims' Rights Week: Fulfill the Promise." http://www.ojp.usdoj.gov/ovc/ncvrw/2003/pg5j.html. Retrieved April 2007.

U.S. Department of Justice. 2007. "Dispelling the Myths." Preserving Life and Liberty. http://www.lifeandliberty.gov/index.html. Retrieved May 2007.

Wessler, Stephen. 2002. "After 9-11: Understanding the Impact on Muslim Communities in Maine." Center for the Prevention of Hate Violence, University of Southern Maine.

Thirty Years of Italian-American Public Employment in New York City and New York State

VINCENZO MILIONE, CARMINE PIZZIRUSSO, ITALA PELIZZOLI
Calandra Italian American Institute, Queens College, CUNY

This paper summarizes thirty years of Italian-American government employment in New York City (NYC) and New York State (NYS). It excerpts part of a study conducted by the National Council of Columbia Associations in Civil Service and the Calandra Institute entitled *Thirty Years of Italian-American Government Employment in New York City and New York State*.[1] The study analyzes the percentage of Italian Americans in 471 NYS government and 462 NYC government occupations, including management and professional, service and sales, skilled and unskilled employment. Another aspect of study about Italian Americans in government was their employment tenure as entry, career or senior-level employees.

Italian immigration to the United States is well documented. Italians who came during the early immigration wave of the 1880s to 1920s worked predominantly in labor occupations and initiated small-business ventures.[2] Language barriers, educational certification, residency, and citizenship all limited Italian participation in government employment. By the 1930s and 1940s, the children of these immigrants spoke English, were American educated, participated in public works projects, and entered the military because of World War II.

Following WWII, many Italian Americans took advantage of the GI Bill benefits, which included preferential recruitment for government employment. Although negative stereotypes about them continued, Italian Americans began entering mainstream society, as they helped fill a labor shortage and improved their socioeconomic status. In the 1950s and 1960s, more Italian Americans completed high-school and post-secondary studies, thus gaining opportunities to compete for government service occupations.

---

[1] "Thirty Years of Italian-American Government Employment in New York City and New York State." (The Calandra Italian American Institute, City University of New York, January 2007).

[2] Richard Gambino, *Blood of My Blood* (New York: Doubleday, 1974).

In the 1970s Italian Americans in NYC and NYS governments organized Columbia Association fraternal organizations, predominantly within such service occupations as police, fire, and sanitation. The Columbia Associations provided an opportunity for Italian Americans in these government occupations to unite and mutually help each other for recruitment and promotions. The fraternal organizations raised funds and provided members with scholarships and direct assistance when needed. The National Council brought all of these civil service organizations together under one umbrella to give Italian Americans a single voice.

ASSESSING ITALIAN-AMERICAN REPRESENTATION IN GOVERNMENT

The study reported here used U.S. housing and population census data for 1980, 1990, and 2000.[3] Prior to the 1980s, no government employment data was collected about white ethnics, and so we have virtually no information about Italian Americans in city or state public employment. Only through head counts and membership in the Columbia Associations did Italian-American representation become known. More reliable data became available with the release of the self-identification ancestry data from the 1980 decennial Census survey, but unfortunately, no resultant analysis of the data occurred to improve hiring practices of Italian Americans in the NYC and NYS governments. By the 1990s, with the establishment of the research unit of the John D. Calandra Italian American Institute, it was able to conduct the first-ever study of Italian-American public employment at the city and state levels, using the available ancestry data.[4]

In 1994, the National Council held a conference involving the Columbia Associations and the Italian-American community to 1) discuss the study's findings on the under-utilization of Italian Americans in NYC and NYS governments, and 2) develop outreach efforts to attract more Italian Americans at the entry level. The proceedings of this conference, entitled "Italian Americans in Civil Service: Getting Our Due or Becoming Extinct?" provided a platform from which to bring the problem to the attention of the Italian-American community and government

---

[3] U.S. Census Bureau, *Housing and Population Data: 1980, 1990, 2000*.

[4] Vincenzo Milione, "Statistical Profile of Italian Americans in Civil Service in the Nineties: New York City and New York State," paper presented at conference of the National Council of Columbia Associations in Civil Service, City University of New York, 1994.

leaders. The idea for a conference on the status of Italian Americans in civil service grew out of the perception that, because of stereotyping, the needs of the Italian-American community were not being addressed. These discussions developed against a background in which disparate impacts and government retrenchment proceeded apace as the demographics in NYC changed.

The 1994 Italian-American civil service study found that during the 1980s, Italian-American government employees were underemployed in city and state occupations. This study demonstrated that in NYC government, Italian Americans were under-represented in approximately 7 out of 10 NYC government occupations and that, in particular, Italian-American women were under-represented in more than 80 percent of government occupations employing females. Similarly, in NYS government operations, approximately 70 percent of occupations under-represented Italian-American male and female workers, compared to their average percentage of representation within the NYS workforce. The spectrum of Italian-American groups in attendance also demonstrated that the feeling of being "put upon" and "discriminated against" was wide-ranging and deeply felt.

MEASURING ITALIAN AMERICANS IN GOVERNMENT IN THE NEW MILLENNIUM

As Italian Americans entered the new millennium by year 2000, they had more than 50 years of government experience although, as stated earlier, we lack specific data about their first few decades of post-WWII government employment. However, with the advent of the Italian-American ancestry data from the 1980 decennial census (representing achievements in the 1970s), the 1990 decennial census (representing those of the 1980s), and the 2000 decennial census (representing achievements in the 1990s), we have a statistical profile for the past 30 years of Italian Americans in NYC and NYS governments.

While most Americans, including Italian Americans, receive a short census data questionnaire every 10 years, about 1 out of 20 receives a longer questionnaire that seeks much more detailed information. In the short version Italian Americans could only identify themselves as "White" and therefore were not part of an actual headcount of Italian Americans in the total U.S. population. In the smaller, representative sample, the more specific socio-demographical questions include the respondent's self-identification of ethnic ancestry, which can include multiple ancestries. The respondents who answer "Italian" as one of their ancestral roots (first or second generation) serve as the base to extrapolate the total number of Italian Americans in the United States. It is through this ancestry question that Italian Americans are identified not only in government but also in other industries and ranges of life.

There are about 471 occupations in the state and 462 occupations in the city classified in the census data within the private sector, federal government, self-employed occupations, family-run businesses, and city and state governments. The governmental occupations listed in the census data include not only direct government hiring but also positions in sectors affiliated with government such as transit authorities and public universities.

THIRTY YEARS OF ITALIAN-AMERICAN EDUCATIONAL ACHIEVEMENT

Italian-American educational attainment improved between 1980 and 2000. The proportion of those with less than a high school degree decreased 50 percent. While Italian Americans with only a high school degree decreased a few percentage points, the general ratio of 1 out of 3 Italian Americans with only a high school degree remained constant. Italian Americans with postsecondary education increased greatly in the last 30 years, as the percentage of those with some college education doubled and the percentage with bachelor's degrees tripled during this time period. Graduate post-secondary education also increased greatly, with the percentage of Italian Americans in NYC and NYS with post-graduate studies nearly doubling.[5]

THIRTY YEARS OF ITALIAN-AMERICAN GOVERNMENT EMPLOYMENT

The availability of U.S. census data with the self-identification of Italian-American ancestry provided an opportunity to compile a statistical profile of their proportional representation in each occupation and within NYC and NYS government employment since the 1970s. The longitudinal study of employment trends from 1980 to 2000 documents a generational change in the Italian-American presence in city and state

---

[5] "Thirty Years of Italian-American Government Employment in New York City and New York State," *op. cit.*

government, as many Italian Americans who entered government service in 1970s were most likely the senior-level employees we found in 2000.

EMPLOYMENT OF ITALIAN AMERICANS IN GOVERNMENT

Occupational responsibilities in NYC and NYS governments range from unskilled labor tasks to public community service, to highly-specialized managerial and professional decision-makers. The skilled and unskilled job occupations in government—such as boilermakers, carpenters, electricians, and mechanics—require specialized vocational skills with minimal education requirements. Many early Italian immigrants found opportunities to work in these occupations because, although unable to speak English and/or lacking sufficient education or acceptable educational credentials, they did have excellent vocational skills. Documenting this as the experience of the Italian immigrant workforce entering the infrastructure of the NYC government is 1970 census data showing Italian immigrants in NYC government occupations constituting nearly 40 percent.[6]

Government service occupations include fire, police, and sanitation. Many children of the early Italian immigrants who were able to attain secondary education in the United States were competitive for these positions. In fact, the Italian Americans in these occupations founded the Columbia Associations for mutual fraternal support. Management and professional positions include administrators, accountants, lawyers, engineers, and other professional positions. Some of the early Italian immigrants were able to use their high school and post-secondary training in Italy to enter these positions. In reflecting their job tenure longevity, the Italian-American workers in city and state government were defined as follows: Entry: 16 years old–32 years old; Career: 33 years old–50 years old; and Senior: 51+ years old.

ITALIAN AMERICANS IN NYC GOVERNMENT

Table 1 shows the percentage of Italian Americans in NYC government management and professional, service and sales, or skilled and unskilled occupations. In 1980, the larger portion (44 percent) of the Italian-American

---

[6] Vincenzo Milione, "Occupational and Educational Attainment of Italian-American Professionals in NYC" Pp. 153-175 in *Italian Americans in Transition*, edited by Joseph V. Scelsa, Salvatore LaGumina and Lydio Tomasi (Staten Island, NY: AIHA, 1990).

city government workers was in service occupations. By 2000, 48 percent were in managerial and professional occupations. However, in 2000, a large portion (1 out of 3) of Italian Americans in city government operations was still in service occupations. There was a much smaller portion of Italian Americans in government in skilled and unskilled occupations in 2000, with only 1 out 6 compared to 1 out of 4 in 1980.

TABLE 1
Italian Americans in New York City Government by Occupation Category

	1980	1990	2000
Management and professional	13,122	17,515	21,140
Service and sales	18,424	18,512	15,973
Skilled and unskilled workers	10,634	9,500	7,222
Entry	11,440	11,951	11,079
Career	17,240	21,487	22,051
Senior	13,500	12,089	11,205
Total Italian-American government workers	42,180	45,527	44,335

Much of the advancement of Italian Americans in the managerial and professional occupations is due to the increases in educational attainment within the Italian-American community since 1980. The distribution of Italian Americans among entry, career and senior positions has not changed since 1980, indicating again stability once Italian Americans enter city government employment.

Chart 1 shows the percentage of Italian Americans in city government compared to that in the overall Italian-American work force in New York City for 1980, 1990, and 2000 in relation to changing demographics in New York City's overall population. The first bar is the percentage of Italian Americans in city government. The second bar is the percentage of Italian Americans in all elements of the NYC workforce. The line connecting the bars shows the change of the percentage of Italian-American population in NYC since 1980.

CHART 1
New York City: Percentage of Italian-American Employees in New York City Government vs. Total Workforce

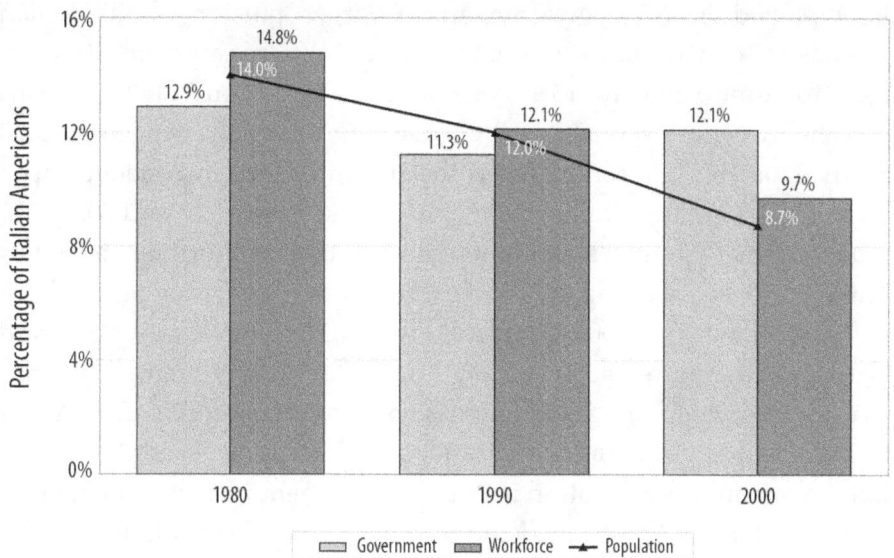

In 1980, Italian Americans constituted 14 percent of the NYC population and 14.8 percent of the NYC's overall workforce. However, Italian Americans in government in 1980 were slightly underrepresented with 12.9 percent of NYC government employees and by 1990 the percentage decreased further to 12 percent. During this same period, however, a corresponding decrease occurred in the Italian-American workforce (12.1 percent) as well as in the percentage of Italian Americans within city government (11.3 percent). In 1990, Italian Americans in government compared to the overall Italian-American workforce in NYC, continue to be somewhat underemployed. In fact, the 1994 study of Italian Americans in government details the numerous occupations in which Italian Americans were not included or were underrepresented.

The Italian-American exodus from NYC continued to 2000 with the overall Italian-American population decreasing to 8.7 percent, with a corresponding decrease in the percentage of Italian Americans in the NYC workforce (9.7 percent). However, in 2000, the percentage of Italian-American representation in NYC government increased to 12.1 percent, greater than the percentage of Italian Americans in the NYC workforce. In 2000, then, unlike the decrease in the percentage of Italian Americans in

NYC government given their exodus from the city, their percentage in city government increased and was subsequently greater than their percentage in the city workforce. For the first time, overall, Italian Americans were not underemployed in NYC government. A larger portion of the Italian Americans in the workforce was employed in NYC government, from 9.9 percent to approximately 13.9 percent. In 1980, 1 out of 10 Italians Americans was employed in the NYC government, which changed by 2000 to nearly 1 out of 7, a period when the Italian-American resident population in NYC decreased from 1 out of 6 in 1980 to 1 out of 12 in 2000.

The National Council's awareness and outreach efforts in the 1990s contributed to maintaining this increased Italian-American presence in NYC government in 2000, despite the Italian-American population decrease. Furthermore, at this same time, an unprecedented Italian-American leadership in government provided accessibility for Italian Americans within government operations. Unlike prior years, the overall Italian-American representation in NYC government increased in spite of decreases in Italian-American demographics in NYC. This is not to say that there are not many occupations where Italian Americans are not included or under-employed in NYC government.

ITALIAN AMERICANS IN NYS GOVERNMENT

Within the State of New York, Italian Americans have constituted the largest ancestry population at about the same population percentage over the last 30 years (16 percent in 1980 to 15 percent in 2000). For those who moved from NYC, the majority of Italian Americans left for metropolitan suburban communities on Long Island and in Westchester County, sometimes increasing the residents of Italian ancestry in those communities to 25 percent or greater. Others moved to New Jersey, which also has a large Italian-American presence. For New York State, the Italian-American presence has remained about 1 out 6 residents since 1980. While Italian Americans are dispersed throughout the state, approximately 30 percent of the total resides in NYC, and approximately 40 percent of all Italian Americans are in the downstate area and within commuting distance of New York City.

The number of Italian Americans in NYS government operations in 2000 was 56,813, approximately 15,000 more than in 1980. From 1980 to 2000, those in government management and professional occupations doubled from 14,565 to 29,739. Italian Americans in service occupations increased slightly during this period, and those in skilled and unskilled occupations decreased slightly (see Table 2).

Similar to the Italian-American distribution in NYC government, in 1980 the larger portion (50 percent) of Italian-American, NYS government workers was in service occupations. By 2000, 52 percent of Italian-American state government workers were in management and professional occupations, while another large portion, 1 out of 3, was in service occupations. A much smaller portion worked in skilled and unskilled occupations in 2000 (1 out 10), compared to 1 out of 7 in 1980.

TABLE 2.
Italian Americans in New York State Government By Position Tenure and Percent

	1980	1990	2000
Management and professional	35%	45%	52%
Service and sales	50%	42%	38%
Skilled and unskilled workers	14%	12%	10%
Entry	41%	30%	23%
Career	35%	49%	54%
Senior	24%	21%	23%
Total Italian-American government workers	100%	100%	100%

Much of the advancement of Italian Americans in the managerial and professional occupations is due to the significant change in the educational attainment of bachelor and post-graduate degrees within the Italian-American community since 1980. However, the change in distribution of Italian Americans among entry, career, and senior positions does flag a concern for their future representation in NYS government operations. Whereas 41 percent entered state government employment in 1980, only 1 out 4 Italian Americans did so in 2000. The large percentage who took entry-level positions in 1980 resulted in a substantial proportion of career employees in 1990 and 2000, when nearly 1 out of 2 was a career employee.

In Chart 2 the first bar in each three sets is the percentage of Italian-American state government employees and the second bar sets are the percentages of Italian Americans in the state workforce. The horizontal line connecting the bars shows the percentage changes since 1980. In 1980, 16.3 percent of the entire workforce in all classes of employment was of Italian ancestry, while only 12.9 percent of the NYS government employees were of such ancestry. However, 30 years later the Italian-American workforce slightly decreased with statewide demographic changes, but Italian-American representation in NYS government agencies increased to 14.8 percent. Within the census data, no statistical difference exists between the percentages of Italian-American state employees and of the total state Italian-American workforce. Moreover, Italian Americans have steadily increased as a NYS government presence since 1980, and in 2000 reached equity in relation to their percentage in the state workforce.

CHART 2
New York State: Percentage of Italian-American Employees in New York State Government vs. Total Workforce

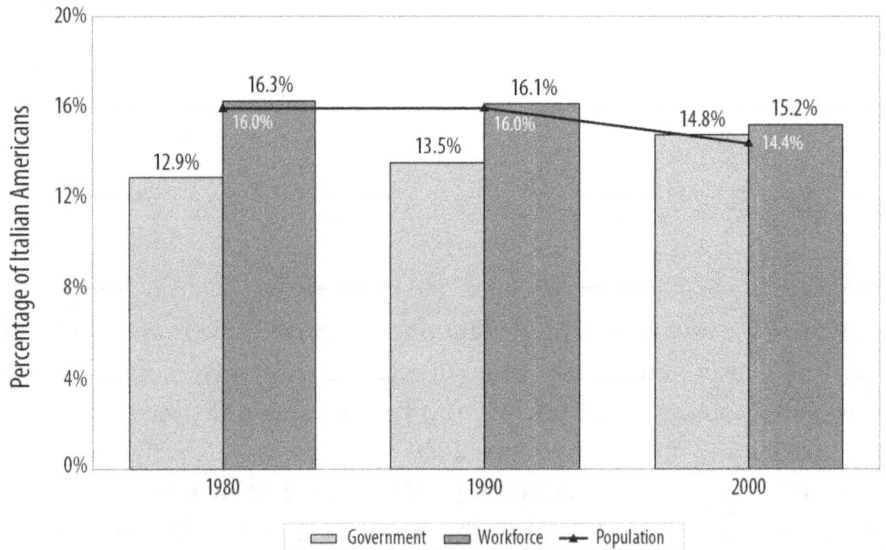

Since 1980, the percent of the Italian-American workforce within NYS government has been increasing, from 3.4 percent to 4.5 percent in 2000. However, whereas 1 out of 7 Italian Americans in the NYC workforce is in city government employ, only 1 out of 20 of the NYS Italian-American workforce is represented in the state government.

No major attrition of Italian Americans from NYS occurred since 1980, keeping the percentage of Italian Americans at approximately 16 percent over the past 30 years. Many of the Italian-American achievements of workforce equity in state government positions were the result of the additional hiring of 15,000 Italian Americans since 1980. Most of these new Italian Americans in state government are in management and professional occupations, reflecting the higher educational achievements in bachelor and post-graduate degrees.

UNDEREMPLOYMENT OF ITALIAN AMERICANS IN GOVERNMENT

Italian Americans in NYC government in 2000 have achieved equity with the Italian-American workforce in many occupations, even though Italian Americans were, overall, underemployed in state and city government in the 1980s and 1990s. Much of this success is due to the political visibility and gains in educational achievements since the 1980s as well as to the outmigration of Italian Americans from NYC.

However, many government agencies and select occupations in these agencies still under-employ or do not employ Italian Americans, as evidenced wherever the percentage of Italian Americans in government is less than that of the general workforce. The federal government considers an occupation as under-utilized when its hiring is less than the qualified workforce for that occupation. This is its means of determining disparate treatment of a protected class of workers within the evaluation guidelines established by the U.S. Office of Civil Rights and Equal Employment Opportunity Commission.[7]

In the NYC government's 327 occupations, approximately 60 percent (197), employ Italian Americans. In the NYS government, Italian Americans are employed in 74 percent of the state's occupations (264 of the 357 total).[8] This study was limited to the grouping of government occupations across agencies and departments. However, further vigilance is needed *within* the individual government units to ensure that Italian Americans are not kept from employment opportunities in those agencies. A particular anomaly to the past 30 years of Italian-American

---

[7] Federal Contract Compliance Manual; United States Department of Labor, Employment Standards Administration; Office of Federal Contract Compliance Programs; November 25, 1998

[8] "Thirty Years of Italian-American Government Employment in NYC and NYS," The Calandra Italian American Institute, The City University of New York, January 2007.

employment progress in the city and state governments is the City University of New York (CUNY). CUNY four-year colleges are considered as state government employers and the CUNY community colleges are considered as city government employers.

CUNY has been historically in the forefront in addressing Italian-American employment among its faculty, administration, and support-classified staff since the 1970s.[9] In 1976, the blatant underemployment of Italian Americans at the university and discriminatory practices resulted in the designation of Italian Americans as a protected class within CUNY according to federal affirmative action guidelines. This was a sincere and unique effort by the CUNY Chancellor and Board of Trustees to use the federal affirmative action procedures for increasing the presence of Italian Americans among CUNY employees.[10] Unfortunately, the federal affirmative-action procedures were never used or implemented to target Italian-American employment applicants in order to increase the number of Italian Americans in the CUNY workforce. However, as a result of the Italian-American affirmative action status within CUNY, faculty and staff data have been collected for Italian Americans employed in the University since 1978. CUNY is the only city or state agency to have detailed information about its Italian-American faculty, staff, and students.[11]

Chart 3 shows how the Italian-American instructional staff changed annually at the City University of New York from 1978 to 2005. Instructional staff positions at CUNY are comparable to the managerial and professional occupations within city and state government. Italian Americans on the instructional staff constituted about 6 percent of the

---

[9] Francis N. Elmi, *The Invisible Minority: A History of the Italian-American Struggle for Justice and Equality at The City University of New York 1993/1994*. Faculty Fellow Report. The John D. Calandra Italian American Institute Queens College/The City of University of New York. December 9, 1996. Unpublished paper.

[10] See Robert J. Kibbee, memorandum sent to CUNY Council of Presidents, December 9, 1976, Office of the Chancellor, The City University of New York; Joseph S. Murphy, Memorandum to the Council of Presidents, Italian Americans at The City University of New York," December 9, 1986, Office of the Chancellor, The City University of New York; and Matthew Goldstein, Memorandum sent to College Presidents, November 15, 1999.

[11] See: Judge Constance Baker Motley, Opinion on Motion for Preliminary Injunction Scelsa v. City University of New York, 92 CIV6690 (NY Dist. Ct. 1992); Affirmative Action Summary Data by College, Sex and Ethnicity: Instructional Staff, University Affirmative Action Office. The City University of New York 1978 to 2001; The City University of New York Affirmative Action Staff Utilization Analysis for Italian American Faculty and Staff: Review and Comment; Calandra Italian American Institute, 2006.

work force in 1978 and remained at that level in 2005. Chart 3 also shows that during the same thirty-year period, other protected category populations, using the federal affirmative action procedures, increased their percentage at CUNY from approximately 20 percent of the workforce in 1978 to about 40 percent in 2005. Because no affirmative action plan was implemented for Italian Americans, no increase in the percentage of Italian Americans among management and other professional occupations at CUNY occurred.

CHART 3
City University of New York, Total Instructional Staff

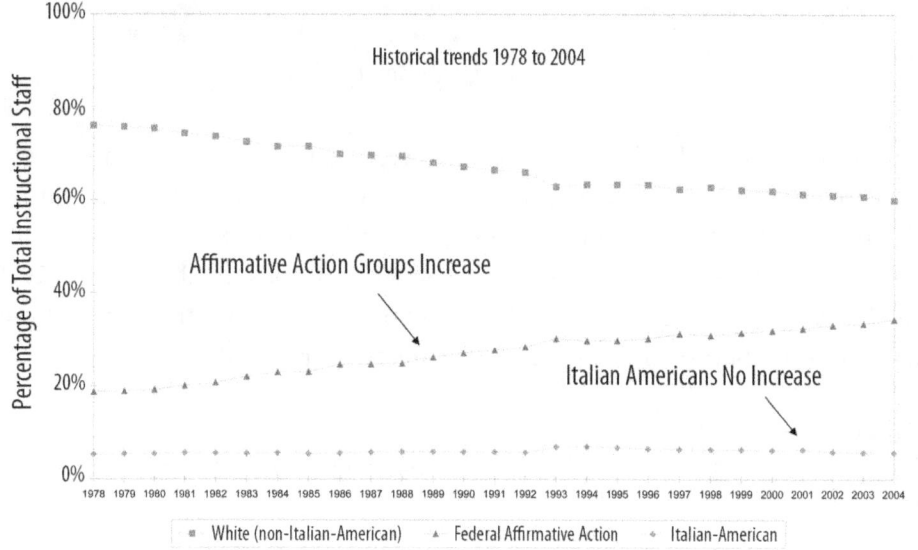

While Italian Americans did well in 2000 within many government occupations, they have been under-utilized at CUNY. Thus, the progress made by Italian Americans in NYC and NYS government occupations during the last three decades did not extend to the City University of New York (see Chart 4). The percentage of Italian Americans in the CUNY instructional staff is half the rate of the managerial and professional Italian Americans employed in NYC government (12 percent) and even less compared to the 15 percent Italian-American representation among state government employees at that level.

CHART 4
Italian-American Representation in Government Agencies, Management and Professionals

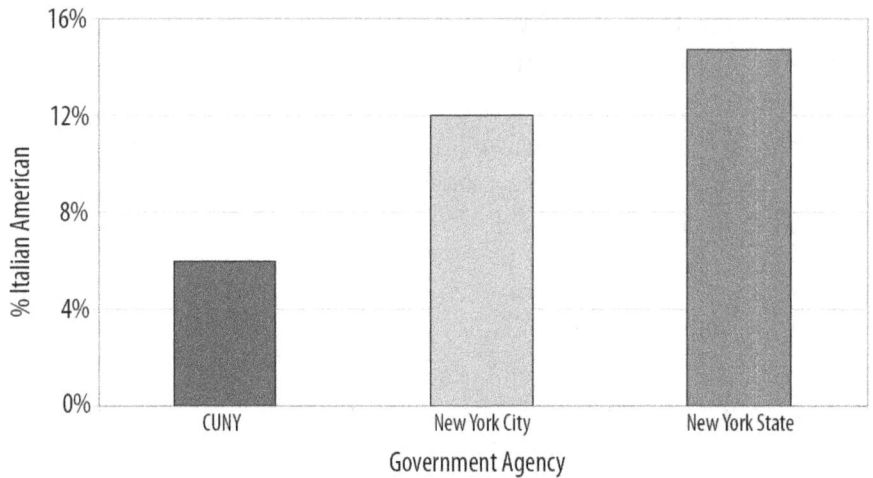

Since 1978, CUNY has also collected employment data on the classified support staff, analogous to the service and skilled and unskilled occupations within city and state governments. Chart 5 shows the annual percentage of Italian Americans in classified job titles at CUNY from 1978 to 2005. The percentage of Italian Americans among the occupations decreased by half from 8.1 percent in 1978 to 3.7 percent in 2004.

CHART 5
City University of New York, Total Italian-American Classified (Civil Service) Staff
Reference: University Affirmative Action Office: City University of New York 1978 to 2004

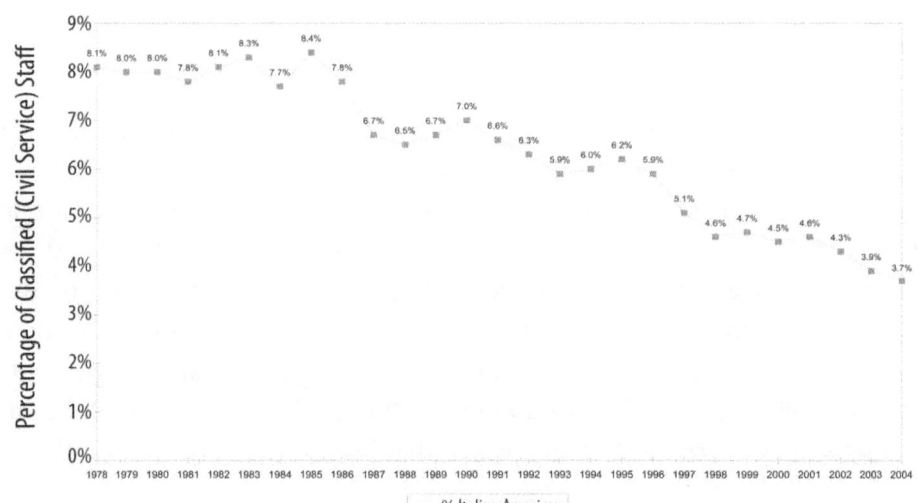

Chart 6, in turn, compares the percentage of Italian-American classified staff at CUNY to comparable occupations in the NYC and NYS governments in 2000. Since Italian-Americans constituted 12.1 percent of city employees at this level and 14.1 percent among state employees, we should expect that CUNY—once again both a city and state agency—to have a similar presence of Italian Americans. However, not only were they greatly underemployed in the 1970s when designated a protected class within CUNY according to federal affirmative action guidelines (20 percent in city government vs. 8 percent at CUNY), but in 2005, they continue to be greatly underemployed, with only 3.9 percent of the CUNY classified staff of Italian ancestry.

CHART 6
Italian-American Representation in Government Agencies, Classified (Civil Service)

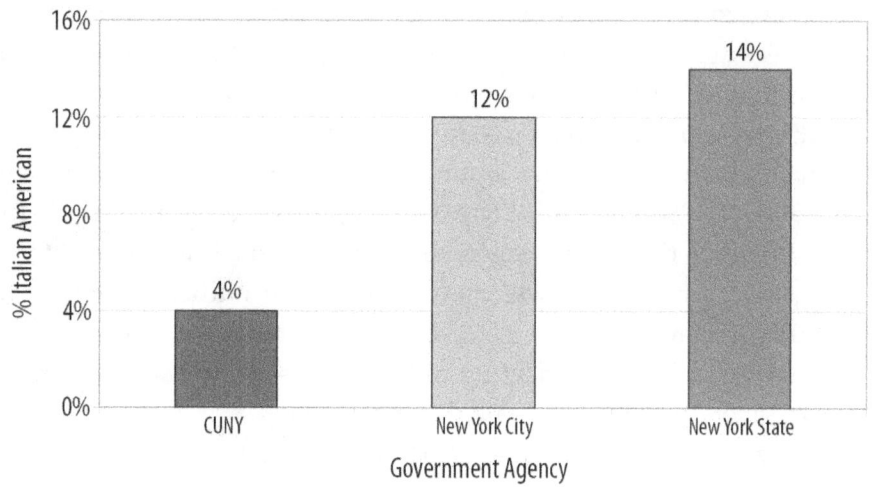

SUMMARY AND ASSESSMENT

This essay has summarized 30-plus years of the representation of Italian Americans in NYC and NYS government operations among entry, career and senior-level Italian-American employees in skilled and unskilled occupations, service occupations, and management and professsional occupations. Notably, Italian Americans greatly improved in educational attainment from 1980 to 2000. The rate of those with less than a high school degree decreased by half. Those with only a high school degree decreased a couple of percentage points but still remained at 1 out of 3 Italian Americans. Those with post-secondary education increased significantly in 30 years, the percentage of those with some college education doubling and the percentage with earned bachelor's degrees tripling. Graduate education also increased greatly, nearly doubling.

Italian Americans were underemployed in NYC and NYS positions in the 1980s and 1990s, but they achieved equity by 2000 with the percentage of Italian Americans in the general workforce within many government occupations. They were underemployed in 1980, when Italian Americans were more numerous, with 1 out of 7 NYC residents of Italian-American ancestry as compared to 1990, when Italian-American population demographic changes decreased the Italian-American presence to 1 out of 9 NYC residents. The demographic loss of Italian Americans in New York dropped further by 2000, with 1 out of 12 NYC residents claiming Italian ancestry. Much of the greater equity in the percentage of Italian-American employment in NYC government vis-à-vis the total workforce was less the result of increased new hiring of Italian Americans as it was from the demographic attrition of Italian Americans in NYC. A large portion of Italian Americans who remained in New York City were employed in city government.

No major attrition occurred among Italian Americans living in New York State since 1980, instead remaining at approximately 16 percent for 30 years. Much of the Italian-American advancement toward workforce equity in state government was the result of the additional hiring of 15,000 Italian Americans since 1980, most of them in management and professional occupations, reflecting their increased educational attainment of bachelor and post-graduate degrees.

The City University of New York is an example of how some government agencies may still under-employ Italian Americans in many occupations. CUNY, as a governmental agency, has been underemploying Italian Americans even though they constitute a protected class within CUNY according to federal affirmative action guidelines. This reality stands in contrast to the increasing percentage of Italian Americans in NYC and NYS government positions since 1980 and their achieving equity in the total workforce.

Acknowledgements

We thank Joseph Guagliardo, President of the National Council for Columbia Associations in Civil Service for his support of this project by providing a student scholarship to Daniel Guadiello, La Guardia Community College, to assist with the data compilation. His contribution to the history of Italian Americans in government helped to guide the statistical analysis. We appreciate, over the years, the participation of other Columbia Association members for their suggestions in documenting the Italian-American government experience, including John Milotti and Robert Agnoli. In addition, we appreciate the contributions of the Honorable Jack Como, President of the Italian American Legal Defense and Higher Education Fund, for an oral history of Italian Americans in government in the post war years and for promoting equal employment opportunities for Italian Americans in government.

In addition, we appreciate the research assistance from Dr. Joseph V. Scelsa, Vice President for Cultural Affairs, and Cav. Maria Fosco Director for Administration and Community Programs and Vice President of the Italian American Museum, for help over the years in collecting data and documenting the Italian-American government experience. Dean Anthony Julian Tamburri provided valuable oversight and editorial review. We also appreciate the information research assistance of Ms. Marianne McCauley, the administrative assistance of Rosaria Musco, and the secretarial assistance of Phyllis Tesoriero.

PART FIVE
The World of Work

The Idea of Work in the Postmodern Age

MARIO ALDO TOSCANO
University of Pisa

One of the most important subjects of public debate in Europe nowadays is *work* and the relationship between work and life. To make sense of it, a sort of hypothetical comparison between Europe and the United States seems to be useful and instructive, forcing, in a way, the differences between the two situations, while at the same time defining the special character of each of them.

In this sense we have adopted a Weberian procedure which leads in the end to the *ideal type*. Our thesis is that in Europe we are moving toward a process of marked and dramatic *individualization of work*. This expression appears rather incomprehensible in the States. Specific cultural and historical reasons help explain the difficulty in giving the same degree of meaning to this phenomenon both in Europe and the United States.

The fact is that in the States work has been always a matter of individual domain and management, with a significant impact on the social context. The individual dimension is specifically evident in a great deal of activities, from the everyday training of trade unions, to the negotiation of work conditions between workers and corporations, from the character of political parties to the behavior of representatives in the elective bodies, from the ideology of self-made man to the perspective of social mobility, from the religious organizations to the conception of property, from capitalistic entrepreneurship to the meritocratic practices. Most importantly, social policies have a special individual focus in the United States.

In a word, we can perhaps speak of *jobs instead of work*, with jobs being *pieces* of work. The ideal and abstract—philosophical, if you wish—pressure of work as the way of individual presence and existence in the world is somewhat reduced to a pragmatic consideration of what someone does in his biographical circumstances and career. This is not to say that work is underestimated; it is only a sign of a different attitude toward work in the context of a different economy of life, and of a hierarchy of values. It is, in the long run, connected to the perception that work is not at all denied to anybody who has the will and desire to look, using one's network of opportunities, for a job. This is the approach to suit the individual worker, and in a way invent it while waiting for what is not yet realized, although potentially expected. The condition is that the system is dynamic and the public deeply respects private initiative.

Europe comes from another kind of experience. The workers' movement, from the beginning of the industrial era, has been always strong and associated with the evolution and involution of capitalistic organization of economy and society. Class consciousness has achieved legitimization on a public level: and work has been the core of a *Weltanschauung*, which has obtained special results in modelling political constitutions and fundamental laws. Remember, for instance, the first article of the Italian Constitution: "Italy is a democratic republic, founded on work." Work was the social question, and affected socialism and society, in a sense contributing to the building up of a social and sometimes socialist society.

The Italian Constitution states that work is a right: the right to work. The implication is that the State, as the general government of society, has to secure the right to work, and therefore provide work itself. The ethics of work is thus associated with the goal of the State. This idea of work is also philosophically intensive; work is the way for an individual to make oneself effective, giving meaning to one's existence in the world. There are few religious, but many secular implications in such a concept.

What is the situation now? Analytically speaking, we can state the issue in simple terms: it is the relationship between *what someone does* and *what someone is*. This relationship has been always consistent and especially significant.

As we know, under all latitudes and ages, manual work and intellectual work have been separated and associated to a different quality of human capabilities and, to tell the truth, of human qualities and, in the end, of humans themselves. The division of labor resulted in complex layers of social stratification, and on this terrain, the idea and practice of citizenship played out. It is clear that this was an important theme to the ancient Greeks: they attributed great value to intellectual work and underestimated manual work. Plato's doctrine of the soul is a spectacular transcription of the common sense and culture of the era. And we can say that in Greek mythology all the heroes and heroines have an intellectual physiognomy, and even the twelve labors of Hercules were hard tasks, energetic but not manual.

It was only the beginning of the story, which lasts for a long time. In the Middle Ages, workers are in the community but not completely included in the city. We have discovered the masses who built the pyramids, as we have discovered the masses who erected the gothic cathedrals, but none of these subjects had any literature about them during their times. We discovered, as we say, those masses because there were important processes which happened and changed the perception of things. Overall, the rise of capitalism and the process of industrialization have improved the meaning and given modern dignity to the concept of work.

Two different directions advanced in Europe and in the States. The capitalist individual was recognized in Europe on the basis of the Protestant Ethic *and* on the secular ethics of Machiavellian virtue and fortune, but in the States mainly on the grounds of the Protestant Ethic — that is, the individual. At the same time, however, the idea of work as mass work advanced, equally decisive for the success of production and the development of the social system as a whole. But while in the States individual inspiration influenced the idea of work in general, in Europe the notion of mass work affected the general idea of work, resulting in two different implications. In the United States, the value of individuality gave strong legitimization to the capitalist system and great support to capitalist society; in Europe mass work reduced the value of individuality, lowered the legitimization of capitalist dimensions, and promoted the socialist connotation of society. Work thus had a much stronger public impact in Europe, with several important consequences.

First of all, in Europe the stability of work largely constituted the meaning of work, and the meaning of work connected to the *duration* of work. Work in its duration sustained and shaped personal identity; and in the long run was the fundamental factor of social stability in the system. Today, however, the stability of work is being questioned by a great amount of events which are not controlled by any one national system. Globalization affects all systems and new strategies are needed.

In contrast, because the United States conceptualized work on a traditional individual base, it now needs to find new adjustments that are not external to the general culture. In Europe it is more difficult. Flexible work inclines towards precarious work, with irradiations to the entire system. The *advocatio ad societatem* of the previous period must be supplanted by the *regressio ad individuum*, considered as a regression in general. The problem is a problem of radical change of culture, politics, and organization of life. The old forms of collective thinking and acting must be integrated or removed.

The ultimate implication of the instability of work is instability in general. On a large scale, this has to do with the identification of the agencies of governance of the world. History seems to be dominated by random forces and elements, and old movements based on work no longer have sufficient power. What factor is going to take supremacy is an open problem for Europe; surprisingly enough, it is less a problem for the United States, where work enjoyed the common and popular semantics of job, or, rather, jobs.

References

Accornero, A. 1997. *Era il Secolo del Lavoro*. Bologna: Il Mulino.

Bauman, Z. 1991. *Moderinity and Ambivalence*. London: Polity Press.

Beck, U., Giddens, A. and Lash, S. 1994. *Reflexive Modernization. Politics Tradition and Aesthetics in the Modern Social Order*. Cambridge: Polity Press.

Beck, U. 2000. *Il Lavoro nell'Epoca della Fine del Lavoro. Tramonto delle Sicurezze e Nuovo Impegno Civile*. Torino: Einaudi.

Bobbio, N. 1990. *L'Età dei Diritti*. Torino: Einaudi.

Durkheim, É. [1893] 1996. *La Divisione del Lavoro Sociale*. Milano: Comunità.

Giddens, A. 1991. *Modernity and Self-Identity*. Cambridge: Polity Press.

Sennett, R. 1998. *The Corrosion of Character. The Personal Consequences of Work in the New Capitalism*. New York: Norton.

Sennett, R. 2006. *The Culture of the New Capitalism*. New Haven-London: Yale University Press.

Toscano, M. A. 1988. *Marx e Weber. Strategie della Possibilità*. Napoli: Guida.

Toscano, M. A., ed. 2007. *Homo Instabilis. Soiciologia della Precarietà*. Milano: Jaca Book.

Weber, M. [1920] 1976. *Sociologia della Religione*. Torino: Utet.

Weber, M. [1922] 1958. *Il Metodo delle Scienze Storico Sociali*. Torino: Einaudi.

Employment and Social Inclusion: A European Perspective

RACHELE BENEDETTI
University of Pisa

The concept of social inclusion has recently assumed a new centrality because of its multidimensionality and dynamism. With this concept, indeed, we define not a state, but a process, useful in understanding and analyzing the actual meanings of inequality and vulnerability. Yet even as these features led to study of the process of social inclusion through its opposite and complementary concept, social exclusion, a new debate about social inequality developed in a European context around the dialectic between exclusion and inclusion. Originating in France in the 1970s, the concept of social exclusion assumed in the 1980s a broader European dimension, one that defined a new approach to face socio-economic challenges.

Serge Paugam (1996), one of the primary theorists of social exclusion in France, explained the development of this concept in three temporal steps in relation with the French socioeconomic dynamics, but the process he describes can extend to all European realities. In his analysis, social exclusion grew as unemployment increased and remaining employed became a precarious situation for other workers. Rene Lenoir's book, *Les Exclus* (*The Excluded*, 1974), popularized the concept of social exclusion and this concept assumed a new dimension with the transformation of the labor market, becoming in the 1980s, and even more so in the 1990s, the framework through which to analyze the emergence of social vulnerability and new types of poverty.[1]

---

[1] Even if the question is often very critical in the sociological debate, the concept of social exclusion can become a new, interesting manner to study the problem of poverty with a more dynamic and multifaceted approach. Paugam, in particular, explains the relationship between poverty and social exclusion with the elaboration of three ideal-types: *pouvreté intégreé, pouvretè marginale* and *pouvreté disqualifiante*, where the first type is more similar at the traditional kind of economic poverty, while the second puts its attention both on the problem of traditional poverty and exclusion and the third is specifically connected with the new 'social question' of vulnerability, insecurity and exclusion.

With the concept of social exclusion, the analysis of inequality, typically connected in industrial society with employment structure and social stratification, shifts now to a more complex, multidimensional reflection about both economical and social-relational problems, in a dynamic and fluid perspective.

But when can we affirm that the process of social exclusion is complete? When, in other words, do individuals define themselves out of the social system?

There are numerous interpretative patterns. In Robert Castel's analysis, for example, social exclusion occurs in three steps: complete integration in the social system, then vulnerability, and finally the absence of social relations.[2] In this pattern social exclusion stays in the middle of two alignments, an economic axis and a socio-relational axis, where the first is defined from the active and secure participation in the labor market and the second from belonging to a social network. Also Wilson[3] and Kronauer[4] develop a similar approach; for them the *status* of "out," of excluded, is the outcome of two co-present features: marginal economic position and social segregation.

Krekel's approach is particularly original; he applies the center/periphery pattern (generally used in world-systems analysis), to analyze the inclusion-exclusion dynamic as a process of unequal access to material and symbolic resources.[5] It is important to underline that, despite the different approaches, exclusion is explained as an outcome of a multidimensional process, a combination of economic, social and relational aspects, but also individual and collective elements.

EXCLUSION IN THE EUROPEAN CONTEXT: COMPARISON WITH THE U.S. CONTEXT

As we have seen, the dialectic between inclusion and exclusion represents the most important concepts in the present European debate about social inequality and vulnerability. But why does social inclusion-

---

[2] Robert Castel, *De l'Exclusion Comme État à la Vulnérabilité Comme Pocessus*, in *Justice Sociale et Inégalités*, edited by J. Affichard and J.B. de Foucauld (Paris: Ed. Esprit, 1992), pp. 135-148.

[3] Cf. William. J. Wilson, "Public Policy Research and the Truly Disadvantaged," in *The Urban Underclass*, edited by Christopher Jencks (Washington, DC: The Brookings Institution, 1991).

[4] Martin Kronauer, "'Esclusione Sociale' e 'Underclass': Nuovi Concetti per l'Analisi della Povertà," in *Vulnerabilità, Inclusione Sociale e Lavoro*, edited by Vango Borghi (Milan: Franco Angeli, 2002), pp. 37-63.

[5] Cf. R. Krekel cited in Kronauer, *op cit.*, pp. 40-41.

exclusion become so important in European societies?[6] We think its success comes from some specific issues.

As we have underlined at the beginning, social inclusion is a dynamic concept that describes a process. As Ranci said, "In its original meaning, social exclusion doesn't identify a specific social group, but the existence of specific social processes, that lead, more frequently than in the past, to situations of disadvantage." From this perspective, social exclusion defines a discontinuity in the social structure and it faces the problem of new social dualism between in and out (2002:21).

Furthermore, social inclusion emphasizes the multidimensional nature of present discomfort, one that includes both employment and different aspects like house, health, social relations and integration. So, this concept also becomes a framework through which to analyze the process of the "corrosion of middle-class," seen as one of the more critical trends in contemporary European societies.

Actually, there are some critical aspects linked to the question of the contemporary society as a dichotomist society. To some authors, such as Castel, the approach of social exclusion, calling its attention on the dialectic in-out, trends to hide the problem of the erosion of middle class, which is one of the more evident aspects of post-industrial society[7].

Without getting into this theoretical debate, we would like to underline, on the contrary, how this perspective of social inclusion as a multidimensional process can be useful in exploring new social trends and dynamics in a larger perspective where employment plays an important role in improving participation and integration.

This dialectic defines a specific European dimension. In the Anglo-Saxon context (especially in the United States), the current debate about inequality and new types of poverty centers on the underclass. As social exclusion, *underclass* too is a new concept in social analysis. Borne in the United States in the 1960s to call attention to the existence of a persistent poverty during strong economic growth, *underclass* assumes in this context a specific dimension, strictly connected with the challenge of unemployment (similar to the European concept of exclusion).

In the 1970s the success of this concept resulted from media exposure

---

[6] For these subjects, see in particular A. Woodward, M. Kohli, *Inclusion and Exclusion in European Societies* (New York: Routledge, 2001).

[7] Cf. Robert Castel, "Le Insidie dell'Eclusione," *Assistenza Sociale*. 3-4 (December 2003): 193-208.

that shifted attention to the marginal existences of metropolitan disadvantaged groups. Here, *underclass* assumed a new behavioral and racial dimension (Procacci 1996) that specficially included blacks and Hispanic immigrants. In the 1980s social scientists expanded the concept of underclass, adding to the original racial dimension a stronger spatial connotation; more and more, the underclass became a specific problem of central cities, particularly in poor immigrant and black communities.

In comparison to social exclusion, the underclass concept displays strong parallels but important differences as well (see Table 1). The two concepts define new socially unequal space and shapes, and they award especial importance to marginality and the social isolation process. Most particularly, social isolation assumes significance in the exclusion framework, resulting from weak or precarious employment, whereas in the underclass frame, social segregation is linked with minority integration.

The most important difference between the two concepts concerns the analytical approach to inequality problems. Exclusion, as we have said, describes a process, whereas underclass defines a state in which social positions are already stabilized and spatial dimension is specially stressed. Social exclusion framework, in contrast, tends to define an imprecise, wide, and fluid category that emphasizes the in-out dualism.

TABLE 1
A Comparison of the Concept of Social Exclusion and Underclass

SOCIAL EXCLUSION	UNDERCLASS
Analogies	
▪ New shapes of social inequality ▪ Marginality and social isolation ▪ Centered on employment	▪ New shapes of social inequality ▪ Marginality and social isolation ▪ Employment strictly connected with immigrants, integration
Differences	
▪ Dynamic process ▪ Fluid and width category ▪ Dualism in-out ▪ Unemployed	▪ State ▪ Spatial dimension ▪ Structured social positions ▪ Immigrants and black men

From this comparison we get different social categories too, particularly in the United States, with the excluded often represented by black and Hispanic inhabitants of deprived areas. In other words, the underclass represents the most marginalized groups, easily identifiable and labeled. In the European context, the debate around social exclusion calls attention to all social groups weakly integrated in the labor market and it describes a large fleeting area of vulnerability, in which new types of marginality keep developing.

In Europe, then, employment is the *trate d'union* of all reflection about inequality and it becomes the most important factor of social participation and the integration process, as well as the pillar of a wider and stronger social cohesion strategy, as discussed below.

FROM EXCLUSION AS THEORETICAL DEBATE TO INCLUSION AS POLITICAL PRACTICE

The European dimension of inclusion/exclusion synthesizes the success of these two concepts in terms of 1) *multidimensionality* (e.g., economic, social, relational, psychological; 2) *dynamism* (exclusion as social process); and 3) a *strict connection with labor market change* (e.g., flexibility, precariousness, growing unemployment).

This concept of inclusion emerges in the European Union in the 1980s during the Delors presidency, and it becomes an instrument of social cohesion, especially with the Lisbon process that utilized an integrated strategy for economic growth and social development. This integrated strategy has strengthened since 2001, with NAP/inclusion[8] and Open Method of Coordination (OMC)[9], which simplify social protection and inclusion policies, calling attention to some specific aspects. In particular, in 2007 the Joint Report on Social Protection and Inclusion reduced the goals to three:

1. Full participation in society and guaranteed access to resources, rights, and services;
2. Promoting active inclusion and fighting poverty;
3. Strengthened governance of social inclusion policies.[10]

These goals divide into many sub-dimensions, but it is possible to

---

[8] The National Active Planes are annual reports in which member states explain policies, activities and advancements in the process of social inclusion, in relationship with EU goals defined in European Commission council of Nizza and Laken.

[9] The OMC is a work method defined during the Lisbon process to improve cooperation between member states, and focuses national policies on some specific and common goals. The open coordination is based on: common definition of goals; definition of means to measure evolution and results of this process; benchmarking to improve best practice diffusion.

[10] Cf. EC, *Joint Report on Social Protection and Social Inclusion* (Brussels 2007).

individualize one common, transversal axis that represents the core of all European policies on social inclusion: employment. Indeed, employment becomes the principal dimension to improve full and active participation in social life and, at the same time, it is the most important guarantee against poverty and exclusion risk. In this view then we can note the attention given in recent years to active inclusion policies, that is, policies in which the right of all people to have an active role in the social process is strictly linked with both providing that activation and a strategy of responsibility for subjects at risk of exclusion.

These intervention policies find a specific relevance within the present labor market, characterized by improving flexibility to where the worker is often exposed to unemployment and vulnerability. That's why in the EU, *employability* and *flexicurity*, the two concepts about to be discussed, are successful and serve as the pillars in the definition of an integrated, multidimensional inclusion and social cohesion strategy.

EMPLOYABILITY

Employability is a concept created in the mid-1990s with the birth of the European Employment Strategy (EES) that seeks to establish policies to make unemployment systems more active and to increase the skills of workers. When EES began, employability mainly was a recovery instrument for unemployed people, but progressively it became a bigger strategy to face emerging changes. So, we can say that from a recovery mean, employability became a preventive mean, involving many different dimensions. Its activity principally concerned the fight against unemployment, particularly long-term, youth unemployment, but also the access or re-integration into the labor market trough training, education and the promotion of dialogue among the various social components[11].

In short, we can say that employability is a multidimensional concept in which its material and relational dimensions offer insights into a discussion about social inclusion and integration. In its more recent meaning of global approaches to address social change, analysts tend to frame employability as a social process from a multi-dimensional perspective to understand better its intervention aspects (EC 2000).

A first consideration concerns the integration process. Since 1999,

---

[11] On this point, three specific goals of employability are: modernizing education and training systems, reducing dropouts from the educational system, and active monitoring of the unemployed by offering training plans.

officials have focused on the employability of disadvantaged groups and, in particular, on the capacity/possibility for them to have an active role in the labor market. The second concern is less about a new intervention area and more about giving attention to the organizational process and encouraging a partnership among employers, training agencies, and other social agencies, particularly with involvement at the local level.

Another important employability aspect is adaptability to technological change in the relationship between workers and this new knowledge, certainly a strategic factor in the inclusion process. Here, the dialectic of inclusion-exclusion changes: exclusion is no longer explained as a residual phenomenon involving only traditional marginal social groups (the poor, immigrants, ethnic minorities), but also becomes a critical threshold that is crossed more easily, especially by those vulnerable groups exposed to growing job security risks. From this perspective, the adaptability to the technological change and training improvement need to reduce the gap between those who can use new technologies and those who are excluded from them.

In short, the dialectic between employment and exclusion is becoming more complex. In the contemporary context, indeed, not only does employment itself represent the goal of the social inclusion process, but the new challenge of European social cohesion also involves the integration of a population either weakly or only partially in the labor market. It thus becomes necessary to develop a more global approach to social inclusion, one that goes beyond the simple dichotomy between employed/unemployed and involves the new risk categories: precarious workers, "junk-job" workers, and the working poor.

FLEXICURITY

Flexicurity recently entered into the core of European debate about the interplay between the welfare state and the labor market, in other words, the discussion about reforming the European social model. Facing such new challenges as globalization, transition to a knowledge-intensive economy, aging trends, and the social inclusion and integration process, those promoting the European social model must rethink its structure and reaffirm its capability to balance the social and economical spheres. This model, in spite of European internal national differences,[12] "is the outcome

---

[12] Traditionally, we can distinguish four national typologies of European welfare: the Scandinavian, the Anglo-Saxon, the Continental and the South-European model (Cf. G. Esping-Andersen, *Three*

of a long and complex historical process trying to combine social justice with high economic performance."[13]

However, the actual transition of European societies requires reforming the social model and developing a bigger strategy to face the challenges confronting 1) transition into the labor market; 2) social dialogue and improvement of social partnerships; and 3) active policies for social inclusion. In this way, flexicurity becomes the core of a social model reform because it joins employment and social concerns into a more integrated strategy.

But what exactly *is* flexicurity? The principal idea behind this concept is that the flexibility of the labor market and the security of workers are not contradictory, but can actually be mutually supportive. Instead of the traditional dichotomist idea of flexibility for employers and security for employees, it offers a more interdependent perspective where flexibility and adaptability can be positive for both employers and employees if coordinated with active policies, training, and educational programs to effectively improve workers' skills. In this context, the process of flexicurity is a negotiated course of action between labor and management and its desired outcome should be the improvement of social cohesion and sustainable employment.

As Madsen (2006) says, we can interpret the dynamic perspective of flexicurity through three different approaches: a political strategy; an historical social process; and an analytical framework. Before discussing these three approaches, we should first mention that this concept of flexicurity is not a new idea, but rather, in some European countries at least, of a long-standing political and social practice.

FLEXICURITY AS A POLITICAL STRATEGY: THE EU POLICY

The Expert Group on Flexicurity (EGF)[14], established on September 2006, defines flexicurity as a new way of looking at flexibility and security in the labor market and, more precisely, "as a policy strategy to enhance,

---

Worlds of Welfare Capitalism, Princeton University Press, 1990). These typologies became more complex in the most recent years, because of the European enlargement, but the four models remain an important guide into welfare state analysis (Cf. C. Hadjmichalis and D. Sadler, *Europe at the Margin: New Mosaics of Inequality* (New York: Wiley, 1995).

[13] Maria G. Rodrigues, *References and Tools for Policy Choices* (Lisbon: ISCTE, 2006), p.4.

[14] The expert group was set up by DG Employment, Social Affairs and Equal Opportunities (DG EMPL) and consisted of seven experts chosen on the basis of their academic record and of their relationship with social partners. The group's main task is to monitor the flexicurity theoretical debate and practice in EU and OECD countries, but also advise the European Commission about preconditions of flexicurity, adequate indicators and specific members states' situation.

at the same time and in a deliberate way, the flexibility of labor markets, work organizations and labor relations on the one hand, and security–employment security and income security–on the other."[15] The Expert Group's analysis gives a strong emphasis to two aspects: active labor market policies that include training, education, and lifelong learning activities, and secondly, a social security system providing income support but also combining work with care to improve equal opportunities and gender equality.

This approach puts the accent on the acquisition of a new employability mentality, as illustrated by this statement in the same document: "Encouraging flexible labor markets and ensuring high levels of security will only be effective if workers are given the means to adapt to change, to stay on the job market and make progress in their working life."[16] The flexicurity approach thus seeks to provide new securities to offset the insecurities created by the contemporary economic and labor market transition. The average European productivity gap in comparison with the EU's main competitors, its labor market segmentation, and its at-risk-poverty rate are all still too high. Also, its unemployment and precarious employment rates represent the most important challenges that the European welfare systems must face. Flexicurity, in this context, defines a positive strategy because employers would have flexibility to anticipate and respond to market changes, while employees would have better possibilities to combine work with private responsibilities.

The success of this model requires a dynamic security perspective, not just a simple protection against job loss but also provision for workers to "enter, remain and progress in employment throughout the life-cycle" (EC 2007). Given this perspective, the strategy of flexicurity centers around four components: 1) flexible contractual arrangements; 2) active labor market policies; 3) reliable and responsive lifelong learning; and 4) modern social security systems. In addition, this model assigns a specific role to improving a productive and supportive social dialogue.

---

[15] EGF, *Flexicurity Pathways*, Interim report from the rapporteur presented at the Stakeholder Conference on Flexicurity (Brussels, 2007), p. 2. EGF assumes Wilthagen's definition of flexicurity. More recently, Wilthagen defined flexicurity as "a degree of job, employment, income and combination security that facilitates the labor market careers and biographies of workers with a relatively weak position and allows for enduring and high quality labor market participation and social inclusion, while at the same time providing a degree of numerical timely and adequate adjustment to changing conditions in order to maintain and enhance competitiveness and productivity" (Cf. .Wilthagen and Rogowski, 1994; 2004).

[16] *Ibid*.

This policy strategy of flexicurity closely relates with the European Employment Strategy, itself modelled after the revised Lisbon Strategy that promotes an active response to the challenge of globalization.

FLEXICURITY AS A GRADUAL, HISTORICAL PROCESS: THE DANISH CASE

If the European Union principally defines flexicurity as a specific political strategy, this concept emerged as the outcome of a long historical process, where economics and culture played an important role. In Denmark, flexicurity has long represented the pillar of its collective bargaining system and welfare state structure. This pattern, also called *competitive solidarity*, is the result of social compromises between employers and trade unions since 1907. Indeed, this historical agreement has dominated the Social Pact that still governs industrial Danish relationships, where employers have considerable latitude in hiring and firing, while employees enjoy extensive protections against the risk of job loss.

FIGURE 1
The Danish Golden Triangle

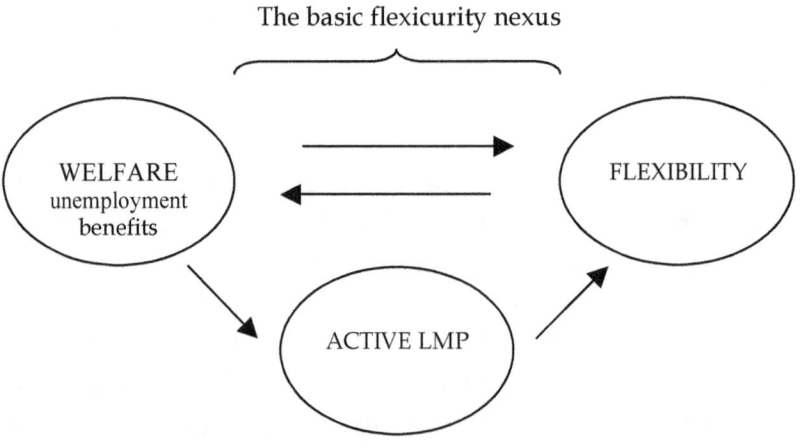

Source: Ministry of Employment, *Social Cohesion and Flexicurity*, November 2005.

Since the 1990s, the Danish flexicurity model, often called the "golden triangle," involves a relationship between welfare and flexibility on its main axis, while active labor market policies (ALMP) create an integrated and dynamic dialectic between high employment mobility and social safety (see Figure 1).

The Danish flexicurity pattern represents an interesting hybrid between "the flexible, free-market welfare states characterized by high numerical flexibility (liberal hiring-and-firing rules) and the generous Scandinavian welfare regimes of high social security (relatively high benefits levels)."[17]. However, Danish flexicurity serves as a good reference model because of its tradition of social agreement based on democratic comparison, cooperation, and dialogue among all social parties. In particular, the local and decentralized dimension becomes important as it seeks in critical times to improve social dialogue and to strengthen the process from the bottom up, in a context of balance between competitiveness and social sustainability needs.

FLEXICURITY AS A FRAMEWORK: THE TLM APPROACH

Finally, we can also see flexicurity as an analytical framework. From this viewpoint, we can use flexicurity to compare different labor market systems and its close relationship to another important labor market approach, the transitional labor market.[18]

Obviously, this short analysis cannot get into detailed European comparisons. Still, thanks to the concept of transition in the labor market, we can define a multidimensional approach that emphasizes both some transversal European trends and elements that are essential in the functioning of the European welfare state. The key assumption in the TLM approach, as developed by Schmid, is that "the borders between labour market and other social systems have to become more open for transitory states between paid work and gainful non-market activities which preserve and enhance future employability."[19]

This approach identifies six distinct transitional spaces increasingly typical of our post-industrial society: 1) transitions between different kinds of employment (full-employment, part-time employment, fixed-time employment, etc.); 2) transitions between dependent or self-employment; 3) transitions between employment and unemployment; 4) transitions between education or training and employment; 5) transitions between productive but unpaid private work and paid market work; and 6) transitions from employment to retirement.

---

[17] Madsen, *Flexicurity: A New Perspective on Labour Markets and Welfare States in Europe*, p. 7

[18] Cf., in particular, recent studies of Madsen and Gazier.

[19] Günther Schmid, *Transitional Labor Markets: A New European Employment Strategy*, discussion paper, October 1998, p. 2.

The TLM approach seeks to transform the motto "making work pay" into "making transitions pay," where the former tries to push people into the labor market while the latter emphasizes job quality, training and competence accumulation, and individual autonomy of the employed or unemployed[20]. Four principal criteria define a "good" transitional labor market: 1) empowerment (the labor market must empower individuals faced with challenges and critical events in their work life); 2) solidarity and sustainable employment (the labor market must support transitions with active measures, unemployment insurance and employability promoting programs); 3) sharing responsibilities and co-operation (the labor market must enhance synergies between all social parts and stimulate local networks); and 4) co-ordination and efficiency through decentralization (the labor market must define a new balance between central levels and local agencies).

In other words, assuming that employment transition will be a normal condition in the future, the TLM approach tries to improve the capacity and/or possibility of individuals to fight against the new social risks in order to enhance their participation in the process of social inclusion. However, can this approach actually face such a big challenge? As we said about flexicurity, we see this approach not as a simple recipe, but as a framework, as a vehicle to promote a sustainable change in the construction of a new individual and collective social safety.

CONCLUSION

We have called attention to some elements that assume specific relevance in the current debate about social policies in Europe, both from a theoretical point of view and in their political, practical implications. However, the goal of this analysis is not to offer a solution to the social and employment questions linked with present transitions in the labor market. On the contrary, we seek to spur reflections about the new challenges and new social risks, starting from the strategies and different approaches developed on this subject in the European context.

All the elements just discussed (employability, flexicurity and transitional labor market) must be interpreted both as possibilities and also as challenges in the process of social inclusion. The risk, however, is to

---

[20] For example, one of the most important elements in this approach is the combination of working time reduction with life-long learning.

interpret these concepts from a utopian perspective, as solutions to all current social change problems. Instead, we should explain employability, flexicurity and the TLM approach, in the Weberian context, as ideal types. They provide a key role in guiding and orienting us in this process, not by defining one solution, but by opening the process of coping with social change in a more cooperative and active approach towards social inclusion and participation.

References

Castel, Robert. 1992. "De l'Exclusion Comme État à la Vulnérabilité Comme Processus." Pp. 135-148 in *Justice Sociale et Inégalités*, edited by J. Affichard and J.B. de Foucauld. Paris: Esprit.

——. 2003. "Le Insidie dell'Esclusione." *Assistenza Sociale* 3-4:193-208.

Council of Europe. 2007. *Joint Report on Social Protection and Social Inclusion*. Brussels.

Council of Europe. 2001. "Promoting the Policy Debate on Social Cohesion from a Comparative Perspective." *Trends in Social Cohesion*. Brussels.

EGF. 2007. *Flexicurity Pathways*, interim report from the rapporteur presented at the Stakeholder Conference on Flexicurity, Brussels.

Esping-Andersen, Gøsta. 1990. *Three Worlds of Welfare Capitalism*. Princeton, NJ: Princeton University Press.

European Commission. 2007. *Joint Report on Social Protection and Social Inclusion 2007*. Brussels.

Gazier, Bernard. 2006. *Flexicurity and Social Dialogue: European Ways*, working paper, Paris 1 University and CNRS.

Hadjmichalis, Costis, and David Sadler. 1995. *Europe at the Margins: New Mosaics of Inequality*. New York: Wiley.

Kohli, Martin. 2008. *Inclusions and Exclusions in European Societies*. New York: Routledge.

Kronauer, Martin. 2002. "'Esclusione Sociale' e'Underclass': Nuovi Voncetti per l'Analisi della Povertà." Pp. 37-63 in *Vulnerabilità, Inclusione Sociale e Lavoro*, edited by Vando Borghi. Milan: Franco Angeli.

Madsen, Per Kongshøj. 2006. "Flexicurity: A New Perspective on Labour Markets and Welfare States in Europe." Paper presented at the CARMA Centre for Labor Market Research, Aalborg University, May 18.

Paugam, Serge. 1996. *L'Exclusion l'État des Savoirs*. Paris: La Découverte.

Procacci, Giovanna. 2002. "Underclass e Esclusione Sociale nel Dibattito Odierno sulla Povertà." Pp. 85-102 in *Vulnerabilità, Inclusione Sociale e Lavoro*, edited by Vando Borghi.

Ranci, Costanzo. 2002. *Le Nuove Disuguaglianze Sociali in Italia*. Bologna: Il Mulino.

Rodrigues, Maria G. 2006. *References and Tools for Policy Choices*. Lisbon: ISCTE.

Rogowski, Ralf, and Ton Wilthagen. 1994. "The Rediscovery of the Individual in Labour Law." *Reflexive Labour Law: Studies in Industrial Relations and Employment Regulation*. New York: Springer.

Schmid, Günther. 2006. "Social Risk Management Through Transitional Labour Markets." *Socio-Economic Review* 4(1):1-33.

Wilson, William J. 1990. *The Truly Disadvantaged: The Inner City, the Underclass, and Public Policy*. Chicago: University of Chicago Press.

Wilthagen, Ton, and Frank Tros. 2004. "The Concept of 'Flexicurity': A New Approach to Regulating Employment and Labour Markets." *Transfer* 10(4):166-186.

The Industrial Districts: The Case Study of Santa Croce sull'Arno (Tuscany)

SOFIA CAPUANO
University of Pisa

Prada, Gucci, and Ferragamo are a few of the best-known international Italian brands. Most people can only imagine the kind of work that goes on behind these big names. Accordingly, the objective of this paper is to reveal the type of Italian organization at the top end of the market, that which allows Italy to compete on a global market. To do so, we must first discuss the Italian economy before examining the industrial district phenomenon.

THE PHENOMENON OF THE INDUSTRIAL DISTRICT

Alfred Marshall appears to be the first person to use the term "industrial district" in *The Principles of Economics* (1952). Marshall writes of a "thickly peopled industrial district."

In his original formulation of the industrial district, Marshall envisioned a region where the business structure is comprised of small locally owned firms that make investment and production decisions locally. Firms, in the economies of scale, are relatively low in the number of people that they employ. Within the district, substantial trade is transacted between buyers and sellers, often entailing long-term contracts or commitments.

Since the 1980s, the term has taken on other meanings, deriving from an important element of dynamic industrial development in northern Italy, where, after World War II, clusters of small and medium-sized enterprises (SME) experienced extensive growth. Industrial districts are a powerful source of wealth for different categories of "actors" operating in the territorial areas hosting a business cluster.

In the Italian industrial scenario, the industrial district (ID) constitutes a peculiar model of production deeply rooted in the social context. As a matter of fact, the district is a socio-territorial entity characterized by the active presence of both a community of people and a group of firms in a naturally and historically delimited area (Becattini 1990). Therefore, the territory represents not only numerous physical factors but also a socio-economical and cultural environment, which becomes a critical infrastructure of communication upon which district relations are based (Micelli and Di Maria 2000).

Some of the main features of the district are the capacity for innovation and the flexible structure of production and workflows. In such a reality, tacit knowledge seems to represent the central resource upon which the competitive advantage of the district itself is based (Belussi 2000).

From a structural point of view, the industrial district can be considered as a network of institutions, associations, and small and medium enterprises located in a specific geographical area and normally characterized by a high capability for innovation and self-organization (Biggiero 1998). This definition particularly underlines the dimensional aspect of district firms, which are closely interconnected among themselves through vertical and horizontal networks. The district itself as a whole can be considered as a hyper-network, composed of a network of other networks that tie the firms between themselves and to the institutions (public bodies, professional associations, trade unions, etc.). Inside the ID, Biggiero (1999) identifies three levels of multidimensional patterns of interaction. At the first level, we find networks of firms composed by SMEs (mostly district firms) and by leading firms (multinationals or bigger sized firms or innovative SMEs). A second level of interaction is individuated in relationships that occur among these firms and associative structures such as consortia, trade associations and real services providers. The third level of interaction involves district firms, associative structures and the local institutions such as municipalities, provincial and regional governmental institutions, schools and universities, banks or other financial service providers. The multidimensionality of those networks resides in the different layers in which relationships occur. Indeed, all the above-listed actors interact with each other at economic, social, cognitive and symbolic levels, by creating dense and recursive patterns of interaction.

In the Italian experience, such phenomena have proved to be an important source of excellence for many networked small and medium enterprises. Although in Italy business clustering has always been a spontaneous rather than a planned phenomenon, in order to promote local economies in the past 15 years, public institutions have been inclined to establish formal policies to foster the start-up development of industrial districts. Industrial districts in Northern Italy have a precise location and are highly specialized, for example, Prato in woolen fabrics, Sassuolo in ceramic tiles, Brenta in ladies' footwear, and Santa Croce sull'Arno in leather goods.

The success of SME-based Italian districts was one of the factors that motivated economic development organizations across the world to adopt cluster promotion (that is, a network of firms cooperating to achieve a common objective) as an approach to stimulate growth and job creation. Industrial districts are relevant economic phenomena for other countries, where they may take on different configurations.

A number of regions have grown into enterprise zones, because of their growth, competitiveness, agglomeration patterns, and certain similarities to the model of the industrial district provided by Marshall, or its Italian variant (Piore and Sabel 1984). The most well known North American examples are the regions of Hollywood, Silicon Valley and Orange County, although many others have also been studied. Scholars have identified in the UK the area between London and Bristol, and in France, the areas of Grenoble, Montpellier and Sophia-Antipolis.

In any case, it seems fair to say that industrial districts are mainly an Italian phenomenon, and have played a large part in the country's economic development and growth. "Unity is our best weapon," goes an old Italian proverb, and empirical evidence shows that many Italian small-medium enterprises have taken this popular advice to heart by success-fully linking their strategies to those undertaken by other companies located in their geographic area. As a result, small business clustering has proven to be an important lever for growth, especially for those small-medium enterprises having structural difficulties in pursuing strategies aiming to increase the size and target of their activities.

The typical production model of the current Italian economy dates back to the 1970s, when the rapid expansion of small firms gave rise to the industrial districts that still represent the engine of the Italian economy. Many scholars have addressed this intriguing phenomenon. Their research has furnished a deep understanding of the peculiarities of this socioeconomic model, stimulating widespread debate among economists, geographers, sociologists, historians and business scholars as to its relevance as a model for the Italian economy and society. Additional research has addressed the Italian variant of the Marshallian industrial district. Sociologists see the district as a relatively stable community providing a strong local cultural identity and giving the local people a feeling of belonging.

It is difficult, however, to propose a single model of an Italian district, given the variety of organizational and relational forms that exist in the different districts. Nevertheless, it is possible to single out some salient features that have characterized the districts since their development in the 1970s. We can characterize the district as a socio-territorial entity characterized by three main factors: a community of individuals; a population of firms; and a naturally and historically bounded territorial area.

Community of individuals makes explicit reference to the internal social structure of the district. Such structure is reinforced by a homogeneous system of values diffused within the district, invigorated by daily interaction and transmitted from generation to generation, thanks to a system of institutions and rules (firms, spread families, technical schools, churches, political parties, etc.). *Population of firms* regards the economic aspects of the district's reality and identifies a spatial concentration of numerous small and medium firms in a geographically delimited area (Paniccia 1998).

The economic environment of a district as a population of geographically adjacent firms also presents peculiar features. First, within the district a radical fragmentation of the value chain takes place. Brusco (1990) underlines that, generally, a vertical division of work exists rather than a horizontal one, which favors the appearance of such peculiar dynamics as a vertical cooperation joined with a horizontal competition, although the latter is also characterized by a main common interest, that is, the survival of the district.

In this kind of environment, the fact that the division of work between firms prevails over the division of work within the single firm reinforces the reciprocal interdependence of organizations and favors the perception of the local industry's peculiarities, and particularly, of the human capital, which is requested and developed as if it were common property. Such a reality also favors the expectations of long-time collaborations between district firms and therefore a reduction of opportunistic behaviors. Second, the fragmentation of the productive system leads to a high degree of specialization in the single phases of production and to high flexibility and capability of adjustment to the market's requests (Piore and Sabel 1984), which has determined the success of the district model in the Italian economy in the past few decades.

Another important feature of the Italian district model is the manner in which districts create, accumulate and spread knowledge (Becattini and Rullani 1993). Most of the knowledge that circulates within the districts has a tacit nature, deeply tied to the experience of individuals who are in the center of the production dynamics (Micelli 2000). Therefore one can talk about contextual knowledge (Belussi 2000), meaning the collective result of a slow process of knowledge creation, experimentation, know-how, interpretation and transposition of abstract knowledge. This type of knowledge develops from the continuous interaction in the workplace, from repetitively carrying out the same activities over time, and from acting within the same environmental complexities. Consequently, firms are deeply rooted in the territory and its supplies, within the context of an essentially communal infrastructure sharing a specific language and local culture that constitutes the base of the district (Micelli 2000). Strongly influencing the process of innovation within the districts, therefore, is the economic structure of the districts (their flexibility and high specialization) that, from the relational point of view, makes it a collective phenomenon "that is realised through a social process of diffusion that is centered in the sharing of the same social environment" (Micelli 2000:162).

In Italy, since the beginning of the 1990s, the role played by the regions has become crucial. In the past decade, each Italian region has assumed the function of both legislator and policymaker. A challenge the regions now face, in outlining their industrial districts' policies, is to link two different elements: making better laws and implementing sound policies.

The European Commission has undertaken a similar approach to regional development policies. In fact, the 2000-2006 Community Support Framework focuses on integrated projects as a pool of actions covering different sectors and sharing the same objective of territorial development. Therefore, this approach requires an implementation perspective based on complementary and coherent needs.

The industrial district concept cannot be confused with that of a technological district. Although both kinds of districts may significantly involve SMEs, in a technological district the main actors are generally different entities (i.e., larger and smaller firms, research institutions, universities, science parks, incubators, etc.). In Italy there are more than

200 industrial districts, concerned mainly with textiles, fashion, leather and the production of furniture.

CASE STUDY: SANTA CROCE SULL'ARNO'S INDUSTRIAL DISTRICT

One of the most important Italian industrial districts is the one in Santa Croce sull'Arno. From the research carried out on the district in Santa Croce sull'Arno, we can find some common elements.

Fashion is the most important activity in Tuscany, with its 27,000 firms and 150,000 workers representing more than 37 percent of the total export market. The region has two main production sectors: textile and leather manufacturing. Behind the glittery shop windows of big brands like Prada, Gucci, Ferragamo, and the glamorous Pitti catwalks in Florence, there is a solid production system so typical of this area.

Santa Croce sull'Arno contains 50 percent of the regional production of leather, with a total of 1,500 firms with a total turnover of 700 million Euros. The industrial area of Santa Croce produces 35 percent of all Italian tanned leather and nearly 90 percent of sole leather. The goods produced are of medium-high quality: mainly men's, women's and children's leather shoes. The best known name is Salvatore Ferragamo, whose shoes are exhibited in many museums all over the world. Tuscany also represents two-thirds of the national production of leather clothing. As for leather accessories such as bags, wallets, purses and belts, suffice it to mention two names: Gucci and Prada.

The leather industry district of Santa Croce sull'Arno is made up of small-medium enterprises which employ a total of about 10,000 people. Those local firms focused on leather tanning provide 98 percent of the national production of shoe leather soles, and 35 percent of national production of leather goods for the footwear and clothing industries.

Today, the district actors are implementing a project, to which both the University of Pisa and the Fiat Research Centre participate. Such projects aim to find innovations in material use and in production processes. This initiative was needed in order to respond to the crisis emerging from an uncertain condition of the global market, specifically a drastic reduction in demand associated with the lower consumption in Southeast Asia, particularly in Hong Kong, where 20 percent of the district's export is marketed.

Among the main factors positively affecting the creation and growth of industrial districts is a fragmented and linear structure of industry, which encourages a high division of labor and specialization in firms, encouraging strong and stable relationships with a close network of suppliers. Other factors include business longevity in a given territory, and a strong sense of belonging to it; the availability of raw materials, and a skilled labor force in the district; the opportunity to create synergies between the reference industry, and the production of related machinery; proximity to universities and research institutions; and increasing trust between firms, though they might be competitors.

The main factors causing a crisis in the district are an excess of focus on internal growth to increase control on firms; cultural rigidity, leading to an excess of focus on past practice, rather than on new competitive systems and processes; and an excess of focus on formal/bureaucratic issues.

References

Becattini, G. 1987. *Mercato e forze locali: il distretto industriale.* Bologna: Il Mulino.

Becattini, G. 1990. "The Marshallian Industrial District as Socioeconomic Notion." Pp. 37-51 in *Industrial Districts and Inter-Firm Cooperation in Italy*, edited by Frank Pyke, Giacomo Becattini and Werner Sengenberger. Geneva: International Institute for Labour Studies.

Becattini, G. and E. Rullani. 1993. "Sistema Locale e Mercato Globale." *Economia e Politica Industriale*. 80:25-49.

Belussi, F. 2000. "The Generation of Contextual Knowledge through Communication Processes. The Case of the Packaging Machinery Industry" in *The Bologna District*, paper presented at the conference *"Intervention Strategies for Territorial Identity and Marketing,"* L'Aquila (Italy), November 10.

Biggiero, L. 1998. "Italian Industrial Districts: An Evolutionary and Institutionalist View." paper presented at the conference *"The Future Location of Research in a Triple Helix of University-Industry-Government Relations,"* New York, January 7-10.

Biggiero, L. 1999. "Markets, Hierarchies, Networks, Districts: A Cybernetic Approach." *Human Systems Management*. 18:71-86.

Marshall, A. 1952. *Principles of Economics.* London: Macmillan.

Brusco, S. 1990. "The Idea of Industrial District: Its Genesis." Pp. 10-19 in *Industrial Districts and Inter-Firm Cooperation in Italy*, edited by Frank Pyke, Giacomo Becattini and Werner Sengenberger. Geneva: International Institute for Labour Studies.

Micelli, S. 2000. *Imprese, Reti e Comunità Virtuali.* Milan: Etas.

Micelli, S. and E. Di Maria. 2000. *Distretti Industriali e Tecnologie di Rete: Progettare la Convergenza.* Milano: Franco Angeli.

Paniccia, I. 1998. "One, a Hundred, Thousands of Industrial Districts. Organizational Variety in Local Networks of Small and Medium-sized Enterprises." *Organization Studies*, 19(4):667-699.

Piore M.J., Sabel C. 1984. *The Second Industrial Divide.* New York: Basic Books.

Rullani E. 2000. *Tecnologie della Conoscenza e Distretti Industriali. Due Linee di Evoluzione.* Pp. 203-223 in Micelli, S. and E. Di Maria. *Distretti Industriali e Tecnologie di Rete: Progettare la Convergenza.* Milano: Franco Angeli.

Life Histories at Risk: Work and Identity in Flexible Capitalism

VINCENZO MELE
University of Pisa

We must regard uncertainty and insecurity in light of the phenomenon that in Europe, the United States, and throughout the global economy is generally referred to as "work flexibility," which, according to some authors, is accompanied by a more generalized change in the *regime of accumulation* of the capitalist economy (Harvey 1989).[1] In this framework of ongoing debate, social scientists examine the phenomena of uncertainty and insecurity mostly in relation to *environmental* threats (global warming, typhoons, etc.) and to security threats stemming from war and terrorism.

In contrast, German sociologist Ulrich Beck (1992), in his theorization of the "risk society," emphasized the risks to individual life conduct and histories posed by the so-called "second modernity."[2] What does he mean by this? Beck ascribes the threat to individuals' ability to determine their personal life histories to the phenomenon of *individualization*, "the historical process contrary to socialization (*Vergesellschaftung*)" (Beck 1992:115). While individuals have been progressively liberated from the social constraints of industrial society (class, rank, nuclear family, roles linked to the status of male and female gender), there has been an emergence of "individualized forms and conditions of existence that force men, in the interests of material survival, to make themselves the center of their own plans and life conduct" (Beck 1992:113). "In this case, individualization means variation and differentiation of lifestyles and ways of life, in contrast to the thought underlying traditional categories of the society of large groups: classes, rank and social stratification" (Beck 1992:113).

---

[1] U.S. sociologist David Harvey examined the link between what he defined as the "regime of flexible accumulation" and post-modern cultural change. Harvey's economic analysis is based mainly on the work of the "regulation school" of economy, notably that of M. Aglietta.

[2] A great body of work exists on the concept of risk from the point of view of the social sciences, so great, in fact, that 'risk study' almost qualifies as a discipline in itself. See, for example, the work of the sociologist Niklas Luhmann (1991), and the anthropologist Mary Douglas (1992).

Marking the "second modernity," therefore, is a true de-standardization of lifestyles that also became more diversified, particularly in consequence of changing work patterns. In the industrial era, salaried work, together with the family, represented the "axis of life conduct," the coordinated system within which the individual's existence unfolded. Today, with transformation of the "post-Ford" industrial system and the supposed end of the "mass society," this system has been radically called in question.

More and more, individuals are left alone before society, deprived of the necessary tools to orient themselves, which once derived from patterns, habits, and behavioral models handed down from one generation to the next. Moreover, jobs themselves have become more and more individualized, far from the recognizable work typifying industrial society (factory, office worker, industrialist, etc.). Such a situation is highly ambivalent: on the one hand, it potentially offers great freedom to individuals, while on the other, it binds their lives to extremely variable, changing social factors, such as the vicissitudes of the labor market, training opportunities, and institutional frameworks. It is precisely for such reasons that it is worth reflecting further on the relations between *work* and *modern identity* and how the risk that uncertainty in the former affects formation of the latter.

Although largely neglected in discussions of the transition of our age, which cast doubts on "work as the key sociological category" (Offe 1985), work, in fact, still represents one of the major factors in modern individuals' ability to formulate a personal, stable identity, one which enables them to become fully socialized, the bearers of rights and duties and, moreover, *recognized* from the perspective of their personal abilities and dignity.

Work and *identity* are two terms generally encountered separately in today's philosophical and social science debates. Although many social analysts from varying perspectives, and with varying degrees of insight, have tackled the subject of contemporary individuals' difficulties in maintaining coherence and stability over time, rarely do they associate the problem with the subject of work and work's changing face in modern social processes.

A good example in this regard is the classification made by Jürgen Habermas in his *Theory of the Communicative Action* (1984-87), which defines work as an "instrumental action," a merely functional, reproductive activity, and hence completely irrelevant (or nearly so) to the makeup and expression of individual personality. Personal realization actually comes about in the *Lebenswelt* (a term taken from phenomenology), that is to say, the cultural and symbolic world of daily life.[3] Habermas nevertheless recognizes that a relation does exist between these two spheres and must be studied. Even if "work" does not necessarily coincide with "interaction," a relationship exists between the two on which "the process of formation of the spirit as well as the species substantially depends" (Habermas 1969:47). It is interesting, therefore, to analyze the interrelations between work and modern personality, to try to understand what problems and risks to contemporary subjective identity may stem from its becoming more flexible.

WORK AND CHARACTER IN INDUSTRIAL MODERNITY

In recent years, U.S. sociologist Richard Sennett provided arguably the best treatment of the relevant issues. In his now-classic book, *The Corrosion of Character: The Personal Consequences of Work in the New Capitalism* (1998), he focuses on the "*liaisons dangereuses*" between new work patterns and the consequent risks to the development of personal identity.[4] He uses the term *character* in a highly pregnant sense, to include all the connotations that current usage would ascribe to "personality" as well. There is, however, a distinction: whereas personality "concerns desires and sentiments which may fester within, witnessed by no one else," the concept of character instead:

> focuses upon the long-term aspect of our emotional experience. Character is expressed by loyalty and mutual commitment, or through the pursuit of long-term goals, or by the practice of delayed gratification for the sake of a future end. Out of the confusion of sentiments in which we all dwell at any particular moment, we seek to save and sustain

---

[3] Habermas makes a clear distinction between instrumental action and communicative action, stressing how instrumental actions are based on empirical knowledge, are organized according to technical rules and have specific work tasks to fulfill: They are rational insofar as they achieve ends, defined under given conditions, through the use of means suitable to such ends. On the other hand, communicative actions consist of symbolically mediated interactions among individuals, that is, through language, and organized on the basis of rules that define mutual expectations of behavior. For a criticism of the concept of work as an "instrumental actions." see Krahl (1971) and Honneth (1980).

[4] Actually, Sennett has devoted more than one book to the subject of the formation of modern individual identity. *The Corrosion of Character* is merely a small pamphlet, a 'long essay' based on "heterogeneous, informal sources," which should be viewed in light of his more important works, such as *The Fall of Public Man* (1974) and *The Hidden Injuries of Class* (1972).

some; these sustainable sentiments will serve our characters. Character concerns the personal traits which we value in ourselves and for we seek to be valued by others (Sennett 1998:10).

Character, therefore expresses permanent, or at least long-term, personality traits, without which it would be hard to imagine anyone immersed in a social fabric, who is *recognized* as such by himself and others.

In order to trace the origins of this sense of character—its special link to western culture and its development in parallel to the modern concept of work—we must return to an historical classic of sociological thought, Max Weber's *The Protestant Ethic and the Spirit of Capitalism*, written in 1903-05. Sennett himself suggests this source for western character, when he states, "As an economic history, *The Protestant Ethic and the Spirit of Capitalism* is riddled with errors . . . As the critique of a certain character type, however, both its purpose and its execution are coherent" (Sennett 1998:105). In fact, this work was long regarded as an attempt at interpreting the development of capitalism in contraposition to the alternative of Marxism. Given the recent debate over the transition to post-modern society, which has cast light on the connection between Weber and Nietzsche, it is possible to discern in Weber's work a reflection on the formation and maintenance of the self in an age of change (Goldman 1988).

In the context of such a reading, the two key terms are *Beruf* (at once "profession" and "vocation") and *Persönlichkeit* ("personality" or "character"). It is precisely the twofold connotations of the term *Beruf*, comprising the "profession," "occupation," and "work" performed in industrial society, as well as one's "vocation" or "calling" that explains its inextricable link to the concept of "personality." By virtue of its religious connotations, *Beruf* is well-suited to forming one of the basics of the sense of existence and individual identity. Ultimately, one of Weber's main aims was to propose a conception of "vocation" and "personality" that would present his contemporaries with the only hope of living a life endowed with sense in an age pervaded by cultural disorientation and desperation. In this sense, the *Protestant Ethic* can be considered the basis for Weber's subsequent search to find a vital, binding, and effective ideal of the person, in both public and private life. Weber's conception of vocation and personality reached its acme (and its ethical-political consequences) in his political writings and famous lectures on *Sciences as a Vocation* (*Wissenschaft als Beruf* 1917) and *Politics as a Vocation* (*Politik als Beruf* 1919), in which he attempted to reformulate his notions of vocation and personality by presenting them as a remedy for Germany's crisis in political and spiritual leadership.

This is one of the reasons why Weber's thoughts remain so topical with regard to the ongoing transformations in today's workplace. His work can provide some insights into understanding the link between work and personality, and the *risks* to the development of individuality inherent in the rationalization process of modern culture. It should not be surprising that Weber's concept of *Beruf* was not limited to the context of liberal middle-class professions. As pointed out by English historian Edward Thompson (1978:121), in the nineteenth century even the most disadvantaged workers (poorly employed, unemployed, or continuously switching jobs from one day to the next) strove to define themselves as weavers, blacksmiths or farmers, using terms such as "career," "profession," and "job" in a broader sense than would be accepted today.

Here, our interests lie not so much in the validity of Weber's thesis on the "elective affinity" (*Wahlverwandschaft*) between the "spirit of Christian asceticism" and modern *Beruf*, but more in the description of character and personality that emerges wherefrom. Even the harshest repudiation of Weber's thesis on the role of ascetic Protestantism as the crucial factor in the spirit of capitalism cannot undermine the validity of the formulated hypothesis with respect to the need for a new *character* that the rise of capitalism brought about—a new form of personality that within its interior bears the elements of innovation, of rational methodical action, and of a new self. The type of modern personality ideally suited to capitalism and, more generally, to the spirit of modern rationalization (of which capitalism is the economic realization) is found in the great entrepreneur, in the modern scientist, and in the politician. Such a character portrayal holds true even if we ascribe its development to other historical and cultural sources. *Entrepreneur, politician,* and *scientist* represent the three "ideal types" of *Beruf* in the spheres of economics, the sciences, and politics, respectively, even though such spheres may at first sight appear distinct and governed by different "gods" within the framework of the modern processes of rationalization and differentiation.

For Weber, the "professional" (Berufmensch) is a new man, formed and educated by Protestant asceticism, which drives him toward rational, systematic behavior and control of his professional life. This represents an overturning of the "natural" order, by which the aim of work and duty is to satisfy needs. In the perspective of an individual's leading a "good life," that is, one based on the harmonious development of a comprehensive personality, such a drive may even seem "irrational." Such is the "spirit of modern capitalism," which indeed finds its most suitable expression in modern capitalist enterprise.

From the perspective of the relation between work and personality, such a "life conduct" (*Lebensführung*) requires giving up one's "natural self," and defining oneself, rather than through a channeling of the desire to accumulate boundless wealth, by *domination* of the desire itself. Prime examples of this can be found in Weber's depictions of the first great entrepreneurs. They represent models for the new character types and personalities, made necessary by the birth of modern capitalism, which would take on a significant *ethical* quality even for the present day and age.[5]

The consequences of this professional spirit, however, were evident not only in its effects on entrepreneurs and businessmen, but also on workers. Weber maintained that considering work as a profession became as characteristic for the modern worker as the corresponding concept of profit for the entrepreneur. Only work performed as if it were an absolute autonomous goal — a profession — produces that which is required, and such a mentality is not a nature-given thing.

As much as Weber's conception of *Beruf* can be considered "idealistic," or even literary, it is impossible to deny its descriptive power with respect to the working conditions and work ethic prevailing during the times of Henry Ford, that is to say, in a productive system based on long-term planning, certain markets and predictable demand (Harvey 1989). In Weber's sense, *Beruf* reveals the importance of work intended as "narrative" and the character development made possible by organized, long-term efforts. In the "disenchanted" modern world (*Entzaubert*), traditional religious narrative — original sin, redemption and salvation — gets replaced by profane narrative, that of "career," whose end is to deliver subjectivity from absurdity and fragmentation. The concept central to Weber's conception of *Beruf* is *sense*: faced with the lack of historical philosophies and the polytheism of values, which fragment individual life — in the sense that there are no given "absolute" values binding on an individual and all of one's spheres of action, but only "local" values — work constitutes the unifying narrative for the personality. Weber was well aware of the fact that the spirit of modern

---

[5] According to Goldman these "are the true objects of Weber's interest in this work and actually have great prominence in his explanation" (1988: 48).

professionalism had religious and ethical origins, but mature industrial society appeared entirely devoid of such ethics. The Puritans were motivated by the glory of God to live a professional life at the service of higher ends; nowadays when

> it is not necessarily felt subjectively as simple economic pressure, the individual today generally ceases to reflect on it. In the United States, where it has been given most freedom, acquisitiveness, stripped of its religious and ethical meaning, tends today to be associated with purely competitive passions, which often give it the character of a sporting contest (Weber 1958:171).

The capitalist lifestyle and modern personality stem from inspirations and influences of an ethical-religious nature, but such influence is soon spent to give rise to a self-perpetuating mechanism. Weber, in his later writings, expresses his desire for a return to the ethical values of *Beruf* as work-vocation, viewed as a "demon who holds the fibers of our very life" (Weber 1946:156), a sort of eminent code in everyone's life, an "individual law" that each gives himself and must follow, not because it is sanctioned by external authority, but as a law that springs from the particularity and individuality of each life. Modern professions take on the paradoxical role of "necessary pretense," in the sense that, despite the awareness of their inadequacy as governing values for one's entire existence, they must, lacking any other equally valid values, be accepted. The fulfillment of the "daily duties" we have chosen, a sense of *Sachlichkeit*, that is impassioned devotion to a "cause" (*Sache*) and the objective logic governing it, are the virtues that Weber attributes to the entrepreneur, politician, and scientist, though they hold for every working activity, even the humblest. Perhaps, the solution to the modern identity crisis lies in the inner strength that allows us to model ourselves, in that strength of character that makes it possible for us to adhere to the "spiritual discipline" of our profession.

TRANSFORMATION TO THE FLEXIBLE IDENTITY

For Weber, work, in the sense of a methodical, rational "life conduct" inspired by the "demon" of inner vocation, represents the final attempt to save the self from modernity's inherent drive towards dissolution of the individual. However, the circumstances in the current era, which some observers define as post-modern, appear different. In a 1983 essay, German sociologist Claus Offe, reflecting on "work as the key sociological category," maintained that, given the heterogeneity of what we mean by work in today's service-oriented society, it is impossible to identify a single type of rationality for all work activities. However, Offe's dismissal of the work-oriented society, soon echoed by others such as Gorz (1989) and Rifkin (1995), appears a bit hasty. Although industrial work is no longer central or so visible in western societies, the "spirit of capitalism" tends to extend to all spheres of life without an ethic or social class to drive its development. In this regard, Beck speaks of capitalism as a "second modernity" and "classless capitalism" (Beck 1992:34).

Zygmunt Bauman described the ongoing transformations toward a *postmodern* culture with an eloquent metaphor: the modern individual would be transformed *"from pilgrim to tourist."* While "the modern 'problem of identity' consisted in building and maintaining a solid, stable identity, the post-modern 'problem of identity' is above all how to avoid any and all kinds of fixation and how to leave open possibilities" (1995:27).

The metaphor of the pilgrim makes explicit reference to Weber's *Protestant Ethic*. Bauman defines the Protestant as the characteristic figure of modern man, a product of industrial society. In fact, Protestants became pilgrims of the interior world, taking on intra-worldly life as their task and professional duty as the instrument with which to attain salvation. In his view, the "disenchanted" world of science and technology became a desert without rich, meaningful places or seductive temptations. Impersonality, frigidity and emptiness rose to the status of virtues in an attempt to ward off the world's temptations and make the external world meaningless and devoid of any value. Nevertheless, maintains Bauman, today's world is inhospitable for the pilgrim. Not only have lifelong jobs disappeared, but present-day professions and jobs, which characteristically appear out of nowhere and fade into nothingness, can hardly be construed in terms of Weber's "vocations."

Work and identity are thus clearly divorced. The "pilgrimage" of the temporary or intermittent worker is no longer a heroic or holy choice, but little by little, transformed into aimless wandering without the ultimate goal that gives meaning to the pilgrimage. In fact, it is distance that enables plans to exist, for space–time coordinates are the vectors of life sense and identity. Distance measured in terms of time allows building and giving meaning to identity; it gives shape to the deferred gratification that marks the beginnings of personal development and the formation of identity. However, the act of deferring gratification (despite the momentary frustration) provides the stimulus for constructing identity only if there is faith in the linearity and cumulativeness of time and trust that the future will repay savings with interest. Without such trust, economic activity and a market could not even be imagined.

The life histories of the new "flexible" workers are different from those of past generations that unfolded in the cumulative "linear time" of a career or, in any event, within a relatively predictable framework, enabling them to measure an increase in savings and overall improvement in lifestyle. It was not only enrichment of their material lifestyle, but also human and psychological experience, as life unfolded as a linear narrative.

What instead characterize "flexible" contemporary life histories are the fragmentation and the unpredictability of work patterns, which threaten the possibility of creating a *narrative* to define it. The consequence of such impossibility is difficulty in attaining some form of "mastery" (or of *governance*, as Foucault might have put it) over the course of one's own life, even in purely symbolic terms. This process of conferring sense to one's life actually helps the individual come to terms with the errors of the past, while it stimulates acting in the present and looking toward the future. And, above all, it helps the individual to bear the eventuality — ever more frequent in the world of flexible work — of failure.

> But there is little room for understanding a breakdown of a career, if you believe that all life history is just an assemblage of fragments. Nor is there any room for assaying the gravity and pain of failure, if failure is just another incident (Sennett 1998:133).

The ability (and possibility) to gather the events of one's own life (at work and elsewhere) together in a plot or storyline has a restorative and healing capacity on the self, especially when the events are sources of stress and fragmentation.

The taboo towards, and obsession with, failure in contemporary "flexible" capitalism actually stems from the fragmentation and discontinuity of current work patterns. If an individual has enough proof of concrete results, of a life course endowed with some continuity, then that person runs less risks than when, by virtue of discontinuity in the work sphere, one cannot manage to hold one's own life together or even give it a sense: "Failure can come about . . . when the journey . . . reveals itself to be endless and pointless" (Sennett 1998:133). This is one of the reasons why it is so difficult to appease feelings of failure with money.

Money, by its very nature a *universal means* (Simmel), cannot provide sense. Thus, when the failure consists of losing the purpose around which one's very existence was centered, money can be no more than a mere palliative.

Some distinctions given in contemporary philosophical writings enable a more precise definition of what is meant by "strength of character," which in contemporary circumstances is fading. Emmanuel Levinas (1981) distinguishes between *maintien de soi*, the maintenance of oneself, and *constance à soi*, loyalty to oneself. The former preserves identity over time, while the second is the basis for *virtues*, such as honesty with oneself, even with regard to one's own defects. Self-loyalty also has a social dimension and implies responsibility towards other people. The "corrosion of character" (Sennett) characteristic of contemporary flexible capitalism consists precisely in the collapse of the conditions facilitating this second characteristic of the self.

Overall, the socioeconomic system breeds indifference in a multitude of ways: indifference towards human effort (given the financial market mechanism of "winner takes all," with a minimal relationship between risks taken and remuneration); indifference as a state of systemic lack of trust in others; and lastly, the indifference of companies towards their employees, who can be summarily dismissed. The consequence is that no one is indispensable, and precisely for this reason, nobody feels responsible. If no one is relying on me, I am not answerable to others for my actions. To be reliable, we must feel that someone else needs us, and in order to feel this, that *someone else* must feel some sort of need. The question "who needs me?" is a character question on which contemporary capitalism raises serious doubts about the answer.

> This is the problem of character in modern capitalism. There is history, but no shared narrative of difficulty, and so no shared fate. Under these conditions, character corrodes: the question "Who needs me?" has no immediate answer (Sennett 1998:147).

From a different theoretical approach, Axel Honneth (1996) stresses that, without some form of *recognition* from society, individuals risk being abandoned to the solipsistic cult of individual interiority. Honneth (inspired by a school of thought tracing its origins to Hegel and Mead) holds that formation of personal identity is determined by the "other's glance," in the sense that the grounds for our individual realization are based on the recognition (or the "scorn") that others demonstrate with regard to our personality. The realization and evolution of personal identity does not happen in the air-tight vacuum of freedom from all social bonds, but rather within the context of meaningful communicative social relations, which—as Habermas neglected (cfr. Honneth 1980)—develop largely in the sphere of work.

SUSTAINABLE PERSONALITY

Faced with nihilism and fragmentation, Weber expressed the hope that professions could once again be guided by rules of "ethical conduct" binding on both the individual and the collectivity. This is not an attempt to reaffirm or vindicate the ethical value attributed by Weber to work, but to stress that work is not merely the role that individuals are called on to play in society. It represents something more than the simple autonomous actions of the individual:

> This something more that distinguishes true from autonomous conduct is its being somehow connected to the center of the social actor's personality and expressing at least some of its aspects. True conduct brings the unique personal identity of the actor into play, rather than the culturally or socially shared identity (Ferrara 1999:72).

For most flexible workers, profession and work have no constructive value, as they do not allow for the possibility of formulating a work "narrative" that involves projection towards the future and responsibility towards others. Without any "distance" in time, it is impossible to speak of projection, meaning or, hence, identity. The *short-termism* prevailing in the majority of labor market sectors seems to preclude this out of hand.

Is it legitimate to consider that work today—given its plurality and fragmentation—no longer has anything to do with "character" or ego consciousness? Despite the complexity of modern subjectivity and the great number of its affiliations, the sphere of work still remains the *de facto* decisive sphere for recognition, socialization, self-esteem, and self-definition. It remains the field in which the "decisive plays" for definition of subjectivity take place—the struggle for its possible emancipation.

Modern subjectivity has probably always surpassed work, as well as the pre-established roles in society. It is likewise probable that a "society of chosen time and multiactivity" (Gorz 1999:107) can—or rather, according to Gorz, *must*—be based on a repudiation of work and the pre-established roles of society. However, by separating the two spheres (*identity* and *work*) of current social conditions, we risk not only ignoring a fundamental aspect of the modern personality (albeit not the only one), but also not understanding the roots of that *character corrosion* denounced by Sennett.

The *risks* consequent to life histories formed under the conditions of flexible work are those feared by Christopher Lasch (1985) when he speaks of the "minimal self" prey to the immediate gratifications of consumerism, malleable and permeated with the impersonal organs of mass society. The inability to defer gratification to a future time leads to a tendency to expend the personality in immediate satisfaction (hyper-consumerism, drugs, etc.). Furthermore, the inability to gather up life events into a coherent plot leads to a lack of "experience," in the sense of wisdom, and therefore ultimately, to an essentially endless adolescence, never achieving autonomy and consequently needing recourse to aid from external authorities (experts, psychotherapists, etc.). Individuals' fragility and difficulty experienced in coherently assembling life experience makes them susceptible to the seductions of the unchanging (and unchangeable) "integral" identities, typical of fundamentalist doctrines.

Perhaps countering such trends requires introducing a concept of "sustainable personality" (analogous to the concept of "sustainable development"), which modern capitalism should foster as a precondition for fundamental human rights. Such a construct should, moreover, be founded upon the right to a minimum level of coherence in life experience, to the deferment of gratification and to the establishment of reciprocal relations.

References

Andolfi, Ferruccio. 2004. *Lavoro e Libertà: Marx, Marcuse, Arendt*. Reggio Emilia: Diabasis.

Bauman, Zygmunt. 1995. *Life in Fragments: Essays in Postmodern Moralities*. Oxford: Blackwell.

Beck, Ulrich. 1992. *Risk Society: Towards a New Modernity*, trans. by Mark Ritter, and with an Introduction by Scott Lash and Brian Wynne. London: Sage Publications. Also *Risikogesellschaft: auf dem Weg in eine andere Moderne*. Frankfurt am Main: Suhrkamp, 1986.

Bodei, Remo. 2002. *Destini Personali: L'Età della Colonizzazione delle Coscienze*. Milano: Feltrinelli.

Douglas, Mary. 1992. *Risk and Blame: Essays in Cultural Theory*. New York. Routledge.

Ferrara, Alessandro. 1998. *Reflective Authenticity: Rethinking the Project of Modernity*. New York: Routledge.

Gorz, André. 1989. *Critique of Economic Reason*, trans. by G. Handyside and C. Turner. London: Verso. Also *Métamorphoses du Travail: Quête du Sens: Critique de la Raison Économique*. Paris: Galilée, 1988.

Gorz, André. 1999. *Reclaiming Work: Beyond the Wage-Based Society*, trans. by Chris Turner. Cambridge, UK: Polity Press. Also, *Misères du Présent: Richesse du Possible*. Paris: Editions Galilée, 1997.

Goldman, Harvey. 1988. *Max Weber and Thomas Mann: Calling and the Shaping of the Self*. Berkeley: University of California Press.

Habermas, Jürgen. 1969. *Technik und Wissensschaft als Ideologie*. Franfurt am Main: Suhrkamp.

Habermas, Jürgen. 1984-87. *The Theory of Communicative Action*, trans. by Thomas McCarthy, 2 vols. Cambridge: Polity. Also, *Theorie des kommunikativen Handelns*. Frankfurt am Main: Suhrkamp, 1981.

Harvey, David. 1989. *The Condition of Postmodernity: An Inquiry Into the Origin of Cultural Change*. Oxford, UK: Blackwell.

Honneth, Axel. 1980. "Kritik an Habermas' Trennung von Arbeit und Interaktion." Pp. 185-233 in *Arbeit, Handlung, Normativität*, edited by Axel Honneth and Urs Jaeggi. Frankfurt am Main: Suhrkamp.

Honneth, Axel. 1996. *The Struggle for Recognition: The Moral Grammar of Social Conflicts*, trans. by Joel Anderson. Oxford. UK: Polity Press. Also, *Kampf um Anerkennung: Zur Moralischen Grammatik Sozialer Konflikte*. 1992. Frankfurt am Main: Suhrkamp, 1992.

Kurz, Robert. 1991. *Die Verlorene Ehre der Arbeit*. Nürnberg: Krisis.

Lasch, Christopher. 1979. *Culture of Narcissism*. New York: Warner Books.

Lasch, Christopher. 1985. *The Minimal Self: Psychic Survival in Troubled Times*. London: Pan Books.

Levinas, Emmanuel. 1998. *Otherwise Than Being: Or Beyond Essence*. Pittsburgh, PA: Duquesne University Press.

Luhmann, Niklas. 1991. *Soziologie des Risikos*. Berlin: Walter de Gruyter.

Offe, Claus. 1985. "Work: The Key Sociological Category?" Pp. 129-150 in *Disorganized Capitalism*, edited by John Keane and Claus Offe. Oxford, UK: Polity. Also, "Arbeit als Soziologische Schlüsselkategorie?" Pp. 13-43 in *Krise der Arbeitsgesellschaft*, edited by J. Matthes. Frankfurt a. M.: Suhrkamp, 1983.

Rifkin, Jeremy. 1995. *The End of Work. The Decline of the Global Labor Force and the Down of the Post-Market Era*. New York: Tarcher/Putnam.

Sennett, Richard, and Jonathan Cobb. 1972. *The Hidden Injuries of Class*. New York: Vintage.

Sennett, Richard. 1974. *The Fall of Public Man*. New York: Vintage.

Sennett, Richard. 1998. *The Corrosion of Character: The Personal Consequences of Work in the New Capitalism*. New York: Routledge.

Thompson Edward. 1978. *The Making of the English Working Class*. New York.

Weber, Max. 1946. "Politics as a Vocation," "Science as a Vocation." Pp. 77-128 and pp. 129-156 in *From Max Weber: Essays in Sociology*, translated and edited by H.H. Gerth and C. Wright Mills, New York: Oxford University Press. Also, *Politik als Beruf, Wissenschaft als Beruf*. Berlin: Duncker & Humblot, 1919.

Weber, Max. 1958. *The Protestant Ethic and the Spirit of Capitalism*, trans. by T. Parsons. New York: Charles Scribner's Sons. Also, *Die Protestantische Ethik und das Geist des Kapitalismus*. Berlin: Duncker & Humblot, 1904-05.

Work Harassment as Health Risk Regime

NOELLE J. MOLÉ
Princeton University

Characteristic of this millennial age of security and insecurity, some scholars suggest, is a new kind of risk-centered social order in which social, political and economic fields are undergirded by the management of uncertainty and risk (Simon 1987, Beck 1999, Clark 2003). Sociologist Ulrich Beck (1992, 1999, 2000) conceptualized this global "risk society" — signifying the massive shift in which the prevention of risks gain primacy over the elimination of existing social problems and ills. Risk regimes operate through new strategies and techniques of governmentality in which "governments, corporations and professions govern through risk" (Isin 2004:220) and "manage insecurity" (Rose 1996:37). That is, risk becomes the new plane upon which citizens encounter social protections, welfare and collective belonging (Beck 1992). Importantly, risk society rests on citizens' growing capacity to individualize risk.

This paper seeks to chart one critical way in which risk, uncertainty and fear manifest themselves in the health of workers and how the institutionalization of a new illness shows the biomedical side of risk regimes in contemporary Italy. I am interested in theorizing a particular biopolitical convergence: the connection between neoliberal restructuring of Italian workplaces that led to the sharp decline of long-term job stability and how worker-citizens view and experience their health in relation to what Italians call "mobbing," understood as the psychological harassment of workers. More broadly, I situate the emergent discourse and practice of mobbing in terms of Italy's "precarious" (*precario*) labor market, one stripped of labor protections and safeguards by neoliberal labor policies beginning in the 1990s.

For Italians, the idea of a "precarious" labor market refers to the process of rendering the labor market fraught with risks and uncertainties for the average worker. It is a process entailing psychological unraveling of fear, suspicion and conflict among workers, in no small part because of the rapid process of neoliberalization. Italy's historically protectionist workplace in which workers had been offered secure, lifelong positions has been restructured by a new array of job contracts and expansion of privatized employment services passed in the 1997 Treu Laws and 2003 Biagi laws (Ferrera and Gualmini 2004). Italy's labor market has played a crucially important role in the making of citizenship and political subjectivity because the worker-citizen has been profoundly central—foundational—to the state structure and social protections (Holmes 1989, Blim 1990, Horn 1994). In fact, Italy has what is called an "occupational welfare system," where membership in particular occupational groups is the essential component of garnering welfare protections (Koenig-Archibugi 2003:102). The labor market in Italy rests on an elaborate apparatus of protections and rights, which allow for Italians to hold and retain long-term job positions (Ginsborg 1990, 2003; Ferrera and Gualmini 2004). Consider, for example, that 45.8 percent of Italians held the same jobs for more than 10 years in 2005, compared with the 8.2 percent European average (*ANSA* 2005).

Certain standard employment contracts such as the lifelong contract or "undetermined time contract" (*contratto a tempo indeterminato*) have been likened to being enclosed in a "barrel of steel" (*botta di ferro*)—nothing can get through it. In other words, it is both legally challenging and costly for companies to dismiss workers with such contracts. However, because of recent legalization of non-standard employment contracts, employers can, for the first time, populate the workforce with semi-permanent workers holding "casualized" job contracts. As a result, workers holding lifelong contracts, in addition to workers holding semi-permanent positions, are forced to grapple with a volatile and fast-moving labor market. Here, I have adopted Saskia Sassen's (1998) notion of the "casualization of labor," to refer to the "expansion of what are typically considered casual or unsheltered jobs" and "the weakening role of the firm in structuring the employment relation" (Sassen 1998:146). Unlike protectionist labor regimes that rely on strong employer-employee relations, casualization facilitates a process in which individuals, rather than firms, manage their employment and, therefore, adopt socioeconomic risks.

THE EMERGENCE OF MOBBING

It is within this broader social, political and economic shift that we must understand the emergence of first, mobbing, and, in turn, the codification of the mobbing-related, work-related illness. For many Italians, mobbing (*il mobbing*) may be a deeply familiar and salient term. But for many English speakers, it is, quite likely, entirely unfamiliar. In 1984, a Swedish psychologist adopted the English term mobbing for human behavior, a term previously reserved for describing animal pack violence. In the 1990s, German psychologist Harold Ege (1996, 1997, 1998) applied the word specifically to group harassment and ousting of a worker, and the term caught on throughout Europe. Ege opened what has become a preeminent clinic and research institute on mobbing in Bologna, calling it PRIMA, the Italian Association against Mobbing and Psychosocial Stress. The most common definition is long-term harassment, isolation, and humiliation of a worker by one or more co-workers or supervisors, often with the goal of coercing this targeted worker to resign (Ege 1998).

Mobbing is a word and concept that is recognized throughout Europe — it's called "mobbing" in Germany, "moral harassment" in France and "pesten" in Holland. In the Italian language, mobbing has various synonyms including "psychological violence" (*violenza psicologico*), "moral harassment" (*molestia morale*), and even "psychological terrorism" (*terrorismo psicologico*). In my research on mobbing, I found that mobbing included a wide array of practices such as: job transfer, unpredictable workloads, new work assignments, excessive checks, hostile colleagues — practices that have increasingly become characteristic of the late capitalist workplace. Indeed, in popular imaginaries, it seems to be defined less by vexing practices carried out by an actor or group, than by the psychophysical effects of merely having worked in the new labor market, particularly one in which protection and stability have become scarce.

Despite its elusive definition, mobbing has received national and international attention, lending itself to local, state and transnational investment and attention to the problem. In 2001, the European Parliament issued a directive to member states to reduce mobbing, and estimated it affected at least 12 million people in Europe (Di Martino and De Santis 2003:139). In Italy, mobbing has become the center of a veritable social movement: there are hundreds of mobbing clinics offering assistance to victims, mobbing websites and scholarly literature, university courses on mobbing, regional programs for mobbing prevention, a feature film entitled "Mobbing: I Like to Work," (*Mobbing: Mi Piace Lavorare,* BIM Productions, 2003), and a new class of mobbing specialists including lawyers, doctors and psychologists. Importantly, mobbing is often linked to illness in public discourse and expert analysis (Ege 1998, Di Martino and De Santis 2003). In 2000, the Minister of Health, Umberto Diesi, listed cigarette smoking and mobbing as Italy's top national health problems, adding that mobbing was "a mass phenomenon" affecting as many as two million workers in Italy alone.[1] In 2003, the new illness, "Psychological and Physical Disturbances from Mobbing and Organizational Coercion," (*Disturbi psichici e fisici di mobbing e la costrittivita organizzativà*) or what I have dubbed in English, "Organizational Coercion Pathology" (OCP), was codified. A mobbing-related illness has, in fact, become a way in which worker-citizens can sue employers for mobbing or gain insurance benefits from bodily disruptions that result from hostile work environments.

LIVING IT ON THE SKIN

The medical codification of OCP follows, necessarily, from a cultural belief that mobbing disrupts psychophysical health. During my 2004-5 field research in mobbing clinics, classes, and two corporate sites in the city of Padua, I found that most workers, whether male or female, link their cases of mobbing to a variety of physical or psychological reactions. Identifying herself as a mobbing survivor and activist, Lidia Vetri has co-run an "anti-mobbing" clinic since 1997.[2] One afternoon, a middle-aged man came and asked to be a volunteer. Noting her evident disinterest, I asked why she didn't want extra help. Lidia glared at me, horrified, and said in all the years that she was suffering from mobbing, no one had offered her help. She continued, "I've used myself up in this lifetime . . . I know I will not grow old because it [mobbing] is something I will always carry with me." She leaned closer to me and yanked up the arm of her sweater: "I've lived mobbing on this skin! On this skin!" (*Ho vissuto mobbing sulla pelle*). Lidia's painful experience of being mobbed was understood and experienced in terms of permanent bodily trauma — trauma she believed would shorten her life. Underpinning this were cultural understandings of the body that made translating such an embodied knowledge and experience into words seem nearly impossible.

Pino Arturini is a 47-year old municipal police officer whom I met at

---

[1] "Il mio decalogo per vivere bene." *La Repubblica*. (13 December 2000).

[2] All names used in this paper are pseudonyms selected by author.

Lidia's mobbing clinic. He had a long career with the police department, but trouble began when he was promoted to vice director yet was suddenly left with neither work assignments to complete nor officers to coordinate. The new title, he explained, was a just a trap to mob him. Likening himself to a "ghost who wanders the halls of his workplace," he explained how he was shut up in a room and left only with the civil and penal code to read. Pino collected various medical certificates documenting his trauma, which for him had been bright red spots that appeared all over his body, anxiety and depression, and the loss of ten teeth in six months. Pino has taken various sick leaves from work. In the process of building his legal case of mobbing against the city, Pino was suing for biological damage.

I also met Cinzia Vertieri at another mobbing clinic outside of Padua. She works in the corporate division of a global textile company and described how she had been mobbed for the past seven years by a colleague, who was in fact beneath her on the company hierarchy. The young woman would torment Cinzia by talking about her on the phone and embarrassing her in front of colleagues. Cinzia felt very strongly that this was mobbing and related it to the company's recent lay-offs and factory closures. Feeling deeply isolated from other colleagues, Cinzia was disturbed even to talk about this ongoing experience. In addition to depression and anxiety, Cinzia reported hand rashes and sleeplessness.

These cases of mobbing defy an understanding of the body as bounded, and reinstate a notion where the body's "skin," through which social trauma is lived, is a socially mediated process. In her work, Aihwa Ong (1988) explores how amid rapid economic change in Malaysia, young Malay women working in industrial factories began to experience forms of spirit possession. Ong (1988) elucidates how "struggles over the meanings of health are part of workers' social critique of work discipline" (35). For victims of mobbing in Italy, episodes of illness might also be read as a way in which subjects chronicle, and furtively critique, the violations of a deregulated economy that increasingly undervalues the labor of workers. That is, the precariousness of the economy, shifting risk upon individual workers, has serious implications for the health of workers. What mobbing sufferers register is not only the bodily outcomes of extreme stress and harassment, but a more complex negotiation of their ongoing and increasing devaluation. The kind of distress embodied by victims of mobbing emerges in the context of a workplace remapped around fear and anxiety, sharp economic change and the loss of social and economic security.

PROTECTING BODILY INTEGRITY

The work-related illness OCP is also premised upon Italy's occupational legal history and the way in which workers' rights have been defined in relation to mobbing. In 1999, the first legal case filed related to mobbing cited Article 2087 of Italy's civil code and set a precedent for subsequent mobbing cases, particularly as there is no law explicitly for mobbing (Amato et. al 2002:79). Article 2087 of Italy's civil code declares: "The employer is obliged to adopt measures [within the enterprise] necessary to safeguard the physical integrity and moral personhood of employees." Similarly, the designation of OCP rests on the notion that the employer failed to provide for and guarantee the health and safety of workers. For its enforcement, however, the victim of mobbing must prove the existence of persecutory conduct, and that this harassment was the sole cause of incurred physical and psychological damage. Victims of mobbing have received recognition of physical, psychological, moral and even a new category "existential damage" that relates to losses incurred against future potentials and possibilities (Amato et. al 2002). Though this law existed as a form of protection against mobbing, public health institutions were nonetheless left with the challenge of codifying a response to health claims issued as a result of mobbing. That workers' failing health could be legally linked to the employer provided the necessary juridical grounds for the creation of a mobbing-related illness.

ORGANIZATIONAL COERCION PATHOLOGY

The medicalization of mobbing took place on various levels and scales—on the one hand, workers sought help for psychophysical symptoms from clinics and physicians, and INAIL (The Italian Workers' Compensation Authority) sought to codify mobbing in an effort to standardize diagnosis and treatment. In 2003, INAIL named a new psychosomatic disturbance, "Organizational Coercion Pathology." In first defining the illness, the insurance company specifies that "work-related" includes the "organizational structure of work activities" (Relazione del 26 luglio 2001 N. 473/2001). Unlike the term mobbing, the notion of "organizational coercion" bypasses the intentionality of a single mobber and relates physical and psychological symptoms to a generalized workplace environment (Terpolilli 2004:18). The list of practices considered integral to causing this condition very much resemble some of the most common difficulties that have emerged in a precarious work environment: "marginalization from work activity, removal of responsibilities, forced inactivity, unjustified and repeated transfers, the assigning of tasks below qualifications of the employee's professional profile, systematic and structural obstruction to information access and exasperated and excessive exercises of control" (INAIL, Circolare n. 71, December 2003).

Yet in the context of this medical diagnosis, these practices that characterize the late capitalist workplace have severe health consequences. Medical conditions most correlated to OCP include, "anxiety, depression, behavioral alteration, emotional and somatic disturbances," as well as Post Traumatic Stress Disorder. Taken together, the codification of OCP reasserts that workplace practices—fast becoming normalized in Italy—render bodies vulnerable to a host of serious physical and psychological symptoms. Importantly, rather than describe a particularly pathological mobber who engaged in these abuses, the diagnosis of this illness actually related the illness to the "conditions of labor" in and of themselves and the psycho-physical outcomes in workers. One important implication of this formulation is that the "mobber" falls out of the juridical definition, replaced instead by proof of bodily harm. What we see, then, is how this new psycho-physical illness actually condenses and recognizes the bodily and health effects of neoliberal orders and labor structures. It transforms the physical and mental disruptions, precisely those shaped by privatization and the casualization of labor in Italy, into pathologized conditions to be regulated and managed, Workers however, must mediate the high-risk labor market by transforming their economic risk in medically-documented bodily risk.

After defining OCP, however, the public health institute announced that only 15 percent of their 200 cases could be defined as such and, therefore, limited the number of cases that could be insured (INAIL, Circolare n. 71, December 2003). Moreover, in 2005, the TAR Lazio, a high court of Rome, further limited OCP by asserting that the medical diagnosis lacked adequate "scientific evidence," and, as a result, greatly expanded the mandate of proof required by workers for legal cases (TAR Lazio, N. 5454, 4 July 2005). As a result, we see how various organs of the Italian state operate both with and against one another in the story of

OCP. State institutions both recognize and yet limit the ability of workers to make legal and medical claims that hold employers, and indirectly the state, accountable for the human costs of neoliberal labor restructuring.

In this way, medicalization depoliticizes mobbees' claims, and only those workers who can make their claims legible by the state are recognized — excluding those mobbees who can't document their bodily trauma. In turn, and as I found many times in mobbing clinics, the focus lay increasingly on the individual's health and less on the collective health effects of risk at work. As the metaphor of illness becomes more prevalent for mobbing, so too will the salient difference between the worker who adapts to the demands of the precarious workplace as flexible and even morally superior compared to the victim of mobbing who is viewed as rigid and traditional. The legal right that employers "safeguard the bodily integrity" (Article 2087) and are held accountable for mobbing, paradoxically, demands that managers initiate *more* controlling measures in order to avoid being held accountable for workers' ill health. Moreover, such legal precedents may produce a future in which managers justify disciplinary actions and increased surveillance in these terms.

THE FUTURE OF MOBBING

In Italy, accusations of mobbing allow workers to name the abuses and human costs of labor market reorganization, and their own replaceability and devaluation. The codification of OCP in 2003 shows how certain work practices, already in tension with vast neoliberal economic change, became inextricably tied to bodies and health — and deeply pathologized. Episodes of illness might also be read as a way in which bodies register, and furtively critique, the violations of a neoliberalism. Finally, OCP has become a means through which the uncertainties and collective *labor* risks are transformed into and managed as individual *health* risks. As a result, labor disputes might be managed not by union workers or labor ministers, but by public health institutions and medical doctors. Taken together, the emergence of 'mobbing' and its bodily effects represent both an embodied critique of neoliberalism and a problem contributing to an increasingly medicalized management of labor.

Mobbing is a discourse that allows subjects new ways to find political recourse for the injustices and abuses of the neoliberal workplace, and symbolically, of pathologizing Italy's rapid economic and social change.

As one journalist put it, "It seems that Italian offices are, in reality, sick from mobbing."[3] If we return to the origins of mobbing, as deeply entangled with forms of neoliberal economic reform, then we have before us a dynamic meeting point—a traceable fusion between the concrete manifestations of neoliberal capitalism and bodily suffering. The codification of OCP exposes the mental and physical wear on worker's bodies in a flexible work regime, and rewires circuits of contact between workers and the state.

References

Amato, Fabrizio, Maria Valentina Casciano, Lara Lazzeroni, and Antonio Loffredo. 2002. *Il Mobbing: Aspetti Lavoristici: Nozione, Responsibilità, Tutele*. Milano: Giuffré Editore.

ANSA Notiziaro Generale. 2005. "Censis: Decelera Mercato Lavoro, Italiani Pigri d'Europa." 2 December.

Beck, Ulrich. 1992. *Risk Society: Towards a New Modernity*. London: Sage Publications.

——. 1999. *World Risk Society*. Cambridge, UK: Blackwell.

——. 2000. *The Brave New World of Work*. Cambridge, UK: Polity Press.

Blim, Michael. 1990. *Made in Italy: Small-Scale Industrialization and Its Consequences*. New York: Praeger.

——. 2002. "The Italian Post-Communist Left and Unemployment: Finding a New Position on Labor." Pp. 136-149. *Culture, Economy, Power: Anthropology as Critique, Anthropology as Praxis*, edited by Winnie Lem and Belinda Leach. Albany, NY: State University of New York Press.

Clark, Ian. 2003. "The Security State." Pp. 177-188 in *The Global Transformations Reader: An Introduction to the Globalization Debate*, edited by David Held and Anthony McGrew. Cambridge, UK: Polity Press.

Di Martino, V and R. De Santis. 2003. *Mobbing: La Violenza al Lavoro*. Editore: Oasi.

Ege, Harold. 1996. *Mobbing*. Bologna: Pitagora Editrice.

——, ed. 1997. *Il Mobbing in Italia*. Bologna: Pitagora Editrice.

——. 1998. *I Numeri di Mobbing*. Bologna: Pitagora Editrice.

Ferrera, Maurizio and Elisabetta Gualmini. 2004. *Rescued by Europe? Social and Labour Market Reform in Italy from Maastricht to Berlusconi*. Amsterdam: Amsterdam University Press.

Ginsborg, Paul. 1990. *A History of Contemporary Italy: Society and Politics 1943-1988*. Penguin Books.

——. 2003. *Italy and Its Discontents: Family, Civil Society, State 1980-2001*. New York: Palgrave Macmillan.

Holmes, Douglas. 1989. *Cultural Disenchantments: Worker Peasantries in Northeast Italy*. Princeton, NJ: Princeton University Press.

Horn, David. 1994. *Social Bodies: Science, Reproduction, and Italian Modernity*. Princeton, NJ: Princeton University Press.

Isin, Engin F. 2004. "The Neurotic Citizen." *Citizenship Studies* 8(3):217-235.

Koenig-Archibugi, Mathias. 2003. "National and European Citizenship: The Italian Case in Historical Perspective." *Citizenship Studies* 7(1):85-109

Ong, Aihwa. 1988. "The Production of Possession: Spirits and the Multinational Corporation in Malaysia." *American Ethnologist* 15(1):28-42.

Rose, Nikolas. 1996. "Governing 'Advanced' Liberal Democracies." Pp. 37-64 in *Foucault and Political Reason*, edited by Andrew Barry, Thomas Osborne, and Nikolas Rose. Chicago: University of Chicago Press.

---

[3] Ardu, Barbara. "Ecco il Mobbing Veleni in Ufficio." *La Repubblica* (24 July 1999.)

Sassen, Saskia. 1998. *Globalization and Its Discontents.* New York: The New Press.
Simon, J. 1987. "The Emergence of a Risk Society." *Socialist Review* 95:61-89.
Terpolilli, Paolo. 2004. "Il Fenomeno Mobbing e La Costrittivita' Organizzativa." *L'Ispettore e la Societa* 23(6):16-24.

Possibility and Insecurity in the European Learning Society: Considerations on the Italian Situation

GERARDO PASTORE
University of Pisa

Lifelong learning and social development are now high on the agendas of the EU and national governments across Europe. This concern has been generated by economic and social changes across Europe, brought about by the transition to a knowledge society. The significance of lifelong learning for the European Commission is evident in the 1995 White Paper and more recently in the EU Memorandum on Lifelong Learning (2000) and in the Declaration of the European Council made in Lisbon in 2000.

This paper offers a critical analysis of possibility and insecurity caused by learning supply and the multiplication of professional training programs in the European knowledge society. It would seem that while knowledge in working society once represented security, it now seems to represent insecurity. Has there been a shift from illusion to disappointment?

THE EUROPEAN STRATEGY AND THE INTERNATIONAL DEBATE

Starting from a concept of permanent education, put forward in the 1970s by UNESCO, and continuing up to the present day with the most recent documents issuing forth from the European Commission on the subject of instruction and training, a philosophy of education has come to be broadly accepted, one that addresses the entire life span and singles out—precisely in education and training—those tools which fulfill the development of the individual, society and the economy.

People speak about a *learning society* and, in doing so, set forth a need and identify a future that will not be deviated from by whatever the current social changes may be. The plan, from the content of European Community Commission reports, seems to be clear. Having singled out unemployment as the most important problem facing the countries on the continent, it is crucial to find suitable solutions. It is no longer enough to increase Gross Domestic Product in order to raise employment levels. Economic growth requires parallel and so-called "active work policies."

The immediate objective of this European strategy is training and instruction to help prepare workers and school-leavers professionally to face the changeable requirements of the work market. The basic principle at the root of each training scheme, according to the Delors Report (Commission of the European Communities, 1993), must be the valorization of human re-sources throughout their active lives, or to "learn how to learn throughout life." In order to facilitate the passage of school-leavers onto the job-market, broader forms of internships and apprenticeships within companies will be available, coupled with short, practical professional training courses, to be organized in specialized centers.

The White Paper of November 1995, *Teaching and Learning towards the Learning Society* (Commission of the European Communities 1995), reiterates the same issues and states that in order to build a knowledge society, it is necessary to: 1) encourage the acquisition of new knowledge; 2) bring schools and enterprises closer together; 3) combat exclusion; 4) develop proficiency in three European languages; and 5) treat capital investment and investment in training on an equal basis.

This thinking was confirmed and supported by the strategic objectives proposed on the occasion of the Council Summit in Lisbon in 2000, which sought to create an economy in Europe based on the most competitive and dynamic knowledge in the world. It also sought to achieve sustainable economic growth with newer and better jobs and to create greater social cohesion. These same ideas were repeated and repackaged both in the *European Memorandum on Training and Lifelong Learning* of 2000[1] and in the recent Council Summit in Brussels March 23-24, 2006:

> Education and training are critical factors to develop the EU's long-term potential for competitiveness as well as for social cohesion. The search for excellence and innovation at all levels of education and training, in particular through better links between higher education, research and enterprises is crucial. Reforms must also be stepped up to ensure high quality education systems which are both efficient and equitable.

---

[1] Disseminated by the European Commission in November 2000, it aims to identify coherent strategies and practical measures to foster and facilitate permanent learning for all. There are six messages set out in the memorandum: new basic competences for all, greater investment in human resources, innovation in investment techniques and learning, assessment of the learning outcomes, rethinking on guidance and learning that is closer to home.

National lifelong learning strategies should provide all citizens with the competences and qualifications they need, increasingly assisted at Community level by educational and training programmes such as Erasmus and Leonardo. To support greater mobility and an efficient labour market, progress on a European Qualifications Framework (EQF) should also be achieved [. . .] They should be targeted on areas where economic returns and social outcomes are high. Education and Training must occupy a central position in the Lisbon reform agenda, in this context, the Lifelong Learning Programme 2007-2013 will be essential (Council of the European Union. Presidency Conclusions, 2006:6-7).

As regards the idea and the need for a learning society, many scholars put forth their theories and out of this international debate, differing perspectives emerged. According to Hutchins (1970) the learning society is founded on an ideal vision of the future — anticipating something like a new Athens — where technology replaces slaves and where the possibility of access to technological, educational and cultural resources constitutes, for the democratic political order, the basis of development. We find also in the works of Husén (1974) this concept of a *learning* society as an ideal society whose fulfillment becomes ever more urgent. The position of Ranson (1994) too is essentially the same. Ranson states that the indispensable requisites for the construction of a learning society are a new ethics and full democracy.

Hake (1990), Beck (1994), Giddens (1994) and Lash (1994) devote greater attention to reality and social changes in progress. The direction of their investigations would seem to indicate a weakness in social structures which forces individuals to search continually for training to counteract the risks which derive from continuous knowledge obsolescence.

As John Field stated:

Evidently, the learning society is an international phenomenon. It also remains very much a rooted phenomenon, embedded in particular locales and in specific social milieus and networks. It is therefore not surprising if much of the debate has been torn between generality and specificity, between abstraction and concrete experience. The concept of the learning society is perhaps best seen as an umbrella concept, valuable for its heuristic potential as well as questionable for its normative, even utopian content (Field 2007:225).

THE ITALIAN SITUATION

The consequence of the indications and requisites, contained within the European Union's program documents, has been a corresponding increase in the supply of training at all levels. Flexible work practices on one hand and the valorization of human resources on the other have been recognized as the two fundamental strategies to push the economically-advanced countries into competitiveness on a global scale and to deal with developing crisis situations. The development of human resources therefore seems to be one of the main keys to success in global economic competition (Benadusi 1998:23).

The decline of the "job for life" and the need to match the continual changes in work are evidence on which, for more than a decade, many academics have examined (Rifkin 1995, Accornero 1997, Gallino 1998, Sennett 1998). Period-dependent downturns, processes that signal a major break with the past, significantly change the way in which we interpret reality (Foa and Ranieri 2000:5). In such situations, training would seem to be an indispensable condition for transforming flexibility into job opportunities and professional growth.

In Italy, professional training courses have increased by 42,000 in just five years, as shown in the following graph:

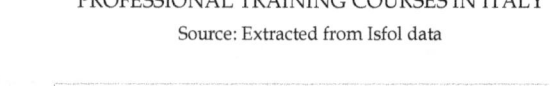

PROFESSIONAL TRAINING COURSES IN ITALY
Source: Extracted from Isfol data

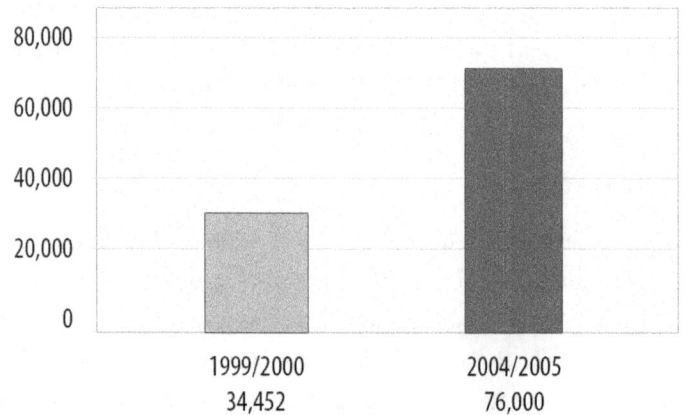

As far as postgraduate training is concerned, the numbers of students continuing their training after university studies is constantly increasing and presently number around 167,000. The following table and the graph show the data on students involved in postgraduate training ordered according to type of course, from 2000 to 2006.

TABLE 1
Italian Students in Postgraduate Courses, 2000-2006

	UNIVERSITY MASTERS COURSES- FIRST LEVEL	UNIVERSITY MASTERS COURSES- SECOND LEVEL	IMPROVING COURSES[2]	PHD COURSES	SPECIALIZATION SCHOOLS[3]	TOTAL
2000/2001	-	-	22,495	21,128	50,224	93,847
2001/2002	3,369	2,324	20,703	26,304	56,458	109,158
2002/2003	8,872	7,101	13,642	29,944	6,4635	124,194
2003/2004	13,009	10,347	14,232	37,906	75,453	150,947
2004/2005	13615	12,615	19,198	37,519	74,464	157,411
2005/2006	16083	21,178	17,238	38,262	74,089	166,850

Source: Ministero dell'Università e della Ricerca (Miur) – Office of Statistics

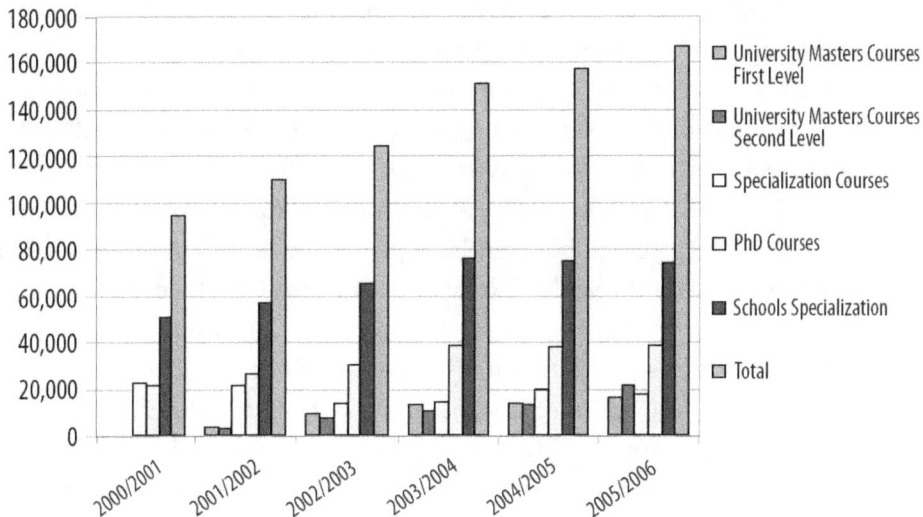

Source: extracted from Miur data – Office of Statistics

New profiles and new qualifications represent a factor of social identity but are also "goods" placed in the job market where the demands of the productive system are in constant change. The main investment in training is naturally from young people who depend on this strategy to

---

[2] These courses do not issue an educational qualification.

[3] These schools issue an educational qualification.

maximize their chances of finding work. However, this is not always a winning strategy, since there does not always exist a balance between work supply and demand. Such a situation makes it difficult to plan for the future and often requires individuals to postpone making important choices, such as living away from home or deciding to get married and have children.

CONCLUSIONS

This analysis has shown that the need to be versatile is gaining ground. This trend signals the fact that Italy may otherwise find it difficult to maintain its competitiveness. Generations of workers held the belief that it is not the preparation that counts but the ability to sell oneself. The new generation is taught that as individuals they are goods produced in the 21st century and that, in order to be distributed, they need to promote themselves. The aim is no longer to work, therefore, but only to be employed. In fact, once hired they may work for such a short time that they do not have the chance to gain sufficient experience to work well or to develop a suitable attitude to their work environment. Just when many begin to dwell upon what it is to work, budget problems may no longer allow for their contract renewal and they have to start again from scratch.

The real problem is that instead of feeling stronger, more flexible and more in line with faster global trends, aspiring workers lose faith in their own abilities. The ontological security that Giddens (1990) speaks about is lessened and their daily lives turn into an ever-questioning existential torment. Daily anguish and insecurity, to quote Zygmunt Bauman (2000), are like the sensation that airplane passengers might feel on discovering that the cockpit is empty and that the reassuring voice of the captain was pre-recorded a long time ago. In an attempt to escape from insecurity and overcome anguish, men and women search for something that they may never find. They may never be certain of discovering either what they have found or what they were looking for. However, they will be certain that whatever they find (whether they were looking for it or not), the fact remains that once they find it, it may not stop them from looking for it again (Bauman 2000:28-30). Therefore, if on one hand this new knowledge stands for a strategic resource, on the other hand it would seem to represent the source of insecurity and unrelenting competition.

Certainly, considering the devaluation of such important guarantees as economic security, job security, political, religious and family membership, training is an answer to a problematic situation. However, there is a threshold beyond which we can argue about the criterion of the rationality of choice and beyond which pathological elements come into play (Pastore 2007:782-783). When a person changes from one pathway of training to another, without any logic to this change, this accumulation of specialization, this accumulation of training, becomes hobby-like and severely lessens any possible future feeling of fulfillment.

Training that does not lead to work is a denial of possibilities and a brake on the constructive development of society. Certainly it is necessary to hold to the idea of *lifelong learning*. It represents a priority factor that fosters economic development, the growth of social cohesion and the struggle against unemployment. But the *knowledge society* is not to be taken lightly. It can be placed within possible reach only as far as it is capable of selecting sectors of reference, the extent to which it can regard territorial and cultural vocations and the extent in which it can make for itself a position of prestige in the division of labor. Unfortunately, the many training providers are not always that strongly congruent with the actual demand for specialized professional competences and often these new qualifications and a brief internship make up an existential puzzle, which is increasingly difficult to put together, between new possibilities and a growing unease in planning for the future.

References

Accornero, Aris. 2000. *Era il Secolo del Lavoro*. Bologna: Il Mulino.

Bauman, Zygmunt. 2000. *La Solitudine del Cittadino Globale*. Bologna: Il Mulino.

Beck, Ulrich, Anthony Giddens, and Scott Lash. 1994. *Reflexive Modernization: Politics, Tradition and Aesthetics in the Modern Social Order*. Cambridge: Polity Press.

Benadusi, Luciano. 1998. "Formazione e Occupazione: Situazione Attuale e Prospettive Future." *Il Welfare del Disincanto: Appunti per il Terzo Millennio*, edited by E. Bartocci. Roma: Donzelli.

Commission of the European Communities. 1993. *Growth, Competitiveness, Employment: The Challenges and Ways Forward into the 21st Century*. White Paper, December.

Commission of the European Communities. 1995. *Teaching and Learning: Towards the Learning Society*. White Paper on Education and Training, November 1995.

Council of the European Union. 2000. *Lisbon European Council. Presidency Conclusions*. March 23-24, 2000.

Council of the European Union. 2006. *Brussels European Council. Presidency Conclusions*. March 23-24, 2006.

Field, John. 2007. "Lifelong Learning and Learning Society: Trends and Prospects in Europe."*New Society Models for a New Millennium*, edited by Michael Kuhn. New York: Peter Lang Publishing.

Foa, Vittorio, and Andrea Ranieri. 2000. *Il Tempo del Sapere. Domande e Risposte sul Lavoro che Cambia*. Torino: Einaudi.

Gallino, Luciano. 1998. *Se Tre Milioni Vi Sembrano Pochi. Sui Modi per Combattere la Disoccupazione*. Torino: Einaudi.

Giddens, Anthony. 1990. *The Consequences of Modernity*. Cambridge, UK: Polity Press.

Hake, B. J. 1990. "Lifelong Learning in Late Modernity: The Challenges to Society, Organizations, and Institutions." *Adult Education Quarterly* 49(2).

Hutchins, Robert M. 1970. *The Learning Society*. Harmondsworth: Penguin Books.

Husén, Torsten. 1974. *The Learning Society*. London: Methuen.

Isfol. *Rapporto 2006*. Milano: Franco Angeli.

Ministero dell'Università e della Ricerca 2001-2007. Ufficio di Statistica. "Indagine sull'Istruzione Universitaria." Accessed February 28, 2008 at http://statistica.miur.it/scripts/postlaurea/vpostlaurea.asp.

Pastore, Gerardo. 2007. "Un'altra Chance. Il Futuro Progettato tra Formazione e Flessibilità." Pp. 769-789 in *Homo Instabilis. Sociologia della Precarieta*, edited by Mario A. Toscano. Milano: Jaca Book.

Ranson, Stewart. 1994. *Towards the Learning Society*. London: Cassell.

Rifkin, Jeremy. 1995. *La Fine del Lavoro*. Milano: Baldini & Castaldi.

Sennett, Richard. 1998. *The Corrosion of Character*. New York: Norton.

Contributors

Contributors

RACHELE BENEDETTI is a Ph.D. sociology student researching the new shapes of social inequality in Europe. Her scholarly interests primarily focus on transformations in the labor market and welfare state, and the inequality dynamics in a comparative perspective, with special attention on the new European member states. Recently, she participated in a research project about the flexibility in the labor market, in which she studied the employment trends and changes in European context and in European projects for social cooperation in Europe.

RITA BIANCHERI earned a Ph.D. at the University of Pisa where she now teaches sociology of the family and sociology of education. She is an active researcher and currently serves as President of the Equal Opportunities Committee. Her principal publications and primary areas of investigation are in women's studies, social policy, the welfare state and the third sector. A visiting scholar at Sam Houston State University in 1997, she has been a consultant for the Department of Social Policies and now for the Department of Equal Opportunities of the Region of Tuscany. Her most recent books include *The Gender Approach in the Workplace* (2008) and *Time of Life and Welfare* (2009).

ANDREA BORGHINI is associate professor in sociology at the University of Pisa, Department of Social Sciences. He teaches political sociology and he mainly investigates topics relating to political and social transformations, both from critical and storiographical approach and with an empirical approach. Among his works *Karl Popper: Politica e Società* (Milan: Franco Angeli, 2000) and *Metamorfosi del Potere: Stato e Società nell'Era della Globalizzazione* (Milan: Franco Angeli, 2003). He is also Director of the Master's program in "Social Entrepreneurship and Territorial Governance" at the University of Pisa.

DOMINIC CANDELORO earned his Ph.D. in history from the University of Illinois. He served as Executive Director of the American Italian Historical Association from 2001-2006, and as its national president from

1984-1988. Recipient of a Fulbright research fellowship to Italy in 1982, he is the author of several articles and five photo history books about Italians, Chicago, and Chicago Heights (Arcadia). Currently an adjunct professor of history at Governors State University, his primary interests are in promoting Italian-American studies as a university discipline, preserving Italian-American culture, and examining the impact of stereotyping. He also is a part-time volunteer program coordinator and librarian for the Italian Cultural Center at Casa Italia, Chicago.

ROCCO CAPORALE received his Ph.D. in sociology from Columbia University, then taught at the University of California at Berkeley, the Claremont Colleges, Manhattanville College, the Partenope University in Naples, the University of Bari (Italy) and St. John's University, from which he retired in 2002. His major publications include *Vatican II: Last of the Councils*, (Helicon Press, Baltimore, 1964); five volumes on *Social Stratification in Developed Countries* (Torino: Valentino Editore, 1975); and editor of *Italian-Americans Through the Generations* (New York: General Hall, 1986) and a nine-volume series, *Mezzogiorno Revisited,* (Naples: ESI Publisher, 1985-2000). He also conducted major research projects in more than twenty countries under grants from the NSF, Ford, Rockefeller, Russell Sage, Agnelli, and Cassamarca Foundations, as well as the Italian Foreign Ministry and several Italian regional governments.

SOFIA CAPUANO has a degree in sociology from the University of Rome and a Ph.D. in sociology from the University of Pisa. Her research interests are in sociological theory, the sociology of work, and sociology of organizations, the latter also an area in which she has taught several seminars. Published articles include "Bauman e il Dibattito sul Moderno," in *Introduzione alla Sociologia*, edited by Mario A. Toscano (Milan: Franco Angeli, 2006), and "Realtà Militari e Società Civile: Indagine sull'Incontro tra due Mondi," in *Mondo Militare, Mondo Civile* (2007).

LUCA CARBONE holds a degree in modern literature and a Ph.D. in fundamental ecology. A contract professor in environmental sociology and project manager for the Faculty of Social Science at the University of Pisa, he cultivates a multidisciplinary approach to the themes of social and global environmental change. Publications include *Razionalità e Dominio: Teoria Critica e Modernizzazione*, a monograph analyzing the socio-cultural connection between "science" and "power" in the modern age; "Disciplina e Informazione," comparing Marx and Weber on the role that militarization plays in the modernization process; and "Traslazioni storico-sociali," on the weight of translation in sociohistorical interactions.

MICHAEL CAROSONE earned a B.A. and M.A. in English from Brooklyn College, CUNY; an M.S. in education administration and supervision from Touro College, New York; and he is pursuing a second master's degree in library science. He taught high school English for eight years and English for four years at Brooklyn College, CUNY. In 2000, he received the National Italian American Foundation's Youth Award for Entertainment, for organizing Brooklyn Film Festivals and Italian American Filmmakers' Showcases. Michael's writing projects include a book on the marginalization of Italian American writers and Italian American literature, a completed book of poetry, and outlines for a novel, memoir, and collection of short stories.

VALENTINA CREMONESINI graduated with a degree in philosophy, and then earned a Master's degree in marketing and a Ph.D. in sociology. She works as a researcher at Department of Social Science and Communication at the University of Salento, where she teaches social theory and collaborates with the chairs of Sociology of Culture and History of Sociological Thought. She has published several papers on sociology of consumption, marketing and advertising, and the monograph, *The Power of Objects: Marketing as a Social Control Device* (Milan: Franco Angeli, 2006).

GABRIELE DE ANGELIS studied sociology and philosophy at the University of Tübingen and Heidelberg (Germany), where he completed his Ph.D. in Philosophy in 1999. He has been a fellow of the Sant'Anna School of Advanced Studies at Pisa, Italy, and is currently a research fellow at the New University of Lisbon, Portugal. He is author of several articles and chapters on the history of social theory and took part in several research projects carried out at the Department of Social Sciences at the University of Pisa.

SIMONE GABBRIELLINI is a Ph.D. student at the Department of Social Sciences, University of Pisa. He is a member of the "Teorie e Metodi di Analisi delle Reti Sociali" Department Section. His research interests are: social research methodology, network analysis, agent-based simulations and online communities. Recent publications include "Il Mercato delle

Flessibilità: Il Caso Italiano," In *Homo Insabilis*, edited by Mario A. Toscano (Milano: Franco Angeli, 2008); "Analisi delle Reti Sociali con R: Il Pacchetto SNA," in *Analisi delle Reti Sociali: Teorie Metodi Applicazioni*, edited by A. Salvini (Milan: Franco Angeli, 2007).

KARYN LOSCOCCO is associate professor of sociology at the University at Albany, New York. Her research and teaching interests focus on social inequality. She has written extensively on the gendered work-family system, particularly in the context of entrepreneurship. Current research projects include: a comparison of women's and men's small business networks and a study of media constructions of race, gender and work-family linkages. She has given many talks in the local community on race and racism in the United States.

PAUL MAGRO received his Ph.D. in Sociology from the University of Notre Dame. His research interests include pre-1924 Italian immigration and crime in the immigrant community. He has also conducted original research on police attitudes and the interaction of race and ethnicity with the criminal justice system with a particular focus on prejudice and racial profiling. Dr. Magro developed his interest in criminal justice as a police officer and later a loss prevention manager for JC Penney. He is a member of the faculty in the Department of Criminal Justice and Criminology at Ball State University in Muncie, Indiana.

VINCENZO MELE is lecturer of sociology at Monmouth University and was visiting professor at William Paterson University in the spring of 2008. He studied in Germany at the Albert Ludwigs University of Freiburg i.B. and the University of Bielefeld. His recent publications include: "New Tendencies in the Theory of Social Action: Touraine, Bourdieu, Giddens" in *Introduction to Sociology*, edited by Mario A. Toscano (Milan: Franco Angeli, 2006); *Forms of Modernity: Actuality of Georg Simmel* (Milan: Franco Angeli, 2007); "Paradoxes of Style in Global Culture: An Analysis from Georg Simmel's Point of View," in *La Società degli Individui* 32 (2008):135-49.

STEFANIA MILELLA holds a Ph.D. from the Faculty of Political Sciences and is collaborating with the Department of Social Sciences of the University of Pisa. She is developing research paths and methodological interests about the themes of the Italian communities abroad and their social capital. Her most recent publication is "Il Capitale Sociale: Analisi Comparata delle Strategie di Misurazione," pp. 203-229 in *Analisi delle Reti Sociali: Teorie, Metodi, Applicazioni*, edited by Andrea Salvini (Milan: Franco Angeli, 2007).

VINCENZO MILIONE is Director of Demographic Studies for the John D. Calandra Italian American Institute, Queens College, CUNY. Responsible for social science research on Italian Americans, as well as institutional research on faculty, administrative staff, and students for affirmative action purposes, he received his Ph.D. from SUNY/Buffalo in civil engineering specializing in socio-engineering systems. He also earned a B.S. in Physics and a M.S. in earth and space sciences from SUNY/Stony Brook. Dr. Milione was conferred honorary doctoral degrees from the Consejo Iberoamericano of Latin American universities, the Universidad Nacional Hermilio Valdizan, and La Universidad Nacional de Tumbes in Peru.

NOELLE MOLÉ received her doctorate degree in cultural anthropology from Rutgers University in 2007, and is currently a lecturer at Princeton University. Broadly conceived, her work focuses on economic and medical anthropology, and specifically, on issues of neoliberal capitalism, mental illness, labor law and structure, and gender and sexuality. For the study in this volume, she conducted fifteen months of fieldwork in Padua supported by grants from Fulbright IIE, the German Marshall Fund, and the Council for European Studies. She is currently working on her book manuscript, entitled *The Precariousness of Mobbing in Italy*.

SONIA PAONE has a Ph.D. in history and sociology of modernity from the University of Pisa, and specialized in social deviation and social security at the University of Padova. A contract professor of environmental sociology for the Naval Academy of Livorno and of urban sociology at the University of Pisa, her publications are *Carcere & Città, Nuove Prospettive nello Spazio Urbano* (2007); "Accoglienza Zero: Le Zone di Trattenimento Come Paradigma della Messa a Distanza," in *Sociologia e Globalizzazione*, edited by L. Corradi and F. Perocco (2007); "Le Trasformazioni dello Spazio Urbano nell'Era della Flessibilità," in *Homo Instabilis: Sociologia della Precarietà*, edited by M.A. Toscano (2007); "Le Nuove Frontiere della Città Panottica," in *Mediterraneo, Città, Culture, Ambiente, Governance, Immigranti*, edited by A. Andelini, (Milan: Franco Angeli, 2007).

VINCENT N. PARRILLO is professor of sociology at William Paterson University, a Fulbright scholar and Fulbright Senior Specialist. He has been U.S. coordinator for four of the five Italo-American conferences. His books include *Strangers to These Shores*, 9th ed. (Allyn & Bacon, 2008); *Under-standing Race and Ethnic Relations*, 3rd ed. (Allyn & Bacon, 2008); *Diversity in America*, 3rd ed. (Pine Forge Press, 2008); *Cities and Urban Life*, 5th ed. with John Macionis (Prentice-Hall, 2009); *Contemporary Social Problems*, 6th ed. (Allyn & Bacon, 2005). He is General Editor of the two-volume interdisciplinary *Encyclopedia of Social Problems* (Sage, 2008). He is also executive producer and writer of two award-winning PBS television documentaries: *Smokestacks and Steeples: A Portrait of Paterson* (1992) and *Ellis Island: Gateway to America* (1991). His scholarly articles have appeared in such journals as *The Social Science Journal, Sociological Forum, Journal of Comparative Family Studies*, and *Small Group Behavior*.

GERARDO PASTORE is a Ph.D. student in the history and sociology of modernity at the University of Pisa, Italy. He is interested in research and in the sphere of social change, paying particular attention to the analysis of study and training pathways in the *European Knowledge Society*.

MARIA GRAZIA RICCI is a researcher at the Department of Social Sciences of the University of Pisa. She graduated in political science and completed her Ph.D. in Sociology of Development. Her research interests include the analysis of the dynamics of modernity and their consequences on the life of individuals. Her recent works deal with the problematic construction of identity correlated to the radical change in the social dimension of memory. Recent publications include *Il Soggetto è il suo Racconto? Identità e Memoria, Presupposti dell'Azione Sociale* (2003); *Memoria e Generazioni* (2005); *Tiempo, Memoria y Modernidad* (2007), *Spazio e Memoria: Luoghi, Non-luoghi e Lieux de Mémoire* (2007); *Flessibilità e Memoria: Il Doppio Volto della Contemporaneità* (2007); *Dall'Ambiente ai Luoghi della Memoria: Identità e Modernità* (2008).

MICHELE ROSA-CLOT holds a Ph.D. in political science from the University of Pisa, Italy, and a Laurea summa cum laude in history from the same university. An Aquarone and Fulbright scholar, he received a M.A. in American history from the City College of the City University of New York. His research interests focus on the history of electoral systems in the U.S. and the broader field of its political and social history, on the cultural and social history of political representation, and history of immigration. He currently works and researches in Brussels, Belgium.

INO ROSSI is professor of sociology and anthropology at St. John's University. His books include editor of *The Unconscious in Culture: the Structuralism of Claude Levi-Strauss in Perspective* (Dutton, 1974); authoring *The Italians at a Glance: Socio-economic Characteristics of the Italian-Americans in New York* (Italian-American Center for Urban Affairs, 1976) and *Community Reconstruction after an Earthquake: Dialectical Sociology in Action* (Praeger 1993); and editing *Frontiers of Globalization Research: Theoretical and methodological Approaches* (Springer 2007). In 1982 and 1985 he was co-recipient of two National Science Foundation grants to study the long-term recovery and reconstruction of the Southern Italian communities destroyed by the 1980 earthquake.

ANGELO SALENTO is a D.Phil. in sociology of law and assistant professor of sociology of law and sociology of economics at the University of Salento (Lecce, Italy). His research deals with social theory, economic and legal transformations, and local development. His most relevant publications are *Post-Fordism and Jurists' Ideologies* (Milan: Franco Angeli, 2003) and *The Field and the Game: Notes on Bourdieu* (Lecce: Manni, 2004).

SARAH SICILIANO teaches communication and marketing at the University of Salento, where she is also a researcher. Her work focuses on the new communication technologies and their socio-cultural impact on the glocalization process. Among her most recent publications are "Ieri e Oggi in Piazza: Bene Culturale e Contemporaneità Attraverso la Fotografia," in *Piazza Sant' Oronzo a Lecce*, edited by Galatina Congedo (2003); *Immagini della Città: Percorsi Inediti a Lecce Tra Passato e Futuro* (2006); "Mediamorfosi dei Beni Culturali," in *Tecnologie e Culture dell'Identità* (2007); "E-muse: Beni Culturali e Contaminazione Elettronica," in *La Vita Online: Strategie di Costruzione del Sé in Rete* (2007).

FERDINANDO SPINA is a Ph.D. Student in Sociology at the Department of Social Sciences and Communication of University of Salento, Lecce, Italy. His main research interests are the deliberative democracy and the sociology of law. His current work focuses on the problems of trust and legitimacy in contemporary Italian democracy.

SUSANNA TARDI is professor of sociology at William Paterson University. She received her M.A. and Ph.D. degrees from New York University and specializes in research methods, racial and ethnic identity, and family. Her research and publications focus on Italian Americans—their cultural norms and values; their contributions to U.S. society; and their historical struggle against defamation and discrimination. She is currently developing an interdisciplinary Italian Studies Program, as well as writing a socio-historical manuscript on the Italian-American experience from immigration to the fourth generation. Professor Tardi has received numerous awards for both teaching excellence and university service.

MARIO A. TOSCANO is professor of sociology and Director of the Department of Social Sciences at the University of Pisa. A past president of the National Association of Sociology (AIS), his books include editing *Homo Insabilis* (Milan: Franco Angeli, 2008) and *Introduzione alla Sociologia* (Franco Angeli, 2006); *Materiali per lo Studio della Cultura e Dei Beni Culturali* (Pontedera, 2004); *Quattro Ricerche sulla Cultura Dei Beni Culturali* (Pontedera, 2001); co-editor with Vincent N. Parrillo of the aforementioned *Millennium Haze* (2000); Spirito *Sociologico* (Franco Angeli, 1998); *Trittico sulla Guerra: Durkheim, Weber, Pareto* (Laterza, 1995); Liturgie del Moderno: Positivisti a Rio de Janeiro (Fazzi, 1992). He also serves as President doctorate in the history and sociology of modernity.

CHRISTINE ZINNI, Ph.D. is a lecturer at the State University of New York at Brockport and consultant for the New York Folk Arts Program. A recipient of numerous video awards, she organized a multimedia exhibit about Italian-American stonecutters and their families, "Writings in Stone and Textile: The Art/Works of Italian Americans from Abruzzo," that was funded by the National Italian American Foundation (NIAF) and will soon be displayed in Italy. Zinni's written works have appeared in *Oral History Review* and *Voices: the New York Journal of Folklore*. Her essay "Cantastorie: The Ethnographer as Storysinger" appears in *Oral History, Oral Culture, and Italian Americans* (Palgrave Macmillan, 2009).

Index

Abruzzese, Alberto, 180, 183.
Abu Ghraib, 267.
Accornero, Aris, 294, 344, 347.
al Qaeda, 73, 187, 257, 260, 261, 263, 265, 267.
Alba, Richard D. 123, 124, 125, 127, 143, 214, 247, 249, 254.
Alberto Italian Studies Institute, 153.
Albrow, Martin, 195, 197.
Alexander, Jeffrey, 194, 196.
Alfedenesi stonecutters, 201-202, 205-213.
Alfonsi, Fernando, 149.
Alleanza Nazionale party, 221.
Allen, Oliver E., 235, 243.
Allen, Theodore, 245, 246, 254.
AltreItalie, 149-150.
Amato, Fabrizio, 336, 339.
America Oggi, 154, 219.
American Communist Party, 233, 236, 237, 239, 242.
American Italian Historical Association, 145, 146.
American Journal of Sociology, 83, 84.
American Labor Party, 233, 236, 242.
Amoral familism, 53, 56, 161, 231, 241.
Anagrafe degli Italiani Residenti all'Estero (AIRE), 219, 222.
Anderson, M.J., 121, 127.
Andolfi, Ferruccio, 328.
Andreotti, Alberta, 49, 51.
Antonini, Luigi, 236.
Appiah, Kwame Anthony, 175, 183.
Appleby, Joyce, 177.
Arato, Andrew, 61, 65.
Arcudi, Bruno, 149.
Arendt, Hannah, 138, 139, 141.

Arturini, Pino, 334-335
Augé, Marc, 140, 141.

Babb, P., 48, 51.
Bacardi, 20-26.
Bagnasco, Arnaldo, 51, 57, 60, 65.
Baker, Wayne E., 191, 193, 197.
Banchelard, Gaston, 214.
Banco di Napoli, 220.
Banfield, Edward, 53, 56-57, 59, 65, 161, 168, 231, 243.
Banks, Mark, 190, 197.
Bankston, Carl L., 119, 128.
Barabasi, Lazslo, 70, 71, 72, 74.
Barbagallo, Francesco, 55, 65.
Barberini, Angelo, 101.
Barbieri, Paolo, 49, 51.
Barolini, Helen, 148.
Barrett, James E., 245, 246, 248, 250, 255.
Barthes, Roland, 11, 27, 183.
Bartlett, Frederic C., 138, 142.
Bauman, Zygmunt, 11, 27, 91, 92, 95, 140, 141, 294, 324, 328, 346, 347.
Bayor, Ronald H., 233, 237, 242, 243.
Bean, Frank D. 122, 127.
Becattini, G., 310, 313, 315.
Beck, Ulrich, 4, 9, 11, 27, 30, 38, 42, 134, 142, 185-197, 294, 317, 324, 328, 331, 339, 343, 347.
Beck-Gernsheim, Elisabeth, 187, 197.
Bellah, Robert N., 88, 95.
Belussi, F., 310, 313, 315.
Benadusi, Luciano, 344, 347.
Benedetti, Rachele, 295, 351.
Benjamin, Walter, 138, 142, 183.
Berger, Peter L., 135, 142.
Berman, Marshall, 132, 142.
Biancheri, Rita, 75, 78, 79, 82, 351.
Biddle, Francis, 260.

Biggiero, L., 310, 315.
BIM Productions, 333.
bin Laden, Osama, 261, 265.
Birnbaum, Norman, 83.
Blau, Judith, 3, 9.
Blim, Michael, 332, 339.
Bobbio, N., 294.
Bodei, Remo, 328.
Boli, J., 193, 197.
Bonilla-Silva, Eduardo, 252, 255.,
Bonomo Albright, Carol, 149.
Bonss, Wolfgang, 185, 197.
Bonutti, Karl, 117, 127.
Bordighera Press, 149.
Borghini, Andrea, 3, 7, 9, 351.
Borja, Jordi, 109, 113.
Bourdieu, Pierre, 8, 9, 11, 27, 44-45, 51, 76, 82, 164, 168.
Boym, Svetlana, 136, 142.
Bozorgmehr, Mehdi, 125, 128.
Brenner, Neil, 6, 9
Briggs, John W., 214.
Brindisi Provincial Council, 62.
Brint, Stephen, 85, 86, 88, 92, 95.
Brittingham, Angela, 262, 269.
Brooklyn Eagle, 239, 243.
Brusco, S., 312, 315.
Buchanan, Marc, 70, 72, 74.
Burgess, Ernest, 83.
Burham, James, 12.
Bush Administration, 261, 267.
Butterfield, Jeanne, 262, 269.

Cacchione, Peter V., 231, 239, 240, 241, 243, 244.
Cagiano de Azevedo Raimondo, 230.
Cahnman, Werner, 85, 87, 88, 90, 95.
Calhoun, Craig, 60, 65.
Camarota, Steven, 268, 269.
Candeloro, Dominic, 143, 351-352.

Cannata, Frank, 153.
Cannistraro, Philip, 144, 150, 151-152, 231, 243.
Capone, Giovanna, 98., 99, 100, 102, 104.
Caporale, Rocco, 219, 352.
Cappello, Mary, 101, 104.
Capuano, Sofia, 309, 352.
Carbone, Luca, 83, 352-353.
Cariani, Giovanni, 230.
Carilli, Teresa, 102, 104.
Carosone Michael, 97, 105, 353.
Cartocci, Roberto, 57, 65.
Casa Italiana Zerilli-Marimò, 153.
Casciano, Maria Valentina, 339.
Cassano, Franco, 84, 91, 95, 161-162, 168.
Cassese, Antonio, 6, 9.
Castel, Robert, 54, 65, 296, 297, 307.
Castells, Manuel, 108-109, 113, 114.
Cavaioli, Frank J., 144, 145.
CENSIS, 55.
Center for Migration Studies, 146.
Centro Studi Emigrazione Roma, 146.
Ceplak, Metka Mencin, 189, 197.
Cerasualo, Agostino, 204, 214.
Chapman, C., 48, 51.
Charles VII of Bourbon, 172.
Chibbaro, Lou, 103, 105.
Chiesi, Antonio, M., 43, 47, 48, 51.
Chtouris, Sotiris, 189, 197.
Ciampi, Carlo Azeglio, 170, 183.
Ciotola, Nicholas, 146, 151.
City University of New York (CUNY), 150, 282-286.
Clark, Ian, 331, 339.
Clinton, William, 260.
Coccia Institute, 153.
Cohen, Jean, 60, 61, 65.
Cohen, Robin, 191, 197.
Colangelo, Jerry, 152.

Coleman, James S., 44, 45-46, 47, 51.
Colley, Ann C., 136, 142.
Community Support Framework, 313.
Congressional Record, 259, 260, 269.
Connell, Raewyn W., 86, 95.
Connerton, Paul, 93, 95.
Corsi, Edward, 233.
Cortese, Aldo, 230.
Covello, Leonard, 144, 145, 204, 214.
Crialese, Emanuele, 247.
Cremonesini, Valentina, 11, 353.
Crespi, Franco, 86, 95.
Croce, Randy, 214.
Culture of poverty, 56, 161.

Dalton, Harlon L., 245, 249, 250, 251, 255.
D'Angelo, Pascal, 148.
Darwin, Charles, 88.
Davis, Benjamin, 239, 240.
Davis, John A., 214.
Davis, Mike, 110, 114.
De Angelis, Gabriele, 29, 353.
de Beer, Paul, 190, 197.
de Certeau, Michel, 169, 181, 182, 183.
de la Cruz, G. Patricia, 262, 269.
de la Garza, Rodolfo, 125, 127.
de Luca, Maria Novella, 175, 183.
De Santis, R., 333, 334, 339.
DeWitt, General John L., 258, 259, 260.
Dedman, Bill, 267, 269.
Defino, Susanna, 214.
Del Giudice, Luisa, 209, 210, 215.
Deleuze, Gilles, 26, 27.
Della Porta, Donatella, 30, 42.
Delors Report, 342.
Denton, Nancy, 249, 255.
Derrida, Jacques, 13, 27.
Di Carlo, Frank, 212.
di Donato, Pietro, 148, 149.

Di Laura, Norma, 207, 210, 215.
Di Laura, Virginia, 207, 210, 215.
Di Maria, E. 310, 315.
Di Martino, V., 333, 334, 339.
Disaster capitalism, 199, 200, 201, 213, 214.
Diesi, Umberto, 334.
Domenici, Leonardo, 180.
Douglas, Mary, 39, 42, 317, 328.
Doyle, Charles, 269.
Durkheim, Emile, 4, 83, 85-89, 95, 294.

Ege, Harold, 333, 334, 339.
Eghigian, Greg, 132, 142.
Elias, Norbert, 85, 86, 95.
Elmi, Francis N., 282.
Elster, Jon, 135, 142.
Engel, Eliot, 260.
Erie Canal, 208.
Esping-Andersen, Gøsta, 301, 307.
Eula, Michael J., 204, 210, 215.
European Employment Strategy (EES), 300, 304.
Europedia, 179.
Executive Order 9066, 259, 265, 269.
Expert Group on Flexicurity (EGF), 302-303.

Falbo, Ernest, 149.
Fante, John, 148.
Faulkner, William, 103.
Feinberg, S.E., 121, 127.
Ferragamo, 309, 314.
Ferrara, Alessandro, 327, 328.
Ferrera, Maurizio, 332, 339.
Festa Italiana, 155-156.
Fiat Research Centre, 314.
Field, John, 343, 347.
Fish, Stanley, 253, 255.
Fisher, Ian, 102, 105.
Flanagan, Owen, 135, 142.

Flap, Henk, 50, 51.
Flexicurity, 301-307.
Floro-Khalaf, Jenny, 145.
Foa, Vittorio, 344, 347.
Fondazione Giovanni Agnelli, 148, 150.
Foner, Nancy, 120, 127.
Ford, Henry, 322.
Fordham University Press, 149.
Fortier, Anne-Marie, 101, 105.
Foucault, Michel, 11, 13, 14, 27, 132, 161, 182, 183, 325.
Fox, Stephen, 260, 269.
Fra Noi, 154.
Frankfurt School, 136, 183.

Gabaccia, Donna R., 209, 215.
Gabbriellini, Simone, 69, 353-354.
Gallino, Luciano, 344, 347.
Gambino, Richard, 149, 242, 243, 271.
Gans, Herbert J., 123, 124, 127.
Gardaphè, Fred L., 148, 149.
Garibaldi Fraternal Society, 237.
Gazier, Bernard, 305, 307.
Gazzetta Ufficiale, 226.
Geertz, Clifford, 160, 168.
Geneva Convention, 267.
Gergen, Kenneth J., 132, 134, 135, 136, 142.
Gerson, Simon, 240, 241, 243.
Ghiardelli, Domenico, 152.
GI Bill, 248, 271.
Giannotti, Gianni, 83, 86, 95.
Giddens, Anthony, 11, 27, 132, 134, 137, 142, 185, 294, 343, 346, 347, 348.
Gilligan, Carol, 135, 142.
Gini coefficient, 54.
Ginsborg, Paul, 332, 339.
Gioia, Dana, 149.
Giordano, Paolo A., 148, 149.
Gladwell, Malcolm, 72, 74.

Glazer and Moynihan, 243.
Goldenberg, Jacob, 19, 20, 27.
Goldman, Harvey, 320, 322, 328.
Gordon, Milton M., 124, 127.
Gorz, André, 324, 327, 328.
Gramsci, Antonio, 56.
Granovetter, Mark S., 44, 51, 70, 71, 74.
Graziadio Center for Italian Studies, 153.
Graziani, Augusto, 161, 168.
Green Party, 35.
Greenya, John, 263, 269
Gualmini, Elisabetta, 332, 339.
Guantanamo, 267.
Gucci, 309, 314.
Gutierrez, David, 119, 127.

Habermas, Jürgen, 26, 27, 53, 60-62, 65, 318-319, 327, 329.
Hacker, Andrew, 249, 255.
Hacking, Ian, 132, 142.
Hadjmichalis, Costis, 302, 307.
Haeckel, Ernst, 88.
Hagan, Frank E. 261, 269.
Hake, B.J., 343, 348.
Halbwachs, Maurice, 138, 142.
Handlin, Oscar, 144.
Hannerz, Ulf, 191, 197.
Harper, R., 48, 51.
Harvey, David, 317, 322. 329.
Hegel, George W.F., 326.
Hermens, Ferdinand A., 239, 240, 243.
Historical Society of Western Pennsylvania, 146.
Hobbes, Thomas, 5, 9
Hobsbawm, Eric, 132, 142.
Hoffmann-Axthelm, Dieter, 133, 142.
Holmes, Douglas, 332, 339.
Honneth, Axel, 319, 326, 327, 329.
Hooghes, Liesbet, 6, 9.

Hoover, J. Edgar, 258, 265, 266.
Horn, David, 332, 339.
Hudson, L., 48, 51.
Hulberton, New York, 201, 209, 212.
Hunt, Margaret, 215.
Husén, Torsten, 343, 348.
Hussein, Saddam, 261.

Ignatiev, Noel, 245, 252, 255.
Il Giornale dell'Arte, 176-177, 183.
Il Progresso Italo-Americano, 154.
Immigrant History Research Center, 146.
Immigration and Naturalization Service, 265.
Impellitteri, Vincent Richard, 236.
Inglehart, Ronald, 189, 193, 197.
International Migration Review, 146.
International Workers Order, 237.
Isin, Engin F., 331, 339.
ISTAT, 54, 55, 65, 79, 82, 222, 223.
Italian American Digest, 155.
Italian American Review, 149.
Italian American Writers Association, 148.
Italian Cultural Center/Casa Italia, 152.
Italian Financial Act of 2002, 176.
Italian Tribune, 154.
Italian Workers' Compensation Authority, 336-337.
Italian Americana, 149.

J. Paul Getty Museum, 170, 174-177.
Jacobson, Matthew, 120, 127.
Jacoby, Stanford, 208, 209, 215.
Jameson, Fredric, 162, 168.
Jane Addams Hull House Collection, 147.
Jedlowski, Paolo, 87, 90, 95, 137, 142.
Jen, Gish, 249, 255.
John D. Calandra Italian American Institute, 103, 105, 150, 271-272.
Joint Report on Social Protection, 299.
Jones, D. Marvin, 251.

Kadushin, Charles, 46, 51.
Kattan, Emmanuel, 137, 142.
Katz, Elihu, 69, 72, 74.
Keefe, Susan E., 118, 127.
Kelly, M., 48, 51.
Kelly, Robin D.G., 236, 243.
Kennedy, John F., 123.
Kennedy, Paul, 191, 197.
Kephart, Janice, 268, 269.
Kessner, Thomas, 233, 234, 243.
Kibbee, Robert J., 282.
Killen, Andreas, 132, 142.
Kirshenblatt-Gimblett, Barbara, 215.
Kivel, Paul, 252, 255.
Klein, Naomi, 199-200, 214-215.
Knorr Cetina, Celia, 187, 197.
Koenig-Archibugi, Mathias, 332, 339.
Kohli, Martin, 297, 307.
Kotler, Philip, 13, 27.
Krase, Jerome, 147, 200, 209, 215, 231, 234, 243.
Krekel, R., 296.
Krimsky, S., 29, 42.
Kronauer, Martin, 296, 307.
Kurz, Robert, 329.
Kushnik, Louis, 250, 255.

La Cerra, Charles, 234, 243.
La Guardia, Fiorello, 233, 239.
La Gumina, Salvatore, 144, 145, 155.
La Progressiva, 237-238.
La Repubblica, 334, 339.
Lasch, Christopher, 141, 142, 328, 329.
Lasch, Christopher, 141, 142.
Lash, Scott, 142, 185, 294, 343, 347.
Lau, Christopher, 185, 197.
Lazarsfeld, Paul F., 69, 72, 74.
Lazio, Rick, 260.
Lazzeroni, Lara, 339.

Lee, Jennifer 121, 127.
Lenoir, Rene, 295.
Leto, Nico, 98, 104, 105.
Leuenberger, Christine, 132, 142.
Levinas, Emmanuel, 326, 329.
Levine, Edward, 232, 243.
Levi-Strauss, Claude, 188, 197.
Library of Congress, 262, 264, 269.
Lin, Nan, 43, 44, 46, 48, 49, 50, 51.
L'Italo-Americano, 154.
Little Italys, 143, 209, 237.
Livorno, Italy, 30, 34-36.
Loffredo, Antonio, 339.
Lohman, Roger, 201, 203, 205, 215.
Loscocco, Karyn, 245, 354.
Loury, Glenn C., 44, 51.
Louvre, 170, 176.
Loyal Wing Club, 211-213.
Luckmann, Thomas, 135, 142.
Luconi, Stefano, 231, 241, 243.
Luhmann, Niklas, 29, 31, 32, 34, 42, 317, 329.
L'Unità del Popolo, 238, 239, 240, 244.

Macro-relational approach, 46.
Madsen, Per Kongshøj, 302, 305, 307.
Magnaghi, Alberto, 163, 168.
Magro, Paul, 257, 354.
Maldonado, Lionel A. 121, 127.
Mambo Italiano, 101, 105.
Manganelli, Giorgio, 64, 65.
Mangione, Jerre, 148.
Mannheim, Karl, 86.
Marcantonio, Vito, 231, 233, 236-237, 238, 242, 243.
Marcuse, Herbert, 136, 142.
Marinelli, Albert, 234.
Marino, John, 155.
Marks, Gary, 6, 9.
Marshall, Alfred, 309, 311, 315.

Marx, Karl, 132, 202.
Maselli, Joseph, 152.
Massey, Douglas, 249, 255.
Mazursky, David, 19, 20, 27.
McNickle, Chris, 233, 235, 236, 243.
Mead, George Herbert, 326.
Mead, Margaret, 137, 142.
Mecca, Tommi Avicolli, 98, 99, 104, 105.
Mele, Vincenzo, 317, 354.
Melucci, Alberto, 136, 137, 142.
Meyer, Gerald, 144, 231, 234, 236, 237, 238, 243-244.
Mezzogiorno, 53-59, 119, 120, 161, 202, 204.
Micelli, S., 310, 313, 315.
Milani, Ernesto, 147.
Milella, Stefania, 43, 50, 51, 354-355.
Milgram, Stanley, 70, 74.
Milione, Vincenzo, 117, 127, 150, 271, 272, 275, 355.
Million Man March, 251.
Minicuci, Maria, 215.
Miranda, Edward J., 234, 244.
Mitgang, Herbert, 235, 244.
Molé, Noelle J., 331, 355.
Mollenkopf, John, 114.
Moncada, Alberto, 3, 9.
Mondadori Press, 149.
Mosca, L., 30, 42.
Motley, Judge Constance Baker, 282.
Murphy, Charles Francis, 234.
Murphy, Joseph S., 282.
Museo ItaloAmericano, 147, 152.
Mussolini, Benito, 220-221.
Mutti, Antonio, 49, 51.

Naldini, Manuela, 78, 82.
Namer, Gerard, 139, 142.
National Council of Columbia Associations in Civil Service, 271-272.

National Institute of Statistics, 54, 65, 222.
National Italian American Foundation, 100, 144, 155, 157.
National Municipal Review, 235, 240, 244.
Nelli, Humbert S., 232, 244.
Neuwirth, Robert, 114.
New Jersey Italian and Italian American Heritage Commssion, 145-146.
New York Red Book, 236, 244.
New York Times, 235, 236, 237, 244, 267, 269.
Newman, William M., 124, 127.
Nietzsche, Friedrich, 7, 320.
Nisbet, Robert, 61-62, 65.
Nitti, Francesco Saverio, 56.
Nora, Pierre, 139, 142.
Notiziario NIP, 226, 230.

O'Brien, Eileen, 252, 255.
O'Brien, John P., 235.
Offe, Claus, 318, 323, 324, 329.
Oksenberg Rorty, Amelie, 135, 142.
Olick, Jeffrey, 89, 90, 93, 95.
Olivo, Grace, 145.
Olmi, Ermanno, 173, 183.
Ong, Aihwa, 335, 339.
Ono, Hiromi, 125, 127.
Open Method of Coordination (OCM), 299.
Oppedisano, Robert, 149.
Osti, Giorgio, 91, 95.

Padilla, Amado M., 118, 127.
Paniccia, I., 312, 315.
Paone, Sonia, 107, 355.
Pareto, Vilfredo, 83.
Park, Robert, 83.
Parker, Simon, 114.
Parrillo, Vincent N., 178, 183, 191, 192, 197, 215, 245, 246, 247, 255, 356.
Parsons, Talcott, 75, 82, 83.

Pasolini, Pier Paolo, 84, 90-95, 96.
Pastore, Andrea, 228.
Pastore, Gerardo, 341, 347, 348, 356.
Paugam, Serge, 295, 307.
Pavalko, Ronald M. 245, 255.
Paxton, Pamela, 60, 65.
Pearl Harbor, 257, 258, 261, 265.
Pelizzoli, Itala, 271.
Penna, Sandra, 94-95.
Periconi, James, 148.
Perlman, Joel, 123, 127.
Petrillo, Agostino, 114.
Piore, M.J., 311, 312, 315.
Pisa, Italy, 36.
Piselli, Fortunata, 45, 48, 50, 51.
Pitti, 314.
Pizzirusso, Carmine, 271.
Pizzorno, Alessandro, 51, 56, 60, 66, 160, 168.
Plough, A., 29, 42.
Polanyi, Karl, 91, 96.
Porcelli, Paul, 147.
Portes, Alejandro, 60, 65, 119, 124, 125, 127.
Powell, Rev. Adam Clayton, Jr., 239, 240.
Powell, Kevin, 251.
Powell, Walter, 200, 208, 212, 215.

Prada, 309, 314.
Primeggia, Salvatore, 144.
Procacci, Giovanna, 298, 307.
Prodi, Romano, 103, 229.
Prodi, Romano, 103.
Protestant Ethic, 293.
Puglia, Italy, 53, 59, 62.
Puleo, Stephen, 246, 247, 249, 255.
Putnam, Robert, 46-47, 48, 51, 56, 57, 58, 59, 60, 65-66.

Radomile, Leon, 144.
Ranci, Costanzo, 54, 66, 297, 307.

Ranieri, Andrea, 344, 347.
Ranson, Stewart, 343, 348.
Reimann, Joachim, 117, 127.
Remotti, Francesco, 159, 160, 168.
Ressler, Steve, 73, 74.
Rete delle Città Strategiche, 180.
Riain, Sean, 6, 9.
Ricci, Maria Grazia, 131, 356.
Richard J. Daley Library, 146.
Rifkin, Jeremy, 162, 168, 178-181, 183, 199, 202-203, 215, 324, 329, 344, 348.
Ritzer, George, 5, 9, 191, 197.
Robbins, Joyce, 89-90, 93, 95, 96.
Robertson, Roland, 5, 10.
Rodrigues, Maria G., 302, 307.
Roediger, David, 245, 246, 248, 250, 255.
Rogowski, Ralf, 303, 307.
Rohrmann, Bernd, 33, 42.
Roosevelt, Franklin Delano, 235, 241, 258, 259, 261, 265.
Rosa-Clot, Michele, 231, 239, 244, 356-357.
Rosaldo, Renato, 136, 142.
Rose, Nikolas, 331, 339.
Rosenthal, Edward, 69, 74.
Rosoli, Gianfausto, 146.
Rossi, Ino, 185, 187, 188, 192, 193, 194, 195, 197, 234, 244, 357.
Roux, Christophe, 57, 66.
Rullani, E., 313, 315.
Rumbaut, Ruben G., 119, 127.
Rutelli, Francesco, 175.
Ryle, Gilbert, 173, 184.

Sabel, C., 311, 312, 315.
Sacco and Vanzetti, 151, 242.
Sacks, Harvey, 17, 27.
Sacks, Karen Brodkin, 245, 246, 248, 255.
Sadler, David, 302, 307.
Saint Rocco, feast, 201, 212.

Salento, Angelo, 159, 357.
Salento, Italy, 162-167, 182.
Salvemini, Gaetano, 56.
Salvini, Andrea, 46, 51.
Sapelli, Giulo, 91, 96.
Saraceno, Chiara, 78, 82.
Sassen, Saskia, 107-108, 114, 332, 340.
Scalabrini Fathers, 146.
Scelsa, Joseph, 152, 275, 282.
Schiavo, Giovanni, 144, 152.
Schirato, Tony, 194, 197.
Schmid, Günther, 305, 307.
Schnore, Leo F., 88.
Schütz, Alfred, 16-17, 27, 139.
Schwartz, Barry, 69, 74.
Sciorra, Joseph, 209, 210, 215.
Scottoline, Lisa, 149.
Seabury, Samuel, 235.
Seligman, Adam, 65, 66.
Senator John Heinz History Center, 146, 151.
Sennett, Richard, 12, 27, 59, 66, 133, 134, 136, 141,142, 294, 319-320, 325, 326, 328, 329. 344, 348.
Settis, Salvatore, 170, 172, 176, 177, 184.
Shapiro, Thomas M., 250, 255.
Shaw, Frederick, 235, 244.
Siciliano, Sarah, 169, 357.
Silver, Hilary, 53, 66.
Simmel, Georg, 60, 66, 86, 137, 142, 168, 326.
Simon, J., 331, 340.
Small, Albion, 83, 84, 85, 94, 96.
Smith, Gordon, 7, 10.
Snijders, Tom, 49, 50, 51.
Social capital, 43-51, 53, 57-60, 63, 123, 125, 189.
Sociology without borders, 3.
Sombart, Werner, 86.
Sons of Italy, 143, 153.

Sorokin, Pitirim, 85, 87.
Sowell, Thomas, 232, 244.
Spina, Ferdinando, 53, 59, 357.
State of the World Population 2007, 111, 112.
Stehr, Nico, 134, 141, 142.
Steinberg, Stephen, 248, 255.
Stiegler, Bernard, 14, 27.
Stone, Wendy, 48, 51.
Stonecutters Journeyman's Association, 208.
Strogatz, Steven H., 71, 74.
Sztompka, Piotr, 59, 66.

Taliban, 267.
Tamburri, Anthony Julian, 105, 148, 149, 153, 155.
Tammany, 233-235, 238.
Tardi, Susanna, 115, 358.
Tarrow, Sidney, 60, 66.
Taylor, Charles, 132, 142.
Tedlock, Dennis, 201, 207, 215.
Terpolilli, Paolo, 337, 340.
The Golden Door, 247.
Thomas, G.M., 193, 197.
Thompson, Edward, 321, 329.
Tirabassi, Maddalena, 150.
Tocqueville, 177-178, 184.
Tomasi, Silvano, 232, 244.
Tonelli, Bill, 148.
Tönnies, Ferdinand, 83, 85-91, 96.
Topp, Michael, 242, 244.
Toscano, Mario A., 56, 66, 171, 184, 191, 192, 197, 291, 294, 358.
Transitional labor markets (TLM), 305-306, 307.
Tremaglia, Mirko, 221, 222, 226.
Tresca, Carlo, 231.
Trigiani, Adiana, 149.
Trivisond, Gilda, 210, 211, 215.
True, Marion, 174.
Tumlin, Karen C., 263, 269.
Turner, Bryan S., 4, 10.

Tuscany, 35, 38, 181, 309, 314.
Tusiani, Joseph, 148.

U.S. Census Bureau, 117, 127, 262, 269, 272.
U.S. Department of Justice, 263, 266, 269-270.
U.S. Office of Civil Rights and Equal Employment Opportunity, 281.
UNESCO, 169, 174, 341.
UN-Habitat, 110-111, 113, 114.
UNICO, 153.
United Nations Development Programme, 54.
United Nations Population Fund, 109, 114.
University of Pisa, 81, 314.
USA PATRIOT Act, 262-263, 267, 269.

Valente Family Italian Studies Library, 153.
Van Creveld, Martin, 7.
Van der Gaag, Martin, 49, 50, 51, 52.
Varacalli, Joseph A., 144.
Vecoli, Rudolph, 144, 145, 154, 232, 244.
Verazzano Institute, 150.
Vertieri, Cinzia, 335.
Vetri, Lidia, 334.
Viesti, Gianfranco, 59, 66.
Voce, 155.
Voices in Italian Americana, 148.

Wacquant, Loic, 11, 27.
Wagner, Peter, 131, 133, 142.
Waldinger Roger, 123, 125, 127, 128.
Walker, James J., 235.
Wallerstein, Immanuel, 90.
Waltzer, Kenneth Alan, 236, 237, 244.
War on Terror, 257, 260-262, 265-266, 268.
Ward, Lester, 83, 94, 96.
Waters, Mary, 123, 124, 128, 246, 249, 255.
Watts, Duncan J., 71, 74.

Webb, Jen, 194, 197.
Weber, Max, 4, 83, 132, 142, 294, 320-324, 327, 329.
Welzel, Christian, 189, 193, 197.
Wessler, Stephen, 263, 270.
Western Defense Command, 258, 259.
Whyte, William Foote, 250, 255.
Wiedemann, Peter M., 33, 42.
Wildawsky, Aaron, 39, 42.
Wilson, William J., 296, 307.
Wilthagen, Ton, 303, 307.
Wood, Gordon, 177, 184.
Woodward, Alison, 297.
World Value Survey, 188, 191, 193.
Worldwatch Institute, 114.

Yans-McLaughlin, Virginia, 215.

Zahller, Alisa, 152.
Zerubavel, Eviatar, 90.
Zhou, Min, 119, 124, 127, 128.
Zinni, Christine, 199, 215, 358.

www.ingramcontent.com/pod-product-compliance
Lightning Source LLC
Chambersburg PA
CBHW082057230426
43662CB00039B/2170